DANCING
TO
DIFFERENT
TUNES

DANCING
TO
DIFFERENT
TUNES
Sexuality and Its
Misconceptions

•

ETHNA VINEY

THE
BLACKSTAFF PRESS

BELFAST

U.S. DISTRIBUTOR
DUFOUR EDITIONS
CHESTER SPRINGS
PA 19425-0007
(610) 458-5005

First published in 1996 by
The Blackstaff Press Limited
3 Galway Park, Dundonald, Belfast BT16 0AN, Northern Ireland

© Ethna Viney, 1996
Typeset by Paragon Typesetters, Newton-le-Willows, Merseyside

Printed in England by Biddles Limited

A CIP catalogue record for this book
is available from the British Library

ISBN 0-85640-570-1

for Michael who gave unswerving support
and
for Michele whose arrival inspired this book

CONTENTS

PREFACE

I have always been concerned by the failure of feminism to reach, or impress, the vast majority of women even in our Western society. Despite the consciousness-raising, the deep, complex insights of the past twenty-five years, so few women are feminists or have made any effort to bring about an end to male supremacy. The reasons are not simple nor are they all attributable to men. There are factors at work that militate against the mobilisation of women in their own cause. I am going to suggest that one reason lies in a flawed definition and interpretation of human sexuality.

Many women have profited from the work of the women's movement, from the gains that feminists have made in their struggle for equality, but the outlook of the vast majority of women remains the same. They will still defer to men, accept a lower status and economic return for their work, allow men to make decisions for them; and in some cases they will even try to denigrate and criticise women who succeed in gaining some measure of personal equality or status.

The anthropologist Margaret Mead claimed that women consent to leave to men the main responsibility for history and for the *spiritual* and *psychological* continuity of the species, because men's self-respect requires it; they need this role in order to counterbalance women's more impressive contribution as child-bearer, to the physical continuity of the species. If that were ever thought to be a valid underlying motive for male domination, nowadays it sounds more like an excuse to justify the subordination of women, or a piece of teleological deduction – a backwards inference that because the present situation serves the purpose of giving men control of history and is important for their self-respect, this is why it came about in the first place. The proposition has no validity in the unequal situation that has developed.

If the majority of women really took part in a revolution against male supremacy, they would be successful. Something is stopping them. It is not the fragmentation of the women's movement, although that has had an effect; it is not the advantage (wealth, status) that some women can gain by 'collaborating' with men, although that too plays a part; there is something else besides inertia that influences women and holds them back that is almost hidden in their complex and image-distorted sexuality.

In the age-old history of humanity, and in the equally long and mainly forgotten history of feminism, sexuality has been an ever-present shadow over the lives of women. They have been defined in terms of it, enslaved or deprived by means of it, reviled and tormented, dismissed and silenced because of it. Yet in more than seven thousand years of philosophical analysis of the human condition, it is only in this century, and more particularly in the past two decades, that adequate study of the nature of human sexuality has been attempted. The study was first undertaken by twentieth-century sexologists and psychoanalysts; but for work more relevant to women's situation, credit must go unequivocally to the women of the present wave of feminism, who, driven by the need to understand their continuing subordination, have been examining the various aspects of their lives and relations with men, phenomena which must first be understood if they are to be changed.

Recent feminist analysis has centred to a large extent on defining female sexuality, as women peeled away the layers of misconceptions that mummified them – misconceptions that existed because the stereotype of female sexuality had been defined in male terms. Progress has been made, but there are still areas of female sexuality that are defined in male terms. Male sexuality requires a similar redefining, for it, too, is the victim of a cultural definition.

On one front sexual politics in the women's movement sent women back into the home to fight their battles alone (the personal is political), and on another, ripped apart the movement with intolerance and aggression, much of it centred on the question of sexuality. In this book I will review some of the more significant literature on sexuality, and will look from a new angle at some cherished beliefs and misconceptions. Is heterosexuality as natural as we think it is, or is it merely a cultural norm? Why is Western society genitally fixated in this particular era? What part does the missionary position in coitus play in defining female and male sexuality? What is the function of the female orgasm? What is the Great O? Is romantic love a confidence trick played on women? Why has motherhood been written out of sexuality and the feminist movement?

ETHNA VINEY
March 1996

1

SEXUALITY
AS WE KNOW IT

In every society sexuality is predominantly culturally defined both in its practice and its scope, regardless of its origins. It is a product of the culture in which we live, and that culture is patriarchal; that is, part of a social system of male domination and female subordination.[1] By 'culture' I mean not just art and literature, but a broader context of the customs, practices and beliefs of our society; the multitude of ways in which we communicate with each other – language, the system of signs which we use to convey meaning (such as dress, body language, advertising or art), the various media of communication, philosophy, our working habits and leisure pursuits, religion, politics, how we solve problems and celebrate success; in short, our behaviour and attitudes, the visible and invisible, conscious and unconscious, rules by which we live.

In Ireland religion has a crucial conscious and unconscious influence: the conscious one of Catholic teaching; the unconscious one of millennia of Judaeo-Christian patriarchal culture which also deeply influences European and North American societies. Religion, as we know it, developed out of a patriarchal, Middle Eastern society at least four thousand years old, which Jesus Christ attempted to reform. His efforts, however, were frustrated by the continuing power of the patriarchy and the spin its representatives put on his message. (If Christ ever wrote down any of his teachings, they have not survived; those who later wrote the early history of the birth of Christianity claimed divine inspiration, which was an old trick of the Jewish patriarchs – God speaking in olive groves and on the top of mountains.) The single greatest influence on our Western culture has been patriarchal religion, of which the last two thousand years have masqueraded under the name of Christianity.

Humans are social beings and culture is important to us; it is a means of bonding individuals and preserving society. Our culture envelops us like a warm and familiar room. It is hallowed by living, dear to us as part of our routine and our past, it feels right. We are slow to reorganise it because it seems that is the way it has always been; we are used to the arrangements. It can exist side by side with change, new ideas and the search for truth. During periods of change, we cling to large portions of our culture, even the awkward or useless bits, almost unconsciously, because it is familiar. It gives us social stability and security, and a framework for our lives; we can all become irritated with, and resist, ideas at variance with our own cherished beliefs.

As we grow up and as we grow older the culture of our society is absorbed by all of us. This process of socialisation could be called 'conditioning', or more pejoratively 'brainwashing', but 'internalising' is a better word; we take in ideas and attitudes and make them our own. We concur, indeed co-operate, with the process of internalisation, and it is therefore something over which we *can* exercise control. Debriefing ourselves, however, is not easy; we need an overriding drive to do so. And even after a successful debriefing, flashes of the old conditioning can return like the hallucinogenic relapses of drug addicts.

As virtually all cultures worldwide are male-dominated and patriarchal, the ideas, attitudes and mores that prevail are those of men. To a considerable extent only the bits of theory that suit patriarchy are absorbed into the culture; and great resistance is initiated to the others, as is evident in the slow progress being made in the struggle to achieve equality for women. The genes passed on by the male in reproduction are celebrated by the convention of using the male surname in our society, yet women inherit genes from their fathers and men inherit genes from their mothers. In art we are only beginning to become aware of the world-view of women, a view which has been drowned by the male vision of the world.[2] We listen to music created by men; when will we hear music created by women? (Not in the harsh and violent sounds of male pop music, but in Enya or The Cranberries.) The interpretation of life through the music which has been allowed to survive by the musical establishment has been mostly undertaken by men, written by men, chosen and promoted by men, according to rules laid down by men.

Men differ from women in the way they view life. The French social anthropologist Claude Lévi-Strauss wrote at the end of his study of primitive societies:

Passage from the state of Nature to the state of Culture is marked by man's ability to view biological relations as a series of contrasts; duality, alternation, opposition, and symmetry, whether under definite or vague forms, constitute not so much phenomena to be explained as fundamental and immediately given data of social reality.[3]

In other words the way *men* see things determines the culture; but women do not necessarily see duality or opposition in all or even any aspects of relationships or life, biological or social; they are more likely to see, or hope for, reciprocation.

Journalist and writer Caroline Humphrey lucidly paraphrased Lévi-Strauss's jargon-ridden definition of culture as follows: 'The advent of culture occurred when men rejected [the] sexual free-for-all. One group of men gave its women to a second, trusting in reciprocity, and it was in this discovery of generosity – for woman was the most precious of all gifts – that culture was born.'[4]

Margaret Mead saw another side of sexual culture in situations where societies were isolated from each other. In one tribe she saw both sexes demonstrating the 'female' qualities of child-nurturing and gentle, caring sexual relations, with no apparent powerful sex drive; in another, the direct opposite – powerful and aggressive sexual relations in both men and women, with a low level of maternalism in either sex; in a third tribe women were sexually dominant and men emotionally dependent. These observations demonstrate that culture shapes in different forms the way humans respond to their basic instincts, and these become the way of life for the people of a particular society.

Rooted deep within our culture is an attitude to women which can only be described as misogyny, a degrading and a downgrading of women based on their sexuality. Many women will say that the men they know are not monsters who degrade or oppress women. They may be right, some men do not; and it is likely that many of the women who are concerned about the problem of oppression will tend to know and favour those men who treat women with fairness. Indeed the oppressors and the degraders avoid engagement with women who challenge their position, or read books like this; they give them a wide berth when seeking a female companion. At the same time let us not forget that even the fairest of men do little to challenge the prevailing culture which is the medium through which the subordination of women works. After twenty-five years of this latest wave of the women's movement, men are still firmly in charge.

For those who do not believe that there is a deeply ingrained streak in our culture that defines and degrades women in terms of their sexuality, I will recount an incident that happened to a friend. She was taking the bus from Heuston railway station to the centre of Dublin, and alongside her bus stood another, a school outing of ten-year-old girls. Seated behind her were two youths who carried on a conversation in revolting detail about the pleasures of raping these schoolgirls when they were ten years older. It is immaterial whether they really meant what they said, or whether they were merely chest-thumping for each other's benefit; they had the ideas and the vocabulary of sexual oppression, *and a cultural context in which to express them.*

We have internalised the definitions and meanings that our culture has assigned to the various aspects of our lives; in particular, where gender and sexuality are concerned. However *defining* something, labelling and affirming its scope, does not necessarily reveal its true essence; and feminists are only now in the process of discovering, under the cultural accretions of millennia, the essential make-up of female, or indeed, human sexuality and gender difference.

GENDER

In their quest for this holy grail feminists have found the need to redefine, or specify, the meanings of words such as 'sex', 'gender', 'sexuality', which have accumulated their own cultural accretions, and have gone beyond their commonly understood definitions. 'Gender' is generally regarded as synonymous with 'sex'. However, in recent times, because professionals such as psychologists, sociologists and anthropologists have introduced precision into terms, the word 'gender' has been given a more rigorous meaning and increased significance in the study of human beings. ' "Sex" is a biological term; "gender" a psychological and cultural one,' says Ann Oakley in *Sex, Gender and Society*. 'Gender, like caste, is a matter of social ascription which bears no necessary relation to the individual's own attributes and inherent abilities.' Robert Stoller, the American psychoanalyst, defined 'gender' as a term that has psychological or cultural rather than biological connotations. If the proper terms for sex are 'male' and 'female', he said, the corresponding terms for gender are 'masculine' and 'feminine'.[5]

Some feminists hold that gender is sexual, that under male supremacy sexuality is the 'eroticisation of dominance and submission', and that these dominant and submissive sexualities are a part of the building blocks in the formation of male and female gender.[6]

It saves confusion if the word 'gender' is used to indicate the different roles, behaviour, practices and attitudes which are attributed to women and to men, and which condition them – the social and cultural edifice which has been erected on a base of biological difference. 'Gender' is no longer synonymous with 'sex', yet sex and sexuality are a part of gender. Gender roles include sexual roles, social roles, economic roles and any other female and male roles where there is a designated difference. Most significantly, gender is an important part of identity. Gender roles are allotted to people on the basis of their biological sex (or in the case of physiological anomalies of their perceived biological sex). Sex is decided on the physical appearance of the external genitals, and internally on the nature of the gonads: women have ovaries; men have testes; women bear children; men do not.

The more old-fashioned analysts who maintain that gender is biologically determined, that our gender depends on which sex we are, meet with fierce denunciation from modern thinkers who insist that gender is socially and psychologically constructed. In fact, many feminists maintain that gender is *purely* social and psychological, while a few (pejoratively called essentialists by the others) subscribe to a belief that femininity has a biological basis. Ann Oakley maintains that gender is totally a social construct and quotes experiments which are said to prove that hormones have no effect on gender identity.[7]

Humans are integrated beings, with minds and bodies that exist in a social context, yet gender is usually discussed in the context of biology *or* of psychology *or* of social formation. The answer is likely to be a combination of all three, with one having dominance at one time or another.

SEXUALITY AND SEX

The word 'sexuality' is also ambiguous and is often loosely used to mean sexual preference. In current terminology it expands to mean

> the quality of being sexual or having sex; possession of sexual powers, or capability of sexual feelings; recognition of or preoccupation with what is sexual.[8]

Ann Oakley holds that the word 'sexuality' describes the whole area of personality related to sexual behaviour.

The word 'sex' is also widely used in a confusing manner. It is used to label the biological difference between women and men, and sometimes to mean the genitals; it is also used to describe sexual instincts and desires, and sexual activity – generally genital intercourse. Germaine Greer gave a comprehensive definition of the modern use of the word in *Sex and Destiny*:

> Sex is actually a magical, suggestive and utterly indefinable idea. It includes gender, eroticism, genitality, mystery, prurience, fertility, virility, titillation, neurology, psychopathology, hygiene, pornography and sin, all hovering about actual experiences of the most intractable subjectivity.[9]

In this book I intend to use the word 'sex' as denoting the biological differences between women and men; for example, female sex, male sex; the word 'sexuality' as meaning possession of sexual powers, or capability of sexual feelings; and the self-explanatory 'sexual activity' for the various manifestations and practices of sexuality.

There are three main theories of sexuality: (1) that it is biological; (2) that it is psychologically constructed; (3) that it is culturally or socially constructed. Some hold that it is one or other combination of two of these factors; none allow for a combination of all three, or for situations in which one or other - biology, psychology, social or cultural environment – gain precedence over the other two.

My thesis is that sexuality is all three, and each should be given its due importance in a unified theory. In practice, as new insights emerge, their apologists tend to focus on each new perception to the exclusion or depreciation of those already existing. They spend so much time and energy promoting their new insight that it becomes for them a single issue. Freud is a particular example; he was so enthusiastic about his discovery that sexuality had a psychological dimension which began in infanthood that he applied his theory exclusively, even though in later years there were indications in his own observations that he saw other forces at work. The origins of life and the whole concept of life indicate that it must be viewed in an holistic manner.[10] Life itself, the life force, is a 'living' example of the dictum 'the whole is greater than the sum of the parts'.

Until the eighteenth century, philosophers and scientists maintained that there was only one sex, in which males represented the archetypal or highest form, and females were lesser or imperfect men. This theory was abandoned with the onset of scientific analysis. Yet if the science of biology has disproved this theory of sex, fallout from the concept persists in the unconscious of our patriarchal society; women are still perceived as inferior. This perception demonstrates how susceptible the psyche is to social and cultural conditioning, and how it can resist evidence.

The twentieth century saw a revolution in matters sexual unknown in historical times. Sexuality, which had been regarded as a purely biological phenomenon, indeed an instinctual imperative, became a scientific study, and the old certainties were challenged by psychologists and sociologists. Women were central in two ways to this revolution: at first women were seen as sexually deficient by these researchers because they were judged by a male standard of sexuality; then the women's movement started to strip away the layers of misconceptions, both social and psychological, that concealed female sexuality even from women themselves. However, the theories of Freud and the post-Freudian psychoanalysts were important; and, although difficult, they were absorbed into the popular definitions of sexuality.

When the new 'sexual freedom' of the mid-twentieth century, the sexual revolution, was examined by the women's movement in the 1970s it was found wanting; it was not the liberation that women had been promised. Since then feminists have taken available information and insights, deconstructed and reconstructed them, and they have advanced the understanding of sexuality at a faster rate than at any time since Freud. Generally they accept that sexuality and gender are socially and psychologically constructed, but most of them ignore the biological genesis of 'sex'.

So, what is sexuality? Is it purely a biological instinct or drive which has a definite, inherent and single purpose such as reproduction of the species or the pleasure of the participants? Is it a bodily drive, the objectives of which have been imprinted psychologically? Or is it a bodily function (drive/ energy) formed by and learned from social influences and pressures? With reference to the last two questions, would a human reared in isolation from psychological or social influences (if that were possible) have a sexuality, and know what to do with it if she or he had it?

If gender is allotted to a person because of her or his biological sex, and sexuality is the expression of that sex, then gender is closely identified with sexuality because of the influence it exercises on it.

Sexuality has influenced the relationship between the sexes more than any other factor, and that relationship has been infected by a male antagonism to women that stretches back through historical times. Misogyny, to a greater or lesser degree and in various manifestations, and its concomitant, male domination, have been a constant strain in human relations. Misogyny is sexism and the suppression of women *because* they are women, and what makes them women but a sexuality that has been constructed on their biological sex. There are two related claims made by feminist theorists: one, that women are oppressed through their sexuality; and two, that male sexuality is at the root of male supremacy or male domination of women. To examine these claims, it is necessary to learn how sexuality is constructed, and why the blight of woman hatred developed in the human race.

The mechanics of change are difficult because of the varying degrees of freedom which women enjoy (or oppression which they suffer) in different parts of the world. While in Western society we worry about feminist philosophy, women are being raped, tortured and exploited all over the world. In many countries women are killed or tortured for campaigning for women's rights. In others, they are mass raped as an instrument of war. It is estimated that between 90 million to 100 million women worldwide are subjected to genital mutilation as a cultural imperative.[11] How does the women's movement tackle such an over-whelming task? How can it counter this appalling sexual violence against women?

The roots of this appalling violence against women lie in a cultural misogyny that has always been with us.

2

'THE TERRIBLE CONTEMPT'

The literature of misogyny is so vast that no summary of sensible proportions could do it justice.

KATE MILLETT[1]

Misogyny is not a projection of women who resent men. That it exists, and has been validated by patriarchal culture at all times, is clearly documented . . .

ADRIENNE RICH[2]

. . . only a culture which harboured a deep-seated hatred of women could produce a mass killer of [the Yorkshire Ripper's] kind . . . The discrimination and denigration and violence that women suffer are no historical accident but linked manifestations of this hatred.

JOAN SMITH[3]

The fact is that the myth [of the Fall of Adam and Eve] has projected a malignant image of the male–female relationship and of the 'nature' of woman that is still deeply embedded in the modern psyche . . . Women as a case, then, are 'Eve' and are punished by a cohesive set of laws, customs and social arrangements that enforce an all-pervasive double standard.

MARY DALY[4]

'What do you see as the fundamental issue?' I asked Rebecca West in March 1982. 'Contempt,' she replied, 'the terrible contempt in which men hold women.'

DALE SPENDER[5]

A history of sexuality is a history of misogyny. There exists throughout the world what journalist Susan Faludi in *Backlash* calls a bedrock of misogyny which flows and ebbs, erupts or is quiescent, depending on whether women are successfully resisting subordination or submitting to it.[6] Because we are not always conscious of it, and because it erupts in extreme form only sporadically, does not mean that it does not exist. Women are tolerated so long as they 'keep their place' and do not encroach on male preserves or privilege. A less pejorative word for misogyny is 'sexism', and it is akin to racism, because men in general do not consider that women are, or can be, persons of the same worth or status as themselves.

Throughout the centuries there has been a tacit, often unconscious, internalised conspiracy of misogyny, which became conscious and manifested itself at various times in history when men enacted laws against women or waged war on them. The virtual universality of misogyny does not mean that all men are raging misogynists; in some it is more pronounced and noticeable than in others. Moreover, and significantly, in some societies a few men have almost eradicated it but for the rags and tatters of cultural conditioning that still adhere to them.

Psychologist Lynne Segal points out that there is no male equivalent for misogyny; the term misanthropy applies to all humans.[7] There are degrees of misogyny, ranging from the milder forms of sexism (such as believing women are inferior, especially those who are outside the magic circle of kith and kin, and resenting any success or achievement of equality on their part), through the stronger and more indelible feelings of contempt and plain hatred, to the serious cases of battering, rape, woman murder and gynocide. (Those who think gynocide ended with the witch burnings of three or four centuries ago, need only look at what happened in Bosnia in 1992; and in the same year the Burmese rape and murder of Muslim women.)

When misogyny is examined, it is always directly or indirectly related to sexuality. When it is manifest in gender situations, such as encroachment of roles, the weapons used against women are sexual, either physical or verbal; underlying every criticism of women is the assertion of their sexual inferiority, the assumption that they are objects designed for men's use. The objectification of women is achieved by sexual acts, attitudes, words and fantasies. This is an indictment of the form that male sexuality takes, the psychological and cultural distortion that male sexuality has suffered. Not alone is female sexuality misrepresented and short-changed by a still-prevailing male interpretation of it, but male sexuality is also distorted and limited by the way it is culturally represented and interpreted.

There is an epidemic of pathological male sexuality abroad, ranging in virulence from sexual incontinence to pornography, rape and the atrocities wreaked on women in various wars around the world. It is found in the way men depict women in popular literature and in the other media of communication,[8] in schools where young males try out on young females the sexual attitudes they have inherited from their culture, in sexual harassment in the workplace, in many other instances of male domination where the method used to belittle women is sexual.

Biological determinists say there is no misogyny, just a natural relationship of domination that exists between male and female. Those who place more emphasis on culture say that it results from a patriarchal society, and requires a change in social practice and attitudes. It is explained by some psychoanalysts, such as Dorothy Dinnerstein and Nancy Chodorow, as the reaction of the male to female domination in childhood, and requires a change in child-rearing practices and, in particular, the establishment of joint parenting. Dorothy Dinnerstein calls in the support of other writers to elaborate on the psychological factors involved: Simone de Beauvoir, Margaret Mead and H.R. Hays, she says, all pointed out that man has magic feelings of awe and sometimes fear, disgust and rage towards all things that are mysterious, powerful, not himself, and that woman's fertile body is the quintessential incarnation of this realm of things.

> Alien, dangerous nature, conveniently concentrated near at hand in woman's flesh, can be controlled through ritual segregation, confinement and avoidance, it can be subdued through conventionalised humiliation and punishment; it can be honoured and placated through ceremonial gifts and adornments, through formalised gestures of respect and protectiveness. History and ethnography abundantly illustrate human use of this opportunity.[9]

Most feminist philosophers reject the assumption that misogyny or domination is natural. From a biological point of view there is no logical reason for misogyny; gender antagonism does not exist among other mammals. Males in some mammalian herds protect the females because females are valuable to the survival of the herd, and males are expendable. Misogyny has existed throughout human history,[10] but history is only an account of the development of the dominating culture, not of the human race, and we now know how biassed it is since we discovered how men have suppressed women's involvement in it.[11]

When we talk about men's contempt for women, we are talking about something of ancient lineage and rooted deeply in our culture. Religion has played an important part in the subordination of women; our culture grew out of religion; our basic religious texts contain its earliest historical roots. The seminal story of European and Near Eastern culture, the myth of the

Fall of Adam and Eve, created by a misogynist society, is fundamentally embedded in the modern psyche. Not alone did the Book of Genesis cast blame on Eve and mete out everlasting punishment to her and her female descendants, it made an attempt to hijack reproduction from women by suggesting that Eve was created from Adam's rib.

The reasons given for devaluing woman were that she was an inferior human and sexually unclean. The Old Testament and ancient Greek, Roman, Hebrew, Islamic, Germanic and Celtic literature testify that she was excluded from war, law, government and religion because of the sexuality of her physical body: her menstruation, uterus, child-bearing, lactation. Aristotle said that woman was a 'deficient' man, able only to supply the 'matter' of the foetus to which the superior male supplied the 'form' and 'soul'. Relics of this belief still lodge in many minds even in this 'enlightened' age.

Pandora, the Greek equivalent of the Jewish Eve, is still with us, toting her box, and releasing all kinds of evil and ruin upon men. In the original myth Pandora's box (or honey-vase) poured out blessings and good things on humanity, but in the eighth century B.C. the Greek poet Hesiod composed a new fable which changed the contents of her vase to all the evils and afflictions of the world and blamed them on women.[12] The Greeks supplied Circe, Charybdis, the Sirens, the Furies, the Harpies, the Gorgons and Medusa to our cultural history – all sexually menacing to the male heroes, and the Greek philosopher Pythagoras alleged, 'There is a good principle which created order, light and man, and a bad principle which created chaos, darkness and woman'.[13] The Romans were not far behind: Horace, Juvenal and Catullus wrote scathingly of women. (In the sixth satire, Juvenal attributed to them every possible irritating and evil habit he could conceive, albeit in an engagingly humorous way.)

These Greek and Latin texts still form part of classical studies in the great universities, studies which have been the *sine qua non* of male education for high office in Western countries.

In the old misogynist tracts we often read of the sexual insatiability of women, their evilness and the need to keep them under control. American psychologist Mary Jane Sherfey's analysis of ancient texts led her to believe that in prehistory female sexuality was intense and insatiable – possibly arising from an early manifestation of the recently rediscovered multiple female orgasm. It was therefore necessary, she said, in the interests of cultural evolution and civilisation, to control it, and that is what men did.[14]

Christianity brought some change; Jesus purported to include women on an equal basis with men in the new religion, as in the Martha and Mary story, but he chose twelve male apostles – at least, that is the account that has reached us. Even in the time of Christ, Gnosticism was beginning to have an influence on the religious preachers who were laying down laws for the moral behaviour of people. Gnosis was a nihilist belief that spread west from Persia shortly before the time of Christ. It held that all material things were evil and from the devil, and only the human soul was good and from God. It was against the body and bodily pleasure of any kind which were believed to entrap the soul and prevent it from returning to God. (There were many different sects, with different beliefs, and while some of them were antagonistic to women as a class, others were not, and allowed women to participate as equal in religious observance.[15])

Paul was influenced to some extent by the more misosynistic strains of Gnosticism and was not going to tolerate any women's liberation in the new Church. 'Let the woman learn in silence with all submissiveness,' he wrote in the *Epistle to Timothy* in A.D. 65. 'But I suffer not a women to teach, nor to usurp authority over the man, but to be in silence. For Adam was formed first, then Eve. And Adam was not deceived, but the woman being deceived was in transgression. Notwithstanding she shall be saved in child-bearing, if they continue in faith and charity and holiness with sobriety.'[16] (Even in this myth the lack of logic is evident: Adam was also a transgressor, so where was his much-vaunted superiority which could have led him to refuse to eat the 'forbidden fruit'?)

Soon the Church Fathers reintroduced the old Hebrew misogyny and with even more vitriol. Only 'they [men] who were not defiled with women' were saved, according to the Book of Revelation 14:4 (*c.* A.D. 96). Women's bodies were polluted, menstruating women were unclean and not allowed near the altar. By the end of the second century of the Christian era, Tertullian was addressing women thus:

> You are the Devil's gateway. You are the unsealer of that forbidden tree. You are the first deserter of the divine Law. You are she who persuaded him whom the Devil was not valiant enough to attack. You destroyed so easily God's image, man. On account of your desert, that is death, even the Son of God had to die.

Jerome, a fourth-century contemporary of Augustine, also held that only men could properly serve God, and that women could 'be called man' if they renounced sexuality and reproduction. The myth of original sin was also shifted by the early Church Fathers from the disobedience of eating forbidden fruit from the Tree of Knowledge of Good and Evil to the first sexual act. Evil was centred in sexuality, and this was later enunciated in the fifth century by Augustine to become Christian dogma. When Adam saw Eve naked he lost control of his body and 'the flesh began to lust against the spirit'.[17]

These hostile statements are significant because they have survived, signifying the survival of an irrational and illogical misogyny down the ages; Christian patriarchs spent a lot of time and energy on their palpable and pathological misogyny. By faulty logic and semantic conjuring they transferred their poor opinion of men to women. Their fear of male sexuality and sexual response became fear of sexuality in general and led to the denunciation of the female. And although women gained somewhat from the Christian ideal of marriage, the idea of woman as flesh, and potentially dangerous to man, helped to incorporate all the older beliefs and practices surrounding women's bodies and reproduction into Christianity. For instance, 'churching', the purification of women after child-birth, was reintroduced in the seventh century.[18]

Fear of Eve, and women, continued in the medieval Church. Women were acceptable if they remained virgins and embraced the life of the cloisters; that is, until the fantasies of a thirteenth-century Dominican priest gave rise to the myth of the fictitious Pope Joan who was undone by sex. Then there was the story of Heloise and Abelard; to this day nothing titillates more than the story of priests and nuns, lay or religious, having sexual relations together or with others (unless it is the sex life of bishops). However, women viewed the cloisters in a different way from that in-tended by men. Convents and nunneries were places where women could be free of the interference of men, where they could have dignity and hon-our, and take charge of their own future, running estates accumulated from foundation grants and dowries.

The Church's general attitude to sexuality continued into the sixteenth and seventeenth centuries. The Council of Trent in 1563 declared that marriage for clergy meant living 'in the filth of impurity and unclean bondage'. In more recent times it has been content to take control of women's fertility and to promote their subordination to men – fathers, husbands, clergy – and usually refrains from overt denunciation of them as limbs of Satan.

The most notorious outbreaks of misogyny were the witch trials which took place from the fourteenth century to the seventeenth century. *Malleus Maleficarum* (*Hammer of Witches*), the report on witchcraft commissioned by Pope Innocent VIII and compiled by two Dominicans, Heinrich Kramer and James Sprenger in 1484, was simply pornography. It was a diatribe against the sexuality of women, a resurgence of the old idea that women were sexually insatiable and could therefore be called witches. It contained allegations of orgies on the witches' sabbath, cannibalism of newborn babies, lewd dancing, drunkenness, intercourse with every variety of creature in every possible position; and, of course, that witches castrated men and copulated with Satan:

> Now there are, as it is said in the Papal Bull, seven methods by which they infect with witchcraft the venereal act and the conception of the womb: first by inclining the minds of men to inordinate passion; second, by obstructing their generative force; third, by removing the members accommodated by that act; fourth, by changing men into beasts by the magic act; fifth, by destroying the generative force in women; sixth, by procuring abortion; seventh, by offering children to the devils, besides other animals and fruits of the earth with which they work much harm.

The obvious conclusion of any post-Freudian observer is that the repressed sexuality of these two men, and of the celibate clergy and scribes of the time, had a pathological effect on them and turned them into psychosexual lunatics.

'Witches' were any women who were 'disagreeable' in male terms; almost any form of 'awkwardness' was enough to condemn a woman if she crossed a man of sufficient power and malevolence. The punishment (death by burning at the stake) was carried out by a misogynist state in conjunction with the Church. Some of these women were heretics adhering to the old pagan religion; some claimed magic powers and many of their spells did indeed relate to sexuality. But most were healers or wise women, herbalists, who helped women to control their fertility by contraception and abortion and therefore ran foul of the male claim to the practice of medicine. Their suppression had consequences for the health and sexuality of all women to the present day.

In *Witches, Midwives and Nurses*, Barbara Ehrenreich and Deirdre English connect the persecution of witches to an organised attack on women in medicine in a male takeover of the profession. In this brief history of women and healing they trace an involvement of women in medicine which goes back into prehistory. In the thirteenth century medical schools became attached to universities, which were regulated by the Church. As women were excluded from universities, they could not become physicians, and only university-trained doctors were given the legal right to practise medicine. These male doctors were expensive and affordable only by the upper classes. There were some women healers among the upper classes, but their activities were resented by their male colleagues, who frequently used the law against them and effectively suppressed them. However, the practice of excluding women from healing and medicine was not universal, nor was it uniformly practised. There were times and places where women healers were acceptable, and others where they were banned.

Women were always the healers, Ehrenreich and English assert, particularly among the poorer classes. These women were resented and defamed by the professionals and before long their persecution became official. Like the more recent pogroms against Jews and Blacks, they suffered a sustained, systematic, official vilification and persecution. Even to this day the word 'witch' is so derogatory that in the *Oxford English Dictionary* the meaning is given as female magician or sorceress who has dealings with the devil; the witch as healer or wise woman is forgotten. (However, *Chambers Twentieth-Century Dictionary*, 1936 edition, links it with the old Anglo-Saxon word *witiga* or *witga*, a seer, implying wisdom and knowledge.)

The research which Ehrenreich and English carried out reveals that even in history as written by one of the persecutors, an English witch-hunter, witches were recognised as healers:

> By witches we understand not only those which kill and torment, but all Diviners, Charmers, Jugglers, all Wizards, commonly called wise men and wise women ... and in the same number we reckon all good Witches, which do no hurt but good, which do not spoil and destroy, but save and deliver ... It were a thousand times better for the land if all witches, but especially the blessing Witch, might suffer death.[19]

(The 'blessing witch' was believed by the Church to be healing by the power of the devil.) The infamous authors of *Malleus Maleficarum*, wrote, 'No one does more harm to the Catholic Church than midwives', and 'If a woman dare to cure without having studied she is a witch and must die.'

On the far-flung western approaches of Europe these islands might have escaped the worst excesses of European misogyny. But no. Witches were executed in England and Scotland in the sixteenth, seventeenth and early eighteenth centuries. Interestingly there is only one record of a witch in

Ireland: Dame Alice Kyteler from Kilkenny, who was accused of witchcraft in the fourteenth century. That does not mean, however, that misogyny was absent from the green island; in Celtic Ireland law codes ranked women with slaves, prisoners and drunks as 'senseless'.[20]

While university-educated, medieval doctors, guided by the Church, were trained in philosophy and theology, as well as the works of the ancient Greek physician Galen and made their prognoses with the aid of astrology, the witch-healers were further developing an already profound understanding of anatomy, herbs and drugs, which was acknowledged by Paracelsus, 'the father of modern medicine', in 1527. He is said to have burned his text on pharmaceuticals, confessing that he 'had learned from the Sorceress all he knew'.[21] Yet the knowledge of women healers was labelled 'superstition', and has given to the language the pejorative byword, 'old wives' tales'.

Obstetrics remained, however, in the hands of midwives, until the advent of the forceps in the seventeenth century, when an attack was mounted by the barber-surgeons, who claimed it as a surgical instrument (by the seventeenth century women were legally barred from surgery). In most countries of Europe, even where laws barring women from the study of medicine did not exist, colleges refused to accept women. Some women who qualified as doctors did so disguised as men. In the United States, where the first woman in the world qualified in her own right as a medical doctor in 1849, there were no legal restrictions on women entering medicine, there was just prejudice.

The profession of healing has suffered greatly from the exclusion of women doctors during the past thousand years, particularly in the area of obstetrics and reproduction. For the past century, since they have won access to education, the numbers of women entering medicine has gradually increased, so that now they are as numerous as men in gaining degrees, but inequality of opportunity has kept all but a very few out of the higher echelons of the profession. The number of women consultants, sureons, professors of medicine is small, and this has meant that the accepted creed and canon of medicine is still male-dominated, and women study and work within the confines of this 'orthodoxy'.

MISOGYNY TODAY

Misogyny is rooted deep within our culture but it is difficult to know where a male 'compulsion' to dominate ends and misogyny begins. Indeed, is the desire to dominate not also a form of misogyny? A significant proportion of men resent women whom they cannot dominate, and what is the root of this resentment if not misogyny?

What form does misogyny take at the present time? Apart from a general resentment among men against women who are not submissive, there is the universal, casual contempt for women other than the specially chosen females within a man's personal orbit: it is 'other' women – secretaries, shop assistants, other men's partners, female colleagues, cleaning women, the 'woman in the street', old women, unmarried women – that men criticise generally not their own sisters, mothers, partners or daughters. At the violent end of the spectrum there is the murder and battering of women by men with whom they may or may not be involved. (In particular, such men batter their sexual partners, and occasionally murder them, when they are angered or irritated by them.)

Boys develop, through identification with their father, what we have come to consider the normal contempt for women. The basis for woman hatred (from minor contempt to major violence) is affirmed in the way boys are reared. Why this is so is another question. Boys are mocked for behaviour or dress which is called feminine, thus sowing the seeds of antipathy to femininity. *Why* should dress be feminised and masculinised? Only because some female dress, such as the skirt, is sexualised. Boys are generally insulated from women's work – wheeling prams, knitting and sewing, cleaning, washing clothes, so how could they grow up other than despising women's work and hence women, and then hating them in the more extreme situations, such as when women claim anything approaching equality with them, or demand rights.

Boys are allowed more 'roughness' than girls; they can get dirty without losing face; girls cannot. If they fight they are not reprimanded, while girls are made to feel anti-social for fighting physically; boys are stopped in case they hurt each other – not because it is undesirable or socially wrong. Grown women fighting physically give rise to titillation or amusement, males fighting are manly. If girls were taught to defend themselves – to fight like 'men' – or if boys were ostracised for fighting, then perhaps one element of difference would disappear. Furthermore, because boys are reared to see women as their servicers, they cannot but feel superior to them.

If the way boys are reared, and their general socialisation, ensures the power complex of men and their woman hatred, it could also work for change. The attitudes laid deep in the psyche of infants could be socialised out of them if the culture permitted. Male pride is built on being different to girls and women, and male antagonism to women is similar to the hatred involved in racism – which always assumes inferiority of the hated one, or hatred of the one considered inferior. Boys grow up feeling that women are inferior and so the step to hatred (as in racism) is short.

It is a shock for women to discover that the courtly gloss put on male/female relations is just a façade, a myth, the reality being very different. Many women go through life without ever probing beneath the surface of the myth; similarly men never question their attitude to women. Just as people can live satisfactory lives hating certain insects yet not knowing anything about them, so can men behave towards women.

Women encounter misogyny in all aspects of their lives but particularly in the male preserve of work outside the home. In *Working Your Way to the Bottom: The Feminization of Poverty*, Hilda Scott demonstrates the resentment of men for women who aspire to equality in the workplace. She relates how the Nobel prizewinner James Watson described the crystallographer Rosalind Franklin in his book *The Double Helix*, the account of how he and Francis Crick won the race for the discovery of the structure of DNA. This achievement was made possible by a crucial contribution made by Franklin, which was not acknowledged:

> Though her features were strong, she was not unattractive and might have been quite stunning had she taken even a mild interest in clothes. This she did not. There was never lipstick to contrast with her straight black hair, while at the age of thirty-one her dresses showed all the imagination of English bluestocking adolescents. So it was quite easy to imagine her the product of an unsatisfied mother who unduly stressed the desirability of professional careers that could save bright girls from marriages to dull men.

Scott points out that Watson's book contained no similar personal description of his other colleagues. Not only did Rosalind Franklin fail to live up to Watson's idea of femininity, she persisted in acting like an independent, highly qualified professional scientist, and not like somebody's assistant. Watson again:

> Clearly Rosy had to go or be put in her place. The former was obviously preferable because, given her belligerent moods, it would be very difficult for Maurice (Wilkins) to maintain a dominant position that would allow him to think unhindered about DNA ... Unfortunately Maurice could not see any decent way to give Rosy the boot.

Rachel Carson, the distinguished ecologist, also suffered because she was a woman. After publication of her seminal work, *Silent Spring*, sections of the chemical industry which felt threatened by the book tried to establish a public image of her as an emotional, reclusive, unstable person, the embittered-spinster-with-an-axe-to-grind syndrome. Luckily she prevailed.

The wide extent of direct violence against women such as rape and sexual partner battering was exposed by the modern women's movement and gave rise to rape crisis centres and women's shelters in many Western countries. This violence is the result of men's need to assert their sexual authority over women, and would not, in other antagonistic circum-stances, be directed against a man. In these cases we are not dealing with the general behaviour of the average man, but only at the extremes can one get a clear statement of the attitudes that exist in varying degrees in most men's behaviour. I will deal more fully with the various explanations and reasons given for misogyny, and with such aspects of woman-hatred as rape and pornography in later chapters.

The depth and strength of misogyny at the present time is difficult to appreciate, because nowadays it is hidden to a large extent. In earlier times it was manifested openly: male writers in the fourteenth to seventeenth centuries (who are those that have survived) described women as vile, inconstant, fragile, cowardly, obstinate, venomous, imprudent, cunning, incorrigible, easily upset, full of hatred, always talking, incapable of keeping a secret, insincere, frivolous, profligate with money, a nag, jealous, contradictory, disobedient and worst of all, sexually insatiable. The work of only a very few women writers have survived from that period, of whom the French woman, Christine de Pizan, is one, and she refuted these slanders against women. She called men's condemnations 'arbitrary fabrication': 'nonsense', 'futile words', 'wicked insults', 'slanders', and the 'lies of a lecher'.[22]

In her scholarly history of women in Western Europe, covering the period 1500 to 1800, Olwen Hufton gives a comprehensive and detailed historical account of the social, legal and domestic control of women that amounted to endemic misogyny in our culture, which erupted into overt cruelty when women 'transgressed' or resisted. She shows how it pervaded all facets of life from the biblical era, through the medieval period to modern times, and was a conscious as well as an unconscious process:

> Eve's contribution to notions of womanhood which stretched from
> biblical times and survived the medieval period intact, might be

summarized as three traditions: that of woman as the agent of the Devil and as temptress; that of woman as a heedless chatterbox, gossiping and garrulous, whose tongue needed to be kept under control; and that of woman as man's downfall, woman as a scapegoat for his (or their joint) mistakes.[23]

3

INVENTING SEXUALITY

We need a short history of modern sexuality if we are to understand and define it, and examine its development in ideology and practice. Michel Foucault's eminent *The History of Sexuality* had only reached the second century A.D. when he died. His was not an analysis of the nature of sexuality; it concerned, rather, what he called 'the deployment of sexuality', or 'a history of the experience of sexuality'. This chapter will deal with the various sexual reform movements, the development of ideas about the nature of sexuality over the past two centuries, and the other elements that led up to the mid-twentieth-century sexual revolution.[1]

Social historians claim the emergence of two new areas of knowledge or science at the end of the nineteenth century as the mainspring of the sexual revolution in the twentieth century. These were the development of psychoanalysis and the emergence of the new 'science' of sexology. Others claim more mundane reasons for this century's permissiveness, but ones which, for whatever purpose, are still a deployment of sexuality:

- the economic boom after the Second World War;
- the commercial importance of women as shoppers and the eroticisation of the housewife as the main agent of consumerism;
- the eroticisation of consumerism and leisure;
- and the extension of the years spent in education.

From early in the nineteenth century the first stirrings of a sexual revolution spread across Europe and the North American continent. At the beginning it crept slowly from one patch of intellectualism to another and was sometimes associated with socialism or feminism. In the second half of the twentieth century it became a flood which engulfed large populations on both continents. The radical sexual movements in the nineteenth century had many different objectives; they included campaigns for contraception and against the double standard in sexual behaviour, where promiscuity and sexual assertiveness was admired in men but despised in women, the various social purity and social hygiene campaigns, and the movements for sexual reform, of which the advocates of 'free love' were the most radical.

Contraceptives – sheaths, suppositories, vaginal plugs and other devices – had been around for more than two thousand years; the word condom, first used in print in 1706, is said to have come from a late-seventeenth-century French physician called Dr Condum. Francis Page was the first known campaigner for contraception; he distributed handbills in Britain in 1823 advocating the use of a sponge in the vagina during intercourse. The philosopher John Stuart Mill and other radical reformers also campaigned for birth control from the 1820s onwards. Several physicians of the time published texts of advice and information on contraceptive methods, but it was not until Annie Besant and the British Malthusian League that the campaign for contraception became a movement. Annie Besant was followed by many others, notably Margaret Sanger in the United States and Marie Stopes in Britain, who became leaders of the movement that finally succeeded.[2]

The availability of contraception was very important not only for a freer expression of women's sexuality but also for their health and wellbeing. Previously the alternative to frequent debilitating and sometimes life-threatening pregnancies was life-threatening abortions. The noted antipathy of nineteenth-century women to sexual activity had its origins in its physical dangers for them as much as in a prudish culture that regarded sexuality as immoral and dirty and therefore not proper for good and pure women. But if contraception released women from physical danger and sexual repression, its opponents pointed out that it had undoubted advantages also for men: it increased their opportunities for promiscuity without responsibility.

The social purity movements in the United States were opposed to contraception, to sexual activity outside of marriage, and they urged continence within marriage. In Britain these movements had slightly different policies; they campaigned for the right of women to say no to sexual advances whether outside or within marriage, and for their right to 'voluntary motherhood', but they, too, advocated continence rather than contraceptive methods. They opposed the double standard, the abuse of women, especially girl children, and the exploitation of prostitutes. These movements feared that contraception would allow men to visit prostitutes without risk, that men would put off marriage indefinitely if contraception allowed sexual licence, and that separation of sexual activity and marriage would threaten that institution and therefore women. On moral and religious grounds, some argued for restraint, while others lobbied for sex education.

The social purity movements have received a bad press in this age of sexual freedom, but a few feminists have defended them as reasonable for women at that time. Sheila Jeffreys restored their feminist credentials in *The Spinster and Her Enemies*, and was roundly attacked by libertarians for finding virtue in their efforts; these movements were, they said, misogynist, class-ridden and patriarchal; they were anti-sexual and too ready to resort to legislation to control sexuality.

It is easy to criticise these early social purity movements from the vantage point of the end of the twentieth century, and to denigrate the women who worked for legislation to control male sexuality. The changes in politics and sexual practice which have taken place during this century are tremendous. A challenge to the double standard one hundred years ago could only be mounted in two ways: prevailing on men either by persuasion or coercion to moderate their sexual activity and have more respect for all women; or by claiming the right of women to adopt male sexual practices. Patriarchy and male power were unrestrained at that time; the infrastructure of feminism was weak; most of the laws which now allow women legal and economic freedom did not exist. They could hardly seek to emulate the behaviour which they deplored in men, so using legislation and persuasion to bring about change presented the most effective means available to them.

The social hygiene movements, initiated mainly by doctors and taken up by some women's groups, advocated public discussion of sexuality, and sex education, but within the established moral code.[3] Both movements provided stepping stones to what we now call the sexual revolution, but they were challenged and disdained by the radical sexual reformers who followed them.

Most famous of the British campaigners was Josephine Butler, who fought against the Contagious Diseases Acts, which were specifically directed against prostitutes, and eventually succeeded in having them repealed. The acts applied to army and navy garrison towns of Britain and Ireland and subjected women, who were suspected of being prostitutes, to summary arrest and, if infected with venereal disease, to confinement in hospital for up to three months. There were no similar inspections of the soldiery or of other men who used these women, although they may have infected the prostitutes in the first place, and subsequently also their own wives. As there was no positive definition of who was a prostitute, in practice it meant any woman, particularly those of the working class, who walked abroad unaccompanied by a man, or who did not behave 'properly or modestly', as defined by the arresting policeman.[4]

The advocates of sexual reform in the nineteenth century were usually the radical thinkers of the time; many were early socialists of the co-operative movement, such as the followers of Robert Owen, Charles Fourier and Saint-Simon. Later sexual freedom, interpreted as 'free love', became an important tenet of socialism and hence Marxism.

The ferment of scientific interest in sexuality generated by turn-of-the-century developments in psychology and sexology was reflected in a corresponding burgeoning of radical and reform movements. In the 1910s and 1920s Greenwich Village in New York City became a testing ground for new experiments in sexual relations, such as premarital and extramarital liaisons and communal living. A feminist influence on this model of sexual liberation laid emphasis on mutual sexual satisfaction, emotional intimacy and intellectual exchange between partners, as well as equal career opportunities for women. Relationships should be close, passionate, affectionate and cerebral, with women and men (many of them writers) both sharing outside interests and the work of the home. But the difficulties of adjusting to these revolutionary changes in lifestyle tipped the seesaw of 'equality' further and further back in favour of men; the model gradually reverted to the cultural norms of the time, man in the public sphere and woman in the private.[5]

The Great Depression of the 1930s and the Second World War interrupted these social experiments, and when urban America resumed its search for sexual liberation it was informed by the laboratory experiments of the mid-century sexologists. These, in turn, spawned the 'sex advice' books and the 'wife-swapping' experiments of the 1950s, where the new sexual permissiveness was shorn of everything but mechanistic sexual activity.

In revolutionary Russia the 'free love' advocated by Alexandra Kollontai was seized upon, gloated over and distorted by the international media. Her ideas on sexual freedom were misinterpreted and treated with ribaldry and sneers in a patriarchal plot to discredit her. Her real political contribution as Commissar for Social Welfare and as an influential member of the new Communist administration lay in legislation for the protection of mothers and children, and in the actual organisation of practical help for them.

Kollontai's ideas on sexual liberation were intellectual. Her 'free love' was not 'free lust' but 'love–comradeship', involving 'equality in relationships ... mutual recognition of the rights of others ... (and) comradely sensitivity, the ability to listen and understand the inner workings of the loved person'.[6] In November 1917, immediately after the revolution, at the instigation of Kollontai, the new Soviet Union introduced simplified civil marriage and divorce. In 1920 it reluctantly legalised abortion, allowing free abortions in state hospitals as women's elementary right, because it was the only generally available method of birth control.[7]

In Britain there were the brave experiments of Dora Russell, Stella Browne and some of their contemporaries, who were attempting to break the mould of 'the legal, domestic and sexual bondage from which feminist pioneers were trying to escape and deliver their sisters'.[8] These experiments with free love (or as Russell described it in 1925, 'the mutual nature of sex-love ... free and full on either side') were, however, the prerogative of privileged and educated women. Such an affirmation of sexuality was remote from the material conditions of working-class life in the 1920s. Leonora Eyles found 'many of the [working-class] women she spoke to regarded sex as a chore not a pleasure ... [they were] paralysed with fear about the economic and physical danger of pregnancy'.[9] Therefore, of great importance were the various organisations lobbying for the general availability of contraception and/or abortion.

From the turn of the century, against great opposition, attempts were being made in Europe and North America to make contraception generally available and to legalise abortion. Opposition was motivated by several different interests: in the United States the White Anglo-Saxon Protestant (WASP) ascendancy feared that a declining birth rate would threaten their numbers and therefore their dominance in the land; men everywhere feared that it would enable women to achieve independence; the Churches feared moral decline.

The motives and objectives of birth-control organisations also differed: some were eugenists seeking to limit reproduction among the 'lower classes'; some were Malthusians,[10] who feared a growth of population which would give rise to poverty and disease; and some were both and wanted 'not quantity but quality'.

The world's first birth-control clinic was opened by Dr Aletta Jacobs in the Netherlands in 1882, and at the turn of the century clinics were also providing contraceptives in Germany and the Scandanavian countries. In Britain there were no laws prohibiting the use of contraceptives, but advocates of contraception were prosecuted under the Obscenity Laws which eventually fell into disuse in the years after the First World War but were later used against homosexuals.

By virtue alone of her book *Married Love*, a treatise on foreplay and orgasm published in 1918, Marie Stopes could be included with the early sexologists, but she is best known as an advocate of contraception. Dr Stopes, who was a botanist and fossil scientist, deplored the unscientific approach of both women and men to marriage. In her book she popularised the ideas of the early sexologists and proclaimed that women were just as sexual as men, but they needed stimulation to enjoy orgasm. She was influenced to some extent by Edward Carpenter, a turn-of-the-century social reformer and advocate of personal freedom, and like him she had some unusual ideas (she argued, as he did, that semen and orgasm were necessary for women's health). Marie Stopes opened the first birth-control clinic in Britain in 1921, and by the end of the 1930s the medical establishment had reluctantly accepted a role in birth-control advice.

British laws applied in Ireland until independence was gained in 1921, and even later, until such time as the government of the new state repealed or amended them, or enacted new ones. Therefore, the situation in Ireland with regard to contraception was the same as in Britain but for one important difference: the strength of the Catholic Church. For the overwhelming majority of the population any form of 'artificial' birth control was not entertained on moral grounds, and the new state determined that it should stay like that. In the 1929 Censorship Act it became an offence to advocate contraception; and in 1935 the Criminal Law Amendment Act prohibited the importation or sale of contraceptives (it was unimaginable that they might be manufactured in the country). The situation remained the same until the Family Planning Act of 1979 which permitted the sale of contraceptives to married people over eighteen years of age on a doctor's prescription. Almost immediately this law became unworkable and it is now tacitly accepted that contraceptives are freely available to all, although not legally to those under eighteen.

All Catholic countries were opposed to any form of birth control, but contraceptives were available in France until 1920, when they were outlawed in order to raise the birth rate; they were not legalised again until 1968. In Germany in 1933 the Nazi regime closed family-planning clinics and, in what Kate Millett called 'the brood-mare theory of women', launched a programme to increase the birth rate. Contraception was illegal in the United States during the first decades of this century; the Comstock Law of 1873 made it an offence for any person or agency to give information on contraception to anyone for any reason. Margaret Sanger was arrested when she opened the first birth-control clinic in New York in 1916. During the twenties and thirties, underground distribution of contraceptives and their widespread use meant that the law became unworkable.

The sexual reform movements of the past two centuries also advocated the right of women to abortion, which, though illegal in most countries, existed everywhere and at all stages of history, even in Ireland. Sir William Wilde, surgeon and father of Oscar Wilde, referred to the practice in a lecture to the Dublin Obstetrical Society in 1849. First, he raged against the 'herb doctress' as a charm-working crone, a *cailleach* who 'would have been burnt in Scotland with the "witch's branks in her mouth"'.[11] Then he referred to 'procured abortion, instances of which frequently come under the cognisance of the medical man and the magistrate'. The she-quack, he said, in association with certain mystic ceremonies and pagan rites, 'administers the most drastic purgatives and emmenagogues, of which aloes and gamboge are the chief ingredients. Certain herbs and plants, particularly rue and savine pulled in a particular manner ... are believed by the country people to effect a like end.' He continued: 'Can we wonder at the ignorant Irish girl wishing to conceal her shame by the destruction of her offspring, in a country acknowledged to be one of the most moral in Europe, and where caste is more certainly lost by the circumstances of pregnancy before or without marriage than in any other, when in lands boasted to be the most civilized, induced abortion, even among married females, in the upper ranks of life, is spoken of in society without reserve?'

Over the past two thousand years the Christian Churches have oscillated on the subject of abortion. In pre-Christian times the ethics relating to it were articulated by Plato in *The Republic* and Aristotle in *The Politics*; abortion was allowable in order to control the fitness and the size of the population. In the Christian era it was first mentioned in the third century by Tertullian, who called it murder, but early Christian theologians continued to follow the Aristotelian precepts and allowed abortion within forty days of conception in the case of a boy or eighty days in the case of a girl, the stage at which they believed the soul entered the unborn child. (How the sex of the foetus should be decided is not known.) Pope Sixtus V proclaimed all abortion as murder in 1588, but three years later, in 1591, his successor, Innocent IX, reverted to the old forty-days Aristotelian model. It was not until 1869 that Pope Pius IX reintroduced Church law banning all abortions. For roughly four thousand years of historical times, and under two thousand years of Christianity, abortion has been forbidden by the Catholic religion for only 130 years.

Abortion was made illegal in Britain and Ireland under the Offences Against the Person Act of 1861. It was also illegal in most European countries and in the United States under nineteenth-century legislation. In the last twenty-five years the United States and most European countries have legalised it, and Ireland is in the process of legalising very limited abortion. It was legalised in Britain in 1967 and then with some restrictions, and the British system is one of the most liberal in Europe.

THE EARLY SEXOLOGISTS

By the turn of the century two developments were about to give the sexual revolution an intellectual basis which would launch it into the twentieth century: sexology and psychoanalysis. Until the twentieth century the general (and educated) belief was that sexuality was a biological phenomenon, an instinct with certain reactions and manifestations. Psychology and another child of the nineteenth century, sociology, were already having an influence on the way human behaviour was interpreted, and once Sigmund Freud related psychological development to sexuality, a new enlightenment entered the discussion. The newer ideas of psychology and sociology, however, did not replace biological premises completely. Many biologists, and a new hybrid, sociobiologists, held on to their theories that biology is the sole source of human behaviour, and some of them have had more of an influence on people's perceptions than they deserve.

Looking backwards from the 1990s it is probably safe to say that at no other time in history, in no other century, has there been such an excruciating examination of sexuality and the mechanics of sexual activity, so many words written in scientific or pseudo-scientific enquiry, so much erotica and pornography. Some writings have survived from other times: the sexual ribaldry of Boccaccio's *Decameron*, from the fourteenth century, more direct tracts like the Kamasutra, an ancient Hindu text translated by Sir Richard Burton in 1883, and the works of the Marquis de Sade at the end of the eighteenth century. But if a previous century produced any substantial body of work on sexology, it was destroyed before our time in one of the cold rages of puritanism. Sexology, as the study of the mechanics of sexual activity, is therefore, as far as we can say, a development of the twentieth century, started by nineteenth-century researchers.

One of the earliest sexologists was Richard von Krafft-Ebing, a nineteenth-century German neuro-psychiatrist who made a study of pathological sexuality. With *Psychopathia Sexualis*, published in 1886, he became the founder of modern sexology and was severely criticised for openly publishing matters relating to sexuality, particularly perverted or pathological sexuality. In the prevailing culture of his time, he was considered disreputable, and that reputation has clung to him. He is rarely mentioned in current texts.

Freud was not the first person to allocate sexuality a central role in personality formation. Krafft-Ebing described sexuality as 'the one mighty factor in the individual and social relations of man', but one which could 'degenerate into the lowest passion and the basest vice'. The gratification of the sexual instinct, he said, seems to be the primary motive in man as well as beast. Like Freud, he believed sexuality was powered by a strong natural instinct, but Freud saw in deviancy not vice but regression to infantile sexuality.

Predating and pre-empting the sexologists of this century, Krafft-Ebing recognised the importance of the clitoral orgasm; but that valuable piece of knowledge was mislaid under the cloak of disapproval that concealed his work, and had to be rediscovered by Masters and Johnson in the 1960s.

There were many sexologists by the end of the nineteenth century, and of those the American Havelock Ellis was the most famous and probably the most significant. A contemporary of Freud's, he was a great admirer of Krafft-Ebing and agreed with him that sexuality was a biological drive that was central to human life. He saw sexual behaviour as driven by an inner natural instinct, one of almost overpowering and uncontrollable strength. His first work was a seven-volume treatise, *Studies on the Psychology of Sex* (1936), which, regardless of the title, was more concerned with categorising sexual activity than with defining sexuality. He is credited with being a liberator of sexuality; he dragged it out of the Victorian closet, elevated it as a special human activity and called it an art form. More significantly, for a long period he influenced twentieth-century sex-advice literature, and in particular, the international bestseller *The Joy of Sex* by Alex Comfort.

Ellis held that sexuality was the centre of identity and that there were innate biological differences between the sexes which were immutable, hence the existence of separate roles for women and men. This article of faith begs the question: why then has it been necessary to *impose* restrictions on the lives of women if their roles are dictated biologically?

He is strongly, and correctly, criticised by feminists for erroneous ideas about male domination and female masochism which were (and are still) current in male culture and in pornography. He asserted that the natural form of sexual relations between women and men was male domination and female submission. Domination, according to him, included aggression, capture and bondage, and the infliction of pain. Submission in women was natural, he claimed, because of women's innate masochism; it was the way to true female sexuality and satisfaction. This idea of domination and submission was promoted in *The Joy of Sex* and continues as a fallacy in the study of sexuality. In more recent times psychoanalysts have realised that male domination and female submission in sexuality are psychologically and culturally constructed, and where female masochism exists it is as pathological as male masochism. If pain is identified with sexual satisfaction, then women are likely to run the risk of becoming masochistic, just as men who associate childhood sexual arousal with spanking enjoy whipping in adulthood.

Ellis's thesis was seriously dangerous for women. His ideas induced a tolerance of sexual abuse and rape, even a disbelief that either existed. If, as he claimed, women enjoyed aggression, violence, bondage and pain, then there was no crime. His study of sexuality was unashamedly male-centred, and geared towards maintaining a status quo of male domination in sexual relations. However, in a break with traditional mores he allowed that women had a right to sexual pleasure.

Ellis was very concerned about motherhood, not for any satisfaction it gave to women but in the interests of the improvement of the race. He was a leading light in the eugenics and racial purity movement of the early part of the twentieth century. Women were the mothers of the race and the women's movement of the twentieth century, he said, should direct itself to an 'enlightened culture of motherhood' in order 'to breed a firmly-fibred, clean-minded, and self-reliant race of manly men and womanly women'.

He dismissed the early feminist claims for equality, saying that leadership was not natural for women, and economic equality was impossible for them because of child-bearing and child-rearing . Because this attitude is still used to exploit women, feminists, then and now, unfortunately countered these arguments with a knee-jerk reaction: they included the biological and sexual phenomenon of motherhood in the negative, cultural forces oppressing women. In this they ignored the fact that motherhood for most women is a powerfully rewarding and supremely satisfying experience. If motherhood were not so important for women they would not barter their freedom for it.

4

RANSACKING THE MIND

Psychoanalysis, as created by Sigmund Freud (1856–1939) and further developed by his followers, is one area of study which tried to define sexuality, and it accorded a central and major role to sexuality in the formation of the person. Apart from being a theory of psychological development, psychoanalysis is also a therapy for treating psychological disorders by investigating the interaction between the conscious and the unconscious elements of the mind. Psychoanalytical investigation is made by free association: patients talk about their emotional problems, often starting with dreams, and allow ideas to flow spontaneously until a blockage occurs; the psychoanalyst then focuses on this point of resistance as a clue to some part of the problem.

Psychoanalysis, its theorists say, is first of all about the human being within human culture, and psychoanalytic study begins at the point at which the small human animal initiates her/his first psychological act and becomes a social being. This point is the source, the origin, of the child's humanity and sexuality. Secondly, psychoanalysis is about the relationship between human sexuality and the unconscious.

Freud's theory of sexuality developed and expanded in the course of his work and lifetime. Much of what he said and wrote was reinterpreted by him in later works; therefore it is not always easy to make definitive statements about his beliefs. He began in 1895 by defining sexuality as a sexual drive (libido), which emanated from a biological sexual instinct (which we must assume as genital).[1] Later he extended sexuality to all bodily pleasures and to feelings of affection and tenderness, and 'libido' became 'psychic energy'. He said that sexuality shaped the person's psychological make-up and character. The process, which started when the infant discovered physical pleasure, was shaped and moulded by the interaction between the infant and her/his parents, concerning the satisfaction of her/his needs and demands. Freud believed that sexuality was so powerful that it influenced the whole of life.[2] Because Freudian thought has influenced our perceptions of sexuality to a much greater extent than any of us realise, it is necessary here to take a look at the basic principles of his work.

Freud made several important and influential contributions to psychology, of which the most significant was the role of the unconscious element of the psyche, or mind, in human behaviour. His map of a person's psyche divided it up into the *conscious*, which is all that we are aware of, and the *unconscious*, as a mixed bag which contains all the primitive drives and impulses that influence our actions (the id), plus ideas, memories and emotional charges which have been suppressed and consigned to the unconscious. The psychic energy which fuels these drives he called the libido, which is primarily the instinctual sexual drive. Later he added the ego and the superego to this map.

The ego is a partly conscious and partly unconscious part of the psyche which acts as intermediary between the unconscious drives (the id) and the external world. It controls the excessive drives of the id and exercises an awareness of reality, of the compromises necessary in a world of other human beings.

The superego, which Freud described as an ego-ideal, is the conscience of the ego which judges its performance and is the part of the psyche which causes guilt and suppresses or represses drives and unwelcome thoughts and incidents, consigning them to the limbo of the unconscious. In childhood the superego is strongly influenced by the outlook, attitudes and behaviour of the parents.[3]

In other words, because the drives influence our actions and the libido is the energy which fuels the drives, Freud held that sexuality was the motive force, the engine which powered the personality of the person. Furthermore, the process of development began with infant sexuality, infantile desires and conflicts, which were suppressed and stored in the unconscious, and persisted into adulthood. He maintained that the infant has desires, and these are related to, or arise from, the satisfaction of needs; desire is born because the child remembers the satisfaction that is related to the need. He held that the child actively pursues sexual/sensual pleasure, and that this was evident to any attentive mother or nursemaid. In his time this was a sensational and controversial theory:

> Sexual life does not begin only at puberty, but starts with plain manifestations soon after birth... It has been found that in early childhood there are signs of bodily activity to which only an ancient prejudice could deny the name of sexual.[4]

He further maintained that the sexuality of the adult man or woman, and the psychological turmoils of later life, could be traced to various emotional, sexual crises of infancy and childhood. These crises were (1) frustration of infant desires; (2) the Oedipus complex in both girls and boys; and (3) in girls, penis envy and the clitoral–vaginal transference.

FRUSTRATION OF INFANT DESIRES

The infant's bodily pleasures, said Freud, were at first dispersed throughout the body, and related to any activity which gave the child sensuous or natural pleasure, such as the satisfaction of hunger, evacuation, and the enjoyment of warmth or physical contact. He described infant sexuality as 'polymorphously perverse', by which he meant that infants derive pleasure not only from their sexual organs, but many other parts of the body lay claim to the same sensitivity and afford them similar feelings of pleasure.[5] Some post-Freudians explain Freud's term 'polymorphously perverse' as referring to an infantile sexuality that is undifferentiated and capable of an infinite variety of partial fulfilment; some go further and say that Freud was equating adult sexual perversion with activities that were normal for the infant at some stage of its development. Freud defined 'perversions' as sexual activity which 'has given up the aim of reproduction and pursues the attainment of pleasure as an aim independent of it'.[6] (In our modern world much of our pleasure-seeking sexual activity has long ago escaped the pejorative designation 'perversion'.) He later referred to the early years of the infant's life as bisexual:

> Sucking the mother's breast is the starting point of the whole sexual life, the unmatched prototype of every later sexual satisfaction, to which phantasy often enough recurs in times of need.[7]

Freud believed that the infant enjoys and desires a sexual pleasure from the ministrations of the mother (or whoever attends to her/his physical needs of feeding, cleaning and clothing); and these desires for bodily pleasure are directed as love towards the mother (or mother-figure). At various stages in the development of the infant, these pleasures are located in turn in the mouth, the anus and the genitals. When they are frustrated (by the withdrawal of the breast in the oral phase, by the struggle between mother and child that takes place in toilet training in the anal phase, or by being made to stop 'playing with themselves' in the phallic phase), the child experiences feelings of rage and hostility towards the person who frustrates them. But this person is also the mother–provider, and the hostile feelings conflict with the feelings of desire/love already focused on the mother. Freud believed that the child represses these hostile feelings, that they become part of her/his unconcious, and later affect adult behaviour, laying the foundation for a possibly neurotic or psychotic adult sexuality. These sexual activities 'are linked to psychical phenomena that we come across later in adult erotic life – such as fixation to particular objects, jealousy, and so on'.[8]

Unresolved conflicts during any of these phases, Freud held, result in personality problems in later life. Fixations occur in each case if the child's instinct and the defence mechanism which she/he sets up to cope with the conflict are not in balance. For instance, if the child become's fixated in the sucking stage of the oral phase she/he remains a dependent personality as an adult; if the problem occurs in the biting stage then the result is an orally aggressive person. Fixation in the anal stage, due to conflict over toilet training, also takes two forms: the anally expulsive child was likely to become messy, wasteful and extravagant; the anally retentive child (which is the one we hear most about in conventional wisdom) becomes compulsively neat and tidy, and places an inordinate value on the acquisition of money and power. The phallic phase, where the child discovers masturbation, is resolved by the Oedipus complex; if it is unresolved, or only partly resolved, if the boy does not end up by identifying with his father, or the girl with her mother, then this situation, Freud maintained, leads to a retarded sexual development which gives rise to perversions such as voyeurism, fetishism, sadism, masochism, et cetera, and the 'inversion' homosexuality.

OEDIPUS COMPLEX

Until the age of four or five, when the child discovers that women are different to men, he has no concept of a different sexuality. (Freud's Oedipus complex applied only to males. When he tried to apply it to females he ran into difficulties and error.) It is only when the child resolves his sexual attachment to his parents that the small boy achieves an individual sexual identity, and develops a new attitude towards his own sexuality and towards the opposite sex. At the onset of the Oedipus complex the boy recognises his father as a rival for the attention and affection of his mother, and he feels jealous and hostile towards him. He associates parental displeasure at his infantile erections with this hostility, and fears castration by his father as a punishment for his sexual feelings towards his mother. The boy's castration anxiety becomes unbearable and he represses both his desire for his mother and his hostility towards his father, pushing them deep into his unconscious. Then the boy identifies with his father whom he perceives as powerful and as having the same (sexual) equipment as himself, and detaches from the mother, who in his eyes is already castrated. At this point the oedipal phase comes to an end.[9]

> It is the fate of all of us, perhaps, to direct our first sexual impulse towards our mother and our first hatred and our first murderous wish against our father. Our dreams convince us that this is so. King Oedipus, who slew his father Laius and married his mother Jocasta, merely shows us the fulfilment of our own childhood wishes. But, more fortunate than he, we have meanwhile succeeded, in so far as we have not become psychoneurotics, in detaching our sexual impulses from our mothers and in forgetting our jealousy of our fathers.[10]

This was Freud's explanation of the emergence of adult sexuality, and indeed one might ask how the child knows of the incest taboo, or about coitus. In a later work (*Totem and Taboo*) Freud replied to that question himself. The answer lay, he suggested, in a racial memory trace of an original actual castration of sons by the father, or a fantasy of such an event, transmitted in the genes from primitive man.[11] An even simpler answer than the 'evolutionary' one (treated with disdain by anthropologists) was provided by some post-Freudians (see next chapter) and went something like this: Dad has power. I have a penis like Dad's, so I have power, or I will have power when I grow up.

Freud's Oedipus complex only applied to the boy child. When he tried to apply it to the small girl he got out of his depth. He then had to formulate a thesis that required her to transfer her desire from mother to father by introducing 'penis envy' – a female phenomenon which has dire significance for women (according to Freud in his 1933 essay, 'Femininity'). It is the cause of modesty and shame in women who wish to hide their 'deformity'; it leads also, he said, to jealousy, passivity, masochism, narcissism and other psychological defects like lack of a sense of justice, less capacity for sublimating instincts, and less intellectual capacity.

FREUD'S THEORY OF PENIS ENVY

As the little girl discovers the difference between the sexes, she finds that she has not got a penis, that her equipment is lacking. Realising that her mother is similarly deprived, she blames her for their shared 'catastrophe' and transfers her infantile desire to her father. The discovery that the clitoris is an 'inferior' organ facilitates the girl's transfer of her active sexuality from that organ to the vagina; she moves from an active to a passive phase of sexuality. The little girl stops masturbating and waits for a penis-waving male to provide her sexual satisfaction:

> Quite different are the effects of the castration complex in the female. She acknowledges the fact of her castration, and with it too, the superiority of the male and her own inferiority; but she rebels against this unwelcome state of affairs.[12]

Freud knew about clitoral stimulation, but did he know about the clitoral orgasm? He was dealing with repressed women, women who had been moulded by a patriarchal attitude to female sexuality and were neurotic as a result, so there were gaps in his experience and awareness. He knew how a man felt, and his work was based on, and tested against, his own male feelings; but he had no concept of how a normal woman felt.

He went on to assert that the girl's penis envy and longing for a penis is converted into desire for a baby as a penis substitute; when a woman gives birth, she is partially fulfilled, particularly if the baby is a boy with the longed-for equipment. Furthermore, Freud held that a mother's pleasure in physical contact with their children was a substitute for the repressed sexuality (and longing for a penis) of the oedipal stage.

This absurdity was perpetuated for fifty years until consciousness-raising let the cat out of the bag and women declared emphatically and scornfully that they did not want a penis, that a womb was much more satisfying. Generations of women since Simone de Beauvoir, many of them psychologists, have demolished the penis-envy theory, or transmuted it into a metaphor for envy of male prerogative. Indeed, as Freud was so obsessed with his penis, one is forced to ask was this a pathological condition? (Jung suggested that Freud was 'emotionally involved with his sexual theory to an extraordinary degree'.[13]) Later writers like Eric Fromm have suggested that he had oedipal problems himself:

> Freud had an attitude characteristic of the nineteenth-century middle class, which was more concerned with having than being. His deepest fears were

always of losing something one has, a love object, a feeling or the genital organs.[14]

That may be a little too dismissive; males fear castration above all else, and as Freud had no idea how a woman feels, his extrapolation from castration complex to penis envy may have been just an unfortunate aberration. Perhaps we should take Freud at his word in his essay, 'Femininity':

> If you want to know more about femininity, enquire from your own experience of life, or turn to the poets, or wait until science can give you a deeper and more coherent information.

Throughout his writings Freud referred again and again to his ignorance of female sexuality – its 'impenetrable obscurity', the 'dark continent for psychology', 'the riddle'; and to women – 'you are yourself the problem'.[15]

Freud approached the phenomenon of female sexuality and female psychology with the firm understanding that woman was a castrated being, inferior to man and lacking all that is best in the male. (Assertiveness, he held, was a male attribute; and he told his pupil Marie Bonaparte, who possessed it in large measure, that she was bisexual and therefore more capable of understanding men. Woman, he said, resented this situation and the resentment caused her psychological problems.) Unfortunately, his male superiority complex and the inescapable male bias of his attitude to women and of his approach to their psychology and sexuality (his pejorative language, for instance) enrages us and is likely to blind us to the real insights which were Freud's contribution – his theory of male sexuality, and some almost casual insights into women, such as his references to maternal sexuality, that have been largely ignored in the subsequent development of psychoanalysis. His penis-envy theory has some validity if it is seen as a metaphor for envy of male status, that women were dissatisfied with the inferiority assigned to them by men, or with the social power arrogated by men, but as a theory of female sexuality it is mistaken.

The development of sexuality progressed, according to Freud, through a latency period (roughly from the age of five to twelve), then into a narcissistic period, and finally, as hormonal development approached maturity, the sexual (libidinal) drive was directed outwards towards a 'love-object'. That is, of course, for boys. Girls, he said, entered a stage of repression in which they accept their 'castration', 'the wound to their narcissism', and change from a 'masculine' to a 'feminine' sexuality. This is when woman's sense of inferiority is developed.[16]

Freud believed that the libido was constantly striving for pleasure, and that pleasure was release from the tension which built up because of the needs of the various instincts: pleasure derived from the satisfaction of the instinctual drives, be they sexual, physical hunger or whatever. This led him to the belief that the relief of sexual tension in orgasm (which to him was the biological goal of sexuality) was necessary for mental health, necessary to maintain the equilibrium of the person (often referred to as the constancy principle). Frustration of the libidinal drive, in the form of anxiety, love, hate, grief, pain, disappointment or shame, in any of the stages of the young person's development from birth to maturity, Freud held, caused neuroses which could take many forms, such as sexual deviation, fetishness, obsessional behaviour, and anxiety states including depression and even schizophrenia. (It was originally the treatment of neuroses that led Freud to his theory of sexuality.)

On the other hand, Freud regarded a certain level of libidinal repression, when it was sublimated into other activity, as essential for human progress and civilisation. Sublimation of sexual energy into intellectual pursuits like science or the arts, he said, fuelled an ability which the person already had in such fields.[17] In this theory Freud shows a tendency towards making the situation fit the theory. It is just as likely that the process of satisfying the sexual drive *interferes* with or *suspends,* temporarily, achievement in the intellectual sphere, or inhibits that other human characteristic, curiosity and the drive to explore and learn. He presupposes a constant pressure of sexual energy on the person, when the situation might well be that sexual tension builds up only when the necessary stimuli are present. In the absence of an activated sexual drive other human interests come to the fore and flourish because they are given undivided attention.

Although Freud gave primacy to the sexual instinct, and held that sexuality and the pleasure principle were the central driving force of human life, the source of personal identity, he continually tested the pleasure principle against his subsequent discoveries in the development of psychoanalysis. Later he saw that the deferment of pleasure was also a fact, and that as the human infant developed in thinking and knowing, it developed strategies to cope with frustrations; moreover, that it was the repression of sexuality that determined all other areas of psychological development. This was the reality principle which he later refined into the theory of ego psychology; while the id was the source of all drives, the ego was that part of the psyche which dealt with reality, and the superego was the part of the ego that exercised the critical faculty, deciding what was right and what was wrong.[18]

As time went on Freud further developed his ideas. In the earlier stages of his work he gave preference to the instinct for preservation of the species (sexual drive), over the instinct of self-preservation and intellectual development (which includes curiosity or the drive to learn); or else he combined the two instincts into one composite sexual instinct. Later on he modified his views and acknowledged another instinct, which he called the 'destructive instinct' or death wish (which is manifested in aggression and masochism), as equally important in the psychology of the person:

> What we have recognised as true of the sexual instincts holds to the same extent, and perhaps to an even greater extent, for the other instincts, for those of aggression ... The limitation of aggression is the first and perhaps the hardest sacrifice which society demands from each individual ... The holding back of aggression is unhealthy, creates illness.[19]

It would seem that sexual matters meant more to Freud when he was young, and aggression when he was older, a perception that underlines the subjectivity of his theories. Aggression, of course, has been connected with male sexuality, and I will come to that later.

Freud also believed that a measure of the same sublimated sexual energy was necessary to counter the aggressive drive or death wish. As the 'destructive instinct', this psychological phenomenon would seem to deny the existence of the instinct of self-preservation. But perhaps the destructive instinct is the pathological side of self-preservation.

Freud regarded the family as a hotbed of sexuality, an institution based on reproduction, and therefore motivated by the sexual instinct. Motherhood was sexual; childhood pleasure was sexual. Freud said that the high point of a woman's sexuality was giving birth to a son, the acquiring of a penis of her own; not the actual birthing process but the state of motherhood of a penis-bearing infant. Giving birth to a girl was also, he suggested, a penis substitute, but not as satisfying. In this theory he was mistaken but only slightly askew; giving birth *is* the high point of a woman's sexuality. His male sexism (or sexual neurosis) embellished this germ of insight by insinuating a male dimension. Freud also realised that motherhood, the nurturing of a child, was a sexual experience, and it is now generally accepted that breast-feeding is so; but he also held that the pleasure mothers get from bodily contact with a child is also sexual, not in a genital way but like the diffuse sexuality which he attributed to the pre-oedipal stage of the child's development. In more recent times women writers have written of, and acknowledged, the diffuse nature of female sexuality, and approached the idea of a maternal sexuality, even if they skirted the suggestion that birthing is also a part of female sexuality.[20]

Freud points out that what is called sexuality outside psychoanalysis relates only to a restricted sexual life, which serves the purpose of reproduction and is called normal.[21] Juliet Mitchell, a British psycho-analyst, elaborated on Freud's statement and outlined the concept of human sexuality which is currently held in post-Freudian psychoanalysis. Sexuality in psychoanalytic terms, she says, is not to be equated with genital activity nor is it the simple expression of a biological drive. It is psychosexual, with psychological significance beyond any biological drive. Psychosexuality is a range of conscious and unconscious fantasies that produce pleasure – a pleasure that is more than the satisfaction of any basic physiological need. She says:

> Only with great difficulty – and then never perfectly – does [psycho-sexuality become] what is normally understood as sexuality, something which appears to be a unified instinct in which genitality predominates.[22]

For psychoanalysts, she continues, sexuality is deeply involved in the development of human beings; a person is formed through their sexuality, and a psychoanalyst could not subscribe to the sociological theory which holds that a person is born with their biological sex, to which society adds a socially defined sex/gender, masculine or feminine. Most post-Freudian psychologists would hold the same view as Juliet Mitchell.

Freud was a genius, but we should not expect perfection or absolute truth, if such exists, from geniuses; if they open up new avenues of knowledge they fulfil their function. It was mainly his unshakeable patriarchy that flawed Freud's work, but he was not as narrow in his perceptions as many who came after him. He defined sexuality in terms of biological (the sexual drive) as well as psychological principles (although he tends to interweave the biological element into the psychological), and he was approaching the idea of a sociological or cultural dimension to the formation of sexuality at the end of his days. In his final work Freud acknowledged, if tangentially, the influence of the social environment when he introduced the idea of the superego,[23] which is the structure in the unconscious built up by early experiences, on the basis mainly of the child's relations to her/his parents, and it functions as a conscience. It criticises the thoughts and actions of the ego, causing feelings of guilt and anxiety, when the ego gratifies, or tends to gratify, primitive impulses. The superego, then, must be the psychological effects of social formation. Freud has been criticised for his biologism, although towards the end of his life he tried to separate psychoanalysis from biology;[24] but he has not been credited for his admission of culture into the structure.

It is a pity that, for some of his followers, many of Freud's theories are carved in stone and Freudian analysts today try to make his every idle thought relevant. He made an enormous contribution to the under-standing of the human psyche, but he was not infallible. He made great discoveries, but not everything he propounded was great or even correct. He had an arrogant pride in his ideas, which made it difficult for him to accept any input from others who disagreed with him. It wasn't hard to diverge from Freud's teaching, because he was in a process of constant learning himself, and he often absorbed the ideas of the dissenters and included them later in his own revisions, while remaining implacably opposed to the authors.

He has been called a biological/psychic determinist; yet he does not say that sexuality is psychologically constructed as did some of his followers, but rather that sexuality constructs the psyche. His final summation of his theory of sexuality starts as follows:

> (a) Sexual life does not begin only at puberty, but starts with plain manifestations soon after birth.
>
> (b) It is necessary to distinguish sharply between the concepts of 'sexual' and 'genital'. The former is the wider concept and includes many activities that have nothing to do with the genitals.
>
> (c) Sexual life includes the function of obtaining pleasure from zones of the body – a function which is subsequently brought into the service of reproduction. The two functions often fail to coincide completely.[25]

The idea that sexuality has a broader canvas than the genitals, that it is 'polymorphous' or diffused, is a part of Freud's theory of infant sexuality that deserves more examination. Before the sexual revolution of the 1960s a polymorphous sexuality existed in 'petting'. It is an idea that recovers significance in lesbian experience and in the writings of some feminist philosophers such as Luce Irigaray.

Prior to Freud, sexual activity had two interpretations: reproduction and pleasure; he added another: sexual activity as a normal bodily function. Freud's theories, difficult as they may seem, form the foundation on which practically all later work on the definition of sexuality in psychological terms has been based. Nothing has replaced them; later specialists have followed, or reacted to, or reinterpreted his work; and the psychoanalytic definition of sexuality has had a strong influence on current, popular thinking.

Freud misread female sexuality because he filtered it through his own male feelings. It was not long before penis envy was called into question, as was the female Oedipus complex. And let it be said – not for the first time – that the study of psychological disturbance is not the best way to discover the genesis of sexuality or to study the healthy psyche.

5

SEXUAL RADICALS
AND RADICAL SEXUALISTS

The theories of the post-Freudians were sometimes more difficult and complex than Freud's original work. There were many distinguished post-Freudian psychoanalysts, and not all totally agreed with Freud. I will mention here only those who had a significant influence on the events that led to the sexual revolution of the mid-twentieth century. Post-Freudian psychoanalysts tended to divide into two categories on the basis of sex (with some slight overlapping): male analysts who clung to a male interpretation of sexuality and female analysts who were seeking a more satisfactory definition of female sexuality.

Most of the early psychoanalysts continued to regard sexuality as a biological drive which became operative at birth and was of particular significance in the psychological formation of the person. Alfred Adler (1870–1937), a contemporary and colleague of Freud's, diverged from the Freudian theory of sexuality. He believed that sexuality was but a part of the make-up of humans, and he laid more emphasis on intelligence in their development. He saw the human person striving for superiority: the man (with his innate superiority) strove for greater achievement, 'the will to power'; the quest for superiority in woman (with her inferior femininity) took the form of striving to be a man, what he called 'the masculine protest'. Male or female, the individual reached towards the superiority of being a man. He replaced Freud's theories of penis envy and castration anxiety with his own theory of socially induced psychological conditions. He saw women as psychologically castrated, and men as fearing psychological castration, rather than Freud's biological equivalent. Girls and women, he held, did not envy boys and men their penises, they envied the status which was conferred on them by family and society.

Adler moved away from the idea that the sex drive was the overriding influence on the psychology and personality of the individual. He saw culture and socially determined attitudes, rather than biological instincts, as the causes of behaviour both normal and neurotic. In Freudian terms, where Freud gave primacy to libido, Adler gave primacy to ego. In other words, Adler believed that human sexuality, among other human characteristics, was formed by a combination of our social and cultural environment and our reactions to it, and it was only one part of human personality. This line of thought has persisted among some psychologists to the present day.

Apart from his sexist attitude towards women, which was cultural and of his time, Adler's introduction of intelligence into the process of development from infanthood to adulthood brought some realism to ideas that were sexually centred. He did not deny a role to sexuality but removed it from centre stage.

Gustav Jung (1875–1961), who collaborated with Freud in the early years, parted company with him also on the question of sexuality. Jung believed that sexuality was a bodily drive, but only one manifestation of the energic processes (which was his broader definition of the libido). His concept of the libido was that it was not exclusively sexual, but generalised energy which found its outlets in growth, reproduction and all kinds of activity. He rejected the oedipal complex, regarding it as a metaphor for the developing independence of the child. Freud strongly disapproved of Jung's 'symbolic' interpretation of the Oedipus complex, and the two were never reconciled.

Like Freud and Adler, Jung was no supporter of equality for women. He believed that in the unconscious there was a male and a female principle in each person, *animus* and *anima* which were the male and female archetypes:

> No one can evade the fact that in taking up a masculine calling, studying and working in a man's way, woman is doing something not wholly in agreement with, if not injurious to, her feminine nature. Those women who can achieve something important for the love of a thing are most exceptional, because this does not agree with their nature. The love of a thing is a man's prerogative.[1]

Jung became more and more metaphysical, even mystical, as he advanced in years. He believed that not only had humans an unconscious but that they were part of a collective unconscious, and that it was from this collective unconscious that the primordial qualities of wisdom, darkness, evil, love and so on were drawn. Some of Jung's ideas such as the concept of the *anima*, the feminine aspect of man's psyche, and the *animus*, the masculine aspect of a woman's psyche, are still important in modern psychoanalysis.

Erik Erikson (1902-) is an American post-Freudian who also began to recognise the influence of culture and social formation in the psychological make-up of the person, but only for males. Adolescent males, he said, form a sense of identity and self-awareness from the previous experiences of the older generation, if they are well guided by them. As for females, they are totally the product of their biology, their sexuality is their identity. The experience of adolescent females is concentrated into getting a man (or if it isn't, it should be), and they do not develop their identity until they succeed in doing so.

And why is the formation of girls, according to Erikson, so different from that of boys? Girls have wombs, 'a productive inner bodily space safely set in the centre of female form and carriage', an inner space 'destined to bear the offspring of chosen men and with it, a biological, psychological, and ethical commitment to take care of human infancy'. The idea of an inner space arose from an experiment in which he noted that girls and boys used space differently in construction play: 'the girls emphasised inner space and the boys outer space'. He interpreted this discovery as innate, the result of their different biologies (projecting genitals in the boys, internal organs in the girls), rather than the result of social conditioning.

Maternity, 'that everyday miracle, pregnancy and childbirth', was very important to Erikson. This inner space, he declared, must be constantly filled if women are to be fulfilled; each menstruation is 'a crying to heaven in the mourning over a child; and it becomes a permanent scar in the menopause'. He defined women only in terms of their sexual biology; they could have some education but it must end when they found a mate and became mothers, which was their destiny and the source of their identity. Behind men's insistence on male superiority, he said, was an age-old envy of women because they are sure of their motherhood while men can only guarantee fatherhood by restricting women. Women should be satisfied with the creativity of maternity and not try to compete with men in other creative activity.

In the Freudian mode he held the theory that women were innately masochistic (because of their biology - painful periods and the pains of childbirth), a dangerous theory that has contributed to a continuing, dogmatic attitude in this century towards childbirth and female health, and hence to women's oppression. It was their own fault, he claimed. They have let themselves, he said, be 'confined and immobilised, enslaved and infantilised, prostituted and exploited'. They could, however, change that situation if they stopped hankering for a penis and applied themselves 'to the purposeful competent pursuit of activities consonant with the possession of ovaries, a uterus and a vagina'; and they should stop taking a masochistic pleasure in pain and learn to stand it and understand it as a meaningful aspect of human experience in general and of the feminine role in particular.[2]

This rubbish could only be perpetrated by a man. These are not the emotions of women, they are a *male interpretation* of women's sexuality based on the sensations and emotions of a male sexuality which considers itself dominant. But, believe it or not, for long Erik Erikson was credited with having summed up the modern, male, 'informed' attitude to female sexuality. Nevertheless, out of all that self-delusion and male conceit, he may have had one glimmer of inspiration: the 'inner space' is an important element of female sexuality; and Erikson maintained that this inner space made a sense of inadequacy in women impossible. In this he had a point; the 'inner space' as the centre of a woman's sexuality is the reason for her satisfaction in being a woman.

Another group of post-Freudian analysts, sometimes called the sexual radicals, were the most powerful and immediate influence on the sexual revolution of the 1960s and provided it with an intellectual and political validation. Of these Wilhelm Reich and Herbert Marcuse were the most influential.

Reich (1897–1957) was a pupil of Freud's who later became a Marxist. A middle-European who emigrated to the United States, he was a libertarian who advocated freedom from authority which, he said, gave rise to class-ridden societies. Although he subscribed to the aims if not the practice of communism, he believed that the roots of authoritarianism and patriarchy were not to be found in the capitalist system but in the human psyche during sexual development. It was repressed sexual energy, he said, that gave rise to authoritarian structures.

Sexual repression and morality, said Reich, caused anti-social behaviour, and therefore the need for authoritarian structures to control it. Total sexual liberation and freedom would put an end to anti-social behaviour and remove the need for these controlling power structures. Regular orgasm would ensure mental health (Freud's constancy principle) and would not only liberate the individual from a sexually crippled state, but would also confer self-respect; it would free 'the genital man', enabling him to resist authority and refuse to submit to the rule of a few powerful men.

Self-regulation should replace moralistic authority; the young man would cut his losses with a 'moralistic girl' and find one 'who was strong enough and healthy enough' to deal with her moralising parents and society.[3]

Furthermore, sexual repression, he said, was imposed on children by their parents; if children were reared together from the age of three, free of fixation on their parents, and without the influence of their parents, they would develop an entirely different sexuality, a liberated sexuality, and a liberated and assertive personality. (An artless theory of child psychology, by a psychoanalyst who never worked with children; a theory disproved by various studies of children over whom parents exercised little or no control. Such children were found to be violent and aggressive in their ordinary behaviour, with little self-control or regard for the rights of others, not just sexually but in all areas of life; they considered themselves outside society, and only looked to their peer group for approval.)[4]

Like all male psychoanalysts, Reich's theory of ideal sexuality was male-centred, genital, or, more precisely, penis- and orgasm-centred, a freedom to fuck indiscriminately and interminably. It was all he knew from his own subjective view. His ideal was, in fact, a restricted, distorted sexuality; his aspirations were the result of the cultural repression against which he was rebelling. Is Reich's 'genital' character not an extremely anti-social man – for it can only apply to a man – fixated on a very limited style of sexuality? So many of the male sexual radicals were like genital junkies, who could not see beyond the next fix. In the mid-thirties Reich turned his attention to what he called 'biogenesis' or 'biophysics', and he spent three years trying to measure the bioelectric charge of aroused genitals.[5]

It was Reich who coined the term 'sexual politics'. He advocated sex-education classes, and radical sex therapy clinics for teenagers, whose sexual liberation would then undermine the repressive nuclear family and the capitalist state. His ideas appealed to the protesting left-wing youth of the sixties, to the hippie generation and to the young feminists of the sexual revolution. All of them saw the answer to their oppression in a liberated sexuality. Reich's, and later Marcuse's, ideas also formed the basis of the feminist attack on the family.[6]

The Frankfurt School, a group of psychologists, philosophers and sociologists who were attached to the Frankfurt Institute of Social Research, created what was called 'critical theory' - a blueprint for society not unlike Reich's, inspired by the works of Freud and Marx, but unlike Reich, they were Marxists who moved to Freud. Among them was

Herbert Marcuse (1898–1979), a philosopher and influential voice in the emergence of the sexual revolution.

Marcuse differed in some respects from Reich in his ideas. He rejected the view that regular orgasm would get rid of the power structures of capitalism, pointing out that sex itself became a commodity in capitalist society, and time has proved him right. He favoured a broader interpretation of sexuality, one which was not confined to genital activity and included the release of pleasure in the whole body. Like Freud, he saw perversions as a rebellion against reproductive genital sexuality.

Marcuse also held Freud's theory that a certain amount of repressed sexuality was necessary, not just to be sublimated for creative purposes, as Freud held, but for the individual to exercise control in her or his life. Where resources are scarce, he said, life must be organised, and this requires some repression of rampant sexuality. (In an ideal society, he believed, advanced technology would liberate people from labour and leave them free to enjoy their sexuality.) However, he thought repression was carried too far. This 'surplus repression' of sexuality served only the interests of the power groups and their social control of human society.[7] The main agency of repression, he declared, was the nuclear, patriarchal family, an institution whose function was to repress sexuality and confine it to procreation in the interests of industrial development. He claimed that industrialisation had enslaved people in what he called 'pleasant forms of social control and cohesion' by confining sexuality to procreation in an attractive and woman-serviced family life, or alternatively to a bachelor sexuality, free and unhampered by emotion or commitment, thus reducing and weakening erotic energy ('repressive desublimation').

In the bachelor scenario, Marcuse said that sexuality is not repressed because that would cause discontent; but it is not liberated because that would undermine the disciplines necessary in industrial and commercial work. Rather, permissiveness is offered as a luxury, in advertisements, in glossy magazines, in films, as a reward for success in the affluent society. But it is a degraded sexuality, promiscuously confined to uncommitted, impersonal encounters, and devoid of emotion; a distorted and degraded image of male sexuality which exploits women, casting them in the role of mindless, pneumatic dolls, mere playthings which are the reward for success.

The anti-establishment ideology of Marcuse and Reich and their patently accurate analysis of the technocratic society, had enormous appeal for the radical young of the sixties. These were, to a large extent, the privileged offspring of the affluent society, often university students, alienated by the culture in which they found themselves, and in search of 'honesty', 'freedom' and 'justice'. They rejected the lessons of history (in fact, with justification, they rejected history itself as dishonest), and saw themselves in isolation from the corrupted world around them. In a way, the same can be said of Marcuse.

Marcuse saw his utopia as the next stage in human development. The old order of social control had served its purpose of developing technology, placing people in control of nature and abolishing scarcity. This auto-mated, industrial society would free everybody from all but a minimum of work, it would liberate them to indulge in pleasure, and the libido (energy) thus released would be transformed into new and hitherto unknown human relationships. In Marcuse's utopia, his unfettered workers would be the long-awaited dictatorship of the proletariat. It would be an Arcadia of 'libidinal rationality', where the pleasures and joys of the flesh would be taken for granted. People could devote their energies and interest to socially useful work and artistic creation; the liberated erotic energy would turn instead to development of the mind and intellect, and a new and higher level of rationality.

A lovely idea, but Marcuse's concept of the *work* from which people would be liberated was one viewed from the groves of Academe. It was also industrial work and work as done by men. It was not the servicing work which is overwhelmingly done by women. Neither did it take into account the work of controlling the technology, or indeed of passing on the knowledge necessary to maintain or replace the technology which would relieve the human race of work. He did not say who would rear the children and clean up. He was writing in the period before the outbreak of twentieth-century famines, and before ecological awareness that the resources of the planet were finite, and that pollution and ecological degradation placed limits on their exploitation.

Marcuse's ideas appealed to the re-emerging feminist movement in his diagnosis of the patriarchal family as a source of repression, but, unlike Reich, he did not say what would replace it. Marcuse wrote in a generalised and abstract way, attempting to establish a basic principle of existence which would inform later developments; he touched base with reality when he admitted the utopian nature of his thesis and asserted that only by means of a revolution brought about by alienated youth could the new, sexually liberated society be established.

Both Reich and Marcuse, however, performed a useful exercise. Most of us spend so much of our time dealing with jobs, home, social relations and ambitions, that we have little time for the analysis of our sexuality, for discovering whether it is imposed, repressed, underdeveloped, over-developed. This is, to some extent, what Reich and Marcuse, in their different ways, were talking about. But neither were they disinterested observers; they were no less manipulative than those who controlled sexuality in the interests of power or economic advantage. Their aim in liberating human sexuality was to overthrow the power structure of the capitalist system – a laudable purpose. But theirs was a self-centred idea of the rights of the individual; they gave no thought to what would happen when the freedom of one person conflicted with the freedom of another. This is the situation that arises at the beginning of all societies, and it is the reason that people make a social contract with each other, limiting each other's freedom in the common interest. Reich and Marcuse may have wanted to start a new order, but who was to say that power blocs would not arise again and enslave the people, as happened in the Soviet Union.

Linking sexual freedom to socialism has been a phenomenon of this century and the last, and one that is incongruous because there is no more regulated political system than socialism. If social, political and economic life is regulated in the interests of the common good, then the regulator of sexuality should be justice. To date, power, not justice has been the regulator.

THE WOMEN PSYCHOANALYSTS

Among the early post-Freudians were some distinguished women, Anna Freud (1895–1982), Marie Bonaparte (1882–1962), Karen Horney (1885–1952), Helene Deutsch (1884–1982), Melanie Klein (1882–1960). They worked mainly with children, and here we are concerned with their theories only in so far as they relate to sexuality. These women were active in the first half of this century and, with one exception, in varying degrees they brought a woman's point of view to the Freudian definition of sexuality; most of them developed Freud's Oedipus complex in a much more likely and more acceptable way. Anna Freud made no new contrib-ution to the definition of sexuality; she did not deviate from her father's teachings and continued throughout her life to fight his battles against the 'heresies' of such as Karen Horney and Melanie Klein.

These women psychoanalysts made mistakes and were often wrong. Many of them wrote from the point of view of subordinate woman, not as the assertive independent-minded persons they must have been. They seemed to be mesmerised by the parameters of the male-defined science which they promoted, but, among their theories, all of them had insights which were important. Some of these mistakes and insights have survived in post-Freudian psychology and like Freud's have also been absorbed into Western culture. Karen Horney's 'womb envy', and Melanie Klein's theory of the infant's love–hate relationship with her/his mother, are examples of their better insights. The latter led to the very influential object-relations theory of male domination of women, one of the most important developments in psychology this century (see chapter 6).

Important insights often get lost in the clash of battle between intellectuals; each one holds on grimly to treasured theories with a possessive pride not unlike Freud's, and they reject whole bodies of work when they disagree with some portion of it. In recent times, revision of the work of early psychoanalysts has allowed researchers to winnow out some of these insights. This is happening mainly among feminists attempting to construct a true definition of female sexuality, but male thinkers have also joined in the hunt. From their labours, and the new knowledge that such work stimulates, the truth may yet emerge. If these early women psychoanalysts had suspended for a time the use of Freudian theory and listened to their own biology, they might have gained even more enlightenment.

Helene Deutsch and Marie Bonaparte both held that masochism was an intrinsic, biologically determined part of female sexuality. Since pain was associated biologically with women, they said, particularly in menstruation and childbirth, but also in the breaking of the hymen, then enjoyment of pain was part of their make-up. Deutsch also held that masochism in women was repressed libidinal energy, due to the devaluation of the clitoris – an aspect of penis envy; that this energy was regressed into a desire to be 'castrated', and was later sublimated into child-rearing.[8] She went even further and claimed that labour pains were essential to make a mother feel attached to her baby. To her, motherhood was important to a woman's self-realisation and satisfaction, provided that she really wanted a baby and the conditions were favourable. At the same time she was proposing that women avoid erotic pleasure in coitus:

> In the light of psychoanalysis, the sexual act assumes an immense, dramatic, and profoundly cathartic significance for the woman – but

only under the condition that it is experienced in a feminine, dynamic way
and is not transformed into an act of erotic play or sexual 'equality'.[9]

The best that can be said about Deutsch is that she was fumbling around in
the dark looking for explanations that would fit with the literal interpretation of Freudian theory. But she had some useful insights: she was
not impressed by the theory of penis envy in girls, and was quite perceptive
where the psychosexual angst, the psychological and sexual conflicts, of
adolescent girls was concerned.

Marie Bonaparte also remained in the classical Freudian camp, but she
added a distinctly female dimension to the dogma. In a paper called
'Passivity, masochism and femininity' she referred to women receiving
sexual pleasure from the whole body; she reinstated the clitoris as part of
adult female sexuality, and supported the idea of female orgasm.[10] But she
carried the idea of passivity and masochism in women to a ridiculous extreme. Both were present, she said, 'primordially' in the female cell,

> whose mission is to await the male cell, the active mobile spermatozoan
> to come and penetrate it ... Thus the fecundation of the female cell is
> initiated by a kind of wound; in its way the female cell is primordially
> 'masochistic'.[11]

I'm afraid Bonaparte was moulding the biological evidence to suit her
thesis. She even classed coitus as flagellation by the penis, and the rougher
the better. I can only surmise that on the subject of passivity and masochism
Deutsch and Bonaparte were speaking out of the suppressed frustration of
their own subjection.

Karen Horney was a feminist whose ideas have strongly influenced parts
of the present-day women's movement. At first she followed Freudian
orthodoxy on penis envy and the sexual development of the little girl.
Later, in 1939, she moved from the classical Freudian viewpoint to include
social and cultural influences in the development of sexuality; but she
believed that the child was born with an innate femininity or masculinity.
She also revised the oedipal theory, saying it only occurred when the child
was neglected by the parents; and she interpreted penis envy in a more
metaphorical way, as resentment against female subordination.

On the question of men's fear and distrust of women (as the basis of
misogyny), her explanation was not so satisfactory. Using the Oedipus
complex to explain men's attitude to women, she said that because of the
thrusting ability of his penis, the small boy knows instinctively about
intercourse, knows that there is a female organ to be penetrated; but he

'feels or instinctively judges that his penis is much too small for his mother's genitals and reacts with the dread of his own inadequacy of being rejected and derided'.[12] This is a dubious theory of heterosexual attraction, and Horney provides no evidence to support it. Perhaps she was dealing with disturbed children who witnessed adult sexual intercourse, or who were sexually abused by adults.

Her most memorable contribution is that of womb envy. The boy, she said, comes to idealise women because of his mother's ability to 'fulfill all his expectations and longings'; this turns to envy of these capabilities, and envy of her ability to produce children. Both girls and boys, she said, desire this power, but the little boy will never achieve it. Womb envy, she continues, is the reason why men establish 'state, religion, art and science', and why they keep women out, by characterising them as inferior. When a new baby arrives in the boy's family, the event must have a significant effect on him, she said. Not only has he been superseded, but his omnipotent female mother, not his male father, acquired this new human. The girl knows that she will one day be able to equal her mother's feat; the boy knows that he cannot.[13]

In the same paper she refers to the struggle between the sexes:

> It is in the interest of men to obscure [the fact that there is a struggle between the sexes]; and the emphasis they have placed on their ideologies has caused women, also, to adopt these theories.

These were revolutionary ideas in the twenties and thirties. However, at that stage Horney also believed that women were innately passive and masochistic, and that was why they submitted to men. Later she changed her mind and said that passivity and masochism were culturally, not biologically, induced; they resulted from woman's dependence on men and men's desire that woman be passive, so that they conform with the male idea of their sex. Women, she said, have adapted themselves to the wishes of men and they believe that their adaptation is their true nature. Men, she maintained, belittle women by devaluing femininity and maternity, and by revaluing and enhancing masculinity and male genitality.[14]

Melanie Klein was another woman who challenged Freud's concept of female sexuality. The infant, she claimed, was not just a bundle of instincts, but was involved from the beginning in relationships. This starting point in Klein's thinking was eminently sensible, but she went further. Like Horney, she ascribed a distinct female or male sexuality to the infant from birth, and asserted that the girl infant desires the father's penis and instinctively knows that she is receptive to it, first orally then vaginally. Fear of retaliation from her mother leads to her suppressing or renouncing this vaginal eroticism in favour of clitoral excitement.[15]

I find this difficult to accept. How did Klein arrive at this conclusion? Was it from the study of disturbed child patients? Here she is imposing an adult form of sexuality on children. While they may have embryonic feelings of sexual excitement, they couldn't possibly include the amount of detailed knowledge which would be necessary for the reactions which Klein (and Horney) attribute to them. It is much more likely that if Klein and Horney came across examples in their case studies of early vaginal excitement and intimate knowledge of genital activity among the children they treated, that these children were remembering early cases of child abuse, such as the insertion of a finger (the father's?) in the vagina, or the penis in the mouth, or perhaps a more serious form of sexual abuse, such as vaginal or anal rape.

Until recently child sexual abuse was neither accepted nor acknowledged. In the 1890s Freud developed a 'seduction' theory which held that neurosis was the result of sexual abuse in childhood. However, the idea that children could be abused in this way by loving parents and siblings upset him so much that he rejected the thought, and put the claims of his patients down to fantasy. He recorded his recantation in a letter to his friend and fellow physician, Wilhelm Fliess, in 1897. This rejection of the seduction theory was attacked by the Swiss psychoanalyst Alice Miller in 1981 and by two Americans, writer Florence Rush in 1980, and psychoanalyst Jeffrey Masson in 1984.[16] We now know that sexual abuse of children takes place much more frequently than anyone suspected.

Melanie Klein's explanation of a female form of the Oedipus complex, as the little girl's female sexuality desiring the father's penis, does not tally with the level of emotional development which she attributes to the infant in her later work. Her theory of 'splitting', which is the work that led to object-relations theory, concerned the general psychological development of the child and had a Freudian starting point: the mother–infant relationship in the first year of the child's life.

From birth, Klein declared, babies have feelings of satisfaction and dissatisfaction, or love and hate. These are connected with their bodily functions, and are the diffuse sexuality (or sensuality) of the infant – oral, anal and genital satisfaction or deprivation. Klein says that infants have mixed feelings about their mother from the start. At first they identify with the breast and relate to it in two ways: it is good or bad, it invokes love or hate, depending on whether it is gratifying them and giving pleasure, or being denied and frustrating them. Then as infants develop they realise that the breast is mother, another person, an object, who is both the object of love and hate. This conflict of emotions, the anxiety it generates and the stress of the hatred, causes babies to 'split off' the aggression they feel and transfer it, or project it on to the mother: they feel that the mother hates them. This gives rise to anxiety that the mother will attack them. Klein called this the 'paranoid-schizoid position', and said that it also applies to babies who are bottle-fed, who relate in the same way to the mother. This emotional turmoil, in the child's relationship with the mother, is repeated in the anal and genital phase of development.[17] Klein maintained that the child's good feelings towards the mother are also projected on to her, and a balance between the bad and good feelings is necessary for the normal development of the child.[18] It is on this analysis of the mother/child relationship that object-relations theory is based. This theory is of great significance in the psychology of the adult person, particularly in relations between men and women, and, according to some of the feminist psychologists who come later, in the oppression of women.

One criticism that can be made about all psychoanalytic theories is that they cannot stand up to the rigours of scientific method, that they are (that curse word of the scientific establishment) 'anecdotal'. However, science has no other method for investigating psychology, and with such empirical evidence, mistakes can be made. I think it is possible that Melanie Klein was mistaken in the analysis of some of her case studies on children. Some of them are uncommonly like evidence of sexual abuse, which is not at all unlikely as she was dealing with disturbed children.

During the 1920s Klein was involved in controversy with Freud and his more orthodox followers over what constituted female sexuality. Despite his declared openness to new ideas and his development or correction of his own,[19] Freud accused Klein, and the other women analysts, of confusing the psychic with the biological. The controversy, which centred on Klein's interpretation of psychoanalysis, continued throughout the thirties and into the forties, and after Freud's death was carried on by his daughter Anna. This led to a situation during that time, that not only did the women psychoanalysts have to defend their theories against the male psychoanalysts, they also had to defend their place in psychoanalysis.

However, by the mid-1920s it had become evident, even to his most ardent followers, that Freud's definition of sexuality could not be satisfactorily applied to women; whatever its merits, it was a definition of male sexuality. We must not forget that Freud and the early psychoanalysts tended to form their theories to a large extent on their experiences with psychologically disordered people, and on their own experience, and they can only surmise what is the 'normal' situation. The women psychoanalysts, Karen Horney, Melanie Klein, (and in spite of all their short-comings) Marie Bonaparte and Helene Deutsch, tried to devise a more rational construction for the formation and definition of female sexuality. Later there were others, such as Erik Erikson, who were able to benefit from the work of the sexologists, Alfred Kinsey, and William Masters and Virginia Johnson. But all were handicapped by confining themselves to parameters laid down by Freud, limits that he himself, towards the end of his life had been ready to modify.

6

THE CHILD IS
FATHER OF THE MAN

The 1960s were a landmark in the history of sexuality, principally because of the sexual revolution and the revival of feminism which took place then, but also because the theories of the post-Freudian women psychoanalysts, notably Karen Horney and Melanie Klein, were taken up and developed by other analysts and feminists who produced important texts in the 1970s. Of the two, Melanie Klein was the most influential; her thinking on the relationship between the child and its mother was further developed by two British psychoanalysts, Donald Fairbairn and David Winnicott, into what later became known as object-relations theory.

Object-relations theory holds that the infant develops psychologically not just in response to various instincts but also in its relations with different 'objects' which are separate from it. These relations start from the moment of birth and the most important one is with the mother.

Dorothy Dinnerstein and Nancy Chodorow introduced object-relations theory to the women's movement. Dinnerstein took Klein's ideas and developed them further, while Chodorow developed the work of Fairbairn and Winnicott. Both women arrived at the same destination by somewhat different routes. Their work, its relevance to female and male sexuality and to the parenting of children, became important in feminist psychoanalysis.

In 1976 Dorothy Dinnerstein, an American psychologist, published *The Mermaid and the Minator*, which became an important contribution to the development of psychoanalysis.[1] Her motives in writing the book were not entirely feminist, although it became a seminal text for the women's movement. She wrote it, she said, because she was concerned about the survival of human society, about 'the runaway acceleration of life-anta-gonistic trends in human institutions'. These she attributed to our gender arrangements, what she called 'certain central structural defects in human life', the most significant of which is the fact that 'the main adult presence in infancy and early childhood is female'. Her 'central structural defects' were the relations between women and men and the sexual conservatism which maintained the status quo. The most potent sources of sexual conservatism, she said, were buried in the dark silent layers of our mental life, and it was this very burial that made them potent. To articulate them openly, to see them in the light of full awareness, was a necessary (but not sufficient) condition for growth toward liberty.

She saw 'a crucial gap' in the outlook of social philosophers: they ignored, she said, the important role played by the traditional, interdependent relations between men and women ('our traditional gender symbiosis') in perpetuating the destruction of the planet and the human race. The roots of this situation lay, she argued, in the long infancy of humans, and in the gender and sexual relations that result from an infancy and childhood that is female-dominated. She believed that she had discovered the hidden psychological barriers which prevented women gaining equality. The following is a resume of her thesis. The rule that men can bully and subordinate women, and maintain a double standard in the behaviour of the sexes exists, she says, for many obvious reasons:

- because men consider that it is to their advantage;
- because they want to ensure paternity;
- because they are stronger;
- because women's mobility is reduced when they bear and feed children.

These are the obvious, external explanations for the subordination of women, for their exclusion from 'the ruling of the world'. But the roots of this go back to childhood.

To explain why little boys grow up into men who dominate women, and little girls become women who tolerate subordination, Dinnerstein uses Klein's theory that the child's relationship with the mother plays a crucial part in the development of the person. She argues that given our present arrangements for childcare, which fall almost exclusively to women, children of both sexes have problems in developing their own identity as human beings that are separate from mother. They permanently sidestep the task of working through the feelings of anxiety and persecution involved in this task. In other words, they never grow up; their *perception* of adulthood remains that of the child's fantasy, and they act out this fantasy in their own adulthood. In short, men rule the world and subordinate women because they are trying to escape from their own infantilism, from a conflicting attachment to mother and resentment of maternal authority.

It is every infant's early wish, says Dinnerstein (in a restatement of Klein's theory), to possess mother exclusively, because, in its helpless state, mother is the source of satisfaction and pleasure. But mother is also the source of frustration; the infant is enraged when its desires are ignored by her, or are not satisfied on demand. (Who has not heard the incensed fury of an infant who wants the attention of mother?) These hostile feelings conflict with the child's feelings of love for mother, and worry the child that this hostility will damage mother or drive her away. The infant reconciles this conflict by splitting off the hostile feelings from the loving ones, and keeping them separate. Becoming aware of the autonomy of the mother (that she has other concerns different from those of the infant), combined with the loss of infant omnipotence (the power to have all desires satisfied), is, says Dinnerstein, 'an original and basic human grief'.

Because the mother is so intimately associated with these infantile grievances, because she is the first important piece of the physical world that the infant encounters – the supplier of food, warmth, entertainment, comfort – she is, in the infant's fantasy not only a part of her- or himself but also a part of nature. The father is seen as aloof from these intimate concerns, more of a separate human being, more important because he is dealing with affairs beyond the realm of the familiar home. These different perceptions of mother and father are carried on from infancy into adult life, and lead to women being defined (by both men and women) as inferior persons, belonging more to nature and the home than to the affairs of the world, and who do not belong among that sector of humans who are intellectual and achievers. These achievements are the prerogative of father, the male, who is not connected with disturbing infant fantasy and grievances. The fact that this fantasy gets mixed up with real life also gives rise to the perception that women are closer to, and more identified with, nature, that men are more transcendent (intellectual, scientific) and superior to nature.

In the next stage of forging an identity little boys develop along different lines to little girls. This happens, according to Dinnerstein (in her interpretation of the Oedipus complex), because of our parenting practices and because of our intersexual relations. Between the ages of two to five years, when the small boy perceives that his mother is a member of the sex for whose affections he must compete with other males, he stops identifying

with her and begins to identify with his father. His growing attachment to
this newly interesting and powerful male parent represents solidarity with
his own sex, a solidarity which is important to him in coming to grips with
the world, and in gaining membership of the wider and more exciting
community of men, where heroes live, enterprises are planned and public
events are organised. He finds that his tie with his mother becomes an
obstacle to more grown-up ties with his own sex. This new difficulty in
the boy's relations with his mother is then likely to coalesce with the lon-
ger-standing grievances of infancy.

The little girl's oedipal development is different. She identifies with her
mother as being of the same sex; she will, one day, become a mother and
'carries within herself a source of the magic early parental richness'. Already
she is playing mother with dolls. But her grievances against her mother also
cause her to turn to her father, and develop an attachment for him. Early
rage at the first parent (mother) is used in the oedipal stage by the boy, says
Dinnerstein, to consolidate his tie with his own sex, and by the girl to loosen
her tie with hers.

In the present child-rearing arrangements, where mothers are solely or
almost solely responsible for their care and nurture, children never resolve
their love–hate relationship with their mother; nor do they attain a proper
detachment from her or assertion of their own independence. That, says
Dinnerstein, is why misogyny is prevalent, why women have tolerated
male domination, and why both female and male sexuality is stunted. Her
answer to this predicament is to have fathers share equally in the care and
nurture of children. So long as mothers are cast as the child-carers and
child-rearers then women will always be seen as nurturers to the human
race; and because mothers in rearing also restrain and discipline children,
women will always be regarded by them as an enemy who frustrates their
self-development. Dinnerstein writes:

> So long as the first parent is a woman, then woman will inevitably be
> pressed into the dual role of indispensable quasi-human supporter and
> deadly quasi-human enemy of the human self. She will be seen as
> naturally fit to nurture other people's individuality; as the born audience
> in whose awareness other people's subjective existence can be mirrored; as
> the being so peculiarly needed to confirm other people's worth, power,
> significance, that if she fails to render them this service she is a monster,
> anomalous and useless. And at the same time she will be seen as the one
> who will not let other people be, the one who beckons her loved ones

back from selfhood, who wants to engulf, dissolve, drown, suffocate them as autonomous people.[2]

Why? Because, says Dinnerstein, woman (in the form of mother) is the first person to oppose our will, showing us that we are not omnipotent, that we can be thwarted by other living creatures. In our first real contest of will we find ourselves, more often than not, defeated. The defeat is always 'intimately carnal', related to bodily needs; and the victor is always female. Women 'bear the brunt of a profound, many-faceted early filial spite'. Men, she continues, express this rage against early maternal power directly, in arrogance against everything female. Women express it directly in distrust and disrespect towards other women, and indirectly by accepting male authority. 'So the essential fact about paternal authority, the fact that makes both sexes accept it as a model for the ruling of the world, is that it is under prevailing conditions a sanctuary from maternal authority.' This 'filial spite' has warped both female and male sexuality.

At this this stage I should point out that Dorothy Dinnerstein's thesis is still valid even if one does not subscribe fully to either Freud's or Klein's idea of the Oedipus complex. The conflicting feelings endured by the infant in relationships with the mother could take place without the sexual content attributed to them by either Freud or Klein.

Dinnerstein's theory, which makes mothering responsible for the psychological problems that influence the way humans organise their lives, has been used to blame women for the ills of the human race. Through no fault of Dinnerstein's, that is a perverse and selective extrapolation, as illogical as the language we use to describe the relationships between parents and children, where 'mothering' means caring and rearing, and 'fathering' means begetting. It is anti-woman because of the illogicality of blaming women for the results that flow from their own exploitation. Moreover, the idea of co-parenting is not just a tactic to remove inequalities in relations between women and men, but a balanced way of ordering society, so that children grow up with a realistic experience of both sexes.

Significantly for this book, in dissecting male–female relations Dinnerstein analyses both male and female sexuality in a different and perceptive manner. She says that women suppress their own sexuality in order not to alarm men: women realise that for men heterosexual love is laced with emotions which are a return to their relationship with the mother, a relationship which, as we saw, contained frustrations and conflicting feelings. Women sense this, or learn it, and try to re-create the early mother–infant atmosphere; they avoid frustration, by not being demanding. If a woman unleashes her own sexuality, says Dinnerstein, she can recall to a man his infant frustrations and even cause impotence. Therefore she holds back, or does not seek, satisfaction. She calls this 'the muting of women's erotic impulsivity'.

Men also, she maintains, sense their own vulnerability. Women can evoke for them 'the unqualified, boundless, helpless passion of infancy and bring out the soft, wild, naked baby' in them. One way that they cope with this is by having sex-segregated institutions – 'secret societies, hunting trips, pool parlours, wars' – which provide sanctuary from the impact of women, or where 'they can recuperate from the temptation to give way to ferocious, voracious dependency, and recover their feelings of competence, auto-nomy, dignity'. But they need more safeguards. One is to renounce deep feelings for women – to keep love superficial; another is to dissociate its physical from its emotional possibilities.

She describes how this ambivalence in male heterosexual love derives from infant experience, from the conflicting emotions directed against the mother – love and rage (grateful love and greedy rage). Men deal with this difficulty by sorting out the conflicting ingredients into two kinds of love, one tender and the other sensual (lust). Lust carries all the angry, predatory impulses from which the protective, trusting side of their love for women must be kept insulated. A man, Dinnerstein says, may keep tender and sensual love separate by expressing them towards different women, or towards the same woman in different moods. He may largely bury one and give direct expression to the other; or he may mute all tender feelings for other people and bury himself in his work.

Women, she says, do not have this problem because while they may suppress their feelings, they are not afraid of them. Love for their mother is associated with intimacy; therefore intimacy and love, to them, are inseparable. This has a disadvantage, says Dinnerstein: the 'hapless tend-ency of women to melt into a feeling of emotional closeness with any man who manages to excite them sexually'.

Because of the way child-rearing is organised, children permanently sidestep the task of developing a more realistic sense of themselves and of the mother, and of recognising their independence and separateness from her. And because the mother is the ever-present powerful 'boss' in childhood, both boys and girls grow up to be men and women who harbour strong, almost always unconscious, anti-female feelings. These childish attitudes (of unsatisfactory separation from the mother and the deep psychological resentment of power in women) continue into adulthood, causing problems in human relations which will persist, she says, until men share with women the early, intimate parenting of infants and young children:

> Only when this happens will society be forced to find ways to help its members handle the impulses of greed and rapacity that now make man 'wolf to the man' ... It is at this point that the human projects of brotherhood, of peace with nature, and of sexual liberty interpenetrate.

Some feminists blame motherhood in a more simplistic way for women's exploitation and inequality: they claim that men dominate because women are handicapped by their reproductive capacity (their sexuality). They make these claims without examining *why* women have babies. Some say that women reproduce because they are brainwashed, because the culture, or their psychology prevails on them to do so, and the answer lies in taking control of their own fertility, in the provision of child-care facilities. Few of them allow that women have a biological drive to reproduce as part of their humanity. Dinnerstein recognised the sexuality of motherhood, and its biological base:

> What makes motherhood reliable is that the erotic flow between the child and its female parent is primed by a set of powerful postpartum mechanisms, mechanisms which prime not only women, but also simpler she-mammals, to nurture and protect their young.

The example she gives is the physical response of a mother to a baby's hungry cry which is milk let-down, and uterine contractions. The biological content of the desire to have children, she points out, has been interpreted, mediated, masked and reshaped by other factors in a woman's decision to have and nurture children.

When Margaret Mead maintained that woman consents to leave to man the main responsibility for historical continuity of the species, Dorothy Dinnerstein says that this is only part of the answer, because women have never been satisfied to be excluded from the public arena and have struggled for centuries to claim involvement. On the other hand, men have always interfered in the private arena allocated to women, by endeavouring to control women's fertility and sexuality as a way to dominate them.

Why have women not rebelled and overturned male domination of the world, and the consequent distortion of sexuality? Because, says

Dinnerstein, female power is the earliest and most profound example of absolute power experienced by the human being. Power of this kind, concentrated in one sex and exerted at the outset of life over both sexes, is far too potent and dangerous a force to be allowed free sway in adult life. To contain it, to keep it under control and harness it, is a vital need for every mother-raised human. Both men and women run in horror from a return to the sway of 'mother', and therefore prefer male leadership in adult life. The solution, she reiterates, is shared parenting and the ending of female domination of infancy.

The theory that men's feeling of superiority to women, their desire to escape women's control and to dominate and punish them, has its roots in mother-dominated childhood is persuasive. It also provides an achievable means of changing the situation. Still, the solution is not all that simple; it would be as difficult to persuade the majority of men on this planet to share in child-rearing as it has been to involve them in housework.

Joint-parenting means equal involvement with the child in all aspects of its daily life, in nurturing and training, in cuddling and contests of will, in all the interactions that severely test patience. Crèches are not the answer if women still have the sole responsibility for child-rearing. How would such a change in male culture take place? If at first (as is already happening) a few men share the nurture of their children, would these children later revert to the predominant culture and so wipe out their initial advantages? What would induce other men to follow suit?

Humans have the unique (psychological) ability among the animal species to remember the past and to project into the future, the unique (social and cultural) ability to pool knowledge and to build social structures. Therefore, the dictates of our biology, our biological imperatives can be (and some-times are) altered by psychological and social imperatives. There is what Dinnerstein describes as 'our species' most characteristic, vital, and dangerous gift: our gift for enterprise, for self-creation'. The human being of today is different from the human being of 10,000, 1,000, or even 100 years ago. The arrangements we make in our lives, the way we look at things, our ambitions, all change and develop or regress, but two factors are constant: women still control child-rearing and men still control the world.

There are some slight differences in the way that Nancy Chodorow uses object-relations theory to call into question the traditional mothering role of women.[3] She maintains that the mother influences the gender development of the infant by the way she relates to her or him. She identifies with a daughter, as does the daughter with her mother, and a daughter's gender identity continues to merge with that of her mother; there is no separation (although women covet men's power and status, few women want to be men). On the other hand, the mother relates to her young son as different to herself and thus encourages his separation from her; the boy constructs his masculine gender by rejecting the feminine, and as that identity is negative, it is therefore more insecure, more precarious, than the gender identity of the girl. (Yet very few men, because of the power and status they enjoy, want to be women.)

The result, she says, is that girls grow up with a continuing sense of themselves as merged with others, while boys are alienated from others. She maintains that co-parenting would produce children who would identify with the same-sex parent, and individuate from the opposite-sex parent. They would therefore grow up more independent individuals and have more balanced relationships with both sexes.

Chodorow believed that motherhood (that is, the art of mothering) was learned, that a man or another woman can substitute for the biological mother in the rearing of a child. That may be the case from the point of view of the child's physical welfare; but even then the limits to the mother love of the biological mother will usually go far beyond that of a surrogate. Chodorow does not take into account the great attachment of women for their children, an attachment that contains biological (hormonal), as well as psychological elements, relating to the carrying, formation and nurturing of the child in the womb for nine months and later in infancy. If natural mother love is strongest, for the biological reasons given, then this leads to the question of whether, in a situation of joint-parenting, mother nurture would outweigh father nurture, and whether that would matter so long as the father had a significant role in both nurturing and the discipline of rearing. These ideas of Chodorow and Dinnerstein are one of the arguments against single-parent families, which are almost always single-mother families.

Some object-relations psychologists, such as Winnicott, maintain that mother-dominated parenting produces women ideally suited to the rearing of children, and men suited to affairs of the world; and they criticise women for claiming equality with men to the detriment, they say, of their children.[4]

Shared-parenting is a theory that finds favour with feminists because it provides what looks like a simple formula for changing the situation, for altering men's attitude to women. But observing those couples who started valiantly to co-parent over the past decade or so, it is evident that very few persevered. It seems to be just as difficult to achieve sharing in child-rearing as it has been to achieve other feminist aims such as equality of opportunity, pay or respect.

Chodorow's ideas were adopted by the new feminist therapy movement of the 1970s. In 1976 Luise Eichenbaum and Susie Orbach set up the first Women's Therapy Centre in London, combining psychoanalysis and feminist thinking in a programme of help and advice for women whose psychological problems were, they believed, the result of male domination. They were also concerned to bring psychology to bear on the internal difficulties of the women's movement which were caused by personality differences, and which they saw as resulting from women's own insecurities.[5]

Some commentators saw the failure of co-parenting less in men's reluctance to co-operate than in their refusal, both as workers and employers, to change work practices; and to social changes (due to divorce, desertion and the increasing number of women who choose single motherhood) that have left women rearing children alone.[6] But if the social context militates against equal parenting, it will also militate against other (legal, et cetera) solutions. It would appear that the social context is the intransigence of men.

Some reformers promote shared-parenting because it might stop the debilitating effects which men have had on world affairs, and bring women's influence to bear on them instead.[7] If women and men have different modes of thought, for whatever reasons, there is an overriding necessity for both modes of thought to be used in tandem in ordering the affairs of life and the world, and to ensure that both modes of thought are developed in both sexes. And I am inclined to think that in many women both modes of thought are developed (in, for instance, all these women writers on psychology, philosophy, et cetera, which I've been reading).

Chodorow herself falls into the trap of exclusive specialisation; she explores the psychological influences on gender and sexual formation while ignoring the other elements that go towards their construction. She acknowledges biological and cultural elements (in addition to the psychological) in mothering, in women's desire to mother, and in the role mothering plays in the subordination of women, but goes on to ignore the biological sexuality of childbirth and the sensual/sexual elements in the relationship between mothers and children (breast-feeding, bodily contact).

The denial of these powerful forces accounts for the failure of psychological and cultural solutions to the problems posed for women by motherhood. That is not to diminish the psychological and cultural influences on the formation of human gender and sexuality. However, all other mammals establish their gender and sexual identities biologically with some small cultural influence. (The young tom-cat has female parenting, yet he goes off and acts like a tom.) Is it not therefore reasonable to assume that some biological influences remain in the behaviour of humans?

Some women writers (Janet Sayers, Ann Ferguson, Juliet Mitchell, et cetera) challenge Chodorow's theory that girls 'merge' so effectively with their mothers that as women they lack assertiveness. Like Dinnerstein, they support their challenge by pointing to the struggle of women for autonomy and equality in the women's movement, and, indeed, to the assertiveness of the writers themselves. Others say that women's assertiveness and independence are often concealed as a result of internalising society's stereotype of women.

On the other hand, assertiveness can occur in girls who escape mother identification, or because of some other 'failure' of the usual pattern in mother–child relationship, such as being displaced by another baby. Deposed girl children may learn more separation and individuation, or learn to identify with their fathers, and hence acquire independence. In a world where women are denied economic equality, the biological drive to have children, and subsequently the need to support them by whatever means possible, may have (indeed, has) generated an acquiescence to subordination that is political. If the situation is as simple as that, then the will to resist can be found.

There were other women psychologists and psychoanalysts, and feminists using psychoanalysis, who were dissatisfied with Freud's definition of female sexuality and who made valuable contributions to the new debate. In the early seventies Mary Jane Sherfey (who had worked with Kinsey) wrote that the popular conception of a woman's sexuality was male-defined, and that the definition was wrong. She astonished the world and alarmed the male population by the assertion of women's ability to have multiple orgasms.[8] Her claim was based on the research of the sexologists, Masters and Johnson, and she went on to describe the physiology of this phenomenon.

Using this research Sherfey constructed a theory of female sexuality as an uncontrolled faculty, so anti-social that it justified male domination in the interests of a species that lived in community. The ability to have multiple orgasms, she said, did not evolve for, and was not suited to, a culture of settled families, and this was proof that women were not 'biologically built for the single spouse, monogamous marital structure or for the prolonged adolescence' which exists in present society. It suited a time when women had their children in their late teens and early twenties.[9]

Sherfey's theory had the virtue of starting discussion among women about a new assessment of female sexuality, and even about such wild subjects as parthenogenesis, the development of babies from a woman's ovum alone without the benefit of male sperm. (Maybe not so wild in the light of recent developments in reproduction.) Her more useful description of the physiology of the female orgasm was used by Shere Hite in her famous *Hite Report on Female Sexuality*.

The German psychoanalyst Alice Miller has worked mainly with children and it was she who awakened the world to the scandal of child sexual, physical and psychological abuse.[10] She rejected Freud's theory of the sexual drive in infant sexuality, saying that it is an adult concept of sexuality, and that calling a child's pleasure sexual is an adult concept. She suggests instead that the child experiences pleasure in her or his own body, curiosity about the bodies of others, particularly those of the opposite sex, and jealousy of the intimacy of the parents. Her thesis is a blend of a polymorphous sensuousness (rather than sexuality) and object-relations theory.

She explains the castration complex as a boy's pleasure in his penis and fear that he will be stopped from playing with it; and a girl's penis envy as the fact that she is told that he has one and she hasn't. She points to the intensity of a child's physical sensations in general (including oral and anal), the power struggle of toilet training, and the adjustment to, or defiance of, parental power.[11] Miller's theories give pause for thought. All memories of childhood emotions are very strong, often stronger than those of later experiences. Alice Miller's ideas do not invalidate Freud's theory of the construction of sexuality, they just call it by a different name.

The post-Freudian psychoanalysts of the object-relations school were the most influential in the English-speaking women's movement. But the French school of psychoanalysts, called Lacanians, also became important: Jacques Lacan and his students, Juliet Mitchell in the United Kingdom;

Julia Kristeva and Luce Irigaray in France; and Alice Miller in Switzerland. Others made valuable contributions, but these women had a significant effect on the search for a true definition of sexuality and for the causes of male domination.

7

FREUDIAN
FIELDS OF FRANCE

Jacques Lacan (1901–81) declared that other psychoanalysts, particularly the women, had lost the way because they were interpreting Freud through other ideologies such as Marxism, existentialism or humanism. He would return to the purity of the master and reassert male ascendancy. Then he promptly set about reinterpreting Freud through his own ideology of structuralism[1] and 'language',[2] maintaining that sexuality and language were the basis of culture, of the systems which humans have constructed and within which they live. He is usually referred to as a post-structuralist which is a more radical form of structuralism.

Lacan trained first as a physician, then in the late 1920s he became interested in psychoanalysis. He saw himself as the prophet, even the messiah of psychoanalysis after Freud, and this messianic streak caused severe rifts between him and the analysts of the French establishment. His theories (which are more metaphysical than Freud's) are important here because they have had a significant influence on the women's movement.

Lacan was strongly influenced by the work of Claude Lévi-Strauss, the French philosopher, anthropologist and structuralist. Lévi-Strauss gave up academic philosophy because he believed that anthropology provided better material for the study of human culture, but he carried with him the methods of analysis and the structures of classical philosophy – a male way of looking at things.

He declared that the incest taboo, which leads to the prohibition of marriage within the tribe, was the foundation of kinship and hence of culture. This was a male culture, he said, because 'the reciprocal bond basic to marriage is not set up between men and women, but between men and men by means of women, who are only the principal occasion for it'. Woman, he held, is never more than the symbol of her line and of the authority of her father or brother, which extends back from her new home to her brother's village. He also maintained that incest was the link between anthropology and psychoanalysis because of the prevalence of incestuous dreams or fantasies among the patients of psychoanalysts.[3] (Lévi-Strauss obviously picked his point of entry into the development of culture to suit his male vision, because it is much more likely that the first cohesive kinship group was the mother and her child, and culture developed as she taught her child the increasingly rational and intelligent means of survival. Other anthropologists and social theorists agree that women invented culture but propose a variety of scenarios.)[4]

Adopting Lévi-Strauss's theory of culture, Lacan identified the incest taboo with the Oedipus complex of Freudian psychoanalysis, and declared the castration complex as the foundation of sexuality. His theory is as follows. Desire is the first manifestation of sexuality. Desire arises from the absence of pleasure and creates in the infant the first 'memory-trace' which is lodged in the unconscious. It is at this point that the biological baby diverts from the animal world and starts to become 'human'. This memory-trace of desire is the first signifier, the first attributer of meaning, in the life of the new baby. This is the point at which the social and psychological life of the new human begins.

But life, according to Lacan, is defined by other signifiers. While sexuality (through desire) initiates humanity, it is when the child recognises the presence or absence of the penis that differentiation of the sexes occurs and sexual identity is established. This comes about at the oedipal stage of development when the boy fears castration by his father as punishment for (incestuously) desiring his mother. The penis referred to in Freud's Oedipus complex is physical and biological, but Lacan interpreted it as social and cultural, using the term 'phallus' (denoting male power as represented by the possession of a penis). The phallus, he said, signifies 'the law of the father', which is the incest taboo and its by-product, the allocation of wo-men in marriage by men. Recognition of sexual difference, he said, is recognition of the different status of women and men; masculinity and femininity are then formed by the culture through language. Lacan rejects the idea that masculinity and femininity were biological.

He links the castration complex with language as follows: the child desires the mother; the phallus ('the law of the father') represents or signifies the mother's desire, and so he identifies with the phallus; but when he discovers the absence-of-the-power-of-the-phallus (castration) in the mother, he represses his identification with it into his unconscious and seeks substitutes (symbols) for it; this is how the child enters the symbolism of language.[5]

Within all this obscurity, Lacan was saying that the combination of incest taboo and castration complex generates language because of the dissatisfaction they cause in the infant. It is language that designates one masculine or feminine. Language is the sublimation of dissatisfied desire, and the language is structured by patriarchy – 'the signifier is male'. From the moment that the castration complex takes hold of the infant, language shapes sexuality. And language also shapes attitudes, the grid or framework through which people see things; it provides the ideas and categories that people use to impose meaning on their lives and surroundings and make sense of their situation.

This theory of language is correct in so far as it goes, but other factors enter the scene: emotions, the psyche and intellect. Humans are thinking, feeling beings, and they can change the interpretation of language. Indeed language and communications continually change their meanings, and feminists have made brave efforts to hasten change in what they call 'the language of oppression'.

Lacan's structuralist logic defined female sexuality under patriarchy as an 'absence of sex', and asserted that 'femininity' has a meaning only when contrasted with 'masculinity'. Yet, conversely, he also held that male identity needed a female object in order to establish itself by reflection or contrast, and women play along with this situation which he called 'the masquerade'. But he did not believe that this position was unchangeable; he suggested that feminists 'unmask the masquerade', overthrow patriarchy and patriarchal language, and discover suppressed female sexuality.

Herein lies his appeal to feminist theorists. If sexuality was constructed by patriarchal language, if femininity was a mask donned in response to patriarchy, then one could be changed and the other removed. Feminists who rejected Freud accepted Lacan's interpretation of Freudian psychology because it offered hope for the success of their objectives.

However, I fear his phallic castle is built on sand. Neither he, nor Freud, could give a satisfactory explanation of the castration complex. Where did it come from? Who was the paternal figure that first threatened castration? Presumably there had to be sexuality, sexuality had to exist, in order to require or produce a castration complex. Was this merely a biological sexuality? All that Freudians and Lacanians can say is that it is prevalent in the dreams of those they've analysed. Furthermore, Lacan does not provide any answer for what masculinity would be like if it were not reflected in femininity, nor for the new femininity or female sexuality behind the masquerade.

It is not difficult for a woman to pick holes in some of the statements made in Lacanian theory, and I am not the first woman to point out that his thinking is phallo-centric, based on phallic egoism, putting maleness at the centre and defining all else in relation to it. It all depends on where you stand; it could be said that from a woman's point of view, masculinity has meaning only when contrasted with femininity, or, as Chodorow said, that masculinity is negative and therefore fragile because it is a rejection of femininity.

The castration complex, real or imagined, can conceivably be held to relate to the sexuality of the small boy, but the problem with all Freudian psychoanalysts is that they try to pull and punch it into a theory that also applies to the little girl. Because he claimed that the child's first awareness of sexual difference is the presence or absence of a penis, Lacan defined woman as an 'absence of sex'. Only a male who cannot conceive of an active sexuality other than his own could talk about the lack of a penis as castration. The small girl has no reason to believe that possession of the penis is an advantage; she may see it as an ugly protuberance rather than a desirable protrusion. In childhood she is more likely to be proud of her identification with the mother, whom she will see as more powerful and relevant than the father in her life. There is no reason to assume that recognition of phallic power is universal. I did not, as a child, consider that male power was superior to female power. It came as a great and unpleasant surprise to me when I had left childhood behind, to discover the true state of affairs, that men 'ruled' the world. It is the male (and presumably also the male child) who values the penis. I cannot speak with authority for either, but they are both adequately represented by all those male psychoanalysts who have been telling us for the past hundred years about phallicism.

Lacan was the victim of his own theories in two ways. As I said earlier, he condemned the theories of the women psychoanalysts as polluted with ideologies, yet he himself reinterpreted Freud through the science of linguistics, which he held to be patriarchal, and what is patriarchy if not an ideology? Furthermore, as a post-structuralist he asserted the influence of the communicator (writer/reader, speaker/listener) on the meaning of the text, yet he sees nothing wrong with the fact that his interpretation of female sexuality is male in concept, structure and attitude. He bombarded us with male language; he used male images, a male concept of sexuality to achieve this theoretical erection!

He defines psychological life as if biology did not exist. This was a man carried away by the idea of his own transcendence who forgot that he was also a biological being. He is another example of the 'genius' confined to the tunnel of his discovery, and of the scientific method breaking down the object of study into components, and then generalising from the particular. Lacan took no account of the biological information – nameless/unexpressed – that is contained in genetic transmission, in the genetic bank. He also underplayed social influence; he ignored the fact that language arises from social situations, and is changed not only by feelings but also by imagination and changing social structures and situations. He took language as a given fact imposed by society on each new human.

Lacan's attitude betrays an overweening desire to annihilate women from the psyche of the species. Whether he suffers from Karen Horney's 'womb envy' or Dorothy Dinnerstein's unresolved grievances against the mother, he has a large chip on his shoulder. Using words from what he admits is phallic language, he makes women disappear:

> There is no woman who is not excluded by the nature of things, which is the nature of words, and it must be said, if there is something they complain a lot about at the moment, that is what it is – except that they don't know what they are saying, that's the whole difference between them and me.[6]

The influence of language in psychoanalysis, as in other areas of life, cannot be denied. But when some psychoanalysts and other scientists talk about human anatomy and refer to a woman's clitoris as an atrophied penis, this is male-centred, sexist language. If the situation is viewed from a female-centred (also sexist) point of view, one could say that the penis was a distorted clitoris, grossly over-developed to the point of deformity.

Lacanian theory attracts feminists because it presents a manageable goal. If language and culture are the bulwarks of patriarchy, then they can be tackled, perhaps not easily but with some prospect of success. It is better than having to fight something like biology. Women of the seventies, who were attempting to define their own sexuality (among other status problems), were seduced away from the main substance of the task by quick-fix solutions such as reforming patriarchal language, when that language was more likely a symptom of the problem rather than the problem itself.

Juliet Mitchell, the distinguished British author, socialist and psychoanalyst, combined socialism and psychoanalysis in her theories. She saw patriarchy and capitalism as the two systems that caused the subordination of women (socialist feminists tend to mix their theories of feminism with their political beliefs). She introduced an understanding of Freud to English-speaking feminism, and saw psychoanalysis 'not as a recommendation *for* a patriarchal society, but as an analysis *of* patriarchy'. Freud, she held, had been dismissed by the new wave of feminists because they had misinterpreted him; but if they re-examined his writings, using the insights of Jacques Lacan, women would understand how their sexuality was formed under patriarchy and then they would be able to transform society. Freud's theories, she said, were concerned 'with how the human animal with a bisexual psychological disposition becomes the sexed social creature – the man or the woman'. Freud, she maintained, did not refer to physical bodies in his theories of the Oedipus complex and penis envy; they were both symbolic:[7]

A psychoanalyst could not subscribe to a currently popular sociological distinction in which a person is born with their biological gender to which society – general environment, parents, education, the media – adds a socially defined sex, masculine or feminine. Psychoanalysis cannot make such a distinction: a person is formed through their sexuality, it could not be 'added' to him or her.[8]

Lacanians are being disingenuous when they interpret the phallus as *symbolising* male power, because the origin of the symbol is biological and a potent instrument of biology. Psychoanalysis deals with the psychological aspects of sexuality, but they cannot be divorced from the biological or the cultural. In other areas of life there are interactions between the psychological and the biological, take hunger and its satisfaction, so why isolate the psychological aspects of sexuality from its biological and social aspects? What is Lacan's 'law of the father' if not culture? And if culture is not part of the social environment, then what is it? It seems to me that this confusion is created purely by semantics, and the construction of the psyche and social formation are intermingled and interdependent. Indeed, Freud said, 'sociology . . . dealing as it does with the behaviour of people in society, cannot be anything but applied psychology'.[9]

Luce Irigaray holds that psychoanalysis is a male discipline, and, in their own interests, women should construct psychoanalytic models that suit them. She has degrees in both philosophy and linguistics, and is also a psychoanalyst who studied under Lacan in Paris. Strictly speaking, Irigaray is not a Lacanian, as she was expelled from his school for disagreeing with him, and is highly critical of aspects of both Freud's and Lacan's psycho-analysis. She says that Freud underestimated the power of womb envy, which may be stronger than the desire to relate sexually to the mother. She also holds that female sexuality is quite different from its present definition which is a male one:

> *woman has sex organs more or less everywhere.* She finds pleasure almost anywhere ... the geography of her pleasure is far more diversified, more multiple in its differences, more complex, more subtle, than is commonly imagined.[10]

She maintains that a woman's sexuality is not confined to genital sexuality, that it is a 'sort of expanding universe', which is restricted by male domi-nation. Irigaray is Freudian in so far as she sees an inevitable difference between female and male sexuality because the girl and the boy relate in different ways to the mother: the girl identifies with her; the boy separates from her. The boy rejects the mother in order to grasp her; the girl wants to stay united to the mother. There is no cure, no solution, for this difference, she says, and the best that can be hoped for is that each will see and admire in the other characteristics that they do not possess themselves.

In Irigaray's theory there is an explanation of why women combine emotion with sexuality, why women replace the mother with a husband or partner, and expect the reciprocation of love from that man that they received from the mother. Her ideas also explain the difference in women's and men's reaction to intercourse: men penetrate, ejaculate/orgasm and withdraw, and women resent the withdrawal because they enjoy the closeness and identification of the union. How many times have we heard women complain about the 'wham, bang and not even thank you ma'am' school of heterosexual sexual activity.

Irigaray says that since women are branded as sexual commodities by a male-oriented society, a tactical separatism in which they could find their own voice and become economically independent – political lesbianism – is an indispensable stage in the escape from sexual subordination; but not as a permanent solution. Renunciation of heterosexuality, she maintains, would only 'involve a new prison, a new cloister, built of their own accord'.[11]

Irigaray's theory of female sexual difference has not been appreciated by English-speaking feminists for reasons that have little to do with her ideas:

her style is difficult and often enigmatic, so most of her work has not been translated; her emphasis on difference in female sexuality caused her to be dubbed a 'biological essentialist' by a movement more interested in establishing similarities between women and men. It is unfortunate that she has been ignored, because her ideas are first steps towards developing a female psychoanalysis that would benefit everyone.

Julia Kristeva, although Bulgarian in origin, teaches in France and is also in the French sphere of psychoanalysis. Like Irigaray she is involved in post-structuralist linguistics, but her analysis of sexuality has more appeal to many feminists.[12] Kristeva refuses to be called a feminist although her work is used by feminists in so far as she provides a theoretical basis in psychoanalysis for androgyny, which became important in one strand of the women's movement. Her thesis is that femininity should not be identified with biological woman, nor masculinity with biological man; that sexual difference begins in the pre-verbal stage of development when the infant is non-verbally involved with the mother. This non-verbal stage of experience with its emotions must be transcended so that the infant can become masculine or feminine, and this takes place at the verbal stage. But the emotions of the non-verbal stage, she maintains, are never totally transcended and escape to appear principally in art. She has been criticised for assigning no value to women except as maternal machines, providers of the pre-verbal stage of the infant's development which is superseded by the patriarchal and verbal. But in assigning this cradle of sexuality to women, she also recognises the sexuality of childbirth ('the ecstasy of birth') and nurture.

These are difficult concepts, but they are merely differences within psychoanalysis rather than in the wider context. For all psychoanalysts, for Lacan and his followers (to whatever degree), sexuality is constructed psychologically, and sexuality constructs the human person.

We cannot leave French fields without reference to Michel Foucault (1926–84), the French psychologist and philosopher who, whatever insights he had into its deployment, also fell into the male trap of defining sexuality only in male terms. He set out to write a history of sexuality, and had written three volumes before he died. His *History of Sexuality* was not an account of the evolution of sexual behaviour and practices, nor of the development of ideas about the nature of sexuality;[13] it concerned what he called 'the deployment of sexuality', or 'a history of the experience of sexuality'. In the first volume he had only outlined his thesis but without sufficient explanation to convey his purpose. The subsequent two volumes had progressed no further than 'a history of the experience of sexuality' in classical Greek and Roman times, and dealt mainly with homosexuality. There is no way of knowing what he would have said in subsequent volumes had he lived to write them.

Sexuality, he maintained in volume 1, was not suppressed in the nineteenth century and the first half of the twentieth century, as many of us believe; it was, instead, 'deployed' by various power centres, and had been deployed during the course of history. This deployment was engineered by religion, state control, medicine, psychology, families and individuals, through various instruments. These were religious taboos; state laws; the medicalisation of women's bodies; the psychoanalysis of children and control of their sexual activity; the regulation of procreative behaviour in several ways; and the 'psychiatrisation (the pathologisation) of perverse pleasure', that is, of what was called 'perverted' sexual activity, such as fetishism, homosexuality and other practices.

In this deployment of sexuality, he said, sex became 'a problem of truth'. It became a subject to investigate, mainly through confession: confession of sexual activity and fantasy to priests, doctors, psychoanalysts and sexologists. Psychoanalysis and sexology, he said, took over from religion in the twentieth century as the instrument of investigation and control of sexuality. He went on to say that other cultures (China, Japan, India, Rome, the Arabo-Muslim societies) had an *ars erotica* (erotic art); while Western civilisation was the only one to practise a *scientia sexualis*. By making a science of sexuality, power was given into the hands of certain groups, such as doctors, psychologists, legislators, priests, et cetera. The deployment of sexuality also gave rise to 'a deployment of alliance', which included systems of marriage, a variety of kinship ties, and the transmission of names and property:

> Sexuality must not be described as a stubborn drive . . . It appears rather as
> an especially dense transfer point for relations of power between men and
> women, young people and old people, parents and offspring, teachers and
> students, priests and laity, an administration and a population. Sexuality is
> not the most intractable element in power relations, but rather one
> endowed with the greatest instrumentality: useful for the greatest num-
> ber of manoeuvres and capable of serving as a point of support, as a linch-
> pin, for the most varied strategies.

Therefore, it is not a natural phenomenon which has to be held in check, or something obscure which we are gradually trying to uncover, Foucault said, it is a historical construct, 'a great surface network',[14] where arousal and pleasure, intense discussion, controls and resistances, are linked together 'in accordance with a few major strategies of knowledge and power'.

Well, that is another way of looking at it, but while this insight is useful in regarding sexuality as a cultural phenomenon, it is of little help in establishing the nature of sexuality. Foucault declares that sexuality is a construct of power centres, and 'sex' is a necessary invention of sexuality.[15] In fact, he discounted the idea that such a thing as sexuality existed except as a creation of power blocs in order to manipulate people, and he maintained that 'sex' was an invention made necessary by the deployment of sexuality:

> Is 'sex' really the anchorage point that supports the manifestations of sexuality, or is it not rather a complex idea that was formed inside the deployment of sexuality? ... sex is the most speculative, most ideal, and most internal element in a deployment of sexuality organised by power in its grip on bodies ...

Among the main power blocs that regulated and deployed sexuality (family, religion, the state and medical science) Foucault regarded psychoanalysis as an essential part of the modern construction and deployment of sexuality. Psychoanalysis, he held, took sexuality outside the family, set incest at its central core in the Oedipus complex, and found ways to relieve the stress caused by laws regulating it. Foucault would dispense with sex and the meanings attached to it, in favour of 'bodies and pleasure'. He never got around to giving 'bodies and pleasure' a context in the human person.

There is no doubt that, following a certain train of thought (in this case Foucault's contention that sexuality is the product of power centres in their manipulation of people), it is possible to see 'sex' as a necessary invention of sexuality. But this is again the tunnel thinking of the philosopher/terrier running with a bone of logic. It is the nonsense you get if you abstract one element of the situation (in this case the deployment of sexuality), subject it to a philosophical discourse (using logic, one of the principal tools of classical philosophy) and ignore all other factors relating to sexuality. Biological sex cannot exist in a society without causing a sexuality to form around it. Indeed, the interaction of the various elements of relationships between the sexes leads to a very complex sexuality.

While Foucault succeeds in showing that sexuality has always been deployed, there is an inherent fallacy in his denial of the idea that sexuality would have existed without, or before, becoming an instrument of power.

Unless sexuality had an existence and a power of its own, it could not be shaped, deployed or manipulated. Foucault was conditioned by the very deployment which he exposed. Furthermore, the sexuality he wrote about is a male sexuality, and when he stripped it of its cultural accretions, he could find nothing but 'bodies and pleasure'; but what is pleasure but a deployment of sexuality? He was also ignorant of female sexuality which, despite the worst that can be imposed on it, has such a rich bedrock that it survives: women give birth.

His dissociation of sexuality from reproduction and his emphasis on 'bodies and pleasure' are a definition of sexuality that is undoubtedly a construct. It is a form of sexuality already deployed by commercial interests for their own advantage. Foucault's ideas have become influential among some modern thinkers, and have validated the consumerist culture. In *Sex and Destiny* Germaine Greer writes:

> Sex is the lubricant of the consumer economy, but in order to fulfil that function the very character of human sexuality itself must undergo special conditioning. Its connection with reproduction, which is potentially disruptive, must go.

Foucault's great contribution was that he led people to loosen their rigid ideas on sexuality, to broaden their perceptions of it, perhaps to glimpse what it might be if it were released from the constrictions of the rules and regulations made in its deployment by various sources of authority. But while Foucault may be right about the deployment of sexuality, his view of it is a male view, and his subtext is an apologia for homosexuality. As revolutionary feminist Sheila Jeffreys says: 'Foucault's map of the world is simply a male gay map.'[16]

The difference between Freud and many of those who claim his mantle is that he acknowledged a biological person in which the psychological person developed. He included biological sexual activity, as well as instincts, feelings and fantasy in his definition of sexuality. But a reading of Freud's immense corpus of psychoanalytical writings leads to confusion about his stance on the relationship between psychoanalysis and biology. In one place he says, 'Sex is a biological fact which, although it is of extraordinary importance in mental life, is hard to grasp psychologically.'[17] Three years later, in discussing instincts, he admitted to 'biological psychology' or 'the psychical accompaniments of biological processes'. Yet later on he enjoined his readers to separate psychoanalysis from biology.[18]

Later psychoanalysts have abandoned or ignored the biological element, and claim that sexuality in psychoanalytic terms means solely psycho-sexuality – 'a system of conscious and unconscious human fantasies involving a range of excitations and activities that produce pleasure beyond the satisfaction of any basic physiological need'.[19] This confines sexuality to a mindset or psychological cast detached from biology or physiology. I find this casuistic, because the pleasure produced is experienced physically, and the sexuality which they claim is constructed in the infant cannot be divorced from the biology from which it sprung. The mind or psyche mediates between culture and biology; or in Freudian terms, the ego mediates between the culture and the id or the inherited instincts.

Undoubtedly sexuality has an important influence on the formation of the person, if by person we mean the characteristics, attitudes, behaviour, reactions of the specific human ('What kind of person is she?'). But these are not the only influences on the construction of the person. There is, for example, the influence of fear of physical pain, hunger or death: the instinct of self-preservation is stronger than the sexual instinct which retreats in times of danger.

There is an element of faith attached to psychoanalytic theory. How can one test, say, the Oedipus complex or the castration complex? One can only apply their various interpretations to oneself and see whether they fit, and enquire of others in the same manner. This is empiricism. Psychoanalysts would say that such research is useless, that the unconscious suppresses the truth, and while I do not decry empiricism, nor am I a slave to what Juliet Mitchell called 'the contemporary fetishism of measurement as the means to scientific verifiability', the existence of these complexes can only be em-pirical, deduced from the anecdotal evidence of those analysed, and from the analysts own subjective opinion.

Unfortunately, psychoanalysis, this new and exciting area of knowledge, set women back a century. It is understandable that feminists reacted against Freud and his male-centred theories. Often they were reacting against the popular, and sometimes mistaken, idea of what Freud said, those aspects of Freud's thinking that were assimilated into cultural beliefs. Freud advanced the science of psychology and made a significant contribution to humans' understanding of themselves. However, a theory of sexuality built solely on male values and attitudes cannot be correct, it is a mark of male sexuality to value the penis; nor can one built solely on female attitudes. There is a whole world of female sexuality, both actual and theoretical, that is unknown to men, and unexplored (in the theory of sexuality) by women; unexplored physically, too, by them, except by a small minority, among whom are some sexually active lesbians.

Psychoanalysis has been travelling along a road of male bias and mis-apprehension for almost a hundred years. From Freud to Lacan they were priapic, despite their protests that they were concerned solely with the unconscious. Their theories related to men and had limited relevance to women. To make it relevant to themselves, women have got to go back to the beginning, travel the road again, as Luce Irigaray suggested, and find a psychoanalysis that is relevant to female life. Then the two bodies of knowledge can be combined. Some of the women psychoanalysts have attempted to do this, but they try to take too much Freudian baggage with them.

Perhaps they should forget about Freud and Lacan and establish a theory of female sexuality from their own work and personal experience. Why should the phallus because it represents male sexuality have anything to do with the formation of female sexuality? It was only given relevance by men who could not conceive of the absence of the penis, or visualise another kind of sexuality. Psychoanalysts are human with human psyches – male in men, female in women. If psychoanalysis had been developed by women perhaps there would be an elephant's trunk complex and fear of abnormal growths which would seal off the womb; and, perhaps, more prominence given to a corresponding male complex of (Karen Horney's) womb envy. Why should male sexuality be taken as the starting point when male development in the embryo results from an intervention (see chapter 10)? The fact that it has been taken as the starting point may owe more to the less-than-scientific pronouncements of earlier Churchmen who still influence cultural beliefs. Aristotle, that professional misogynist of the fourth century B.C., described woman as an impotent male, 'for it is through a certain incapacity that female is female'. And Thomas Aquinas in the thirteenth century said, 'the production of woman comes from defect in the active power'. The power of woman-hatred or woman-fear has been enduring, a cultural pathology, which transferred to their anato-my the inferiority which was imposed culturally on women. How can any rational person claim that maleness is superior to femaleness on the evidence of their contribution to the species, or on any evidence? The opposite could be posited with arguably more conviction if one wanted to go down an equally irrational road.

There is confusion in the writings of the various post-Freudian psychoanalysts as to what Freud really meant by castration complex and penis envy. These terms are bandied about as if they were being used in the terms in which Freud used them, and as if everyone agreed on what they mean, when they patently do not. Even Freud was ambiguous about them. When the women psychoanalysts (Horney, Deutsch, Klein) questioned the castration complex they fell back on biology and asserted an essential femininity or masculinity in the newborn baby. But they went on to become more concerned with the nature of female sexuality than with the construction of sexual difference.

The child could, conceivably, relate to her/his genital pleasure the feeling of deprivation which she or he experiences when the breast (or the bottle nipple) is withdrawn, she or he could fear that the same deprivation of pleasure could be repeated in the genital area. That would explain castration complex in a psychological way but related to the biological organ. Furthermore, if the castration complex is psychological – in that it does not relate to the actual organs – then its very form, the words used to describe it, are sexist and betray the male attitude and complex behind it. It should be called the male complex rather than castration complex.

The question of whether that other Freudian tenet, penis envy, is a biological statement or a metaphoric one (relating not to the organ but to phallic power) is irrelevant. If it were a biological statement, it would have to be motivated by either psychological or social factors. The fact is that there are few women who would swap their female sexuality for male, especially when they have had a baby. That alone suggests that a factor other than psychology or sociology is significantly involved in sexuality, and only someone prejudiced by a cherished belief would then deny biology. If Erikson's 'inner space' had not been so swathed in patriarchal nonsense it might approach the answer.

As there is a biological principle of heterosexual attraction among all other mammals, there is no reason to deny its presence in humans: it is a basic biological hormonal factor in the make-up of all mammals. The development of the human intellect and, as a result, of human psychology, plus the more complex sociological development of humans (and the complex interaction of the sociological and the psychological) controls and modifies these mammalian instincts, *but does not wipe them out.*

Why are there two biological sexes? What is their purpose? It is not, surely, for pleasure alone. Sexual activity in other mammals is a release of tension caused by hormonal activity activated by pheromones or other triggers; its purpose is reproduction. As a release of tension, it may be called pleasure. Freud claimed that sexual activity in humans was also a release of tension. But tension is a physical phenomenon. The difference between humans and other mammals is the intervention of superior intelligence, which includes the ability to control or modify, not eliminate, physical phenomena.

Sexual difference and response in the human mammal exist basically for the purpose of reproduction, but this basic biology is mediated by, and integrated with, human psychology, intelligence,[20] and culture to form human sexuality which serves other interests such as pleasure. Instincts such as hunger and self-preservation are also mediated by intelligence: hunger has been sophisticated into an immense and diverse culture of food and culinary art; self-preservation into an equally vast culture of clothing, housing and environment. The senses have also been mediated by intelligence: sight into a wide variety of decorative and artistic appreciation and hearing into an equally wide variety of pleasurable sound and music.

This is not to deny the existence of a psychological and sociological dimension in the formation of sexuality, but to restate the biological element and to give it its due place alongside the others. Some psychologists, particularly psychoanalysts, rule out biology as if to defend human intelligence against some animality; some feminists rule out biology because they are afraid of its essentialism or determinism, which would mean, they think, that oppression and subjugation of women was then inevitable. I maintain that the oppression and subjugation of women through their sexuality comes not from biology but from psychological and sociological reasons, and that biology is used as an excuse.

8

THE SEXUAL REVOLUTION

During World War II, an atmosphere of personal freedom, of which sexual freedom was part, swept over Europe and the United States of America. This sounds like a contradiction in terms when at the same time war imposed great restriction on many aspects of individual freedom. It was also a time, however, when women gained a substantial degree of economic and personal independence, if not status. They had staffed industry and 'kept the home fires burning', discovering in the process their previously untapped abilities. They also claimed a large measure of sexual licence. In the immediate post-war years, governments in Britain and the United States were concerned that jobs (and marriages) should await the returning soldiers, and therefore the women who worked in the factories and the offices, on the land and behind the steering wheel, must be returned to the home.

There was also concern in these countries about the state of marriage and the high rate of divorce, the 'breakdown in morality', and the 'sexual incontinence' which had become widespread. In 1948 a committee set up by the British government recommended that grants be made available for marriage-counselling services. Discreet meetings were held with editors and opinion-makers in the media, manuals were written, marriage guidance councils were set up, and a plethora of organisations directed their energies towards the resolution of marital problems on both sides of the Atlantic.[1]

Another force was also at work. Industry had reverted to peacetime manufacture, and consumers were needed for all kinds of personal and household products. Surveys of the time showed that women confined to the job of housewife would buy more goods, so the hidden persuaders of advertising and the media were brought to bear on women.[2] A carrot-and-stick manoeuvre was used to get women back into domesticity: on the one hand, homemakers were glamorised; and on the other, women aspiring to careers were warned of the dangers to their sex lives that would follow. (This tactic was repeated in the 1980s and 1990s.)[3] Meanwhile, the sexologists got to work on improving the quality of women's sexual performance which, they said, would give them the fulfilment they were seeking.

Sheila Jeffreys gives a very good account of that period in Britain in *Anticlimax*. She says that the joy of reading the sexological works of the 1950s is that they 'reveal the naked power politics involved in marriage and sex'. A glance at the popular sexology and sex advice publications of the immediate post-war years on both sides of the Atlantic, makes her point abundantly clear.[4] These tracts unblushingly advocated male domination and female submission, implying (and sometimes stating clearly) with staggering illogicality that equality for women lay in their recognition of male supremacy.

'Equality' as defined by feminists, the sex manuals all agreed, was the main cause of marital problems; marriage was stable when a man was boss in his own house. It would make it easier for discontented wives to accept marriage on a man's terms (they were quite explicit about this) if they found a new enjoyment in sexual activity, hence the official birth of sex advice. Frigidity (in women, of course), the extent of which surprised and alarmed the researchers, became a focus and a challenge to the new engineers of sexual activity; women's reluctance to submit to their husbands, they decided, must be related to their new independence.

In the remaking of the wife, equality for women was redefined: it was equated with equality of sexual enjoyment. Equal, mutual orgasms would satisfy women and keep them from encroaching on the traditional male-held territory of the workplace, as such adventures on the part of women threatened the structure of marriage. Thus was launched the eroticisation of the housewife and a new era in the history of sexuality, when sexual activity became part of housework. Sexology had come of age.

Modern sexology began in the 1950s with Alfred Kinsey and his famous reports; and it took off in the 1960s with William Masters and Virginia Johnson. It is inextricably involved with what became known as the sexual revolution. All three of these researchers regarded sexuality as a biological drive which responded to stimulus, and which was necessary for mental and physical health. Their definitions of sexuality were based (as ever) on the male biological manifestation, for even these more modern sexologists were primarily interested in studying what they called the inadequacy of female sexuality. (I've often wondered if Virginia Johnson revised her ideas when she read the Shere Hite reports.)

Kinsey (1894–1956) was a zoologist (an entomologist, actually, interested in the gall wasp) who, in mid-life in the 1940s and 1950s, changed his academic pursuit to the classification of human sexuality. He collected material for this work from an immense number of interviews, few of which were corroborated;[5] and he applied to this material the classification methods which he had used in his insect studies. His 'science' was un-ashamedly male-centred and related to the mechanics of coitus with which he became so obsessed that he isolated it from the context of all other human relations. He made the not uncommon mistake of scientific specialists by attempting to study one particular focus of interest in isolation from the organism in which it is embedded.

Kinsey regarded the exercise of sexuality as biologically necessary for male health, and it was the *duty* of women to shed their inhibitions, their frigidity and morality in order to allow men their 'natural' sexual freedom. Women, he believed, had a low sex drive and therefore they had little desire for sexual activity. For that very same reason, he declared, they should have no anti-pathy to it; any antipathy to sexual activity was a pathological inhibition. In fact he advocated that women behave more like prostitutes, and if they did not enjoy the role, their reward lay in pleasing the man.[6] Not surprisingly, Kinsey was hailed as a sexual liberator by men and, for a time, women blamed themselves for their sexual shortcomings and were tricked into compliance. He devised a scale to measure the degree of homosexuality, bisexuality and heterosexuality found in the community, and because of overlapping and variations in tendencies from one person to another, he said that the term homosexual should be applied to a behaviour pattern rather than to a person. In this he contributed to a more liberal attitude towards homosexuals.

The Kinsey reports on male and female sexuality became a new gospel in the 1950s. Even Simone de Beauvoir quoted them in *The Second Sex* as an authoritative source. The reports were not challenged for reliability or objectivity until many decades later, and then only on the question of his female respondents being mainly middle class. Kinsey's reply was that it made no difference because 'girls' of all classes were similarly trained to inhibit their sexuality.

His choice of male respondents was wider, but this work was later called into question, this time because he seemed unable to recognise the difference between truth and possible fantasy in the statements which he recorded. Some of his contacts were made on an ad hoc basis, and it has been suggested that some of the wilder material that he collected was likely to be heavily overlaid with fantasy. The American writer Andrea Dworkin quotes one instance from his biography which I have condensed. It was a statement from a sixty-three-year-old man, a college graduate and responsible government employee, who was reputed to have kept an accurate record of his sexual behaviour over his lifetime. He claimed to have had sexual relations with six hundred pre-adolescent males, two hundred pre-adolescent females, countless adults of both sexes, animals of many species, and he had elaborate techniques of masturbation. His grandmother, he said, introduced him to heterosexual intercourse, and his father introduced him to homosexual acts. Of thirty-three members of his extended family, he claimed to have had sexual contacts with seventeen. Kinsey's biographer and collaborator, W.B. Pomeroy, claimed that this uncorroborated statement formed the basis of a significant part of chapter five of *Sexual Behaviour in the Human Male*.[7]

Kinsey was soon succeeded in the 1960s and 1970s by the partnership of Masters and Johnson who were not in danger of being fooled by the fantasies of their respondents. No longer did research depend on verbal or written reports, it now acquired a new dimension – sex laboratories where sexual activity (coitus) was observed in the flesh, so to speak, and recorded by means of electrodes and cameras. (The first experiments in measuring the 'bioelectrical' charge emitted by the skin of the genitals during orgasm were carried out by Wilhelm Reich in 1934.)[8]

Masters and Johnson were interested in orgasm and deliberately sought out subjects whose sexual activity was more than average. They used in their tests only women who had orgasm regularly during intercourse, and who, presumably, had no inhibitions about being observed in action. We owe a lot to those women.

From the thousands of female orgasms observed, Masters and Johnson made a definitive and momentous discovery: female orgasm resulted *only* from clitoral stimulation; there was no such thing as the vaginal orgasm.[9] (What they mean is that orgasm is not stimulated by friction on the vaginal wall but by friction on the clitoris.)[10] Orgasm, they decided, was a matter of mechanics which anyone could learn, and they translated their findings into a therapy available at their clinic. Later it became evident that the missionary position for sexual intercourse – male on top, female flat on her back – was one reason why women were not having orgasms. It has been the reason for the 'frigidity' of which women have been accused in the past (and perhaps yet in the privacy of their lives). *The Hite Report on Female Sexuality* found that less than 30 per cent of the women who replied had an orgasm during sexual intercourse, and of those who did, most achieved it with the woman on top. Other positions such as side-by-side, entering from the rear, sitting up, were also used successfully. It was a matter of complementary body shape: only with some couples does the man's pubic area provide the necessary stimulation of the clitoris.

The 'discovery' of the clitoral orgasm, and the abandonment of the vaginal orgasm, coincided with the sexual revolution. Masters and Johnson captured women's imagination because they refuted the traditional belief in female frigidity. They appealed particularly to feminists because they argued against the double standard of sexual morality, and defended women's rights to sexual pleasure.

In *Human Sexual Response*, Masters and Johnson gave a detailed description of the female orgasm:

Stage I: 'Orgasm has its onset with a sensation of suspension or stoppage. Lasting only an instant, the sensation is accompanied or followed immediately by an isolated thrust of intense sensual awareness, clitorally oriented, but radiating upward into the pelvis. Intensity ranging in degree from mild to shock level has been reported by many women within the context of their personal experience, a simultaneous loss of overall sensory acuity has been described as paralleling in degree the intensity and duration of the particular orgasmic episode ... During the first stage of subjective progression in orgasm, the sensation of acute clitoral-pelvis awareness has been described by a number of women as occurring concomitantly with a sense of bearing down or expelling. Often a receptive opening was expressed. This last sensation was reported only by parous study subjects, a small number of whom expressed some concept of having an actual fluid emission or of expending in some concrete fashion. Previous male interpretation of these subjective reports may have resulted in the erroneous but widespread concept that female ejaculation is an integral part of female orgasmic expression.

Stage II: As the second stage of subjective progression through orgasm, a sensation of 'suffusion of warmth', specifically pervading the pelvic area first and then spreading progressively throughout the body, was described by almost every woman with orgasmic experience.

Stage III: Finally, as the third stage of subjective progression, a feeling of involuntary contraction with a specific focus in the vagina or lower pelvis was mentioned consistently. Frequently, the sensation was described as that of 'pelvic throbbing'.

Women with the facility to express sensate awareness frequently separated this final stage of subjective progression into two phases. The initial phase was expressed as contractile, followed immediately by a throbbing phase, with both sensations experienced as separate entities. The initial contractile feeling was described as localized vaginally, subsequently merging with the throbbing sensation which, though initially concentrated in the pelvis, was felt throughout the body. The 'pelvic throbbing' sensation was often depicted as continuing until it became one with a sense of the pulse or heartbeat.

Only the two phases of this third stage of subjective progression during orgasm afforded positive correlation between subjective response and objective reaction. This correlation has been developed from a composite return of direct interrogation of female study subjects during investigative sessions. The phase of contractile sensation has been identified as paralleling in time sequence the recorded initial spasm of the orgasmic platform.

Regularly recurring orgasmic platform contractions were appreciated subjectively as pulsating or throbbing sensations of the vagina. Although second phase sensations of pulsation coincided with observable vaginal-platform contractions, consciousness of a pulsating sensation frequently continued beyond observable platform contractions. Finally this pelvic throbbing sensation became one with a subjective awareness of tachy-cardia described frequently as feeling the heartbeat vaginally. Subjective awareness of orgasmic duration was somewhat dependent upon the degree of intensity of the specific orgasm.

The female orgasm is 'a psychophysiologic experience occurring within, and made meaningful by, a context of psychosocial influence'. The 'physio-logic' referred to the physical conditions and reactions during the orgasm; the 'psychologic' referred to attitude towards coitus and receptivity to orgasm; the 'sociologic' included the cultural and social factors that in-fluenced the ability to attain orgasm. For the first time sexuality was defin-ed as a combination of biological, psychological and sociocultural factors. Yet, although they made this assertion in their earlier work, their approach to sexuality continued to be biological and behaviouristic. In their writings, they treated sexuality mainly as a biological phenomenon, a genital, mechanical, conditioned reflex, separate from human social relations, and they advocated certain techniques for satisfactory performance.

They believed, like Freud and some of his followers, that frequent orgasm was necessary for the health of mind and body. An orgasm a day keeps the doctor away; and orgasmic equality would solve women's problems. As well as the clitoral orgasm, Masters and Johnson, in the course of their researches, came across two other phenomena of equal importance which linked the female orgasm with giving birth (see chapter 11). Their other aim, they said, was to change the commonly held ideas of what was 'normal' in sexual practice, and bring them into line with what they believed was actually happening.

These ideas were self-fulfilling; by their work Masters and Johnson, and other sexologists, deliberately created a culture of sexuality which encouraged sexual activity and experiment. But they advocated a 'liberation' of sexuality without taking its psychological content into account. By concentrating on the mechanics of sexual intercourse, their perception of sexuality was (once more) male-centred and informed by the prevailing male culture.

Female sexuality in the mid-sixties, in their estimation, was stunted; women should be like that portion of the male population which is ready to couple with anyone, anywhere and at any time. Sexuality should be like conversation, capable of being used as a universal coinage. The ideal was 'the zipless fuck' (so aptly named by Erica Jong), where both partners came together for non-involved or non-relational coitus and zips parted like rose petals. This thesis did not take into consideration the personality, psychology or feelings of those who might prefer to have attraction or some other social context for their sexual relations. It also assumed that, like Pavlov's dogs, humans could be conditioned to pleasurable sexual reflexes.

Kinsey, and Masters and Johnson used stimulus-response psychology; they took their theoretical lead from behaviouristic social-learning theory, a type of psychology that was popular in the United States in the 1940s and 1950s. Like Reich searching for a bioelectric charge in excited genitalia, they used cameras, electrodes and other paraphernalia in an attempt to find what physical evidence identifies the perfect orgasm. Sexologists at this stage were merely technologists observing and instructing sexual activity, advocating methods to improve performance. They decided that improved techniques in sexual intercourse was the answer to better relations between the sexes; that orgasm through proper stimulation of the clitoris was the answer to women's problems. As Germaine Greer said in *The Female Eunuch*, the sex books show that in our society we make love to organs not to people. Other commentators described the sexologists as 'sexual essentialists' who spent a great deal of time seeking the truth of sex 'in biology usually, in the instinct, the chromosomes and hormones, the DNA, the genes, or less often, but powerfully, in psychic energy or unconscious compulsions'.

While still confining their own work largely to the physiology of sexual activity, in the fullness of time Masters and Johnson took note of the current social and psychological studies on sexuality. In *Human Sexuality*, published in 1992 and written in a more popular style, they drew heavily on a broad selection of modern writers, and gave much more emphasis to psychological and sociocultural influences. In this book they explained their early mechanistic approach as a first step in understanding sexuality, and that biology was never intended as an 'endpoint' but rather a beginning.

Women were deceived for a while in the fifties by the official and unofficial efforts to manipulate their sexuality and regulate their lives in the interests of male dominance, but little more than a decade later the young women who were the children of the war and post-war years would not submit to regulation in the same way as their mothers. Meanwhile, the roots of this modern sexual revolution continued to grow, fed by the writings of the sex radicals (Reich, Marcuse, et cetera), psychoanalysis and the new breed of sexologists. It was the advent of the contraceptive pill, however, that gave it the green light and propelled Western youth into the greatest sexual binge in history.

The contraceptive pill was the wonder drug of the sixties. When it was launched in the late fifties, it was endowed with possibilities that surpassed the wildest dreams of quite different categories of women: it was the key to sexual liberation for the swingers of the sixties, and it was a reprieve for married women from the burden of large families.

The sexual revolution brought about an unprecedented cultural sea change in the lives of young people. It altered not only sexual behaviour but also attitudes to what was permissible in society: 'sex' was the new gate-way to freedom and equality, the way to establish one's individual identity. Lust became respectable; everyone was doing it. The sex manuals of the seventies moved on from the marriage advice of the previous decades and followed the new trend; they assumed that all women should be sexually available, and urged on them a change of attitude towards sex. They sought no change of attitude from men, apart from encouraging them to engage in foreplay: male sexuality, in its accepted form, was put forward as the norm. In a mechanistic approach to coitus there were buttons to press, which, if properly operated, would result in orgasm, and that was good for everyone. They made no reference to any Reichian or Marcusian ideas of political or cultural change that would result from this new sexual freedom and release of libido; the mechanics of sexual inter-course were paramount.

Depending on how you read history, feminism was associated with sexual freedom during the various sexual revolutions. Feminism (or aspects of it) informed the Greenwich Village sexual experiments and similar endeavours in the first quarter of this century. It informed European socialist 'free love', although the feminist aspects were lost in the form patriarchal socialism finally took in Europe – Alexandra Kollontai failed to prevail against the weight of male-domination in Russia. There was and is more than a semantic difference between a feminist sexual revolution which seeks sexual equality for women, and the popular idea of 'sexual revolution' that prevailed over the past two centuries.

That popular idea has always been male-libertarian, merely requiring women to drop the guards which, over time, they had developed to protect themselves from the excesses of male sexual dominance. The sexual revolution of the sexologists and the sexual radicals was unashamedly male-oriented, and when the women's movement of the sixties and seventies sought sexual freedom as a right, it was women – not men – who changed. Men continued to crow like cocks on the midden of their sexual privilege, delighted that women were going to make their bodies freely available to them, at no extra cost. John Stoltenberg, American writer and feminist, said that sexual freedom has never been about *sexual justice* between men and women; it has been about maintaining men's superior status, men's power over women; and about sexualising women's inferior status. Essentially, he said, 'sexual freedom has been about preserving a sexuality that sustains male supremacy'.[11]

The sexual freedom that they were offered seemed desirable, at the time, to women who had been oppressed by the double standard. The 1970s feminists who adopted the male model of sexuality were seeking a situa-tion in which they could be as assertive in sexual matters as men. They wanted to be independent and autonomous sexual persons rather than passive sexual objects. Moreover, unlike the sexologists, *they* saw the sexual revolution not just as a reactionary movement against the sexual sub-ordination of women, but as a subversive force (à la Reich), which would undermine the traditional culture that brought about that oppression. Women soon discovered that the 'sexual revolution', whatever its original objectives, had been turned into another way of subverting them to men's designs, that the new sexual 'liberation' did not liberate them from the mould in which male society had cast them. Men, in fact, retained the double standard; they continued to regard women who were permissive as sluts; they still referred to them as birds, tail, strokes, pussy and all the other denigratory terms that show contempt for women. Women found that they were still regarded as objects, not equal persons, only now they were more 'available' to men in the new climate of sexual permissiveness; they had *tacitly* lost the right or freedom to say 'no'. It also became evident that the form of male sexuality that existed *required* the subordination of women.

Women found that they were mistaken in another way: they began to regret the lack of emotional intimacy and commitment in the new sexual arrangements. The new regime sought to exclude an emotional life from sexual relations, divorcing the pleasures of lust, first of all from their source in the endocrinology of the body, and secondly from emotional involvement with the sexual partner. The sexual liberation that promised freedom, a greater awareness and happiness, defeated its purpose by its emphasis on genital intercourse.

The sexual revolutionaries, both female and male, ignored the psychological elements of sexuality, its construction from the close and intimate relations between child and parents. They attempted to deny the psychological and cultural construction of female sexuality which linked it with emotional intimacy. Instead they came down in favour of a biological exercise. This was a mistake made by people who, then and later, were themselves denying a biological element in sexuality and asserting that it was constructed psychologically and culturally. Women who discovered that they could make their own decisions soon began to query the parameters and standards of the sexual revolution. However, many women believed that they did not have a choice, and so they acquiesced to what is now a genitally fixated society.

Who gained from the sexual revolution? Men, of course, because they retained their previous attitudes, and achieved their sexual objectives more easily. Women, to some degree; it did help to liberate women into taking responsibility for their own sexual lives.

Other aspects of life, such as the economic situation of women, did not change so fast. Women's wages continued to be roughly two-thirds of men's, and while the new sexual freedom meant easier divorce as an escape out of an enslaving or brutal marriage, and the stigma which applied to unmarried mothers began to disappear, women ended up rearing children alone on reduced resources. These single-parent families became the new poor, a vast poverty-stricken army of women who assumed responsibility for the next generation while a large section of men evaded it.[12]

It is generally accepted that the sexual revolution of the 1960s, and the counterculture of protest against the establishment which took place in that decade and the early seventies, provided the climate and framework for the emergence of a new wave of feminism. But the ground for a revival of feminism was already being prepared by the writings of women such as Simone de Beauvoir, Betty Friedan and socialists like Juliet Mitchell. (Later, the new feminists went in search of their historical roots and resurrected the works of their early twentieth-century foremothers. They were surprised to find that some of them were still alive and were still active feminists.)[13] As early as 1949 (1953 for English-speaking readers) Simone de Beauvoir, in *The Second Sex*, had chronicled the subordination of women, had declared that woman was regarded as the 'Other' in male consciousness, and that female sexuality was largely a male invention. However, *The Second Sex* was not read very widely in Ireland and Britain until 1972, when the first Penguin edition became available.

SEXUALITY

Although the first texts to revitalise the women's movement in the sixties were to become the classics of modern feminism, they were not concerned with sexuality. One of the earliest and certainly the most read on both sides of the Atlantic was Betty Friedan's *The Feminine Mystique*. It was published in the mid-sixties, and Friedan's only interest in sexuality was in the part it played in the 'feminine mystique', how it was used by housebound women as a tactic to establish their status and as a defence against boredom.

Juliet Mitchell's attempt to reinstate 'the problem of the subordination of women' in British socialism in *Women: The Longest Revolution* referred only to sexual *freedom* and the sexual revolution of that time. Later, in *Psychoanalysis and Feminism*, she brought Freudian psychoanalysis to feminism and helped initiate a discussion on sexuality that went beyond the sexual revolution. In 1970 Kate Millett's *Sexual Politics* set out a whole new framework for a feminist philosophy: sexuality as the politics of patriarchy. She demonstrated through analysis of history and literature that sexuality was constructed by, and served the purposes of, patriarchy, and that women were subordinated by control of their sexuality.

In the same year Shulamith Firestone lobbed a literary grenade into the fervid discussion. In *The Dialectic of Sex*, her minimal demand was the liberation of women from the tyranny of reproduction, by turning to bio-technology – test-tube and incubator-hatching of babies – and the diffusion of child-rearing to society as a whole. If Firestone's modest proposal had Swiftian overtones, her analysis of the female predicament, of ecology, and much of child-rearing, was impeccable. In fact, she was serious, and her mistake was to dismiss humanity, to dismiss biology and psychology, and replace them with technology.

In 1970 also, using the research of Masters and Johnson, Ann Koedt revolutionised sexual activity for women in an article called 'The myth of the vaginal orgasm'. Although the sexologists had reported in 1966 that a woman's orgasm was triggered not in the vagina but by stimulation of the clitoris, it took four years for this information to reach the wider audience of women. Koedt's article was the first great step forward in a new definition of female sexuality. It galvanised the women's movement; they believed that they had found the hidden, repressed well of female sexuality. Not only was this 'new' discovery going to improve the sexual relations of women with their male lovers, it was going to make men redundant: women did not need men, or intercourse, to have an orgasm! Anna Coote and Beatrix Campbell told of 'ill-typed roneoed' copies of the article circulating among British women in the early days of the women's movement.[14] *Shrew*, a London feminist journal, proclaimed that for thousands of years patriarchal conditioning had deceived women about the true nature of their sexuality; a sexuality that was taken from them, distorted and mutilated, then returned to them as passive submission. And then Mary Jane Sherfey added another gem of information, that women could have not just one but multiple orgasms from clitoral stimulation.

A rash of books were published which gave advice to women on how to discover and fulfil their own sexual needs, either by masturbating alone or with another woman. This was still the sexual revolution where sexuality was equated with identity and self-assertion, and divorced from relationships and love. However some feminists were critical of this attitude. In 1983 Judith Williamson wrote in *City Limits*:

> [There] is a tendency to overestimate the power of sexuality, which in recent times has taken on a pseudo-radical role. In modern jargon sexuality 'frees' us; it has become part of a discourse of 'liberation' which makes repression, rather than oppression, the enemy of human happiness.

But is sexuality really the arena in which our wellbeing is determined in power structures in modern societies? And if, indeed, we overestimate its power, what effect does this have? What is the function of an ideology that keeps everyone looking for the meaning of life up their own or someone else's vagina?

Sheila Jeffreys said that this activity cast women in the role of 'mindless, uncontrollable sexual animals'.

In the seventies the women's movement was largely confined to small groups of women teasing out their own experiences in consciousness-raising, discussion, research, study and writing. They read the available texts, digging deeper into the genesis of their situation, and found, in one way or another, that women were oppressed because of their sexuality; or, at the very least, many of the problems of exploitation and inequality stemmed from some aspect of sexuality. A few started to peel away the layers of cultural and psychological accretions, the perceptions, customs and practices with which women's sexuality had been overlaid and inlaid under patriarchy. Some carried on their work of defining female sexuality in conjunction with a general social struggle for equality. Others were so angered to find that, in a way, they were hoist on their own petard by a pseudo-sexual revolution, that they withdrew from relations with men into political lesbianism.

While feminist study and interpretation of sexuality followed three particular lines of enquiry – social, psychosexual and biological – acceptance of a new analysis often depended on whether or not it lent itself to reform. For many something immutable, like biology, would dash hopes of change, so biology was pushed so far back in consciousness that it was forgotten.

What were the definitions of sexuality that emerged? They were many and confusing. As we have seen, some feminist definitions include a view of female sexuality as polymorphous (diffused throughout the body), and of male sexuality as aggressive and genitally-fixated. Some confined it to conventional sexual bodily pleasure; others linked it with motherhood. A small number of feminists define female and male sexuality and gender as biological, some say that both are socially constructed, and others that they are psychologically constructed. Some also reject the idea of an exclusive heterosexuality, and see homosexuality or bisexuality as a valid alternative.

Gayle Rubin, an American feminist and anthropologist, combined anthropology and psychoanalysis with Marxism. She defined sexuality as biological, but transformed by culture and psychology. Her 'sex/gender system' was the arrangements by which a society converts biological sexuality into human activity, and allows sexual needs to be satisfied (in other words, culture). These arrangements demonstrated, she said, the 'mutual interdependence of sexuality, economics and politics'. Rubin owed her reputation to an essay called 'The traffic in women', which adapted to feminist theory Lacan's interpretation of Freud and Lévi-Strauss that the incest taboo laid the foundation for kinship. As the exchange of women between families in tribal society was directed by the male members, principally the father, she said, this reproduced male power; women were moulded by this culture into a femininity that was attractive to men so that they could be exchanged, and in this way gender was formed.[15] (Relics of this culture remain in Church marriage ceremonies where the father of the bride 'gives her away' to the bridegroom.)

While Rubin's incest theory was an important advance on the narrower illuminations of sexuality which gained currency in the seventies, and it explained the cultural and historical way in which the incest taboo might have been put into practice, it did not take into account that there are sound biological reasons why incest is not desirable in any society.

Germaine Greer's *The Female Eunuch*, analysed patriarchy and the control and manipulation of female sexuality, with a dash of antipodean gusto. Nowadays only her libertarian attitude towards sexual activity, her celebration of the sexual revolution of the time, in that particular book, remain in people's consciousness. They forget that her analysis was an important milestone in the women's movement. Germaine Greer's maturing process is evident in all her books; each is written with the insights of the time of her own life at which they were written and her contribution has always been enlightening and corrective.

In the 1980s she was reviled as a recanting feminist for *Sex and Destiny* when, in fact, she was attempting to bring some realism and a more holistic approach to the social, cultural and sexual problems of being a woman, which other feminists were treating in esoteric, exclusive and often narrowly defined ways. Fertility had been regarded by most feminist theorists as nothing but an instrument in the oppression of women, with little regard to women's satisfactions in their own fertility; few regarded fertility as part of a woman's sexuality. Germaine Greer sought to redress the situation and was maligned for her efforts.

Other feminists who travelled a similar road fared better but their message was also ignored. In *Of Woman Born* Adrienne Rich examined the universal oppressions of mothers, but she also extolled the experience of motherhood, indeed its sexuality. Because she recorded the *exploitation* of motherhood, her book became a classic, but her message about its sexuality was ignored. The idea offended against feminist doctrines that maintained sexuality was either psychosexual or sociocultural, indeed that motherhood itself was psychological or cultural. If it was found that birthing was sexual, an erotic experience, then sexuality was also biological, and this was unacceptable. Women had been universally defined in terms of reproduction, exploited as mothers and wives, and feminists had worked hard to change this image. Therefore motherhood was a political problem for them, and the idea that sexuality could be involved in birthing or motherhood was not to be entertained; it would undermine the feminist agenda. Adrienne Rich was not criticised in the mid-seventies; however, she is now called an essentialist, and with Mary Daly and others, has been banished to the fringes of the women's movement:

The fracture of the women's movement in Europe and the United States, in the late seventies and early eighties came about because of the sexuality discussions. The Leeds Revolutionary Feminist Group declared that a real difference existed between female and male sexuality, 'perhaps related to their different reproductive functions'. They also said that women's sexuality was crippled and denied by men's imposition of 'compulsory heterosexuality', and that male sexuality arose from men's need to dominate and exercise power in sexual activity. Socialist feminists, dedicated to social change as the road to equality, disagreed and they parted company. Then the problem of male violence against women, of battery and rape, came to the fore and pushed the social agenda temporarily into the background, replacing it with an attack on male sexuality.

Male violence was alluded to in some of the early literature but it only became an issue in the mid-seventies.[16] Erin Pizzey established the Women's Aid movement in London in 1972 to provide shelters for battered women. It grew to hundreds of centres within a few years, and within a decade women's protests against male violence became worldwide. In 1975 Susan Brownmiller published *Against Our Will: Men, Women and Rape*, which stated definitively that rape was not a crime of passion, it was a crime of power, an attack on the sexuality of a woman to show her who was boss, 'a conscious process of intimidation by which all men keep all women in a state of fear'. (As there are men who deplore rape, and would never rape a woman, I think Brownmiller's statement could be rephrased to read: 'a conscious process of intimidation *by which rapists and those who tolerate them keep all women in a state of fear for the benefit of all men'*.) The first rape crisis centres were opened in the 1970s: Boston in 1972; London in 1976; Dublin in 1979; and throughout Europe during the seventies and early eighties.

The sexuality debate became more complex, and more informed, as new issues emerged. To the protest against male violence was added the campaign against pornography. The major American campaigners on that issue were the feminist lawyer, Catharine MacKinnon, the angry and often ribald Andrea Dworkin and, in more restrained mode, poet Susan Griffin, who examined it in a cultural and philosophical context.[17]

The anti-pornography campaign, surprisingly, caused further divisions among feminists. Some were concerned at the censorship aspect of opposing it, others worried about the right-wing bedfellows that opposition to it entailed. These reservations had echoes of a dubious kind of political correctness; they did not reflect a serious assessment of the reality of pornography and of the effects it has on the status of women and on male cultural attitudes to women.

Out of these campaigns the idea gradually emerged that male desire (as culturally constructed) was based on conquest and submission, an idea that became known as 'the eroticisation of subordination'.

SISTERS, SEXUALITY AND SOCIALISM

The feminists who emerged from the sexual revolution belong to two main ideological camps – socialist feminism and radical feminism – each with a variety of basic beliefs which are hotly defended. There were two other types of feminism, post-Freudian feminism and liberal feminism, both of which spilled over into the other two groups. (In this chapter I will refer especially to three feminists texts: Lynne Segal's *Is the Future Female?*, Sheila Jeffrey's *Anticlimax* and Ann Ferguson's *Blood at the Root: Motherhood, Sexuality and Male Dominance*. There are others of equal importance but these three encapsulate most of the feminist ideas.)

Relations between the various groups were difficult almost from the beginning, and feminists from one group still find it as hard to get the other groups to listen, as to persuade anti-feminists to their point of view. This bigotry is regrettable because in almost all cases it relates to beliefs which are only part of the truth. Women are still searching for the key to their subordination, yet each new insight is rejected by some, or seized upon by others and held up as the true genesis of the subordination of women, or of sexuality, or aggression or passivity, when many causes, some primary, some secondary, others contingent, may exist. Many hold their particular views because these views, of their nature, hold out hope of change. Recently, as feminists become more aware of each other's thinking, writers such as Lynne Segal[1] and Ann Ferguson[2] are making efforts to form a more holistic and comprehensive theory of feminism, which includes the key insights of some of the different philosophies.

It is difficult to separate feminism into different ideologies because so many of their theories overlap, and some theories are shared by groups which are diametrically opposed to each other on other issues: some radical feminists can hold psychoanalytic views, others have Marxist or other cultural views. The post-Freudians can hold socialist views; and some socialist feminists can have a rainbow of views that cross all the divides.

SOCIALIST FEMINISM

Socialist feminists are those who believe that male domination is a social and cultural phenomenon which can be eliminated by changing cultural attitudes and the legal and social system. Many of them were political socialists or Marxists. They were the original women's liberationists in the British Isles, and were the mainstream of British and Irish feminism until some broke away to form separatist groups. Two important influences on the establishment of the Women's Liberation Movement in these islands were Juliet Mitchell's 1966 paper, 'Women: the longest revolution' and Sheila Rowbotham's 1969 pamphlet, *Women's Liberation and the New Politics*. In the 1970s, work, wages and equal status were the demands, and writers like Sheila Rowbotham and many others articulated the true social and economic nature of women's position in society. Socialist feminists believe that male domination is socially constructed, and so society has to be changed. In Britain, for the most part they were women who did not want to abandon their association with left-wing politics.[3]

At the beginning they did not believe that women were oppressed through their sexuality. They said that male power over women, and male exploitation of women, were centralised and institutionalised in state policies, and operated through sexism in the home and in the workplace. These policies ensured that homemakers and carers were kept financially dependent upon men, and that male power was established in the workplace through work practices, wage differentials, restrictive practices and sexist attitudes which kept women in lower-paid work, and militated against their promotion. These sexist policies, socialist feminists said, perpetuated patriarchy.

Socialist feminists were generally pragmatic in their choice of tactics; they tended in those early years to approach the problems of domination by attacking each manifestation of it and seeking to change it. And indeed, in the past two decades, they have succeeded in changing the social climate to a significant degree, yet equality for women has still not been achieved.

While the main aim of socialist feminists is to change the attitudes and institutions of society, they have been persuaded by convincing arguments to look at the role of sexuality, and some of them now accept that it plays a part in the oppression of women. At first sexuality was for them a badge of freedom as they launched their drive for liberation; then it became an issue of protest about reproductive freedom (the personal is political); nowadays they comment on current analyses and theories about sexuality and fit them into their social theory, but eventually they relegate them to the sidelines in their day-to-day battle for legal and social equality. While they may acknowledge that sexuality has a biological base and is socially and psychologically constructed, they then excise biology from the equation as if it never existed.

Lynne Segal is a socialist feminist who has written some of the most important feminist literature of the past decade. In *Is the Future Female?* her analysis of the social and political position of women has been a significant addition to feminist theory, but she has, I think, some blind spots on the question of sexuality. At first she did not consider that sexuality had much to do with the oppression of women; preoccupation with the idea that it had, she believed, was damaging to the women's cause. (In her later books *Slow Motion: Changing Masculinities; Changing Men* (1990) and *Straight Sex* (1994) she modified but did not radically alter this perception.) 'The identification of sexuality as "the primary social sphere of male power"' [as Catharine MacKinnon claimed],[4] Segal said, 'was to have far-reaching, and disastrous effects on the feminist analysis of heterosexuality, lesbianism and the possibilities for combating power relations between men and women'. She argued instead that it was the social arrangements for having and rearing children which created the basis for men's power over women and gave men control of women's sexuality. Yet, paradoxically, she went on to describe sexuality as a powerful force in our lives and agreed that, because it is socially defined and controlled, it *is embedded in all the social practices and institutions that confirm men in their power over women* (my italics).

Segal agreed that sexuality in the sexual revolution of the sixties was male-defined, and that feminists in the seventies faced three tasks: to get rid of the double standard, to establish a more realistic image of female sexuality than that offered by male society, and to gain control of their own fertility. At the same time she believed that the sexual revolution was necessary for the re-emergence of feminism because sexual liberation was a part of the counter-culture that challenged the patriarchal system of capitalism.

Where psychoanalysis was concerned, Segal accepted that object-relations theory could be used to explain many of the most troubling aspects of men's behaviour, such as violence and sexual coercion, and that it could also suggest strategies for change, but she still gave preference to the social and cultural answer. Men's violence towards women, she said, comes from the inequalities of power between men and women as much as from any internal psychic dynamic in men. She believed that it is their economic, political and cultural power over women that has allowed men to abuse women sexually, not that men oppress women through their sexuality. It is a fine point of difference, but the fact remains that men do oppress women through women's sexuality because that is the ultimate control, and it works. Rape, she said, was an expression of anger, inadequacy, guilt and fear of women, all linked with men's attempts to affirm their masculinity. She said that popular perceptions of rape as a response to women's sexuality must be exposed and denounced, because women are entitled to overt sexuality.

Rape may not be a *response* of desire to women's sexuality, but it is an attack on it, a sexual weapon attacking women through their sexuality and oppressing them through it. Furthermore, women's 'entitlement' to overt sexuality is a point worthy of discussion. Sexuality has a role in life but it is only part of a social and political existence, a sentiment with which Segal would concur, yet she is in danger here of defining women through their sexuality. If women are to take an equal place with men in the affairs of the world, either attitudes towards sexuality must change or their sexuality (and men's) must be left outside the arena of these affairs; when men bring sexuality into the workplace it is called sexual harassment. This may be what Segal was attempting to do by leaving sexuality out of the oppression of women. However, on closer examination one finds that sexuality is involved in almost every aspect of male domination.

Lynne Segal is not ardently opposed to pornography. Although she says that pornography encapsulates all that is most distressing and depressing in the portrayal of women's bodies in our culture, she does not agree with Andrea Dworkin that it not only *depicts* but also *creates* the imperial power of men. Segal thinks that pornography, in these days of increasing independence for women, is more likely to be a compensation for men's *declining* power, and she dismisses any links between it and male violence against women. She strongly believes that supporting censorship legislation against pornography would strengthen the powers of the moral right to censor erotica, and sex education, and to persecute homosexuals.

These reasons are not worthy of consideration in the context of the real dangers of pornography: the image of women that it lodges in the minds of men, and the accumulating evidence of a definite link between pornography and sexual violence. In the intervening years since she wrote *Is the*

Future Female? Segal has not changed her mind on this subject; in 1992 in *Sex Exposed* she still maintained opposition to censorship of pornography and was still concerned that anti-pornography feminists would share a platform with right-wing 'moral conservatives'.

One sexual demand of the socialist feminists was control of their own fertility, but only in the context of conception-free sex and the right to abortion. Segal points out that the dominant trend throughout the twentieth century has been a separation between sexual pleasure and conception which has transformed the lives of women. There is no doubt that placing control of their fertility in the hands of women was an important aim, but it left the problem of more equitable, sexual relations between men and women unresolved. In those earlier demands there was also a presumption that the control of fertility would mean that women would not want to have children.

Segal is a pragmatist, and pragmatism can rule out insights that could be valuable in the liberation of women. She is sometimes inclined to dismiss a theory if it makes the situation seem impossible or difficult to change. If that seems unfair to one of the more articulate and, in many ways, sensible of British feminists, I would repeat that she is more concerned with the political and economic situation of women than with definitions of sexuality. She believes that if women achieve social, cultural and political equality then the problems of sexuality will solve themselves. Her future strategy would include: working to give women self-confidence and self-esteem; women joining together for political action; persuading men to change, and to share their equality with women both at home and at work. To her the discussion of the role of sexuality in women's oppression is a distraction from these very important tasks. She has been a significant force in improving the situation of women. But the women's movement has achieved only partial success, and then only for the very few. Something more than the social institutions are inhibiting it, and I think that the answer lies in our definitions of sexuality.

The insightful writings of both female and male homosexuals on the subject of sexuality impelled Lynne Segal to write *Straight Sex*, a spirited defence of heterosexuality in which she took another look at the role sexuality plays in the subordination of woman. For the first time she came to terms with psychoanalysis without, in the end, allowing it to play much of a part in sexuality; and she referred to biology only in relation to the mechanics of sexual relations and the management of fertility. She says that we need another sexual revolution, one that would 'uncover [and fight to change] the social forces which ensure that women's sexual agency is suppressed in contexts of significant gender inequality'. Her emphasis is on sexual pleasure. I would want to add that a new sexual revolution should be undertaken with a better knowledge of the nature of sexuality (both male and female) and its pleasures.

RADICAL FEMINISM

Radical feminism includes revolutionary feminism and political lesbianism, both of which assert categorically that women are oppressed through their sexuality. Under this heading is also found cultural feminism, which often overlaps with ecofeminism, and attributes an *inherently* different gender (and hence culture) to women and men.

A group of New York radical feminists were responsible in 1969 for the first policy statements of the current wave of feminism. The Redstockings, who were socialist as well as radical, issued a manifesto which stated that women were an oppressed class, and that the oppressor was patriarchy. Theirs was a pro-woman line; some were not anti-men – yet; at that time they wanted to reform them. Later groups were more determinedly anti-men, and advocated varying degrees of separatism or political lesbianism, or elevated the biological and cultural differences of women almost to a religion.

Some of the early radical feminists claimed that there was no fundamental difference between women and men, that the ideal would be an androgynous society, one in which roles were abolished. This was more an androgyny of gender roles than of sexuality, a desire for women to share on an equal basis in the status, work and economic freedom of men. It was a rebellion against an entrenched culture that allotted circumscribed and diametrically opposed characteristics, practices, emotions and roles to women and to men. Others wanted to end the necessity for biological distinction by establishing methods of reproduction that were virtually independent of women or men,[5] and the family came under attack from many. All of these strands have survived to the present day; all have valid aspects and some good insights.

However, another type of radical feminism became important in Britain, and declared a sexual war on society. In 1979 Leeds Revolutionary Feminists published a manifesto called 'Political Lesbianism: the Case Against Heterosexuality', a paper which stated categorically that it was through sexuality that male oppression of women was maintained. In blunt language the manifesto said that 'a woman who lives with or fucks a man helps to maintain the oppression of her sisters'; that heterosexual women were 'collaborators with the enemy'. This group was following in the footsteps of New York radical lesbians who, earlier in the decade, had declared a similar war, echoing Ti Grace Atkinson's much-quoted assertion: 'feminism is the theory and lesbianism is the practice'.

Sheila Jeffreys was one of the Leeds Revolutionary Feminist Group who has remained a political lesbian, and whether or not one agrees with separatist tactics, her writings hold valuable insights for all feminists. In 1985 she wrote *The Spinster and Her Enemies* and argued for the feminist credentials of some of the social purity movements of the late nineteenth century. They had been accused by today's feminists of being misogynist, class ridden and patriarchal, and as being anti-sexual, too ready to resort to legislation to control sexuality. (There is great danger in discussing the proposition of curbing male lust or rampant sexuality; one is likely to be bracketed with the conservative right-wing fundamentalists who want to preserve patriarchy, and those who would like to abolish human sexuality.)

In *Anticlimax* Jeffreys saw heterosexuality as a political institution through which male domination is organised. Sexual activity and desire as we know it, she wrote, is the eroticised power differences of heterosexuality, and the sexual revolution was an orchestrated attempt to counter the gains and aspirations of the women's movement. She declares that there is a serious problem in women trying to emulate male sexuality. It is a ruling-class sexuality, she says, which depends upon the possession of ruling-class status, such as objectification, aggression, and separation of sex from loving emotion. (What Jeffreys says is true, but what it indicates is that both female and male sexuality are distorted and culturally manipulated.)

Jeffreys and the political lesbians say that heterosexuality is based on difference, but a quality of difference in which one person (the man) is superior and the other (the woman) inferior; one is dominant, the other dominated. In other words, what is accepted as female sexuality is passivity made erotic, and male sexuality is domination made erotic. In arguments which are the reverse of Segal's they say that the whole edifice of the subordination of women rests on the act of heterosexual intercourse; the family is constructed around it, and the unpaid work of women in the family is disguised 'under notions of love'; all other social relationships are organised in reference to heterosexuality: limits are put on female/male relations unless they are sexual, while sexuality lurks in all female/male encounters; sex roles arise because of heterosexuality. In short, they say that society is structured by heterosexuality. (Michel Foucault's theory on the deployment of sexuality.)

Sheila Jeffreys marshals strong arguments to support the contention that heterosexuality is eroticised power difference. First of all, men bring a social and political power to marriage that is upheld by the courts, the social services and religion – the old head-of-the-house syndrome. (In some countries there have been legal and social changes that have improved the rights of women.) Then, in the interests of maintaining the power relationship, there is a popular taboo in society against a marriage where the man earns less, or is less well educated, than the woman, and where the woman is older or taller than the man. (This is observably true: despite changes in modern society these taboos remain, and men who disregard them are regarded with contempt or as figures of fun.) Moreover, women are trained to serve men, to obey them and make sacrifices for them; they are also trained not to be aggressive or use physical force. This, Jeffreys says, is heterosexuality in the service of male domination.

She refers to a study carried out by criminologists Garrett and Wright in 1975 in which they interviewed the wives of rapists and incest offenders. These researchers found that the wives generally had more schooling than their husbands. These 'powerful' wives, they said, deliberately married men to whom they could feel superior, and the men were driven to sex assaults by their feelings of inferiority. (No need to ask what is the sex of the researchers.) Blame is laid by them tacitly on the wives for breaking the taboo on dominance in women, which is certainly evidence in itself of a male power complex.

The idea of heterosexual desire as eroticised power difference is present in our culture but perceived from a different angle. It is said pejoratively of strong-willed and independent women that they 'de-ball' men, castrate them. Men may generally find it more difficult to *desire* independent women although they may love them. It is an observable fact that men generally avoid obviously independent women, and that often, in turn, independent women dissemble rather than frighten them away.

Jeffreys also points out that some feminists had trouble rationalising their relationships with men in the early years of liberation; some found that desire waned when equality entered the relationship.[6] However, there are many cases where sexuality and sexual relations have become egalitarian and remained satisfactory. In many of these cases sexual relations became less important in their lives; other interests moved up the scale, and intelligence replaced sexuality as the real mark of identity.

Heterosexuality as eroticised power difference is the most interesting part of Sheila Jeffreys's thesis. It is a valuable insight into the politics of existing heterosexual institutions, one that women must appreciate if an equitable form of female/male relationships, marriage and family, is to be constructed. But it is not, as she suggests, the only missing link in feminist theory; other candidates for the title might be joint-parenting of children, the sexuality of birthing, and the biological urge to reproduce. However, feminist analysis of love, sex, domestic work and parenting, male violence, sex roles and the division of labour does not make more sense, or fall into place coherently, when heterosexuality is understood as the system that organises male supremacy. The reverse is more likely to be true: male supremacy organises heterosexuality and both male and female sexuality, and in the process important dimensions are denied to both. The problem is not heterosexuality but patriarchy. It is *patriarchal* heterosexuality that subordinates women and is eroticised power difference, and the *patriarchal* family that is oppressive.

The 'high priests' of the sexual revolution, says Jeffreys, were the sexologists of the twentieth century who urged women to take pleasure from sexual intercourse; this was nothing more than an eroticisation of their own subordination, because an enthusiastic heterosexual response from women was an efficient way to keep them subordinate and to maintain male power. The eroticisation of the single woman, she said, recruited her to the designs of patriarchy in servicing men, and to the designs of capitalism by encouraging consumerism. The experiment ended, Jeffreys adds, when feminists began work on the problem of men's violence to women.

But, I fear, these ideas, however valid, were the result of hindsight, and less than fair to the young women who were brave enough to strike out on their own and experiment. Jeffreys is not the first feminist to hold that sexual liberation is inimical to the liberation of women, and I doubt if the sexual revolution was a conspiracy to maintain male power. It is certainly true that the trend-setting sexologists operated from a male perspective, and naturally took male sexuality as the standard. They encouraged female submission to male sexual aggression, because they believed (from a man's point of view) that it was necessary for a satisfactory sexual relationship. It was also a matter of perception: even normal receptivity could be construed as subordination provided the woman was not too demanding. The result, however, was the same: the maintenance of male power. And if no male or patriarchal conspiracy was involved, men certainly took advantage of the situation.

Undoubtedly, also, commercial interests and the advertising industry seized upon this new and public manifestation of sexuality, and used it as a way of marketing their wares; but they were following a trend not making it. When the sexual revolution which Marcuse had advocated arrived and was subverted to the designs of consumerism, he ruefully watched his ideas being 'co-opted'. Both he and Reich would have been horrified at the subversion of their ideas to justify pornography and the commercialism of sex in the interests of consumerism, not to mention the increased commercialisation of sexual activity itself.

Sexuality has been manipulated (by commercialism and by various power centres such as certain parts of the media) into a dominant position in our culture and into a psychologically unhealthy position in people's lives. Through the medium of genital activity it has almost become more important to our identity than intelligence. Yet we *share* sex and sexuality with all other mammals (indeed with all other forms of life); there is nothing especially human about it except the way we use it. The real *difference* between humans and other mammals lies in the level of intelligence, and it would be more useful if we based our sense of identity on our intellectual capacities instead of on our sexuality.

Sheila Jeffreys confines herself to only one factor in the oppression of women through sexuality: the social context of heterosexual relationships, marriage and the family. She also confuses analysis and tactics, a mistake made by many revolutionaries, and fails to think through the practicality or the end result of the separatist policy which she espouses. Tactics, unfortunately, can become as oppressive as the situation they set out to correct. While political lesbians deplore compulsory heterosexuality they advocate compulsory lesbianism. What are they going to do with men after their revolution? Keep them in ghettos or camps, or in sheds at the bottom of the garden? Even if a significant number of women took the road of separatism, a number sufficient to inconvenience men, then male retaliation would inevitably follow. Men would use force and terror, and win, because they have the resources.

Sheila Jeffreys has an admirable vision for society in which sexuality is divorced from power and liberated. She is unable, however, to visualise what form this society would take. Her strategy is separatist; she does not acknowledge that as heterosexual intercourse is a fact of human survival, for that reason heterosexuality will always be the important and central form of sexuality in society. Her suggested (and valid) alternative to political lesbianism is that male sexuality should be reconstructed, male lust and rampant sexuality curbed. However, if sexuality is defined only in terms of social structures and sexual politics without taking psychology and biology into consideration, then it is being constructed on shifting sands.

Nevertheless, political lesbians have performed a great service to the perception and comprehension of sexuality. They have carried out an experiment in the field and proven that sexuality can be changed. If they can construct a 'new' sexuality, then the present form of heterosexuality is not immutable, and there is no reason why a form more equitable to women (and men) should not be constructed.

As a tactic, over a period of twenty years, political lesbians have achieved very little change (except in so far as some of their insights have raised the consciousness of women in other sectors of the feminist movement). On the other hand, feminists who remained in relationships with men, have made some progress legally, socially and culturally, in changing attitudes among both men and women.

Lynne Segal describes the turmoils and divisions that took place among socialist feminists in the early eighties when the Leeds feminists broke away from their ranks. Segal accused them of biologism. A more satisfactory analysis of sexuality, she wrote, would reject the idea of a sexual essence at the core of women's (or men's) identity, and would also reject the idea of sexuality as the key to change. (In this Segal was excluding a psychological explanation, towards which she is ambivalent, which would have helped explain the relationship between men's desire for power and their sexuality.)

Segal hastened to add that sexual desire for women, or engagement with them, was not what political lesbianism was about; it was a political movement which used the rejection of heterosexuality as a tactic against male domination. This meant, she said, that the message *the personal is political*, which enabled women to see their problems as socially produced, the product of all the ways in which they were subordinated – legally, financially, culturally, socially and sexually – was reversed to become *the political is personal* (meaning sexual), and only served to make women feel guilty for remaining involved in relationships with men. Her analysis owes more to a desire to find achievable solutions and tactics that work, than to rigorous assessment of causes.

She believed that political lesbianism alienated many women; it put heterosexual women (who constitute the majority of feminists and, indeed, all women) on the defensive. They felt that they could not participate in the politics of women's liberation, if the question was whether one was for or against heterosexuality, rather than how to formulate strategies *within* it, or how to reform it. Segal was right, of course, in her criticism of the tactic, and she did acknowledge that political lesbians had performed a service by highlighting male violence against women.

Political lesbianism was a tactic, a political rejection of heterosexuality, rather than inherent lesbian desire. It was chosen by heterosexual as well as homosexual women, and was used as a weapon against male domination. While the majority of feminists did not agree with their tactics, these radical groups stimulated discussion and analysis of the nature of sexuality, both within and outside their own ranks, and have contributed many valuable insights. They have drawn attention to other manifestations of sexuality, and lessened the emphasis on coitus as the pinnacle or core of sexual relations. They have, however, narrowed their vision and confined it to sexuality as a leisure activity, unrelated to reproduction. Sheila Jeffreys dismisses the theories of psychoanalysis which locate the oppression of women in infant and childhood experiences. Like Lynne Segal, she believes that these theories ignore the gender and power differences between the sexes. This is an oversimplification because there is a dynamic and complex interplay between the psychological and the social and cultural aspects of sexuality and gender. Unfortunately political lesbianism alienated many people from the women's movement; the general run of women, influenced by a prurient and aggressively male section of the media, equated feminism with this extreme position. Most feminists distanced themselves from it, treating it as a move which had little chance of success.

Radical feminism took another separatist form, which was called 'cultural' and had a philosophy diametrically opposed to the original androgyny. Cultural feminists say that women, because of their essential femaleness (which is biological and particularly manifest in motherhood) are more caring, more in tune with nature, and generally better human beings than men. They say that there is an essential and cultural difference between male and female sexuality; and that female sexuality is a resource not a handicap. They say that male sexuality is genitally oriented, violent, woman-hating and power-seeking, more concerned with domination and orgasm than with emotional relationships; while female sexuality is muted, diffuse, places more emphasis on intimacy and emotions than on genital sexual pleasure, and is interpersonally oriented because women seek relationships and intimacy.

It is true that the values women attach to sexuality are different from men's. Women do connect sex with warmth, affection, loving, caring; and most men connect sex with male orgasm. But if female sexuality has been repressed by patriarchy, so also has male sexuality, and true female and male sexuality may be both demanding and caring.

Under the cultural banner are collected a spectrum of types from gentle poets to hard-core separatist political lesbians. The main proponents of this ideology in the United States are Adrienne Rich, Mary Daly, Susan Griffin, Andrea Dworkin, Robin Morgan; in the United Kingdom, Dale Spender; and Luce Irigaray in France. Not all of the cultural feminists are separatist or lesbian (political or otherwise).

Mary Daly, a leading light in this cultural movement, is an uninhibited and joyous word-spinner who dissects the language to reveal its perversion and distortion by men, and who urges ecstatic liberation on women. In *Websters' First Intergalactic Wickedary of the English Language* with Jane Caputi, she created a new language with gleeful and her-ethical deconstruction of language, gyn/ecology, hag/ography and the male-ordered society. She is a professor of theology at Boston University, a Catholic who has challenged the Church on its attitude to women, and is described by her publisher as 'unconfined by the teachings of church or man'. She has been dismissed as élitist by some who say she has done nothing to change things, but I think that there is a place in the women's movement for her soaring exuberance, if only for the number of women it has converted to feminism.

Robin Morgan and Susan Griffin celebrate women's 'pacifism, nurturance, ecoconsciousness, and reverence for life' in a metaphysical way, while attributing ecovandalism and aggression to men.[7] As the majority of humankind are universally oppressed, Morgan sees women, and feminism, as 'the key to our survival and transformation'. But critics within the women's movement see her ideas as being overtly sexist, therefore in danger of alienating men and endangering their work for equality. The female qualities she extolled, they say, were socially imposed and are a badge of subordination, the strategies of an enslaved people. Susan Griffin identified woman with nature, an image that other feminists were trying to discount. However, women like Morgan, Griffin, et cetera, saw these qualities as desirable and part of women's femaleness and sexuality.

Liberal and socialist feminists reserve a special indignation for cultural feminists who celebrate woman's difference; they disagree with their philosophy and also with their tactics because they feel that they have opted out of the struggle for equality with men. They describe them as wanting to return to the sexual values of their mothers, values that women always attached to sexuality which, together with respect for women, were destroyed by sexual violence and so-called sexual liberation. Those critics say that they are confusing the old-time respect with equality, and fail to see that it is merely the flip side of violation.[8] However, it would seem to me more desirable to extol female virtues than to ape our 'cultural' men.

Lynne Segal disagreed with the ideas of the cultural feminists who claim that female sexuality is essentially different from men's. They seek, at least in principle, she says, the expression of special female power and values, lifestyle and communities, which are cleansed of the language and values of men, but their emphasis on a women's culture, while personally enriching, keeps them isolated from mainstream politics. The moral superiority (caring, nurturing and lack of aggression) which they claim for women, she feels, is more likely due to a slave mentality which women have cultivated because of their subordinate status. It is also due to the fact, she says, that they do the mothering, a situation that is crucial to the maintenance of their general subordination and economic dependence. Because Segal regards the human condition mainly through a social and cultural lens, she will only admit of a social and cultural interpretation. She fears that inclusion of any innate 'moral superiority' in women will push them back into the Victorian ideology of womanhood and serve to perpetuate male domination.

Her thesis is not good enough. There are, of course, characteristics of existing female culture (and of the culture of our mothers) that have no place in a new feminist philosophy: bitchiness and jealousy of other women, preoccupation with appearance, use of sexuality as a tool. These are the characteristics of an enslaved group. But there are other aspects of female culture such as caring and non-violence which are desirable whether or not they are due to oppression, and which have survived in women despite their subordination.

She does not admit that women have a biological drive to reproduce; and she dismisses the idea that reproduction is part of a female sexuality that

extends beyond coitus to birthing and motherhood. Her belief is conditioned by her own 'brief experience of hell on earth' when she gave birth
to her son. For someone who believes so vehemently in social and cultural
conditioning, it apparently does not occur to her that women may be
conditioned into accepting painful birthing. There is no doubt that they
have been conditioned into resisting the sexuality of giving birth and of
the subsequent mothering. Segal also resists a biological dimension to
women's mothering, and questions whether it has a psychological
dimension. For her mothering is socially constructed, something learned
by girls from their mothers. She says it is possible that nurturing is not part
of female nature but rather women's adjustment to social and economic
arrangements which require them to do the work of caring for others.

The radical tradition has evolved into several different philosophies and
blends of philosophy, travelling, one hopes, towards a pluralist theory of
feminism, sexuality and human relations. Radical feminists can be defined
now as those who focus on male control of female sexuality, who see
patriarchal marriage and motherhood, control over women's reproductive
capacities, compulsory heterosexuality, and male violence as the source and
mainspring of male domination. 'A precept which unites all radical
feminists, is that the fight for women's liberation is *against men*'.[9] But, to
the person-in-the-street, radical feminism today generally means the
extreme of separatism or political lesbianism.

Many of those who criticise these cultural feminists and call them
biological essentialists, are themselves sexual essentialists, such as the
libertarians, at the other end of the spectrum of radical feminism. They are
aggressively sexual, with no limits on preference, and they attack all others,
accusing them of being sexually inhibited. They are strongest in the United
States, with feminist writers like Gayle Rubin, Carole Vance, Alice Echols
among their number. They defend pornography, advocate sado-masochism,
deny any sexual difference between women and men except the anatomical
one, and describe the relationships of the cultural feminists as 'vanilla'. These
women have made no headway in breaking away from male supremacy,
and instead they have brought power differentials and eroticised subordination with them into their new lifestyle. Janice Raymond, a professor
of women's studies, says that the libertarian lesbians are not making a
political statement but are pre-occupied with sexual activity, and their
model of sexuality is a male model. They make no connection, she says,
between sexual activity and the rest of a woman's life.[10] They have made

no significant impression that we know of in the United Kingdom or Ireland.

Sheila Jeffreys attributes the use of psychoanalytic theories to the libertarians, and with great courage takes issue with them about the 'sexual freedom' which they advocate: pornography, promiscuous homosexuality, sado-masochism, fetishism, transsexuality, crossgenerational encounters. If Robin Morgan described pornography as the theory, with rape and male violence against women as the practice, Sheila Jeffreys calls it propaganda for the sexualising of power, for the sexiness of inequality.[11] Neither does she, as a political lesbian, make common cause with male homosexuals. She says that homosexual men ratify and strengthen eroticised dominance and submission, and help shore up a form of male sexuality dangerous to the interests of all women. She cannot see sado-masochism as anything but inimical to women, or countenance child abuse even under the anodyne term, 'crossgenerational encounters'. Heterosexuality and homosexuality, she says, are not sexual preferences, they are socially constructed; and political lesbianism is not just a form of sexual attraction, it is a political strategy for revolution. She quotes the American Radicalesbians: 'A lesbian is the rage of all women condensed to the point of explosion.'

POST-FREUDIAN FEMINISM

Post-Freudian feminists brought a new dimension to the women's movement with psychoanalytic ideas of the construction of adult sexuality and its influence on the behaviour of the person. These ideas also invaded other feminist philosophies and have had an enormous influence on modern feminism. They are represented mainly by feminist psychologists and psychoanalysts, and their ideas have influenced most of the other strands of feminism. The writings of Dorothy Dinnerstein, Juliet Mitchell, Luce Irigaray, et cetera, provide valuable explanations of why women are exploited through their sexuality (see chapter 6).

LIBERAL FEMINISM

Liberal feminists agree with some or many of the views of the other groups of feminists, but they disagree with some of their tactics. They argue that since sexism oppresses both men and women by creating sexual alienation, women should work *with* men to overcome gender roles. Some of the early feminists who were termed 'radical' would now fit more easily into the liberal camp.

Ann Ferguson could be called a liberal feminist. In *Blood at the Root: Motherhood, Sexuality and Male Dominance* she sets out to establish a theory of sexuality that would weave together the key insights of radical feminism, Marxism and Freudianism. Ferguson, as a socialist, agrees with Segal that the sexual revolution was a necessary dynamic for the re-emergence of late-twentieth-century feminism; it was necessary, she says, to challenge not capitalism but 'the traditional patriarchal mores of hetero-sexual marriage and sex for procreation rather than pleasure'.

She agrees also with both radical and socialist feminists when they say that sexuality and motherhood are socially constructed in the interests of male domination; that men control female sexuality in the way marriage and motherhood are organised, in the way women's reproductive capacities are regulated, and in compulsory heterosexuality. She criticises Marxism be-cause it has no adequate theory of either sexuality or motherhood. Marxist theories, she says, do not account for women desiring men and wanting children.

Psychoanalysis, she maintains, has good insights about the formation of gender in early childhood and its connection with sexuality; otherwise, she asks, how would one explain the persistence of male domination even when it does not serve the rational interests of men and women to perpetuate it? (Neo-Freudian feminists hold that women and men are conditioned in the patriarchal nuclear family, and as a result women often make choices that are against their own self-interest.) Freudianism, however, fails to understand, she says, how the political and social contexts of a person's life may cause change. On the credit side, she says, Freud saw motherhood as a sexual experience, but he wrongly interpreted the bodily pleasures mothers ex-perienced with their babies as a substitute for the pleasures of the penis. Ferguson says that women have a genuine interest in motherhood because of the sensual and social union between mother and child, and that this 'sex/ affective energy' is neither a substitute for heterosexual intercourse nor a mere acting out of a desire for male power (a 'penis substitute').

Blood at the Root is written in an academic language which is sometimes as difficult to comprehend as any foreign tongue. She uses two phrases, however, which are essential to her thesis and, indeed, describe very well the concept she is outlining: *sex/affective energy* and *sex/affective production*. Sexual or erotic interest, she says, is only one type of emotional or social interest in others. Sex/affective energy describes both sexual interest and other affectionate attachments, such as friendship, parental and family love, kinship and all kinds of social bonding with others. Since sex/affective energy is not directed into any specific expression, she says, society organises systems which will guide it in desirable directions; this process is called sex/affective production. Therefore, sex/affective production refers to the various systems in society that organise, shape and mould the different emotions that constitute sex/affective energy. This regulation can be carried out in an authoritarian or in a democratic way by the state, religion, economic systems, education, family, and any institutions that decide the customs and conventions of human relationships. Sex/affective production systems organise sexuality, procreation and family care in several different ways: 'by directing sexual urges towards heterosexual relations and non-incestuous ties; by defining the role of the individual in kinship situations; and by laying down the rules of friendships'. These systems also organise all types of work by defining what is culturally acceptable as man's work and woman's work.

Ferguson considers that any one of the components of sex/affective energy – human emotional relationships, friendship, parental love, or social bonding – can be as fully satisfying as sexual intercourse. She describes how the invasion by women of traditional male workplaces, whether factory floor or boardroom, is resisted (even unconsciously by non-sexist men) because it is a threat to the flow of male bonding, which, she says, is regarded by men to be just as important as sexual activity.

She asserts that compulsory heterosexuality is a system of reproduction that ensures the continuance of male domination, and for this reason both male bonding and female bonding must be restricted so that children can receive, in heterosexual families and kinship systems, the social and economic support that they need. Beyond this, she says, many forms of male bonding, including institutionalised homosexuality, are compatible with the preservation of male domination; however, female bonding challenges the precedence that women are supposed to give to relations with husbands or lovers and is therefore discouraged.

For the same reason, she maintains, women who demand equality in sexual encounters with men threaten masculine identity. Like Sheila Jeffreys, but with somewhat different arguments, Ann Ferguson maintains that patriarchal heterosexuality is eroticised gender difference and that it *requires* male domination and female subordination. The principal elements of 'compulsory heterosexuality' for her are: marriage, main-stream pornography, the capitalist patriarchal nuclear family, and prostitution.

She sees two opposing types of sexuality at work in contemporary society, one seeking love and intimacy, the other seeking pleasure, thus causing alienation between the sexes. She blames capitalism for this change because it separated economic production from private life. Pre-capitalist society, she says, organised sexuality to emphasise neither pleasure nor emotional intimacy, but simply to regulate biological reproduction so as to strengthen the extended kinship networks through which economic production was organised. Early capitalism undermined this system by developing the nuclear family, making the man head of the household, and separating the workplace from the home which became the woman's realm. This historical shift, she says, brought with it three important changes in sex/affective production: an emphasis on mother love; the concept of romantic love as a base for marriage; and an emphasis on sexual pleasure between husbands and wives as an important goal of marriage. This situation also brought about a double standard for intimacy and sexual pleasure: mothers, not fathers, were emotionally intimate with their children; wives not husbands were emotionally nurturant of their mates; sexual pleasure belonged to the man. This analysis, she maintains, shows how sexuality was socially constructed.

This is not a new argument, it is the socialist view of history, and Ferguson is merely explaining how sexuality is socially formed and deployed in socialist and Foucaultian terms. While this is a correct historical view, the situation is changing with the industrialisation of housework and women working outside the home; these changes are already having an effect on sexual relationships; for instance, men share in the management of the household to maintain a relationship, and women feel less dependent in a relationship. However, as Ferguson points out, some things have not changed; there are three important cultural conventions that have remained entrenched: girls but not boys are taught to value and develop the skills of emotional intimacy; boys are taught that high performance and aggressive sexuality are a mark of masculinity; the nurturing and bonding carried out by women is not valued. The lives of women, she points out, are still controlled by their sexuality; they must be attractive so that they can achieve the coveted state of marriage, and quite apart from state, religious and family control, the control of their fertility in sexual relations in their own interests remains a constant concern.

In *Blood at the Root* Ann Ferguson has made some progress towards a strategy to combine the different strands of feminism. She accepts that patriarchal heterosexuality is what oppresses women and advocates more egalitarian relationships and a more liberal approach to sexual preference. She also recognises that women have a strong desire for motherhood, and allows that it has a sexual component. She did not, however, draw any conclusions from women's desire for motherhood and the phenomenon that only a tiny minority of women seek a feminist future. Do they feel that motherhood rules out feminism or that feminism is not compatible with motherhood?

Shere Hite, another liberal feminist and author of the famous Hite reports, is a cultural historian and researcher who has made human sexuality her field of study. She was a product of both the sexual revolution and of seventies feminism, and regarded the sex drive as a biological function and sexuality and sexual relations as culturally constructed:

> Our whole society's definition of sex is sexist – sex for the overwhelming majority of people consists of foreplay, eventually followed by vaginal penetration and then by sexual intercourse, ending eventually in male orgasm. This is a sexist definition of sex, oriented around male orgasm and the needs of reproduction. This definition is *cultural*, not biological.

(Shere Hite uses the word 'sex' to mean a broad range of sexual activity as well as biological difference.)

The Hite Report on Female Sexuality, published in 1976, was the first time in the history of sexology where women were allowed to speak out for themselves. The report was concerned with a definition of women's sexuality which was made by women, unfiltered through researchers with a male bias.[12] She distributed one hundred thousand questionnaires enquiring about women's sexual activity and their reactions and attitudes to current practice. Over three thousand were returned. The social distribution of the sample could be (and was) questioned but the geographical spread was above reproach; women in forty-nine states of the United States of America and from seven states in Canada responded. *The Hite Report*, however, was more than just the replies of three thousand women, it was a major exercise in consciousness-raising, and it amassed a body of information that influenced a generation of women because it became a bestseller.

These replies had been made in the early 1970s when the sexual revolution had been in full swing for more than a decade, and Masters and Johnson had challenged the shibboleths of female sexuality. Orgasm was the new status symbol for the sexually active woman, and so was central to Hite's study.

The findings were remarkable. Of the respondents

- 70 per cent did not have orgasm during intercourse;
- 82 per cent produced their own orgasms regularly and speedily by self-performed clitoral stimulus;
- 87 per cent said that intercourse was very important to them.
- The most frequent reason by far for liking intercourse was *affection and closeness*, followed by *reassurance about the relationship*, and *because it gave the man pleasure.*
- All of the women wanted more affection and consideration for their feelings in their sexual relations.

It was a testimonial for masturbation and an indictment of heterosexual relations.

Hite proposed a new attitude to sexuality, one that accorded women the same right as men to sexual pleasure. If sexual activity is for pleasure and intimacy as well as for reproduction, she said, then the fact that the kind of stimulation the majority of women need for orgasm (clitoral stimulus) should be included in its definition, and sexual activity should be re-designed. She concluded that the current definition of sexuality and sexual relations belonged to a world-view that was past or passing.

Significantly, but rarely alluded to in assessments of the Hite reports, Shere Hite was the first researcher to demote sexuality to the ranks, to allot it a role in life which acknowledged the claims of other activities and concerns:

Although sexuality is very important, it is questionable whether it is important in and of itself, apart from its meaning in your life as a whole. The increasing emphasis on sex and personal relations as the basic source of happiness and fulfilment is a function of the lessening probability of finding even partial fulfilment through work ... Sexuality and sexual relationships can be surrogates for (or obscure our need for) a more satisfying relationship with the larger world – for example with work. In a way, as long as we accept this schizoid compartmentalisation of public and private life, we are abrogating our moral obligation to take an active part in the direction of the larger world, and accepting an ethic of powerlessness. Meanwhile, the commercialisation and trivialisation of sex advances further and further into our private lives and obscures their deeper personal meaning for us. In fact we haven't had a sexual revolution yet, but we need one.

A few commentators have put forward the same ideas about the sexual revolution and the encroachment of sexuality and sexual activity into all areas of life, but Shere Hite has never been given credit for her analysis.

The impression one gets from *The Hite Report on Male Sexuality* (1981) on men's attitude to women is that they cannot live with them and they cannot live without them. Most men said that friendships with men were not nearly as fulfilling as a sexual relationship with a woman they loved, and that they did not have close women friends with whom they did not have sex; that a friendship with a woman would (more or less) inevitably lead to sex (they use the word 'sex' to mean sexual activity or almost always inter- course). They defined sex as foreplay followed by intercourse and ending with male orgasm in the vagina. Yet, almost all the respondents said that they masturbated regularly, and that they used pornography; but very few of them said that they had sexual relations with prostitutes regularly, or even frequently.

And what constitutes men's sexuality, what do they want from inter- course? Remarkably, only 3 per cent mentioned orgasm. Most of the men who answered gave 'physical closeness and overall body contact – full- length embracing' as the most important physical element of intercourse, together with 'the feeling of being loved and accepted' and 'of verifying their male identity' – 'intercourse makes a male a man before other men; intercourse is a form of male bonding'. They also indicated a desire to be occasionally the 'receiver during sex', while jealously guarding their pre- rogative of being 'in charge' and dominant in the male/female relationship. Many men complained that women did not seem interested in doing things to them, that they were 'just too passive'; and, of course, their major dissatisfaction, that women did not want intercourse often enough. They also feared impotency. A majority of married men had extramarital affairs because they 'made the marriage workable'. Shere Hite interpreted that as a Freudian attitude towards their wives as mothers.

Like many feminists, Hite interprets sexuality in a broader way than the condensed and narrowly focused genitality in which the (male) culture has come to view it. Because of the diffuse nature of women's sexuality, increasingly being written about by women such as Adrienne Rich, and psychoanalysts such as Luce Irigaray and eloquently by Germaine Greer in *Sex and Destiny*, it is evident that there is a broad spectrum of sexual activity which people can enjoy without impregnation, or even without inter- course. It is also more than likely that male sexuality is not as narrowly focused as is commonly believed. Many of the responses in *The Hite Report on Male Sexuality*, especially those that indicated a desire for more closeness in sexual activity, would lead one to believe that a fruitful field of enquiry would be an exploration of true male sexuality, shorn of the cultural shibboleths with which it is imbued.

Without the accompanying cultural symbolism and pressures, says Hite, intercourse would become a matter of choice during sexual activities, not the *sine qua non*, the dénouement towards which all sexual activities move. Sexual activity does not always have to include intercourse, she says, and it would be much freer if intercourse were not always its focus. However, it has become a male cultural institution, as she describes it in her report on male sexuality:

> Intercourse is at once one of the most beautiful and at the same time most oppressive and exploitative acts of our society. It has been symbolic of men's ownership of women [and] is the central symbol of patriarchal society; without it there could be no patriarchy. [Intercourse] is the sublime moment during which the male contribution to reproduction takes place. [It] is a celebration of 'male' patriarchal culture ... In addition, this cultural institution, this symbolic rite, is attended by another person, a woman. If male orgasm is the sacrament here, the woman functions as the priest ... catering to the series of events which culminates in his orgasm.

The elevation of intercourse in this way on the altar of maledom is guaranteed to make a man feel that his needs (for an orgasm and for stimulation of the penis to reach that orgasm) are serious, worthwhile and important, no less than a 'biological' imperative. Shere Hite points out that women's need for orgasm is neither honoured nor respected in the traditional definition of sexual activity. In fact, women court disapproval for having intercourse. 'It is well to keep in mind,' she concludes, 'how differently our culture has chosen to reward the two sexes for the same activity.'

It should be pointed out here that male orgasm has a biological function in projecting semen into the female reproductive system. Now that female sexuality is, at last, being studied intelligently, and following on the research of Masters and Johnson, we may find that female orgasm (newly released from obscurity) also has a function in procreation, as an exercise in toning the labour muscles.

Apart from the one biological fact that conception requires semen to be deposited in the vagina, most if not all of the cultural ambience in which intercourse takes place is socially, culturally or psychologically defined. If sexuality is to have a due recognition and integrity in people's lives, then a new framework must be devised, perhaps non-penetrative, certainly involving pleasure in bodies (foreplay as an end in itself rather than, as the name suggests, a preparation for 'the real thing'), and other less obsessive practices than 'fucking'.

Segal maintains that the culture is 'deeply anti-sexual' but, like Foucault, I dispute that assertion. The culture *presents* itself as anti-sexual, but, in fact, it expects society to be sexual. As Foucault said, the culture deploys sexuality for various reasons, and it is highly sexualised in a generalised and pervasive way: in the everyday use of a sexual sublanguage; in the continual and continuing sexual objectification of women, assigning them value only in the sexual area; in the linking of sexual prowess and masculinity; in advertising which increasingly has a sexual subtext; in the emphasis on genital sexual activity; in the aura of sexuality that is expected to surround encounters between the sexes; in the role of sexuality in gender identification, the emphasis on sexual attractiveness as a necessary or desired attribute. Granted this sexuality is distorted, even pathological; the very sexualisation of the culture is pathological. Paradoxically, deployment (repressive or not) increases or heightens the obsession with sexuality that pervades society. On the other hand, permissiveness, generally of benefit to men, leaves many women (those who are dependent or lack self-confidence) exploited and unsure of their right to say no or even of the practicality of doing so. Feminists who embraced the new sexual liberation are now preaching 'relationships' and 'emotional' closeness in sexual encounters.

Because culture has shaped sexuality in a way that is pathological, or in a form that we find oppressive, does not mean that we can easily dismiss it. Culture is a very powerful force in our lives, and unpicking the stitches that knit it is not a simple matter. It involves people changing the ways they think and act; actions that they believe are natural and right. Changes like that come about slowly by the spread of ideas; but, as the women's movement has discovered to its cost, the media of communications tire of these ideas and find the backlash to them more interesting.

The idea that sexuality is not a fixed, unchanged and unchangeable phenomenon, the fact that it was not liberated but manipulated by the recent sexual revolution, needs another sexual revolution to penetrate the consciousness of this sexual generation.

10

SEXUAL BODIES

Among the *bêtes noires* of feminist theorists are those writers who associate sexuality in any way with biology, and whom they term 'biological essentialists' and 'biological reductionists'. The scientific basis for what is now called biological essentialism and reductionism, biologism, comes in modern times from zoologists like Desmond Morris (*The Naked Ape*) and Konrad Lorenz (*On Aggression*), and from entomologists like Edward O. Wilson (*Sociobiology*). Their approach to the science of human biology and behaviour, although nowadays modified by Darwin's evolutionary ideas, has a long history which goes back to Plato and his concept of the 'idea' or 'form' or 'essential reality' of an object or concept.

The terms 'biological determinism', 'biological essentialism' and 'biological reductionism' are sometimes used interchangeably in feminist literature to describe a belief that sexuality is purely biological. But, while these terms and the beliefs they describe may co-exist in a biological theory of sexuality, there are differences of meaning between them.

Biological determinism is the belief that every event has a cause, and that given the laws of nature and the previous history of the world, the event in question could not have failed to occur. It rules out other factors such as the psychological, social and cultural influences that result from human intelligence, and asserts that behaviour is determined by the laws of nature alone, that, given their immutability, it cannot be changed. In sexual terms, biological determinism means that sexuality is totally or mainly influenced by biology in a set and definite way which is the way humans conduct their sexual activity at present. Behaviourism, another aspect of biological determinism, aims at the prediction and control of behaviour. It studies both animal and human behaviour, and relies only on objective data, avoiding concepts such as perception and emotion.

Biological essentialism is the philosophical descendent of Platonic essentialism, which held that there were underlying essences in all objects and concepts, and these were constant and different from each other. Dogs have an essence of doghood, trees of tree-ness, humans have a human essence – human nature; and in the context of the present discussion females have an essential femaleness called femininity, and males an essential masculinity. Similarly, concepts such as truth or beauty also have their own essential nature. This was the view of nature held by the Christian religion in its theory of Creation, and by many biologists until Darwin propounded his theory of evolution. The belief that living objects were immutable was modified when the theory of evolution was accepted, but the belief in an essential nature or intrinsic essence remains among some to the present day.

Biological essentialism formed part of the philosophy of some feminist theorists, the belief that women have a different (and better) nature than men. It is an attractive idea, especially when the nurturing and caring virtues of women are contrasted to the aggression of men. In most cases it is compounded with a type of psychological and cultural essentialism, a conviction that nothing can be done about the situation, which has led to feminist separatism and political lesbianism.

Reductionism is different, and is the result of a narrowness of perception. It means that the phenomena of one theory can be accounted for by another existing theory; for instance that the world can be explained in terms of pure science, that psychology and/or biology reduce to physics; or, in the present case, that sexuality reduces to biology and is not influenced by any other factor. It also embraces the view that a system can be fully understood in terms of its individual parts. This mechanistic mindset began with the scientific revolution of the sixteenth and seventeenth centuries, with the fathers of modern science (Bacon, Descartes, Newton, et cetera), and still permeates modern scientific thinking and practice, informing almost all pure science and scientific method. Prior to that, the cosmos, the universe and all its animate and inanimate parts, were conceived of as connected and interrelated in a living unity.[1]

The modern trend to specialise in the study of particular aspects of a subject intensifies the tendency to reductionism; researchers learn about one aspect of an area of study without, or with minimal, knowledge of its interaction with other aspects or with other areas. Students of the physical sciences and intellectual researchers alike follow their narrow avenues of enquiry within specific parameters, a kind of tunnel vision, ignoring the complexities and interactions of the systems within which they study. Theirs is a mechanistic view of science which in this century alone has caused terrible catastrophes: drug blunders (such as thalidomide); the disaster of nuclear armaments; the destruction of the environment.

Those who hold reductionist views of human behaviour base their ideas on their interpretation of animal behaviour: mainly, but not always, on the behaviour of primates. (Some extend the field to include all mammals, and even further into the other subdivisions of animal life such as birds and insects.) They then transfer these interpretations in an homologous and anthropomorphic way to human behaviour, although genetic and embryonic research has shown that similar *physical* features in different species can often arise from different genes and different gene patterns.

Biological reductionism is also used in searching for first causes, by assuming that the present situation of humans or other forms of life is a biological given, and tracing a speculative history for it. This simplistic approach ignores the boundless chaos within which human development took place. Another aspect of it is teleology: a totally dubious method of reasoning, a kind of backwards deduction, which relates the developments and changes which have taken place in the biology or biological behaviour of humans (or of any species) to the purpose that is now served by these changes and developments. For instance, childcare is the natural work of women because they breast-feed the babies, and therefore so also is housework and providing personal service; it is not natural for men to care for children because they are engineers, or tycoons, or hunters.

In the world in which we live the roles of women and men arise for all kinds of diverse, social or cultural reasons, not necessarily related to biology, like the instance given above: women take responsibility for childcare because they breast-feed: they do housework because the children they care for are in the house. It is interesting and often important to know how and why a piece of behaviour arose, but jumping to conclusions based on the present situation is not the way forward.

Modern biologism, the belief that biology explains everything, of whatever hue, would claim descent from Darwin's theory of evolution, albeit narrowly defined. But, despite the advent of Freud and psychoanalysis, and of sociologists and social analysis, a strong strain of biologism has survived into the late-twentieth century; latterly, it has evolved into sociobiology.

Too often, research into human behaviour, and the theories evolved, have been a male preserve and mainly used by men, in a self-serving and self-deceiving way, to legitimise male domination of women. Their approach to research is male-centred, not just because they use the word 'man' to mean the human race (man embraceth woman), but because the context is always the behaviour of men in male situations, whether they be those of power, aggression, sexuality or whatever. It is also remarkable, in the case of those biologists who believe that sexuality is a purely biological instinct, that their purpose always seems to be 'proving' the superiority and natural leadership of men, and the natural subordination of women; that male social domination corresponds to biological dominance.

In fact, recent research on the sexual development of the human embryo shows that in biological terms the female is dominant. The chromosomes X and Y determine the sex of the human foetus, the Y chromosome determining the male sex. Until nearly five weeks after fertilisation, a human embryo lacks any type of sex organs. Then gonads develop which will eventually become either ovaries or testes. Each embryo originally develops two sets of potential reproductive tracts, one female and one male. If the Y chromosome is present, the rate of development in the gonad is accelerated and testes are formed. The rate of development, researchers think, is the key to the development of testes. They believe that the function of the Y chromosome is not to make the testes 'but to provide the conditions which allow the testes to develop – in other words to accelerate the rate of development'. Unless the testes differentiate early the germ cells will proceed to become egg cells and the gonad will become an ovary.[2]

This research makes nonsense of the male-centred biology which for a long time cast the man as the standard and the woman as some kind of aberration. If one wished to continue in that kind of sexist mode one could say, in the light of the above revelations, that the female was the standard and the male an aberration, because women have continued their *biological* task of safeguarding the future of the species while men have made determined efforts to destroy it.

Desmond Morris wrote two popular books on human behaviour, *The Naked Ape* and *The Human Zoo*, which have been responsible for some mistaken beliefs and misapprehensions about the basis of human actions. Take his enumeration of the 'ingredients necessary to make up our present sexual complexity' which is unashamed teleology:

First he had to hunt if he was to survive. Second, he had to have a better brain to make up for his poor hunting body. Third, he had to have a longer childhood to grow the bigger brain and educate it. Fourth, the females had to stay put and mind the babies while the males went hunting. Fifth, the males had to co-operate with each other on the hunt. Sixth, they had to stand up straight and use weapons for the hunt to succeed.[3]

Here Morris makes deductions from current social arrangements to construct a history of social evolution which, as well as being purely speculative, is naïvely male-centred. Are we to infer from his account that women's brains did not grow, and women did not stand up straight, because they were all at home minding the young?

He suggests that our 'fundamental patterns of behaviour ... our feeding, our fear, our aggression, our sex, our parental care' have developed because of basic, biological, genetic changes, rather than 'mere cultural' ones, in the evolution from foraging to hunting–gathering. Furthermore, he maintains that for the mammalian female, the sexual role is essentially a submissive one, and for the male an aggressive one; that men are biologically inclined to be sexually promiscuous, while women are by nature more nurturant. The implication that male domination and superiority is genetically coded since the transition from gatherers to hunter–gatherers is more of Morris's backward deduction. When he talks of the 'exchange of females' between groups of higher primates, he implies a system which is controlled by dominating males, when equally it may be that the females decide themselves to seek males in other groups for any one of a number of reasons, which may, intentionally or unintentionally, help to vary the gene pool. (See note 4 chapter 7 for other possible scenarios.) He also saw female orgasm as 'a pseudo-male response'.

Ivan Petrovich Pavlov is another exponent of biological reductionism who was even more extreme. He denied the psychological dimension in human existence; cognition and emotion were neurological reflexes, he claimed, and the brain provided nerve cells as junctions between stimuli and reflexes. The key to understanding behaviour, he held, lay wholly in physiology. He studied conditioned reflexes in dogs.

The problem which has beset biologists where the brain is concerned is that they cannot study its workings by dissection; obviously it has ceased to function when it is dissected. New technologies have increased the ability to study brain function; but behaviour and learning are still empirical studies with which scientific biologists are uneasy and they confine their researches within the parameters of their own discipline.

Edward O. Wilson drew his analogies from the life of insects, rushing in (too soon) to add new discoveries in genetics to the theory of evolution with ideas that were later proved wrong by genetic research. In *Sociobiology*, Wilson tried to explain social behaviour as an adaptive process controlled by biology. He described sociobiology as 'the systematic study of the biological basis of all social behaviour'. Both Wilson and Morris were old-fashioned, mid-century biologists, set in the ways of anti-psychological, anti-sociological and pre-feminist behavioural research, seeking pre-dominance for biology in human behaviour, and writing at a time when genetic research was in a very early stage of development.

In his early work Wilson totally ignored psychological influences on the way humans behave, and he even believed that culture was genetically controlled. Later in *Promethean Fire*, he modified his ideas, promoting a much more likely theory called 'gene-culture coevolution' which suggested that human biology (genes) shaped the way people lived and behaved (culture), and their way of life in turn caused changes in human biology.[4]

Wilson's writings are full of examples of teleology, such as deciding that males dominated in pre-Homo sapiens, hominid societies, because they dominate today. He also attributed to these dominating, hominid males the characteristics which he believed favour sexual selection today – 'cunning, cooperative, attractive to the ladies, good with children, relaxed, tough, eloquent, skilful, knowledgeable and proficient in self-defence and hunting'. Since these social traits would ensure breeding success, male domination became a strain, he wrote, in the development of humans. These assumptions are no more than conjecture; there are several other conjectures that could fit the proposition equally well, but might not make useful arguments to legitimise male domination.[5] The scientist and science writer Stephen Jay Gould maintains that Wilson's problems arose because he transposed observations which he made on ants, a species of little brain but programmed actions, to humans who are at the top of the intelligence league.[6]

There are other examples of backwards deduction in the writings of both Wilson and Morris. Wilson saw sexual *practices* (as distinct from functional copulation) primarily in terms of a bonding mechanism between a woman and a man, rather than a procreative activity. Non-human female mammals have definite periods of oestrus during which they are receptive to the sexual advances of the male; human females are continuously receptive to the male, and both Morris and Wilson claim that this phenomenon is linked to the development of pair bonding in early hominids; it is just as likely that pair bonding arose out of the original oppression of autonomous women's groups by male groups because it was easier to suppress them by isolating them individually. Furthermore, how do they know that hominid females and their successors *Femina sapienta* were continuously sexually receptive? And one might also ask are women nowadays *biologically* or *psychologically* receptive? There is no scientific knowledge of the evolution of continuous female sexual receptivity; there is only cultural evidence, and that evidence is gathered in the context of the subordination of women, when they, as reasoning beings, might possibly make themselves sexually available for cultural or economic reasons. Furthermore, present-day women are more receptive in their fertile period than at other times during their reproductive cycle.

Research on the female reproductive cycle has been narrowly confined to ways of controlling fertility, and little attention has been paid to the desires or needs of women. For instance, it is known empirically that breast-feeding on demand stops ovulation, but the wider evolutionary and physiological implications have been but sketchily addressed. In present hunter–gatherer societies, whose circumstances are assumed to resemble most nearly those of early humans, mothers feed babies until they are at least two years old, and this seems to provide a measure of birth control. But, then, this kind of deduction is also teleological.

A fairly consistent thread in the theories of these biologists was the link between male aggression and male sexuality. The four 'great' biological drives, Konrad Lorenz said, were hunger, sex, aggression and fear. In his studies on aggression he observed the sexual behaviour of small tropical fish called cichlids, and concluded that mating success depended on a mixture of aggression and domination in the male, and a mixture of fear and submission in the female. Then in a piece of straight biological reductionism he applied the same theory to social and intelligent humans. Lorenz extrapolated human behaviour from that of geese, dogs, fishes, bullfinches, et cetera, as well as primates. But for every primate, avian or insect group that shows domination in males there are others that do not.

In his influential book, *On Aggression*, Lorenz endeavoured to produce a solution to the dangerous situation in which the world finds itself because of the development of nuclear weapons of mass destruction. He sought the answer in biology, in what he saw as the aggressive drive 'bred into man' by the process of evolution. He believed that the intelligent man could control his aggression. (The same motive inspired Dorothy Dinnerstein to write *The Mermaid and the Minator*, but she looked for the solution in human psychology.) Still, Lorenz is not the most reductionist of the biologists; in another instance he admitted that 'reason and cultural tradition' had some influence on human behaviour. He went even further to say that some human physiological abilities, such as the ability to speak, evolved in a way that complemented a specific cultural development such as language. In later work Lorenz was writing about 'creative evolution', and asserting that 'adaptation is a cognitive process'.[7]

In *Beyond Power*, Marilyn French debunks the justifications of these biological reductionists with more intelligence than their authors. She does this by taking the evidence of archaeology, of modern primate study and of anthropology, and constructing from first principles (not from backwards deduction) another probable scenario. Far from being male-dominant, crude, brutal, predatory cavemen, bashing each other over the head and dragging women by their hair, French maintains that early humans were more likely 'gentle and playful, with a society centred on a set of mothers and infants'.

Ideas are changing; there are signs that reductionism in general is becoming discredited. Gunnar Myrdal, the Swedish economist and Nobel prizewinner, spoke of the fog of Western culture within which we live and operate. Cultural influences, he said, have set up our basic assumptions about the mind and the body, and about the universe; our culture influences the questions we ask about these phenomena, the facts we seek, the interpretation of these facts, and our reaction to these interpretations and conclusions.[8] Our problem is that the dominant culture is male.

The scientists and science writers Hilary and Steven Rose describe biologism as only one part of the explanation of the human condition, and an excuse to do nothing about the problems of that condition. Biologism, they say,

> excludes all other considerations, and announces that it has *the* explanation for aggression and altruism, war and class struggle, love and hate. Attempting to change the human condition is then presented as an absurd opposition to both our natural selves and the natural world. The everyday possibility and actuality that men and women have continuously

changed their situation in the course of history is methodically and philosophically excluded. Biologism, for all its apparent scientificity, is thus mere ideology, the legitimation of the *status quo*.[9]

Scientists, scholars and researchers fall into another error of their own making. They tend to elevate their new insight or discovery into proof of an already dearly held premise. For instance, on the question of aggression the biologists and some of the psychologists say that it is a biological instinct; the culturalists and other psychologists say that it is learned. There is some evidence that the answer may lie somewhere between the two beliefs. Why does the child hit out when frustrated? Is this an instinct or something that has been learned? If we learn aggression, is fear something that we also learn? And if it is, what about the production in the body of adrenaline as a response to fear, which gives a strength-enhancing boost to fight or flight? When humans are starving or in great danger, another instinct, self-preservation, takes precedence over the basic sex drive. Is this proof that there is no basic sex drive or that a 'real' instinct, like self-preservation, is stronger? Or is there a biological mechanism (like adrenaline) which suppresses the sex drive? Is Freud's 'death wish' the pathological side of self-preservation? There are all kinds of questions still to be asked and answered.

Biological reductionism and determinism are beginning to lose ground even in the scientific establishment, and feminist ideas with a more holistic definition of human behaviour are taking hold. Some scientists have campaigned vigorously against biologism because they regard it as bad biology used to support dubious politics.[10] This deconstruction or revisionism is taking place in the most unlikely fields, in molecular biology and genetics, areas of study one might expect to be the epitome of reductionism. In *The Selfish Gene* (which proposes the theory that the driving force of evolution is the good of the individual gene rather than the good of the species), Richard Dawkins holds that genes are the dominant influence in most animals. Yet he found that this theory did not hold true for sexuality. He suggested that a male strategy of sexual promiscuity would benefit the survival of male genes, and then qualified this assertion by pointing out that many human societies are monogamous, some are promiscuous and some are harem based. 'What this astonishing variety suggests,' he says, 'is that man's way of life is largely determined by culture rather than by genes.'

The idea of interaction between biology and culture, or that the human species is self-created by means of its intelligence, is not new; yet some commentators resist the idea that biology has an influence on social behaviour (such as the exercise of sexuality). Biology and culture are not separate conditions with one superimposed on the other. Culture becomes inextricably bound up in biology and vice versa so that the final state is different and much more than the sum of the two. Gould says that

> every scientist, indeed every intelligent person, knows that human social behaviour is a complex and indivisible mix of biological and social influences. The issue is not whether nature or nurture determines human behaviour, for these factors are truly inextricable, but the degree, intensity and nature of the constraint exercised by biology upon the possible form of social organisation. ... Our struggle is to find out how biology affects us, not whether it does.[11]

The recently recognised threat to the planet's environment has given impetus to a more holistic approach to the nature of things, at first in ecology, and gradually in other areas of scientific interest. Evelyn Fox Keller, a physicist who writes on women in science, attributes this mode of thinking to Barbara McClintock, 1983 winner of the Nobel Prize for Physiology.[12] She describes her as having a 'feeling for the organism'. In her biography of McClintock, Keller quotes her as saying that the scientist must understand how the organism grows, understand its parts and understand when something is going wrong with it. An organism, says McClintock, is constantly being affected by the environment, constantly showing attributes and disabilities in its growth. In 'Feminism and science', Keller noted men's tendency in science to focus on the independent operation of the constituent parts of whatever phenomena they were investigating, whereas women seemed to be more open to recognising the dynamic interplay of these parts, and had a more holistic approach.[13] Yet every so often a new form of biological reductionism appears, and usually in the service of male domination, as if there existed a great psychological need in some men to hold and express such views.

The writings of biological determinists are so irritating in the way they demean women that it is no wonder so many feminist writers, in fury, threw them out. Unfortunately many feminist philosophers have also been trained in the Cartesian mould (in the mechanistic, scientific philosophy of Descartes), and instead of biological reductionism we get cultural reductionism and psychological reductionism, of which more later.

Is sexuality purely biological? No. It has a strong biological base, an indisputable biological content. After all, sexual intercourse, arousal, erection, orgasm, the physical sexual responses, are biological, and the action of the contraceptive pill is biological, yet it affects the sexual responses which are a mixture of biological and psychological elements. But sexuality (the quality of being sexual, the use and practice of sexual activity, the attitudes and beliefs attributed to the different sexes in the area of sexual attraction) also has a strong cultural content and an equally strong psychological content. These three elements – biological, cultural and psychological – are intertwined and woven together in a complex way in the modern construction which is sexuality. For instance, believing in a biological imperative in the male erection, totally beyond the power of the individual, is biological reductionism, and denies the role of culture and social factors in the fantasies or stimuli which cause and regulate erection. As with life itself, sexuality is more than the sum of its constituent parts.

In discussions of female sexuality biology is out of fashion. Cerebral, intelligent feminists, who know the potential of women, react against the old representation of women as immanent and earthy – identified with nature – and their exclusion from transcendence and intellectual activity. They also realise that woman's biology was and is used to confine her, to limit her involvement in a wide range of activities, to subordinate her. Therefore they emphasise the social, cultural and psychological elements in behaviour, which can be changed, and discount the biological where change would be difficult. Jeffrey Weeks does the same from a male, homosexual point of view. He admits a biological base for sexuality because 'we experience it in our bodies', but then finds biology relevant only in the limits it imposes on the body.[14]

Each child is born a small bundle of nascent biology and psyche (including intelligence) which interacts with the culture into which she or he is born; and the biology does not go away. It is dominant at different times in the person's life; in growth and ageing, in puberty and reproduction, and even then it is moulded by psychological factors, by intelligence, and by the social and cultural environment in which the person lives.

Having said all that about biological determinism, and about the scientific revolution, I must hasten to add that I am not condemning science or technology, only the way our culture misuses them. The greatest achievement of the human race has been the expansion of knowledge which intelligence has permitted it. But the present methods used in scientific research have retarded development, as science historian Caroline Merchant so pertinently describes in *The Death of Nature*, where she points out that human knowledge may end there if childish destruction does not stop.

Similarly, without intelligence and the psychological life it provides, our sexuality would be comparable to that of the other mammals, related mainly to reproduction and the release of tension caused by signals of smell or vision, and only peripherally related to pleasure. Indeed actual sexual congress in most other animals (as distinct from mating ritual) takes place so quickly that it would seem to be less a matter of pleasure than a release of tension. Pleasure for them is sensuous and involves grooming, petting and bodily play.

So, is bodily sensuousness sexual? I think the answer is yes, because pleasure in bodily contact requires a certain amount of attraction, but this is an area of sensual/sexual behaviour that has been neglected and eclipsed by genitality. Lesbian writers have explored it to some extent but it is a subject that could profit from more study. There is an area of bodily pleasure to be enjoyed without exercising the genitals, or proceeding to reproduction, but that does not rule out reproduction as a basic component of sexuality as many of the discourses seem to do. We don't need to populate the earth at present, so there is no reason why sexuality should be directed exclusively towards that purpose, no reason why it should not be enjoyed where it does not exploit others.

11

BIOLOGY RECLAIMED

When feminists omit biology from the definition and analysis of sexuality, they are ignoring the sex drive or, more precisely, sex urge which is a life force. Female sex drive is different to that of the male. Women have ovaries, a womb, a vagina and a clitoris; men have testes and a penis. A woman's biological need, or sex urge, is to fill her womb; a man's is to penetrate and deposit. Primarily, female sex is a preponderance of oestrogen, and male sex of testosterone; that is the basic biological difference. The drive to reproduce is present in all species. Human intelligence learned to control it for psychological, social and economic reasons, and to use it for pleasure; and when sexual activity became equated with pleasure, its other purpose, reproduction, eventually became a social impediment in certain cases, and for individuals at certain stages of their lives.

'Sex', in the language of biologists means sexual reproduction,[1] the fusion of genetic material donated by a female and a male. In fishes this takes place without contact between the female and the male: the female lays her eggs, the male sprays them with his sperm. The importance of each contribution is equal in biological terms. In mammals the male spermatozoa are physically introduced into the female's body, there is a biological process of female and male union before the fusion, and the fused genetic matter remains in the female's body for a period of gestation.[2]

Sexual reproduction in mammals demands more physical and biological involvement of the female, an involvement which lasts from conception until the weaning of the offspring. Mammals feed their offspring for varying lengths of time after birth. Primates breast-feed for longer than other mammals; the chimpanzee, which is the primate most closely related to humans, does not fully wean her young until it is four or five years old.

Reproduction is biological. Biological sex and the organs that denote it are the necessary reproductive equipment of humans. Hormones govern the activities and functions of the body, and different hormones make us experience different feelings. The hormones that control a woman's menstrual cycle and fertility, and the neurological responses to these hormones are biological; sexual arousal is biological – the suffusion of tissue with blood, et cetera – as is the response. The bodily demands of a woman at ovulation are a yearning; the bodily demands of an aroused man are a drive. These biological processes are influenced and manipulated by social and psychological factors; stress, cultural practices, social conditions and attitudes can disrupt or alter them. A man can have a psychologically or physically induced erection, masturbate and achieve orgasm as a natural process of gratification, with or without the physical presence of female sexual stimulus; social or psychological factors can also inhibit this process. Similarily, women can induce orgasm by clitoral stimulation. In both cases response to stimuli, the orgasm, is biological but the connection between stimuli and response is subject to cultural and psychological influence.

In current human culture sexual activity is generally taken to mean genital intercourse, we do not think of pregnancy and childbirth as erotic or sexual, although nowadays it is reluctantly acknowledged that breast-feeding is an erotic experience for a woman. As a result, the cultural definition of female sexuality has excised a central element of a woman's sexuality. Sexuality has been assigned only to that part of procreation that involves active male participation; the element of procreation which involves the female alone has been relegated to the status of illness, and unnecessarily designated as a painful experience: Eve's curse. Furthermore, the link between genital pleasure and maternity – the female orgasm – has been isolated as a pleasurable end in itself, and procreation has been split into sexual and non-sexual parts.

Male orgasm has a biological purpose, to project semen into the vagina, as well as the obvious one of pleasure in the release of tension. Female orgasm is also a release of tension and a pleasurable experience, but I have found no reference in the literature to a *purpose* for it other than pleasure; a woman can have intercourse and conceive without ever having an orgasm. The zoologist Desmond Morris suggested that the human female orgasm helps cement the pair bond by rewarding her for coitus. He also suggested that by exhausting the female it helped to keep her prone after coitus, thus avoiding the risk of losing the seminal fluid out of her vagina.[3] How wrong he was! Firstly, women can experience orgasm without coitus; secondly, orgasm does not exhaust her in the same way as it does a man. However, orgasm could help to draw seminal fluid into the uterus and retain it by the contractions of the vaginal wall.

The sexologists Masters and Johnson noted that some women experienced erotic feelings while giving birth. In *Human Sexual Response* they compared the contractions of the uterus and extravaginal muscles during orgasm to first and second stage labour contractions; the correlation is striking (see pages 91–2). They recorded that twelve women, all of whom had delivered babies on at least one occasion without anaesthesia or analgesic, reported that during the second stage of labour they experienced a greatly intensified version of the sensations identified with the first stage of orgasm.[4] Masters and Johnson also found an indication of another link between orgasm and birthing. In one research project concerning coitus during pregnancy, four women had reported that orgasm had induced labour in the last weeks of pregnancy, and in each case there had been no obstetrical distress. The sexologists were impressed and remarked that it could be of major clinical importance if labour could be induced in this way.[5]

From the birth of my own child in 1969, I had been tentatively examining the idea of the sexuality of childbirth, and in 1989 I floated it in a pamphlet, *Ancient Wars: Sex and Sexuality*. For more than two decades I had been reading feminist literature from the classics of the seventies to the recent studies and theories of French psychoanalysis. I had managed to read Adrienne Rich's *Of Woman Born* in 1977 without registering her references to *erotic* childbirth, and I had missed Sheila Kitzinger who, for almost thirty years has been writing about the sexual pleasure of childbirth. (Feminism is full of such experiences.)

Masters and Johnson regretted that the female orgasm never achieved the status of the male orgasm which has an obvious role in reproduction, and ask rhetorically, 'Why has female orgasmic expression not been considered to be a reinforcement of woman's role as sexual partner and a reproductive necessity?' Why indeed? They did not mention either finding in their 1992 book *Human Sexuality*, nor did they follow up on this information in further research. Their study of the female orgasm was directed towards improving women's sexual response in coitus, the only link they establish between birthing and orgasm is to state that because of the physiological changes that take place in the vagina, the increase in the blood supply to the area, women who have given birth have a greatly improved potential for orgasmic performance. They ignored their own previous revelations, as did subsequent students of their work, and preference was given to extolling the sacrament of sexuality, the coital orgasm.

From these findings it takes no great intellectual leap to deduce that the contractions experienced by women during orgasm exercise the uterus and extravaginal muscles and prepare them for the task of pushing a baby out during birth.

Childbirth and motherhood have had a bad press in the women's movement. Most of Simone de Beauvoir's assessment of maternity in *The Second Sex* was skewed by her own rejection of it, and by the low level of biological and psychological awareness of the condition in the middle of this century. For her, who had never given birth and relied only on hearsay, it was an agonising ordeal. Helene Deutsch said that a woman who had not suffered from her labour pains did not feel the baby profoundly hers; but she also admitted that this could also happen to women who feel their labour pains strongly.[6]

Women are the only mammals who in normal circumstances experience birthing as a traumatically painful experience. Giving birth is a physical exercise involving the use of muscles that may, or may not, have been adequately prepared for the job. The pregnancy and birthing stages of reproduction are areas where cultural attitudes have been particularly powerful.[7] Women have been brainwashed (Mary Daly called it mind-raped) to regard pregnancy as, at worst, an illness, and at best, a period of discomfort; and childbirth as dangerous and intensely painful. The result has been medical intervention in labour, and its 'management' to an unprecedented degree. In reaction to the modern development of techno-logical birth, there are movements, not necessarily associated with feminism, which advocate a return to natural childbirth, but they are still a minority interest. (Grantly Dick-Read, a British gynaecologist, and one of the pioneers of natural childbirth, wrote of the 'ecstasy' of childbirth in 1951.)

Pain can be a subjective or a relative phenomenon. The use of unused muscles can cause pain; they must be toned before they are called into use for any strenuous activity, whether that be a cycle race or giving birth to a baby. Even the process of toning muscles can be enjoyable. During pregnancy the body begins the process of toning the muscles of the womb in preparation for birthing. The female orgasm could well be a more pleasurable part of that toning process.

Some women took the subject of reproductive and health practices into their own hands and sought their own solution. The Boston Women's Health Book Collective grew out of the women's movement, when a group of women who were dissatisfied with the service they were getting from the medical profession, came together in that city in the early seventies to research the facts known about their own bodies. *Our Bodies, Ourselves* was the result. Its references are impeccable and it has an added ingredient – women's own experience uncensored by medical science. As a primer on the reproductive health of women, it has not been surpassed.

There is an excellent account of labour in the Boston Women's Health Book which I will give here (in condensed form) to show that it is a natural muscular activity for which the female body needs to be prepared.

During pregnancy women experience a regular tightening and loosening of the womb muscles called Braxton-Hicks contractions. These contractions are a preparation for labour by toning up the uterine muscles for the task of stretching (thinning, effacement) and dilating the cervix, and pushing the baby down into the vagina. Closer to actual labour there is what is called early or false labour, when the muscular process of dilation is increased. When labour becomes established and is strong and rhythmic, relaxation between contractions enables the body to gather strength for the next one and to allow the body, unrestrained by tension, to take over.

Some researchers now believe that when the birthing woman is relaxed, her body produces its own substances for pain relief, called endorphins, which have a morphine-like effect.[8] Tension and fear may inhibit the secretion of endorphins, causing her to secrete adrenaline instead, which causes tension, slows the labour and makes it more painful.

When the effacement and dilation of the cervix is complete, the uterine muscles change gear into pushing contractions which push the baby out of the womb and into the vagina. Contractions continue when the baby is in the vagina, moving it in a two-steps-forward one-step-back process while the perineum stretches gradually around the baby's head to allow it to emerge.

It is obvious from this description that childbirth is a muscular activity, as natural in humans as it is in other mammals. Yet other mammals do not have pain during birth unless they have suffered injury, or had their physiology distorted by domestication or crossbreeding. 'Domestication' of humans, and particularly the 'domestication' of women, has rendered many so unfit – weakened through lack of exercise, malnourished by poor or adulterated diet, poisoned by chemical pollution and injured by

overwork or incorrect work practices – that their pregnancies need monitoring to detect any abnormal circumstances or situations, and intervention
to a greater or lesser degree to avoid the death of the mother or the infant.

The problems of pregnancy and childbirth are complex and require an
integrated approach to their solution. They arise from several causes,
principally the physical and psychological health of the mother, but also
from a lack of proper pre-natal preparation. The expectant mother's physical health depends on diet, exercise, and a balance between work and rest.
Her psychological health depends to a large extent on real knowledge of the
new, changed condition of her body, not on what can safely be called (and
still remain politically correct) old-wives tales of almost 'unbearable' pain,
of pain 'the like of which the expectant mother has never known'.

In a normally healthy woman, labour should not be more painful than
any other strenuous muscular activity, and should be at least as pleasurable.
In fact the great expulsion process should be (and some women have found
it) orgasmic – the Great O. But, in the same way that intercourse can be
painful for the unaroused, unreceptive woman, so childbirth has become a
sort of rape in reverse where the body is rigid with fear, unrelaxed and
unready for any orgasmic experience. Many women confuse the notion of
natural childbirth with the absence of pain; this is a misapprehension. The
process of labour is strenuous, and it leads to distress when the body is
working against it, rather than with it.

The present arrangements for childbirth – hospitalisation, intervention,
technology – are just as much a cultural construct as the way we dress and
work, and they are imposed on women by playing on their fear for their
own wellbeing and for the safety of the baby. The act of giving birth is
biological, yet the physical, psychological, social and cultural environment
in which it takes place has not been conducive to pleasure in the process. In
its present form childbirth is so hedged around with these psychological and
cultural influences and attitudes that even the most well-disposed woman
approaches it with a baggage of fears and tensions. Furthermore, natural-
birth experts, such as Sheila Kitzinger, say that technological birthing
works *against* the natural rhythms of the body more often than with them,
marginalising the natural biological mechanisms of the woman who,
instead of delivering herself, is delivered of the baby. Dr Peter Wagner, a
paediatrician and former World Health Organisation officer for maternity
and child health services in Europe, said in 1995 that induction and
acceleration should not be necessary in more than 10 per cent of births (the

figures for Irish hospitals were up to 50 per cent).[9]

Because the satisfactions of motherhood (without any *overt* sexuality in birthing) make up for the pain of childbirth, women have continued in ignorance that although it is strenuous there is no need for it to be painful, and they have been denied the erotic pleasure it could afford.

It is very difficult for women who have suffered painful childbirth to accept that it does not need to be so, to accept that they have been conditioned into a psychological approach and the acceptance of a technical system, both of which *cause* severe pain. It is difficult for women who have suffered from the system, and who have had difficult deliveries, to accept that birthing could have been enjoyable. There are no more vehement defenders of painful birthing than women who have been put through it. Every woman who has had a baby is an 'expert' on childbirth. Few will admit that, perhaps, they were 'doing it wrong'; but the conditioning of women has been so complete that even those who are favourably disposed, and they are few, still approach their own labour in a tight ball of tension that ensures pain.

Nowadays, when Western women have fewer children, the opportunity of discovering that childbirth is sexual, and can be a sensual, exciting experience may be over for many of them. On the other hand, some women are disturbed if they experience sexual feelings when they are giving birth, because they feel out of control.

Modern confinement is organised mainly for the convenience of the hospital and the medical personnel involved; above all, it is one in which the control of delivery passes from the woman giving birth to them. The control of nature is the predominant philosophy of modern Western medicine, and scientific intervention whether by drugs or surgery is the essence of medical practice. The natural process of giving birth is subjected to a battery of medical techniques and practices: hospital confinement, supine position (the lithotomy position or upturned beetle syndrome), foetal monitoring, full or epidural anaesthesia, forceps delivery, Caesarean section, induced labour, episiotomy; any one of them necessary in a very small number of cases, but becoming more routinely used to speed things up. For instance, the supine position in the later stages of labour makes intervention by the medical personnel easier, although the opposite, an 'all-fours' position, a leaning forward squatting or sitting position, makes both labour and delivery easier, and reduces the need for forceps delivery. (A few hospitals now offer a choice.)

Why does childbirth need so much intervention? It doesn't. Pregnancy is not an illness which results from sexual intercourse like a sexually transmitted disease. Doctors, and increasingly midwives, trained in medical schools and hospitals, rarely see a normal spontaneous labour and birth, say the Boston women. Medical students, they say, learn about labour during their practical classes and internship by observing a woman who is lying on her back during labour, her bag of waters broken artificially, labour induced, often hooked up to a foetal monitor, drugged or anaesthetised, given an episiotomy, with a possibility of forceps delivery or perhaps a Caesarean section. These students don't know how to relate to a fully conscious, unanaesthetised woman, they don't sit through labour from beginning to end to learn how or what a woman feels, or become acquainted with the rhythm of her labour.

Adrienne Rich says that the loneliness, the sense of abandonment, of being imprisoned, powerless and depersonalised is the chief collective memory of women who have given birth in American hospitals.[10] 'Nobody asks what is the best normal way to deliver', says Beverly Beech of the Association for Improvements in the Maternity Services in the United Kingdom in an article by Patricia McNair. 'When women come into hospital, they are forced to lie on their backs, connected up to machines, and the hi-tech birth begins. When problems begin only hi-tech answers are sought. A Caesarean is the ultimate result of coping with problems induced by technology.' In Brazil, where the rate of Caesarean births is among the highest in the world, women are encouraged to have them in order to keep their vaginas 'honeymoon fresh'. In the United States the figure for Caesarean births lies around 30 per cent, and in the United Kingdom around 15 per cent but is said to be as high as 25 per cent in some hospitals. McNair cited fear of litigation and insurance claims as the main cause for the technological birth.[11]

Hospital confinement makes an illness of childbirth and is necessary only in a small minority of cases. (A figure of between 5 and 10 per cent has been suggested to me by my GP.) In that case it would make economic sense to encourage home births and release hospital beds for those who are ill. If diagnosis of pregnancy problems is as good as we are told it is, then only women who are likely to have complications should be hospitalised. If the new propensity for taking legal action against doctors for mistaken diagnosis militates against home births, then we certainly impose restrictions on ourselves and make life harder by such impositions.

There are many good reasons for the development of the present mode of Western childbirth, such as the reduction of maternal and infant mortality. There are also some cultural roots to the present situation which are of questionable worth. These are buried deep, flowing like a subterranean river from our past history as part of an endemic misogyny and antipathy to female sexuality that is manifest in the development of the practice of medicine in the last thousand years.[12] Nowadays this misogyny is usually buried deep in the unconscious but the cultural structures and practices which it spawned remain with us. Michel Foucault saw the 'hysterisation of women' as one of the four great lines of attack along which the power-politics of sex and the deployment of sexuality advanced.[13] This hysterisation, he said, involved a thorough medicalisation of their bodies and their sex, and was carried out in the name of the responsibility they owed to the health of their children.

A more modern reason for the management of, and intervention in, the process of childbirth is economic. Doctors and hospital managements want to hurry the process in order to maximise the use of personnel and facilities. But apart from administrative constraints some psychoanalysts claim that a perverse psychological influence is at work – Ann Oakley quotes two male psychoanalysts who claim deep-seated womb envy on the part of men. One, Peter Lomas, suggested that the medical treatment of childbirth reeked of dehumanisation of the mother which was related to male envy of women's ability to give birth.[14]

Sheila Kitzinger, a social anthropologist with a woman's insight, is the person who has done most towards trying to make childbirth a pleasurable, sexual experience. She is also a birth educator who for more than thirty years has been involved with the pre-natal preparation of women for childbirth. Undeterred by resistance within and outside the women's movement, in *Woman's Experience of Sex* she proclaimed birthing as a sexual act and lyrically described the process of labour:

> All these sensations [labour contractions] are at their most powerful in her sexual organs. Feelings pour through her genitals ... The uterus, the vagina, the muscles enfolding the vagina and rectum, the lower back, the rectum itself and the anus, the buttocks, tissues around and between the vagina and the anus, and the clitoris are all suffused with heat as if with liquid fire or as if brimful and pouring over with glowing colour.

She goes on to say that the intense sexuality of natural childbirth stands in startling contrast to the institutional setting usually provided for the experience: 'It is as if we were required to make love, pouring ourselves, body and mind, into the full expression of feeling, in a busy airport concourse, a large railway terminus, in a gymnasium or a tiled public lavatory.'[15]

The techniques of natural childbirth which enabled Sheila Kitzinger's clients to experience it enjoyably were already developed by her in *The Experience of Childbirth*. In 1962 she had tentatively arrived at the idea of birthing as part of a woman's sexuality, but in the 1984 edition of her book she declared unequivocally that labour was as much a part of a woman's psychosexual life as puberty, ovulation and menstruation, love play and intercourse, pregnancy, breast-feeding and menopause. There is a flow and rhythm about a woman's life, she said, that is bound up in her sexuality. For far too many women pregnancy and birth were still something that happened to them, rather than something they set out consciously and joyfully to do themselves.

She reports that again and again she has heard women describe the keen sensuous pleasure they obviously experienced when giving birth, and which often surprised them with its delight. Today, she says, birth is treated as a medico-surgical crisis, instead of being a personal, private, intimate experience. She describes the mother as part of an efficient assembly line with procedures which make it difficult for her to discover anything sexual in labour.

Kitzinger believes that the only women who have discovered that birth is a passionate and intense sexual experience are those who have given birth in their own homes, or in rare maternity units where there is unusual flexibility to enable them to behave without inhibition, where they get in tune with their bodies and allow the energy of labour to flow through them.

Her description of modern technogical childbirth, with 'active management of labour', reads like a horror story, but one which is well-known to, and accepted as inevitable by, millions of women. The pregnant woman lies flat on her back with her legs suspended in stirrups; her perineum is shaved 'bald as an egg'. All attention is focused on her crotch as if it were the operative part of a reproductive machine. She will be offered drugs to alleviate the pain but there is a price to pay for this solicitude. Effective anaesthesia, Kitzinger says, makes more intervention possible, and because it interferes with a woman's normal physiological functions, and usually also affects the foetus, it makes this intervention more likely.

Managed birth, she says, involves induced labour either by rupturing the membranes or by using drugs; then electronic monitoring of the foetal heart with an electrode stuck through the mother's vagina into the baby's scalp, and the control of uterine activity by a hormone intravenous drip so that labour does not exceed twelve hours, ten hours, eight hours, or whatever consultants in that unit have decided is the correct norm for dilation and expulsion. If the baby is not born within the time limit set, delivery is affected with forceps or by Caesarean section.

Foetal monitoring, she continues, also contributes to the desexualising of childbirth because the mother is tethered by catheters and wires to electronic equipment. She cannot move freely or even shift position without the risk of interfering with the attachments or the printout of the monitor. 'It is almost as if it is the monitor which is having the baby and all eyes are fixed on it.' But the horror story does not end there; to speed up forceps delivery a cut is made in the perineum to open the vagina; this operation which is called episiotomy has become almost routine in managed labour.[16] The Boston Women's Health Book Collective says in *Our Bodies, Ourselves* that episiotomy is necessary only

- when forceps are used;
- when previous damage to the perineum means that a severe tear is likely;
- and in cases of foetal distress, when the baby must come out quickly and the woman's tissues just won't stretch any more.

In a talk at Boston College in 1981 Kitzinger declared episiotomy the most frequently performed obstetric operation in the West. It is, she said, the only operation performed on the body of a healthy woman without her consent, and represents obstetric power – babies can't get out unless they are cut out. She unequivocally called it a form of ritual genital mutilation.[17] The Boston Women's Collective also maintains that there is no justification for routine episiotomy; yet some consultants, they say, insist on its routine use, and midwives are, as a result, getting insufficient training in those midwifery techniques which can prevent or minimise tearing. For instance, they say, in most births you will have little if any tearing when you are upright, sitting or squatting to breathe or to push your baby out, and resting between contractions .

In recent times epidural anaesthesia has become popular with both birthing mothers and obstetricians. The local anaesthetic used produces regional nerve block, cutting off pain sensation from waist to knee, divorcing the mother from the process of birth and, in the words of the drug companies, making her a more 'co-operative patient'. There are warnings attached by the manufacturers of epidural anaesthetics and Kitzinger quotes from one company's literature which warns users to be prepared 'with facilities for supportive measures to maintain vital functions' such as oxygenation, ventilation, maintenance of blood pressure; and that side effects such as a drop in blood pressure, a speeded up or slowed down heart rate, vomiting, or in rare occasions, convulsions or coma can occur. If the local anaesthetic produces lowered blood pressure in the mother, Kitzinger points out that this can mean reduced blood flow and oxygen from the placenta to the foetus and the slowing down of the foetal heart beat; the result is that foetal monitoring is always necessary when epidural anaesthesia is used. The Boston Women's Collective quote from an article in the *British Journal of Obstetrics and Gynaecology*, referring to studies on babies born in these circumstances which says that they are likely to show lack of responsiveness and 'other minor effects' which persist for up to six weeks.[18] Dr Peter Wagner was also critical of the high use of epidurals (up to 64 per cent in some hospitals in Ireland), and he quoted a report of the American College of Obstetrics which said that 10 per cent of babies whose mothers had an epidural did not get enough oxygen.

When Kitzinger observed what women would do naturally when giving birth, she found that it resembled the motions of other mammals expelling their young. Many women writers are so unwilling to compare women with other mammals that they completely discount women's animal nature. Not so Kitzinger who says that when a woman does what comes naturally, she tends to breathe in very much the same way as other mammals giving birth; and that this is also a breathing pattern which corresponds almost exactly with that of sexual excitement and female orgasm. She maintains that in current practice the pattern of a *male* orgasm – 'stiffen, hold, force through, shoot!' – is imposed on women in labour rather than the wave-like rhythms of female orgasm. Women, she says, push because they are told to do so, as if they were forcing out a large, hard, constipated motion.

On the other hand, she says, if a woman does whatever she feels like doing in labour, moving and breathing in any way she wants to, the second stage can become an intense sexual experience. If she pushes only when she needs to do so urgently, then she feels 'the extraordinary and intensely sexual sensations as the baby's head presses first against her anus and then down through the concertina-like folds of her vagina until it feels like a hard bud in the middle of a great, open peony'. When you read this description of childbirth as the peak of a woman's sexuality, it is like all universal truths, it seems so self-evident I wondered why nobody ever said so before.

Giving birth is among the most significant events in a woman's life. I have yet to meet one who does not recall every detail of the birth of her children; even very old women (and I am now thinking of one who at ninety years of age could vividly recall the experience).

Male-dominated obstetrics, some feminists believe, has been one of the instruments for the sexual oppression of women, used deliberately to frustrate the true fulfilment of female sexuality.[19] If women are a colonised people, said Robin Morgan, then the male-controlled medical establishment is the Colonial Secret Police.[20] That might seem an extreme statement, making horned and hooved devils of gynaecologists and obstetricians who would say that their priority is the safety of the child and the mother. They would point to the improvements in statistics on maternal deaths and live births as evidence of the success of their methods.[21] They would deny the sexual element in childbirth, or say that ethics forbid the involvement of a male doctor in any sexual activity with a patient. They would repeat that a mother's pleasure takes second place to her safety and that of her child; they would say that their techniques have been developed and modernised with great effort and expense; they would say that they know best, that a woman who resists this management is irresponsible towards the wellbeing of her baby, or 'out of her mind'.

First of all, the present body of obstetric practice and techniques was built up by male doctors over the past two centuries, and at all times they have resisted change in their methods. It took almost a century for doctors to accept that they were the cause of puerperal fever in birthing mothers. The modern body of obstetric techniques and practices, including attitudes towards women, evolved out of nineteenth-century gynaecology and the eighteenth- and nineteenth-century mechanistic attitude to science transposed to the human body. Developments in gynaecology and obstetrics have been made by men, many of whose cultural prejudices are as anachronistically intact as some of their practices. Women obstetricians may have more sisterly feeling for the woman in labour, but they have been trained in male methods in a male-constructed profession. Technological birth has become the norm. In 1991, during a power failure in Dublin, a male newsreader announced with great wonder: 'Woman gave birth without electricity!' The medical establishment has ignored Kitzinger's work, although some hospitals have compromised by allowing women to give birth in a squatting position, but they will not concede that it can be less than very painful.

How often do complications occur, how often is technology necessary? One woman general practitioner says in not more than 5–10 per cent of cases; but she still thought that managed birth was not too much of a price to pay for safety in those cases, that it is better for 90 per cent of women to be denied natural childbirth than for the 5–10 per cent to have trouble. And if, for safety's sake, all women have to be submitted to technological child-birth, then why not make it more intimate and comfortable?

Among feminist theorists only a tiny number admit that childbirth is part of the female sexual cycle, or an important element of female sexuality. In that classic text of feminism *Of Woman Born*, Adrienne Rich categoric-ally accepts the sexuality of childbirth. She describes the biological changes that take place during pregnancy, changes which (as Masters and Johnson recorded) greatly increase the capacity for sexual tension and the frequency and intensity of orgasm. The woman who has given birth, she says, has a biologically increased capacity for genital pleasure, unless her pelvic organs have been damaged obstetrically, as frequently happens. She cites other sources who have recorded the erotic sensations of childbirth and goes on to say that there are strong cultural forces which desexualise women as mothers, and 'the orgasmic sensations felt in child-birth, or while suckling infants have probably until recently been denied even by the women feeling them, or have evoked feelings of guilt.' The culture requires, she says, not merely a suffering mother, but one divested of sexuality.[22]

Adrienne Rich also quotes researcher Alice Rossi: 'Biologically men have only one innate orientation – a sexual one that draws them to women – while women have two innate orientations, sexual toward men and reproductive toward their young',[23] and 'I suspect that the more male dominance characterizes a Western society, the greater is the dissociation between sexuality and maternalism. It is to men's sexual advantage to restrict women's sexual gratification to heterosexual coitus, though the price for a woman and a child may be a less psychologically and physically rewarding relationship.'[24]

Lesley Saunders is another of the few feminist theorists who admits birth into female sexuality. She declares that reproduction – menstruation, pregnancy, birth, breast-feeding, menopause – are clearly the most conspicuous way women differ sexually from men and are an integral part of female sexuality. This is hard to accept, she says, because of the struggle *against* cultural history which said that sex should only be a part of reproduction, and that certain social roles should follow from this. 'We have had to fight,' she says, 'to keep them separate so that we could have sex without becoming childbearers', and avoid becoming the 'monogamous property' of a man.[25]

Dale Spender also took a political view of society's attitude to childbirth and motherhood and the way it had infected feminist thinking. It was not women's maternity that was the problem, she said, but the attitudes, social arrangements and power structures in a society controlled by men. If maternity were valued it could be a basis for women's strength rather than weakness.[26] For this view she has been wrongly dismissed as an essentialist.

Germaine Greer considers childbirth a heroic ideal and blames consumerism for its divorce from sexuality. Sex, she says, is the lubricant of the consumer economy, but in order to fulfil that function its connection with reproduction must be severed, and sexuality, which is a feature of the whole personality, must be localised and controlled.[27]

Because motherhood has been used to suppress women, has, in fact, been a major factor in their oppression, many of the pioneers in the new wave of feminism wanted to deny it, curtail it, excise it from female sexuality. Some women might say it is irrelevant that birthing is sexual and erotic – that the bearing and rearing of children are at any rate oppressive for women. They have a point in the present organisation of such matters. But so many women want to have children, and accept men's terms in order to do so, that it must be included in a feminist agenda. Unless feminists want to keep feminism confined to a tiny select band of women, they must take motherhood and reproduction into account.

Rethinking female sexuality to include the sexuality of birth will mean rethinking what is freedom, liberation and equality: the tactics of feminist politics will need to be revised. Women have had to fight to be allowed pleasure in sexual activity, they are now going to have to fight to be allowed pleasure in pregnancy and childbirth. When the biological desire of women to mother is added to the psychological and social pressures on women to conform to male domination there is an even more powerful cocktail than feminists realise. When women began to take control of their fertility there was a great outcry from patriarchal society. If women took control of their own childbirth, undoubtedly the obstetrics establishment would feel threatened; it might also alienate men still further, unless fathers took an active role in the birthing.

The Great O is an element of sexuality that cannot be taken casually. It is not an orgasm related solely to pleasure: the lesser orgasm, whether it be coital or from masturbation, can be divorced from the price ticket (or reward) of a child to rear, the Great O can not. If women could begin to think about the wholeness of their lives, and see birth not just as a result of sex, but as an event in the unfolding of a diverse sexuality, a sexuality that carries on into motherhood, then they might understand why they continue to have children and submit themselves to exploitative situations.

Why do many feminists fight shy of the sexuality of childbirth? Is it because they also ignore or deny the biological urge of women to have children? Do they think that erotic childbirth would increase the enslavement of women; that women would have larger families and thus copper-fasten them in an exclusive role of child-bearers and carers; that they would embrace their chains because of the pleasure involved? To accept that premise is to define female sexuality in male terms (or the terms in which male sexuality is now defined), in terms of an uncontrollable biological urge. Looking at it empirically, women find erotic pleasure in breast-feeding, yet they do not continue to have serial pregnancies to repeat the pleasure.

12

CULTURAL MOTHERHOOD

The bad press which motherhood has endured in modern feminism started with Simone de Beauvoir, and continued until the 1980s when the new wave of feminists found the biological clock ticking on their own desire for children. But even those personal attitudes to motherhood did not change feminists' unworthy neglect of mothers.

De Beauvoir had a jaundiced view of motherhood, saying that while maternal devotion may be perfectly genuine this is rarely the case. She described maternity as usually a strange mixture of narcissism, altruism, idle day-dreaming, sincerity, bad faith, devotion and cynicism, a brew of behaviour which she held to be the result of the woman's situation. The mother, she held, is almost always a discontented woman, sexually frigid or unsatisfied socially, inferior to man, with no independent grasp on the world or on the future. Maternity, she said, is not a human transcendent act; as mother, woman is immanent and not free.[1] De Beauvoir believed that a woman could not have independence and a career of her own if she had to rear a child, so she herself never gave birth. If she had, she would have written with more understanding of motherhood. However, she started a fashion among feminists which lasted for several decades.

Motherhood as an experience and an institution, says the Finnish sociologist, Tuula Gordon, is a fundamental aspect of women's lives; it is also used to provide an explanation and a justification for the subordination of women.[2] Many serious feminist writers saw women's 'biological destiny' as the cause of their subordination. Juliet Mitchell said: 'Woman's biological destiny as mother becomes a cultural vocation in her role as socialiser of children. In bringing up children, woman achieves her main social definition.'[3] And it is this social definition that feminists regret.

Many of these women had problems with their own mothers, whom they saw as enforcing patriarchy and training their children to do the same.

Patriarchy perceived motherhood as the pinnacle of a woman's life and second-wave feminists, in their iconoclastic way, wanted to knock it down. Nell Myers put it succinctly: 'when you are told that your only real value is as a reproducer and you know that isn't so – what can you do initially, but deny that value as loud as you can in order to create some kind of balance'.[4] Feminists of the 1960s and 1970s were too busy with their liberated sexuality and too absorbed in their idea of androgyny to examine the phenomenon of motherhood, and so they blindly rejected it. It was fun being free like men, fighting battles, having ambitions, sometimes winning and achieving success. In their new fight for equality there were other satisfying options to motherhood.

Betty Friedan lifted the lid off the myth of 'the happy housewife', the fulfilled mother, in the United States in 1963. Later on, in these islands, consciousness-raising produced tale after tale of woe describing the situation in which young mothers found themselves. But there were a few voices of reason during the early 1970s. In 1972 Ann Oakley assumed motherhood as a natural part of a woman's life and pointed out that the fault lay with Western culture, which restricted women to that role alone. She named other societies where women could be mothers and take part in other activities without detriment to their children; it was a matter of social organisation. Adrienne Rich drew attention to the exploitation of mothers, but also to their deep satisfactions and to their sexuality of which their relationship with their children was a part. In *Sex and Destiny*, a classic of the 1980s, Germaine Greer wrote lyrically about the deliciousness of children and the rewards of motherhood in Italian peasant society. Those who blame motherhood for women's oppression are in fact blaming the victim.

Dorothy Dinnerstein and Nancy Chodorow wrote about the way our culture regards motherhood, the way it is organised socially, and the effect this cultural interpretation and organisation has on society. Their work was misinterpreted and turned into an attack on mothers. Dinnerstein and Chodorow said that the psychological problems and misogyny that exist in the world, the subservience of women to men, are caused by the arrangement that confines child-rearing to mothers; but detractors twisted it and accused them of blaming mothers and their child-rearing practices for the oppression of women. Their concept was taken out of context by the media, and the other part of it, the absence of men from child-rearing, was rarely, if ever, alluded to; unfortunately few people read the full texts. In fact, Dinnerstein and Chodorow were blaming fatherhood (or the lack of it).

There is a vast literature, mainly feminist, on the subject of mothers and motherhood – 168 texts listed by feminist academic Ann Snitow.[5] Women are allocated the twin roles of sexual beings and motherhood by our culture, yet one is divorced from the other. Here it is necessary to differentiate between motherhood (the state of being a mother) and mothering (the practice of being a mother). Motherhood is a cultural and psychological condition which is biological to the extent that the child was physically formed from the mother's body. Can mothering be separated from motherhood, or does one consequently follow the other? Is mothering a social and cultural practice, or has it a biological content? If motherhood is part of female sexuality, is mothering also part of it?

Some say that mothering is a patriarchal construct. Others, mainly cultural feminists, maintained that whether or not it is culturally constructed, the caring and nurturing characteristics of mothering are desirable traits. There is no doubt that the cultural arrangements of child-rearing are a set of chains oppressing women. At the same time women continue to choose to become mothers, and are bound to their children with strong ties that resist even the greatest of pressures. It is accepted that the act of giving birth is biological, and I have argued in chapter 11 that it is also sexual. What is subject to dispute is whether mothering has any biological content. Some theorists hold that it has, and others that it is cultural.

Conventional wisdom says that mothering comes naturally to a woman when she gives birth unless she is of 'disturbed mind'. (It may be that two instincts are in conflict in the mind of the woman who rejects mothering: the instinct of self-preservation against the instinct of preservation of the species, and her psyche mediates between the two.) If we go back to basics and look at the other mammals, it is obvious that instinctive mothering exists: the cat, the dog, the rabbit, the fox, even the lowly mouse, indeed all mammals mother their young without social or psychological influences, and they stop mothering after a set period of time. In them, lactation has a definite time limit and hence indicates biological elements (hormones) at work. Indeed lactation and the uterine contractions of breast-feeding are biological with some psychological input; what is the letting down of milk by the lactating woman in response to a hungry child's cry but a physical response to a stimulus which is – what? – an instinct, an emotion, a physical sexuality, a psychological sexuality?

Dinnerstein and Chodorow examined the psychology and psychological effects of mothering, but Dinnerstein also makes room for the biological influences:

> What makes motherhood reliable is that the erotic flow between the child and its female parent is primed by a set of powerful postpartum mechanisms, mechanisms which prime not only women, but also simpler she-mammals, to nurture and protect their young.[6]

She goes on to say that the human female does not necessarily need these biological mechanisms because her intelligence tells her that she must nurture the infant, but her mammalian bodily responses carry for the human mother emotional consequences that they do not carry for the cat or the rat; a mother's body tells her, by letting down milk and contracting at its centre, how passionately she is connected to the infant. (In this century breast-feeding became almost a forgotten function in our society, and many women have never experienced this erotic sensation.) Furthermore, she continues, feeling in a woman is shaped by remembrance and anticipation in a way that it is not in a cat or a rat.

Chodorow does not question the reality of women's biological experiences, but she does question whether there is a biological basis in women for caretaking capacities, whether women *must* perform whatever parenting children need. She is not convinced that women have an instinct for mothering, because, she says, there is not enough evidence, not enough research carried out on either humans or animals, and it is not clear that research on animals can be transposed to humans because of the influence of human intelligence and culture.

The only scientific study which Chodorow could find was carried out on rats and it showed that hormones did control parenting behaviour. Female hormones injected into male rats, and female rats that had never given birth, stimulated maternal behaviour in both. This suggests, she says, that hormones connected to pregnancy, parturition and lactation do contribute to caretaking behaviour in rat mothers; but the effect wore off as time went on and disappeared after six months. It is clear (from observation) that a similar condition exists in other mammals, as they make devoted mothers for a period after the birth of their offspring. The period of dependency is obviously related to the physiological development of the particular species. In humans it is longer than in most other mammals, and the initial biological instinct to mother would, of course, be psychologically and socially developed also into the human relationship of parent love and nurturance. There is no reason why these social and psychological influences should eliminate the initial biological elements of mothering.

These observations on a biological content in mothering are empirical although they could be verified scientifically; the case for a psychological basis for mothering is also empirical and just as capable of proof; but that does not diminish the validity or likelihood of both. Chodorow and other feminists act as if a biological influence would damage the psychological theory. It doesn't, but it does make the whole thing more complex.

The difference between humans and other mammals is intelligence and the psychology it produces; intelligence mediates between biology and human attitudes to it. If, as the psychologists claim, the psychology of the adult person is basically formed in childhood, then the woman who mothers is prey to all kinds of psychological influences: memories of her own childhood and the type of mothering she received; conscious or unconscious recognition that mothering gives her power which she may be denied in her society; a yearning, again conscious or unconscious, for the close and loving relationship which she enjoyed with her own mother and which can be re-created with the baby. If, as the psychoanalysts say, these psychological influences have their genesis in sexuality, then the psychology of mothering is very complex indeed. The social influences are also complex but easier to trace: the identification of the little girl with her own mother, the dolls which were given to her to practise mothering, the status of the mother in the home.

Modern feminist thinking on motherhood does not deny the complex psychology of mothering, but is more inclined to see social and cultural influences as its main driving force; however, it does deny a biological element. Lynne Segal recognised that criticism of motherhood in the early days of the women's movement contributed to a silence over many women's pleasure in having children and their strong desires to find fulfilment through mothering. But she took issue with an exclusively psychological explanation of the phenomenon and did not even contemplate a biological element. Women's mothering capabilities, *when present*, she said, may be primarily their adjustment to social and economic arrangements which require them to do the work of caring for others. Young children, she said, are so attractive and rewarding in their joy and delight in the world, in their dependence, in the great love they offer those who 'mother' them, that they could hardly fail to affect women dramatically. But psychological perspectives, she says, obscure 'the painful reality' of women's actual experience of mothering, which includes stress, isolation and the undermining of personal confidence.[7] In this analysis Segal blames mothering for women's oppression not the system that oppresses mothers which is usually the object of her criticism.

In the same way as giving birth is divorced from sexuality, so mothering is divorced from the physical act of birthing, and for much the same reasons: a feeble attempt to wipe away the image of woman as close to nature and earthy; and an attempt to find reasons for women's oppression that are open to change. Above all, the culture holds that motherhood must be divorced from sexuality, regardless of the eroticism involved in nurturing a child.

The weight of evidence points to a desire among the overwhelming majority of women to have a child. This fact must be examined and taken into account in the formation of strategies in the women's movement. Because women make a very heavy personal and physical investment in children, perhaps a higher level of education among women, a greater degree of opportunity for alternative satisfaction in life will mean that more women will decide not to have children or to have fewer. Yet even feminists have resisted the pressures to make them turn away from motherhood, and those women who postpone childbearing because of their careers, do not regret succumbing to their desire to have a child in their late thirties.

On the other hand, why have we got girls and young women who act like motherhood groupies, and opt out of education to become mothers in order to gain some control over their own lives? They could gain control over their lives through training or education; and they could avoid the responsibilities of motherhood by having protected intercourse. Part of the answer is social and cultural: there is not a culture of education among the young women of the social class which overwhelmingly opts for early/teenage motherhood. Another factor relates to identity: in a culture which values women only as sex objects and mothers, it is the way that these girls/young women become adult and achieve status; they also achieve a measure of power over another human being. But, there is more than culture and psychology involved: hormones are also at work, and for uneducated young women with minimal ambitions there is little cerebral counteraction to the biological urges.

Sheila Rowbotham came to terms with motherhood and mothering when she had a child. In 1989 she wrote an article for *Feminist Review* about the shift in emphasis within the women's movement on the subject of what she called 'the sensuous pleasure of mothering'. She was, however, concerned that women should not go overboard about mothering, either condemning or lauding it. 'To dismiss the delights of mothering denies intense and passionate aspects of women's lives,' she said. 'But to elevate these into an alternative ideal is to deny the negative feelings [of motherhood], to return women to the sphere of reproduction and [to] subordinate childless women to a maternalistic hierarchy.'

If we further examine 'the sensuous pleasure of mothering' we find that some women lose interest in intercourse during pregnancy and after giving birth. The psychoanalysts Therese Benedek and David Winnicot explain that phenomenon by saying that the experience of pregnancy and the anticipation of motherhood often cause a woman to lose interest in 'other primary commitments' (meaning coitus) and to concentrate on her own body and developing child. This 'libidinal' shift, they say, may continue after birth, and gratifications from the nursing relationship may substitute for gratifications formerly found in heterosexual involvements. However, they go on to say that women come to want and need primary relationships with children because they want intense relationships, which men tend not to provide both because of their oedipal relationship to women and because of their difficulties with intimacy.[8]

Writer Lesley Saunders quotes from two research projects on the resumption of coitus after childbirth, which were carried out in 1982. One project reported that almost all of the couples had resumed sexual intercourse six months after giving birth, but many of them were still having difficulties. In the other project, almost all had resumed intercourse by three months, but much less frequently than before the couple became pregnant. A few of them described very marked and persistent reductions in sexuality.[9]

The following were comments made to Saunders by women about sexuality after birth:

> Having intercourse was having something done to me.

> Sex seemed a total invasion of my privacy . . . I just want to continue intact . . . My main physical bond is with my daughter – my breasts are for feeding her and not to be caressed by my husband. I get enough feedback from my children and I don't feel the need to be sexually [meaning genitally] fulfilled.

> Although I often didn't want to make love with my husband, I used to fantasise and masturbate in private.

> I just let him get on with it.

> I had intercourse because I wanted the closeness.

I felt sexual very soon after birth; I felt guilty about that.

Women's reluctance (or tardiness) in resuming sexual relations with their partners after childbirth is common. Judith Bell of the Tavistock Institute in London says that this reluctance has both practical and psychological elements: practical because of the amount of work and attention required of a new mother and hence her exhaustion; psychological because the advent of a new baby evokes in the parents conscious or unconscious memories of their own babyhood and its satisfactions and frustrations. She also says that the amount of intervention which women endure during pregnancy and birth is also a factor, that the return of sexual desire takes longer in women who have had invasive and traumatic pregnancies and deliveries.[10]

In research carried out in England and Finland Tuula Gordon interviewed fifty-two women (who were feminists and also mothers) on motherhood as a subjective experience. The sensuousness of dealing with babies and the pleasure of cuddling children was raised by many of the women, and some regarded these feelings as sexual. The eroticism of breast-feeding was admitted, and a few women said that they had less interest in men after children were born. It was, however, an aspect of motherhood that they believed women did not want to discuss.[11]

There is still a reluctance to associate mothering with sexuality, although the sensuousness of breast-feeding is felt in the contraction of the womb. In common parlance one's 'sex' is one's genitals; but what is more sexual than the womb? If there is a rule which says that the vagina is a sexual organ but the uterus is not, then female orgasm transgresses it.

Breast-feeding which is the most obviously sexual relationship between mother and child is regarded in an ambivalent manner in modern Western society. The La Lèche League advocates breast-feeding, for at least one year and up to two if that is possible, as important for the child's health. African women in general, when not influenced by the manufacturers of baby foods, breast-feed their children for up to two years and sometimes more. Throughout the ages breast-feeding was regarded as a contraceptive method, and research in the last century showed that 75 per cent of women did not conceive while nursing.[12] More recent research has been carried out on the efficacy of breast-feeding as a method of birth control but mainly as ethnographic studies on hunter–gatherer tribes such as the !Kung in the Kalahari Desert. However, it has been established that breast-feeding only works as a contraceptive if the feeding is frequent or on demand, and even then the suppression of the hormones that controls ovulation does not last much beyond a year.

In *Only the Rivers Run Free*, Roisin McDonough, Eileen Fairweather and Melanie McFadyean chronicle the hardships of motherhood in what they called 'The women's war' in Northern Ireland. These were hardships that were related as much to the oppression of women in their relationships with men as to the military war situation. Many of the women were stereotypes of the worst examples of the culturally oppressed: they showed poor self-esteem, were exploited sexually in their teens and married early, and were domestic and sexual slaves in male-headed households where men took little or no interest in family matters and exacted deference to their status as master.

However, among accounts of the remarkable forbearance of women with large families (often up to ten or twelve), and of the battered mothers, sometimes pregnant, who arrived at the Women's Aid shelters, there was one small, shining light of hope. It was Mary's account of her discovery of the sensuality of breast-feeding, and the pride it gave her in her own body. She had ten children and breast-fed most of them. In order to share her experience Mary organised seminars for young women to encourage them, too, to have pride in their bodies. Men regard breasts as purely sexual and for their use, she said, but they don't belong to men, 'they have a wonderful function in life that has nothing whatsoever to do with men, or whether they like a 40-inch bust or a 32'.

In the late 1980s and early 1990s the Western media threatened career women who postponed childbirth with barrenness and grave psychological problems.[13] Those women who postponed childbearing, and who later, as the biological clock ticked on, changed their minds, did not regret their decision. In *Backlash*, Susan Faludi could find no scientific evidence that women have psychological problems by postponing motherhood. She found the evidence presented in the media campaign to be unscientific and deeply prejudiced.

Childless women who have other outlets for their interest are better adjusted than women who have been denied self-expression. On the other hand, women who have been confined to child-rearing and an unpaid servicing role are much more in danger of psychological problems, as was evident in the outpourings of the mothers reporting their tribulations in the consciousness-raising sessions of the early 1970s.

Perhaps the term when applied to motherhood should not be 'sexual' but rather Ann Ferguson's term 'sex/affective', which describes other emotional feelings that are not genital. If we explore the sexuality of motherhood, must we not also explore it in relation to fatherhood, which leads us into the minefield of child sexual abuse. In *The Hite Report on the Family* men were worried about hugging or cuddling their children for fear of sexual arousal on either side. This is because men are culturally conditioned to pass from demonstrations of affection to genital arousal; their definition of sexuality is limited to genitality and therefore taboo where children are concerned. If mothers and fathers are to enjoy an affectionate relationship with their children, then sexuality has got to be redefined, and not solely related to genitality.

Some of the feminist writers, such as Dinnerstein, Chodorow and Irigaray, place a value on a mothering culture which they see as a challenge to male domination, an influence for change in a patriarchal world of cruelty, war and environmental degradation. Others, such as Petra Kelly, Susan Griffin and Adrienne Rich, see the 'peacefulness' of women as a natural given; while there are those who see it as the social context of mothering.

Denying the sexuality of motherhood and mothering, does not advance the liberation of women. Perhaps postponing motherhood in deference to a career does do so, but women who do this, or who decide not to have children, are merely accommodating a work culture that militates against mothers; they are doing nothing to change it.

Are women going to have to give up an essential part of their sexuality in order to gain equality? The great majority of women don't want to, and this is why the women's movement has failed to recruit more than a very small minority to its cause. It is why women in general have not rebelled against their oppression, and why millions still drag their feet on liberation and equality; they take the benefits gained by feminism, but hold on to their motherhood. Feminists who write about the condition of women tend to be intellectual, ambitious, and of strong character. They are certainly not timid or easygoing, and may not appreciate how difficult it is for less forceful women to risk their security and that of their children in order to fight for their liberation.

Instead of liberating women's sexuality, some current feminist thinking has remoulded it to conform with a narrow concept of male sexuality centred on genital sexual activity. Meanwhile, women have continued to rear children in difficult and sometimes dangerous situations because their desire for children is very powerful. They may choose the life and role of the dependent mother and housewife in order to have their children because it is easier than carving out an independent role in a competitive and un-sympathetic society. Given the prevalence of misogyny, it is sometimes easier (and perhaps wiser?) for women to adopt a role which gives them both social acceptance and the satisfaction of their children. If some women opt out of the rat race, maybe it's because the rat race is not a good place for either women or men; maybe some women have other priorities in life.

In 1987 a section of women in the German Green Party issued a Mothers' Manifesto which criticised the direction which feminism was taking. They believed that current feminist policy was chasing a form of equality with men which forced women into a male system of 'time-efficiency and stress, hierarchy and elitism'. They said that usually the areas of work which women entered were then culturally devalued; that women who succeeded in this male world were 'superwomen – childless, neutered androgyns'. These German women wanted feminist policy directed towards equality for 'the 90 per cent of women who do three-quarters of society's labour, ie, all its unpaid reproductive work and one-third of its paid labour for paltry reward'.

This development in German feminism parallels that of the cultural feminists in the United States, and even some socialist feminists, but it encountered a historical hazard. Some saw it as a return to the patriarchal Nazi 'mother cult', in which women were confined to the domestic sphere and banned from male preserves in the workforce. The Mothers' Manifesto, however, had some success, insofar as the German Social Democratic Party in their 1988 policy advocated three years of paid shared parental leave, half of it to be forfeited if not taken by the male partner (see Appendix 3). Due to the vicissitudes of politics and changes in government, that policy never became law.

Female sexuality can be summed up as existing on a broad spectrum and involving biology, psychology and culture. It is not genitally fixated and includes intimacy, birthing and mothering. The female orgasm could perhaps be an important biological aid to birthing. Women's sexuality is nurturing and caring and, because of the bond with children, is protective of life. The majority of women demonstrate these characteristics because the influence of childbearing and rearing is strong. If they do not, it may well be because of some psychological problems.

13

SEX AS SERVICE

The link which exists between gender and sexuality is important because the oppression of women through their sexuality often operates by means of their gender roles. Gender roles include sexual roles, social roles, economic roles and any other female and male roles where there is a designated difference, and they are an important part of identity. In *Women: The Longest Revolution*, Juliet Mitchell says that women are defined and identified in terms of reproduction; that they are objectified and controlled through their sexuality; that they have been assigned the role of socialising children, and again been defined and identified in terms of this role.

If women are oppressed by men because of, and through, their sexuality, how is this manifest, and are they oppressed in all their dealings with men? Women have dealings with men in terms of gender and sexuality, and the main ones can be listed as follows:

in personal relationships
- as daughters, sisters, mothers, wives/partners, within the family;
- as lovers;
- as friends;

in the community
- as workers within the home and in the outside world;
- as women-in-the-street;
- as street-women;
- as images of the opposite sex.

It is clear how violence or abuse such as rape, incest and wife-beating oppress women sexually, but there are other not quite so obvious ways that achieve the same end: marriage, prostitution, pornography, commercialisation of female sexuality, the myth of the male sexual imperative, gynaecology and the culture of childbirth and genital mutilation. Before we examine how women are directly oppressed in their sexual roles, I would like to look briefly at how they are oppressed in their social roles and to see if sexuality has any role in that oppression.

In the social sphere there are barriers to women entering the sectors deemed 'men's work': sometimes trade union or craft restrictions (though in the European Union such practices are against the law), sometimes cultural restraints, often both. Despite equality legislation, women frequently have problems of sexual harassment. In fact, women at work outside the home in any sector are in danger of sexual harassment if they are perceived as rising above their station as sexual object. I once heard a man say of a female colleague, 'Her ambition would frighten you'. Consciously or unconsciously, male culture still to a great extent resents a married woman working outside the home. Men give a variety of reasons for this attitude: in times of high unemployment a woman is taking a job from a man; or, generally, she should be at home minding her children. The desire (even need) of men to feel superior to women is probably closer to the truth.

There are other social roles in which women are oppressed, such as exclusion and segregation in various situations, discrimination in wages, problems with gaining entry to power structures, exclusion from male conversations or from the forums which lead to power.

The most prevalent social role for women is housekeeping and child-rearing – the nurturing and socialising of children. The family, as presently constituted, is the most pervasive way in which women are oppressed through their sexuality. Women are trapped in the unpaid, and often unthanked, job of housekeeping for men and children because of their sexuality; because they 'fell in love' with a man, or wanted children, or both.

Marriage, or some form of association between a woman and a man with the object of producing children, is part of every culture. There are various teleological theories about the origins of 'pair bonding', which attempt to give a plausible reason for the development of present-day marriage. However, marriage and the family, as now constituted, are a part of social, not biological, evolution; and human sexuality has been moulded and shaped psychologically and culturally to promote and benefit both.

Culture has prescribed woman's right to exercise her sexuality only in marriage or a partnership relationship with a man for whom she is then required physically to maintain a home. (In recent years some cultural changes in this respect have taken place.) Her role in the family, although

changing to some degree in Western society, still retains the basic assumptions of the patriarchal family: that the woman will rear the children, provide personal service to the family, sexual service to her partner, and do the
housework. 'Patriarchy's chief institution is the family,' said Kate Millett in
Sexual Politics. 'Traditionally, patriarchy granted the father virtually total
ownership over wife or wives and children, including the powers of physical abuse and often even those of murder and sale.' Women were bought or
sold into marriage by the males of their families, and although they worked
for their new families and were the coinage of alliances between clans or
families, they were also bought for their unsullied virginity and their
child-bearing ability – in other words, for their sexuality; and they could
be divorced for infertility.

Socialist feminists who have been influenced by Marx say that women's
work in the home (the biological and social production of bearing and
rearing children, and of domestic labour) supports an economic, social and
political order dominated by men, while at the same time preventing
women from participating directly in that order. There is no real reason
why women should be the sole nurturers of children, and there are very
good reasons why fathers, who share a common interest with mothers in
their progeny, should participate in the task, as Dorothy Dinnerstein and
Nancy Chodorow pointed out. Women can breast-feed and still *share* the
nurturing of children with a partner, yet only in a tiny minority of cases is
provision made in the outside world of work for men to take part in that
role, through paternity leave, work-sharing and other types of reorganisa-
tion of the workplace. There is also no real reason why wives should suffer
enforced economic dependence; the work which they do is valuable and
they should be entitled, *as of right*, to a proportion of the family income if
no other adequate provision is made to pay women for housework and
child-rearing.

Although the rearing of children is regarded as highly important in
human society, yet with schizophrenic illogicality the job has a low status:
a mother rearing children is unpaid if she has a male partner, and has a lower
status than the father of the children who works outside the home; a woman
employed to rear children is also regarded as having a low status and is paid
accordingly. Rearing children is as difficult and stressful as any job done by
a man, yet it is dismissed and made invisible. For the great majority of
women it is rewarded by mere subsistence, low status, and they are rarely
praised for their efforts but frequently blamed. And while a mother derives

great satisfactions from this job, she is deprived of other opportunities in life because of it; principally she is allotted the role of homemaker.

Historically women became homemakers when they developed agriculture and were the preparers of food for their children. Later, in settled societies the task of keeping the cave, the hut or the house habitable also devolved on them. From these primitive roots, this archaic division of labour, the role of women as housekeepers, and the providers of personal service to men, continues into modern times. Why? Because it is pleasant for men, and a considerable advantage, to enjoy such personal service, one which John Stuart Mill called being 'the personal servant of a despot'; but also because it became 'women's work' and has therefore been considered inferior.

The idea that modern marriage is a trade in sexuality (sexual service for subsistence) was recognised by many of the foremothers of feminism (Mary Astell, Mary Wollestonecraft, Anna Wheeler, Harriet Taylor, Barbara Leigh Smith, et cetera). Mary Wollestonecraft was the first to apply the term 'legal prostitution' to marriage. Forgotten women of a century ago, like Elizabeth Wolstenholme, Lucinda Chandler and many others, railed against the legalised, sexual slavery of marriage as then constituted, and only in recent years have some of the reforms which they sought been instituted. In 1909, during the first wave of feminism in this century, Cicely Hamilton wrote *Marriage as a Trade*. She looked at 'love, honour and obey' from the unromantic angle of what the contract meant; and it meant that the husband supported the wife in exchange for 'conjugal rights': sexual and other services.

Women are still defined by the family and, within the family, by their relationship to the men of the group: mothers, wives, daughters. Outside the family they are known by their father's or husband's surnames. The principal relationship between men and women is sexual, and although attitudes are changing, a woman is still defined as wife and having sexual relations with one man (good); and as slag or prostitute and having sexual relations with many (bad). There is no comparable definition for men.

Since the nineteenth century women in these islands have struggled to escape link by link the net of legal disablement inflicted on them by marriage, in which they were the property of husbands and had neither property rights of their own nor the right to leave. Women's rights in marriage came dripping slow, and some were established only in recent decades.[1] Marriage reform arrived in most Western countries during the same period.

In the present wave of feminism many women attacked marriage as servitude for women, despite the more liberal laws enacted in the past hundred years. They were concerned about women's economic dependence, their legal situation in the case of property rights, and control of their own fertility. Although the laws concerning the freedom of married women might have changed, men's attitudes have not always changed. The culture which the Western world had inherited was deeply rooted; a hundred years is short in the context of four millennia. Culture resisted the spirit of the laws and women had to pursue their rights aggressively if they were to claim them. Many did not (and do not) because of the threat to their economic security and that of their children.

Arranged marriages traditional to most societies are an exploitation and oppression of women's sexuality because the woman had no say in the matter; and even if the man had no say, he was still master of his wife. Arranged marriages have reappeared in Europe, particularly in Germany, France and Switzerland, originally with brides bought from their families in poor regions of South East Asia. Since the fall of state socialism in Eastern Europe, the marriage agencies (some three thousand in Germany) have switched to importing women from Poland and other former Eastern bloc countries. They find buyers among retired, divorced and less well-off men, who find it difficult in their own country to get a bed-and-kitchen woman who is uninfected with ideas about 'freedom and rights'. Unlike their Asian sisters, European women make the decision freely to become involved in these arranged marriages. Nevertheless, it is sexual exploitation because the agencies advertise the women's sexual attributes ('super-sexy', 'extremely full bosom', et cetera). It is not known, the reports say, how many of these women end up in prostitution.[2]

There are two aspects to female sexuality: the acceptable one of the 'non-sexual' mother, and the problematic one of the sexually unattached, non-mother; and they are linked by the role of wife (or sexual partner). Men have problems with both: in chapter 6 I show how Dorothy Dinnerstein explains how men keep the mother 'non-sexual' by separating tenderness and lust, and they cope with the sexuality of the unattached woman by making her a sexual object in several different ways. (In chapter 15 John Stoltenberg explains how sexual objectification works.) In more permissive societies these two categories can overlap, and female sexual partners may not escape from objectification by other men, particularly where they evade the legal restrictions of marriage. Woman as sexual object has been around for a long time. One of the most powerful influences on our culture is the Bible, and it defines women in terms of their sexuality; in the Bible, and indeed in the other ancient writings, the emphasis is laid on fertility.

Sexuality deserves and has a right to dignity. Men are seriously upset when theirs is not given due respect; however women's sexuality is constantly attacked and denigrated, and publicly deprived of dignity. Commercialisation of female sexuality proliferated into a mass market since the Second World War when *laissez faire* capitalism set out to corral another area of profit. It ranges from the use of women in sexually titillating advertisements, to prostitution and sexual slavery; in between are found women in commercial and social situations (un)dressed for male titillation; stage shows and films of scantily dressed women; soft-porn magazines, films and videos; strip shows, and hard-core pornography. The most obvious sexual exploitation of women is prostitution; the prostitute is the outlaw of female sexuality.

PROSTITUTION

Some people might see prostitution as separate from the general question of equality for women, and of no relevance to the rest of womankind. But if women must use their sexuality, in the various ways allowed or imposed, to survive in a male-dominated world, and if the bottom of the pit is prostitution, then it is relevant.

Prostitution does not appear on any employment statistics, and only in countries where it is legalised do prostitutes pay taxes. It is known as the oldest profession because men in early cultures classified women of independent sexuality as prostitutes, and then made outcasts of them. The result was the institution of female prostitution, in which women were paid for sexual intercourse but stigmatised and despised for doing so. Brothels are recorded as early as the sixth century B.C., and were used by some ancient states as a source of taxation. At times even up to the fifteenth century attempts were made to force prostitutes to adopt a distinctive dress that would identify them from other women; and at all times they were subjected to violence.

Augustine in the fourth to fifth century put the Christian seal on prostitution, seeing it as a necessary evil: 'remove prostitutes from human affairs and you will pollute all things with lust; set them among honest

matrons, and you will dishonour all things with disgrace and turpitude.'
Thomas Acquinas echoed him in the thirteenth century:

> prostitution in the world is like the filth in the sea or the sewer in the
> palace. Take away the sewer and you will fill the palace with pollution
> ... Take away prostitutes from the world and you will fill it with
> sodomy ... whereas Augustine says ... that the earthly city has made the
> use of harlots a lawful immorality.[3]

Both of these sexual neurotics obviously had a poor opinion of men's self-control.

Mary Daly commented that, in this case, it was only the virtue of 'good' women that was being safeguarded, not the virtue of men or prostitutes. Slave women, however, were never condemned for having sexual relations with their masters, only for trying to influence them because of it.[4]

The situation has not changed. Women are still divided by our culture into 'respectable' women and prostitutes: a neat division that puts one set of women in condemnation of the other and in fear of becoming the other. Meanwhile, some feminist commentators will say of our intersexual arrangements that 'respectable' women sell themselves sexually to one man rather than many. In *Female Sexual Slavery*, Kathleen Barry says that both pimps and husbands make women feel dependent and fearful that they couldn't survive alone; and both separate the woman from her previous life. It is true that a very large number of husbands try to control their wives (and succeed); and if there are many prostitutes that find themselves unable to break away from their pimps, there are also many wives who fear to leave their husbands.

Men have always been equivocal about prostitution: they constitute the demand for it, yet they condemn and persecute the suppliers; they make prostitution a crime for the woman and at the same time regulate it. Surveys carried out in Britain suggest that for every woman involved in prostitution there are at least twenty times the number of men involved as clients.[5]

Historically, and overwhelmingly, women have become prostitutes because they were forced to do so through economic necessity. In more recent times and particularly in the last century much of the supply came from women servants who bore illegitimate children. When below-stairs maidservants became pregnant, they were sacked, despite the fact that they were usually pregnant by one of the males of the household. When the unfortunate young mother could not find other work she was forced into prostitution to support herself and her child. As far back as the eighteenth century, Mary Wollestonecraft pointed out that necessity never drove men to prostitution (although the situation has changed for young, homeless men in modern times). In *The Second Sex*, Simone de Beauvoir gives a catalogue of prostitutes' deplorable conditions in France even in this century, and it is echoed by other writers for other countries.[6] A nineteenth-century English prostitute described it thus:

It is men, men, and only men from the first to the last that we have to do with! To please a man I did wrong at first, then I was flung about from man to man. Men police lay hands on us. By men we are examined, handled, doctored, and messed on with. In the hospital it is a man again who makes prayers and reads the Bible to us. We are had up before magistrates who are men, and we never get out of the hands of men until we die.[7]

Towards the end of the nineteenth century feminists in the social purity movements saw the prostitute as an exploited woman, victim of the notorious double standard of sexual morality because of her economic position, and they sought to stop the trade by enjoining chastity on men. Not all advocates of social purity were so sympathetic, and many spent much energy trying to reform the women.

In many European countries, under the Napoleonic Code of Law, prostitution was legalised in brothels from the early nineteenth century. France had a system of registration of prostitutes and weekly medical examinations. In Great Britain and Ireland the Contagious Diseases Acts of the 1860s virtually legalised prostitution by forcing any woman suspected of being a prostitute to be medically examined, and thereafter, unless her hymen was broken during the examination, she was deemed a prostitute. The Acts were enacted in an effort to curb the spread of venereal diseases, but as only women were examined, they were futile for that purpose. Josephine Butler and the Ladies' National Association Against the Contagious Diseases Laws campaigned for the repeal of the Acts from 1869 to 1886 when they finally won. They were called prudes and moral custodians, but, in Margaret Forster's words, Josephine Butler 'kicked the "double standard" in its most private parts and was hated and despised for doing so'.[8]

In Western Europe, regulation of prostitution in order to control venereal disease ceased shortly after the First World War, and feminist campaigns related to it also ceased. Further east, after the revolution in Russia, Alexandra Kollontai saw prostitution as a social evil caused by 'low wages, social inequalities, the economic dependence of women on men, and the unhealthy custom by which women expect to be supported in return for sexual favours instead of in return for their labour.'[9] In China prostitution was prohibited by the Communist Revolution of 1948, but that does not mean that it disappeared completely from the cities. Crowded living conditions and communal living, however, made it difficult.

A 1981 worldwide survey in developed, developing and underdeveloped countries, found that the overwhelming majority of women who became prostitutes, either temporarily or permanently, did so because of economic necessity, and the great majority died young.[10] Social researcher Eileen McLeod says that there is no way of estimating the real incidence of prostitution in Britain because so many women move into it and out of it when need occurs. Most women, she says, go 'on the game' because of the difficulty of living on low wages or social security payments and to provide money for the needs of children. Some do it because it pays better than other employment open to them and because they want nice clothes, perhaps travel and a good standard of living. According to the survey, at times prostitution did indeed pay better than other work available to women, but in bad economic times the number of women who 'took to the streets' increased, and their individual earnings came down. Prostitution has soared in Moscow since the arrival of the market economy, rising prices, low wages and unemployment. The failure of the Cuban revolution, as current reports would indicate, since the fall of the Soviet Union, has also seen prostitution return to Havana because of 'serious unemployment'. Prostitution continues because men are always prepared to pay more than the prevailing wage for women in order to retain it. If the prevailing wage is zero, then they pay a low rate. They always pay just what will generate and guarantee a supply of women: the law of supply and demand has always operated in the oldest profession.

According to a report produced by the Women's Rights Project and Asia Watch of New York in 1993, ten thousand Burmese women are recruited for work and brought into Thailand every year and then sold to brothels. The report said that thirty thousand Burmese women are living in sexual slavery there until they repay their purchase price from their meagre tips. In 1990 it was estimated that between five and eight thousand women were working in Bangkok in illegal prostitution. Girls from poor families in Brazil, some as young as nine, are offered well-paid jobs in the gold mining areas and are then sold to brothels, where they must work to pay off their plane fare, food and lodging. They are auctioned as virgin prostitutes to the highest bidders who call them 'fresh meat'.[11]

It is a moot point whether prostitution was more prevalent in the nineteenth century than it is today, but the shape and form of prostitution and traffic in women has changed in recent years. It has become internationalised; and where once large cities were the locations of prostitution, now South East Asia has become a 'sex-holiday' destination. The withdrawal of American military from Korea and Vietnam left a surplus of prostitutes in the region; and to add to the number, poor families, particularly in the countryside, sell their daughters to pimps and brothels in the cities.

All armies, wherever they are deployed, have arrangements for brothels and other sexual leisure activities. During the Second World War, the Japanese government provided an 'army' of 'comfort women' two hundred thousand strong from the various occupied territories for sexual service to the army. After the war, the Japanese government assigned thirteen thousand women as public prostitutes to the occupying American army. In 1994 the current Japanese administration finally apologised to the surviving women and offered them a fund of 100 billion yen (Ir £7 million) for cultural and educational programmes in atonement. In Mozambique, where prostitution is illegal and the age of consent is twenty-one, United Nations troops were 'buying sex from hundreds of girls, some as young as twelve' in 1994. During the 1991–2 deployment of United Nations troops in Cambodia, the prostitute population increased from six thousand to twenty thousand and there was a sharp rise in child prostitution. These troops 'helped put Cambodia on the map in regard to trafficking in women', stated a report in the *International Children's Rights Monitor*, 'just as US soldiers had done for Saigon, the Philippines and Bangkok during the Vietnam war'.[12] In the Philippines, where prostitution is nominally illegal, 'sex tours' are a recognised part of tourism.

Robin Morgan told of her visit to the Philippines in 1988 with a delegation from the Sisterhood Is Global Institute, on the invitation of some of the women's groups there.[13] She described the town of Olongapo which was the 'rest and recreation' centre for the United States Navy's Seventh Fleet, then based at Subic Bay, but also advertised in tourist brochures as 'the fun city of the Philippines'. The town's business, worth an annual 500 million US dollars, was prostitution, with street after street of bars, pubs, pornography shops and movie houses, massage parlors, nightclubs, dancehalls, display arenas where women box and wrestle nude, and 'hospitality hotels'. Most of the 'smiling, empty-eyed women who line the streets, lounge in the doorways, and perch on the bar stools' were teenagers, some children as young as nine and ten who were third- or fourth-generation prostitutes. In the back streets, Morgan reported, wo- men's organisations provide shelters for these women when they are battered for trying to run away from pimps, bar proprietors, or brothel owners; they run clinics for them when they sicken, and hospices for them when they are dying of untreated venereal disease or from AIDS.[14] The Irish Columban Father Shay Cullen fought against this illegal trade in women in the Philippines, and interceded in vain with the United States army com- mander to prevent American soldiers from co-operating with it. He was later jailed by the Philippines authorities for his efforts.[15]

Since the 1970s and the rebirth of the women's movement, feminists have changed their attitude to prostitutes, or sex workers, as they are now called. In general they have not become involved in the struggles of prostitutes for status and equality, but they have ceased to regard them as outcasts to be saved, and look on them now as women exploited under a common patriarchy. Prostitutes have organised in many countries,[16] and many of these organised groups want to shake off the label of victim and be rec- ognised as workers, because, they say, like most people, they don't have much choice in the kind of work they do. They resent those who try to 'reform' them, and, like all trade unionists, they don't want to see their job abolished. Like the pro-pornography lobbies, they accuse those feminists who see them as exploited victims of aligning themselves with right-wing fundamentalists.

While tacitly admitting that they don't have much choice, and undoubtedly because they see great demand for their services, these prostitute groups have convinced themselves that they are not exploited, that what they need is the respect, freedom and rights accorded to other workers. They see their work as a 'career choice' and campaign for de- criminalisation and the equal rights and status of sex workers; but they ignore the limitations placed on women's choices and the reasons for those limitations. 'If a woman faces poverty, hunger, sexual abuse, homelessness, inaccessible education, unobtainable medical treatment, or inadequate funds for child care,' says researcher Jane Anthony, 'her possibilities of establishing herself in mainstream culture, or merely surviving, are well beyond the traditional concept of "choice".' Anthony defines prostitution as a victimisation of women with 'the very concrete risks of physical harm', and she emphasises the psychological trauma of 'having one's most private self routinely entered by one stranger after the next, day after day, week after week'.[17]

In *The Sceptical Feminist*, philosopher Janet Radcliffe Richards makes a case for the social acceptance (particularly by feminists) of the sexual services industry. Why should sexual services, providing pleasure for men, she asks, be different from, say, the services of a nurse, or the service provided by a musician whose ability to provide a service is the only aspect of her in which the client is interested? The degradation of women which surrounds prostitution or stripping, or beauty contests, she claims, lies in the surrounding circumstances and not in the act itself: in the public contempt for the activity, in women being forced into these activities through economic circumstances, and because they must suffer endless degradations because of their weak position. There are weaknesses in her arguments because the 'surrounding circumstances' she mentions are inseparable from prostitution. And she takes no account of another factor, personal bodily integrity, which is of basic importance to an individual.

Other feminists want to see prostitution abolished because it is a crime against women, not a crime committed by women. They want legal action against pimps and clients, not against the women they exploit. But, in general, the feminist movement has done very little about prostitution. In more than fifteen years of *Feminist Review*, the distinguished British publication, it has received no more than a passing reference.

In an article called 'Confronting liberal lies about prostitution', Evelina Giobbe of WHISPER[18] wrote, 'dismantling the institution of prostitution is the most formidable task facing contemporary feminism'.[19] It is a patriarchal institution that has been around for millennia, and it has resisted all efforts to be abolished because men, who have the power, have not the will to do so. For instance, the 1958 Merlin Law in Italy was meant to help women out of prostitution by prohibiting the keeping of records on them by the police or health authorities. It did not regulate prostitution but outlawed the making of profit from it by abolishing brothels; it also made it a crime to invite anyone to 'libertinism in a scandalous or molesting manner'; this applied to both prostitute *and* client. In fact, the Merlin Law was never implemented in the way in which it was intended. Few cases were brought against brothel keepers, and then only the names of the women, not those of the clients, were published. Women could not set up a legitimate business for five years after giving up prostitution, and could not get a driver's licence because they did not have a certificate of 'good conduct' from the police.[20] Laws governing prostitution are more honoured in the breach than in the observance in almost every country in the world.

United Nations concern about prostitution which started with the 1949 Convention for the Suppression in the Traffic in Persons and the Exploitation of the Prostitution of Others has moved at a snail's pace; less than half the countries of the world have signed and ratified the convention. Ireland and the United Kingdom (in company with the notorious South East Asian countries of Thailand, Indonesia and the Philippines) have not signed it. In Europe, Ireland and the United Kingdom are joined by the Catholic countries of Austria, Greece, Malta and Monaco in sitting on their hands (the Vatican City, also, has not signed); although the other Catholic countries, Spain, Portugal, France and Italy have ratified it, as well as Germany. However, ratified or not, the convention does not seem to have had any effect. There is no record of any action taken against any country or person for contravention of the convention; traffic in women and prostitution as an industry does not seem to concern United Nations member states or world leaders.

In 1983, again prostitution was identified in a United Nations report as a form of slavery, yet nothing further was done until 1991 when the Coalition Against Trafficking in Women (a United Nations Non-governmental Organisation) and the United Nations Educational, Scientific and Cultural Organisation (UNESCO) proposed another United Nations Convention Against Sexual Exploitation. Nothing has been heard of the initiative since then.

Men make the laws and then cause them to be broken. They make laws that penalise women for prostitution, yet rarely blame men. Only in recent decades have certain aspects of men's role in female prostitution been declared illegal. In 1993 the Irish Dáil passed the Criminal Law (Sexual Offences) Act, introduced by Minister for Justice, Máire Geoghegan-Quinn, in which 'soliciting' as a criminal offence applied to the client as well as to the prostitute. Prostitution is not illegal in Britain, only many of the activities related to it, such as soliciting on the street, living off immoral earnings, keeping a brothel, and, if a woman is designated as a common prostitute, just walking in an area known for prostitution; and the law against kerb-crawling criminalises the male clients as well as the women.

In the last century it was control of venereal diseases that prompted the regulation of prostitutes; in this century it is AIDS. Prostitutes protest that above all others they practise safe sex, unless coerced; but as Cheryl Overs of the International Committee on Prostitutes' Rights admits, it is often impossible for them to insist on safer sex and use condoms because, ultimately, the power lies with the client.[21] In the fight against AIDS some prostitute rights groups have been state-funded to carry out health education projects on their clients.[22]

In recent times it has emerged that a large number of prostitutes in Western society have been sexually abused as children; in their damaged self-image they believe that they have only a sexual value. Before the wholesale revelations of child sex abuse in the 1980s and 1990s, Kate Millett wrote in *Sexual Politics*:

> Prostitution, when unmotivated by economic need, might well be de-
> fined as a species of psychological addiction, built on self-hatred through
> repetitions of the act of sale through which the whore is defined.

14

AN OPPRESSIVE CULTURE

The written word is an important way in which the subordination of women is perpetuated, mainly by making her invisible. The history of men's warfaring culture has been preserved; military and political history get priority in the annals of our species. The disruption and destruction of life, both social and personal, through wars and power struggles, has been made important by men. The preservation of life and the social fabric, which has been mainly the job of women, has been ignored. Women's history is called 'social', downgraded and not recorded, except in uncons-tructed ways.

The male-controlled media, particularly film and television, play a significant part in the perpetuation of unfavourable male attitudes towards women. Media images work in two ways: by reflecting the culture, and by reinforcing it. Pornography (which will be discussed in chapter 15 in the context of male sexuality) is the most extreme form of the sexual oppres-sion of women in the media, but there are other pervasive and insidious ways in which women are debased.

In *Backlash*, Susan Faludi examined some fifty films that were box-office successes in the years 1987-90, in which women were attacked through their sexuality. Career women were portrayed either as predatory 'bitches', both professionally and socially, and as embittered women who either could not get a man, were missing out on having children, or if they had children, they neglected them. The 'nice' women were bland and contented house-wives and mothers. The message was clear: careers were bad for women. Faludi details the scripts that were changed and the directors that were hired to ensure that these were the messages that went out. During that same time, male macho films portrayed men in 'the escalating violence of an endless stream of war and action movies'.[1]

Faludi applied the same scrutiny to television drama series, with similar

result. One of the television series that she researched was the police drama
Cagney and Lacey. Scriptwriters Barbara Corday and Barbara Avedon took
six years to sell the idea to a television company. The idea was rejected
because they said that the women leads were too tough, not feminine or
soft enough, used 'dirty' language ('damn' and 'hell'). *Cagney and Lacey* was
first piloted by CBS as a television feature film in 1981 and was a smash hit, so
the network agreed to do a series, but they continually tried to change the
character of the two women, particularly the single woman, Cagney,
played by Sharon Gless, to make her more feminine and less assertive.
Feminist issues in the series were restricted or censored. It was taken off in
1983, but due to pressure from fans and an Emmy award for Tyne Daly
(Lacey) it was put back on the air. In 1987, despite high ratings, it was
moved to a 'doomed' slot and finally killed. A salutary tale, because
financial success did not save the series from male prejudice.[2]

Faludi also cited a 1987 European Commission report on images of
women in television programmes in EC countries. The researchers studied
twenty-nine episodes of series or serials (including fifteen British pro-
ductions) and found that two-thirds of the female characters were shown
in family roles and only one-sixth at work outside the home; one-third of
female characters were cast in romantic roles compared to only one in fifteen
of the men. This situation arises, no doubt, because the vast majority of
scriptwriters for all television series are men. A cursory examination of
cinema and television today reveals the same situation.[3]

The cinema and video industries are largely constructed on sexual arousal;
the decision makers are male, the ethos is that of male sexuality; the eye
behind the camera is male. As Professor of film Ann Kaplan says, the gaze
is male; dominant (Hollywood) cinema is constructed according to, and
reflects, a patriarchal vision, using phallocentric language and fantasy. Real
women are not portrayed in these films.[4] In most films the frenetic rutting
of male sexual activity is preferred to gentle eroticism.

In the print media, feminism and feminist issues peaked in the seventies,
but the eighties brought the backlash. This happened partly because the
media became bored with long-running stories and situations, and with
'whingeing' women. Stirring up controversy sells copies; 'post-feminism'
and looking at the 'excesses' of feminism made 'news'. But what often
seemed a concerted drive in media editorial to get women out of the
work-place and back into the home was much too dedicated to be
attributed solely to boredom with the women's movement. It is tempting

to say that those whose hands were on the levers of power and control in the media found that they could call a halt to assertive women. Or were they merely trying to get women into the shopping centres? Advertising makes use of the sexual object and the housewife. In a 1992 issue of *Cosmopolitan* an article by a former advertising executive decried the downgraded image of women portrayed in television advertisements.[5] The article described the early days of television commercials when there were only three inter-pretations of woman's place – by the stove, in the lavatory or out shop-ping. The agency jargon used for these advertisements was '2 Cs in a K' (two cunts in a kitchen). This 'male idea of a woman' continued into the nineties until, according to the author, the C in the K turned into the 'dragon in the supermarket' who was unimpressed with the advertising. In a 1990s report of the (British) Broadcasting Standards Council, only 16 per cent of the women shown in television commercials were represented as in some paid employment. The *Cosmopolitan* article did not, however, deal with the use of women's sexual parts to sell goods, and that particular issue was packed with advertisements that featured women's bums and crotches, or had the camera focused on their headless bodies.

We tacitly accept advertisements that insult women as intelligent beings, and in our 'beauty-conscious' world we don't often look behind the façade of cosmetics and clothing fashions to the real meaning of the messages they convey: cosmetics that superimpose a doll's face, suggesting a plaything; and clothes that draw attention to 'boobs' and 'butt'. Female brains are not 'sexy' but legs are. In *I am Mary Dunne*, Brian Moore has his eponymous heroine in self-critical mood, hating 'this sickening female role playing, the silly degradation of playing pander and whore in the presentation of my face and figure in a man's world'.

The 'feminisation' of women by various fashions is little different in intent from the various mutilations that have been practised on women, and suggest a belief that only a mutilated woman is 100 per cent feminine. Fashions change in the ways they are used to oppress women through their sexuality. We are horrified now to hear of the foot-binding of women in pre-revolutionary China to make them more attractive to men. We cannot understand the eroticism associated with the resulting deformed feet, yet women in our society gladly squeeze their feet into restricting shoes and wear high heels to make their feet and their walk sexy to men. Foot-binding and high heels are all part of a rather deviant form of the eroticisation of domination, in this case the restriction of women's physical movement. High-heeled shoes may not be as drastic as foot-binding, but they restrict movement, cause foot and spinal injuries; Western tight skirts and Japanese narrow kimonos also hobble women; the ridiculous distortions of so much *haute couture* are insulting to women's intelligence;[6] and obsession with body shape is often neurotic and injurious to health.

The commercialisation of male sexuality, until recently confined to cinema and the popular music industry, has begun. The liberation of male homosexual culture has opened up a new sector of saleable sexuality. But the perception of male sexuality in advertisements is subtly different: men wear their sexuality as a badge of dominance and glory, and they are accorded the place in society that they claim. Women may try to wear theirs in the same way, but because it is regarded as a subordinate sexuality, they are not admired for it. The male sexuality in the advertisement is there to dominate; the female sexuality to be dominated.

As we have seen in the earlier portion of this book, our culture has led men to consider themselves sexually superior to women. The totem of their domination and claimed superiority is 'the phallus', the symbolic image of the penis. They 'erect' representations of it in their environment from the round towers of ancient Ireland to the minarets of Muslim countries. They play with 'toys' that represent it: swords, guns, cars, et cetera (remember Saddam Hussein's supergun?). Although the 'obey' clause is gone from the Christian marriage ceremony in most countries, there are few marriages where the husband does not tacitly believe that he has conjugal rights which entitle him to regular and frequent sexual genital service on demand.

The myth of the male sexual imperative (that men's sexuality is compulsive and arousal is beyond their control), and its concomitant that men have a right to women, is a strong belief in our culture. Therefore women are advised to be careful not to arouse men, and to keep their own sexuality under control, hidden or suppressed, unless they intend to have sexual relations with them. They should not wear clothes which are considered titillating, or walk in a way that might be construed as sexually suggestive, or walk in certain places, or at certain times.

Women, too, can have urgent sexual feelings, yet the culture *prevents* them from leaping on a man to satisfy them, or even *expecting* a man to satisfy them. The myth of female 'frigidity', or at least that these sexual feelings are less demanding in women, is also part of the culture. Yet women were genitally mutilated not so long ago in our society to prevent them obtaining sexual satisfaction by masturbation; it was the prerogative of men to satisfy women's sexuality.

And some of them are not doing a good job. The position which couples adopt during sexual intercourse became an issue for the newly liberated feminists of the 1970s. The missionary position is the one approved by the Christian Churches for sexual intercourse, and validated by what they call 'natural law'. Artemidorus, a second-century-A.D. writer on matters sexual, declared it the only position according to nature.[7] A French sexologist, confusing cultural traditions with the laws of nature, wrote in the nineteenth century that the man lying on the woman was the natural and instinctive position for sexual intercourse; that 'the peculiar fancy that some wives occasionally experience to take the husband's place disturbs the natural order'.

This commandment has been challenged since the sexual revolution, mainly by women who found in it a symbol of male domination, an arrangement which, if used invariably, kept the woman passive and the man dominant. More significantly, they found that it was not just undemocratic, but a position unfavourable to female orgasm.

That was in the early 1970s in the United States, and I am sure that the situation regarding female orgasm has changed dramatically there since then because so much has been written on the subject. But has it changed in Ireland for other than an informed few, or indeed in Britain? The question about frequency of female orgasm has not been asked in Ireland, and the researchers in the 1994 British survey were coy about posing it. They considered a generalised statement ('Sex without orgasm cannot be really satisfying for a woman', with a list of response options) to be 'less intrusive'. The response was surprising: only 28.6 per cent of women agreed that orgasm was necessary for satisfaction. (Even more surprising, less than half of the men agreed that orgasm was necessary for their sexual satisfaction.) The statement is open to ambiguity, and the responses could mean that women also enjoy sexual activity for other reasons, such as closeness, pleasing a man they love, or whatever. However, it might also be reasonable to deduce that despite the advice in sex manuals and women's journals, women are not achieving orgasm to anything like the extent that might be expected. It would be interesting to know if these women are using the missionary position. If so, then the exclusive use of the missionary position denies women their full sexuality.

Absence of orgasm is not the only reason why women were accused of being frigid; the term is also and more commonly applied to them for reluctance to engage in frequent sexual intercourse. Shere Hite says that women feel exploited sexually, because sexual intercourse provides efficiently for male orgasm, and inefficiently and irregularly for female orgasm, also a man's right to intercourse with his wife on demand symbolises female subservience, or of being owned. Many women's resistance, far from being negative, she says, can be seen as a healthy resistance to being dominated, and to their bodies being owned. In addition, if women believe that men think of them as second class, and value them only as 'helpmates' and sexual partners, this is likely to lead to emotional alienation within the relationship; sex can be their only source of power.[8] On the other hand, perhaps women's less frequent desire for coitus represents a more integrated form of human sexuality that keeps in balance its biological, psychological and cultural constituents. Perhaps female, not male, sexuality is the norm.

If the missionary position is being deposed from the throne of orthodoxy, what about current sexual practices; are some of them oppressive to women? For a 'prudish' world the sexual revolution legitimised sexual practices that had been around for millennia, yet were overtly considered unacceptable in most societies. In examining the role of these practices in the exploitation of women, we must differentiate between those that are part of a sexual culture and those that belong to the basic biology of reproduction.

The most obvious oppressive practice is matter-of-course coitus as a leisure pursuit, de rigueur genital intercourse in heterosexual encounters between women and men; what Camille Paglia put so succinctly when she said: If a woman agrees to accompany a man, she is agreeing to sexual intercourse.[9] There is a widespread, but tentative, feeling among women (feminists and others) that encounters with men should not always be, by definition, sexual; that sexual encounters should not always mean genital penetration, and that there are other satisfying forms of sexual activity. This feeling emerges here and there in the literature, but particularly in the Hite reports. In The Hite Report on Male Sexuality, the impression given by respondents was that intercourse was almost the only way in which men felt free to show emotion or their need for love without being seen as 'weak' or a 'sissy' (see chapters 15 and 16 on male sexuality). Hite summed up by saying that

without the accompanying cultural symbolism and pressures intercourse
would become a matter of choice during sexual activities, not the *sine qua
non*, the denouement towards which all sexual activities move ... Sex[ual
activity] does not always have to include intercourse, and [it] would be
much freer if intercourse were not always its focus.

Cultural prohibitions against anal and oral sexual penetration, which
existed until comparatively recently, have diminished, but not as quickly
or as completely as the injunction against pre-marital coitus. As homosexual practice, both have been tacitly recognised, but few heterosexuals
admit to anal intercourse, although, as Germaine Greer (tongue firmly in
cheek) points out, it could be useful as a method of contraception.[10]

Anal intercourse does not appear at all in *The Hite Report on Female
Sexuality*, nor in *The Hite Report on Women and Love*, and only in the context of homosexual activity between boys in *The Hite Report on the Family*.
It was, however, discussed in *The Hite Report on Male Sexuality* from a male
point of view in relation to penetration with penis, finger or other object.
Most men who had experienced anal penetration of themselves found it
very pleasurable because massage of the prostate gland gave them an
orgasm; they also enjoyed anal penetration of others, both women and
men. The consensus, however, seemed to be that entry was painful for a
woman, but that many women enjoyed it once entry was achieved. The
impression was given that it was practised on women mainly where medical problems existed, in cases of vaginal infection, pregnancy, post-preg-
nancy, or post-D and C (dilation and curettage). Germaine Greer quotes the
eulogy which Kate Millett gave on rectal massage as a lesbian practice; 'Dr
Stopes could hardly write more rhapsodically about the marital embrace,'
she added tartly.

Historically buggery has always existed, and recent research records it
being depicted in the literature and art of ancient Greece and Rome.[11]
Christianity, as constructed by the Church 'fathers', proscribed sexual activity and pleasure in all forms except for procreation. In early nineteenth-
century Britain buggery or sodomy, that is anal penetration with the
penis, was punishable by death (there were fifty executions between 1800
and 1830),[12] but the punishment was reduced to penal servitude for life in
1861.[13] It was legalised between men over twenty-one as 'homosexual acts
between consenting adults in private' in England and Wales in 1967, in
Scotland in 1980, and in Northern Ireland in 1982. It was legalised in
Ireland for persons of either sex over seventeen years of age in 1994, except

when committed on a mentally handicapped person. Anal intercourse remains illegal between men and women in England and Wales, but not in the Republic of Ireland.

In the 1994 report *Sexual Behaviour in Britain*, anal penetration was the least reported form of sexual activity, but, as the researchers pointed out, legal and moral sanctions against it may mean that it is not widely practised, and also that it could be underreported. For the 3.4 per cent of men and 2.9 per cent of women who reported it, anal penetration was an infrequent activity in a repertoire of sexual practices. In the non-judgmental fashion of social researchers, the authors remarked that behaviours previously regarded as socially unacceptable, 'may be increasingly encouraged as alternatives to sexual practices that are riskier in terms of unwanted pregnancy, STD [sexually transmitted diseases] and HIV [Human Immunodeficiency Virus]'. However, researchers have found that the risk of infection is higher from anal penetration than from vaginal intercourse.[14]

The question here, however, is whether it is oppressive to women. First we must ask: who requests it and who benefits from it? The replies of the 11 per cent of male respondents in *The Hite Report on Male Sexuality* who occasionally practised anal penetration with female partners only mentioned one woman who actively sought it. It would seem to be a practice in which some women co-operate in order to please their partners. Sheila Kitzinger wrote that most women who talked to her about what they liked and disliked in love-making said that they did not enjoy anal intercourse.[15] If, as it seems, women are 'submitting' to anal intercourse to please partners, then it is, indeed, oppressive.

Oral sex has been around for a long time. It was condemned in the Old Testament as 'unnatural'. I have not read *The Interpretation of Dreams* by Artemidorus, but Michel Foucault quotes him as saying that fellatio was regarded as 'an awful act' and a moral wrong.[16] In *Psychopathia Sexualis*, Richard von Krafft-Ebbing also condemned the practice, although he did not class it as a psychopathological condition. 'These horrible sexual acts,' he said, were committed by men who were satiated or impotent from excessive indulgence, or by married men of low morality, who wished to prevent pregnancy.

Then came sexology and a rash of sex advice books, and oral sex was out in the open. The idea was abroad that it was an acceptable part of sexual activity; in fact, some of the sex advice books urged fellatio on women. In *Anticlimax* Sheila Jeffreys gives the example of 'J' (author of *The Sensuous*

Woman), who like other sex advice writers of the sexual revolution, told women that they *must* perform oral sex on men whether they liked it or not, because 'your man will love you for it'. 'J' found that most of the women who had got over their revulsion of fellatio enough to allow it, still did not want men to ejaculate in their mouths, but she reminded them sternly of their duty, and said that they should make *a fairly long-term effort* to feel the pleasure.[17] Jeffreys also refers to a campaign in the seventies in the (soft) pornographic magazine *Forum*, which set out to persuade women to accept fellatio. In its letter columns, women offered tips to each other on how to cope with it. Fellatio, said Jeffreys, became a new kind of house-work;[18] but she drew a line between fellatio and 'deep throat', made infamous in the pornographic film of the same name, where the unfortunate woman is expected to swallow the penis; this she describes as throat rape.[19]

The September 1979 issue of *Playboy* had this to say to men on the subject of fellatio: 'You may be holding back because you subconsciously think that coming in a woman's mouth is somehow dirty or wrong. (You are ab-solutely right. That's what makes it so much fun.)' Despite this male approval, in the repertoire of male insults 'cocksucker' ranks with 'cunt' at the top of the league.

Then came consciousness-raising and in *The Hite Report on Female Sexuality* only one woman was unequivocally enthusiastic about fellatio; roughly half of those who answered the question disliked it intensely, and the rest accepted with varying degrees of tolerance because it pleased their partners. Of those women who performed for their partner's pleasure, the majority were graphically adamant that they would not swallow the semen. On the other hand, almost all the women who answered the question on cunnilingus liked to have it done to them, but not if they had to do a 'blow job' in return.[20]

In the early days of the current women's movement, feminists con-demned fellatio as 'inegalitarian' or submissive for women because it ob-jectified them as receptacles.[21] Later some changed their minds; even Sheila Kitzinger in her book *Woman's Experience of Sex* is neutral on the subject. Since the advent of the sexual revolution, there has been a consistent, persistent and insistent promotion in films, books and suggestive ad-vertisements to make fellatio acceptable. The reason is obvious: men like it. In *The Hite Report on Male Sexuality*, 85 per cent of heterosexual respondents gave a resounding 'yes' when asked if they liked fellatio (the figure for homosexual men was 97 per cent). Many modern women believe that they will be regarded as 'old-fashioned' or 'repressed' if they refuse; and while 'oral sex' is spoken of and written about relatively freely, women's objections to it seem to have gone underground. Sally Cline explains that culture leads us to choose some sexual acts by praise and reward, and to reject others by scorn or condemnation. Therefore individual sexual acts like kissing or oral sex have to be understood in terms of the prevailing cultural codes; and there is often a gap between what women do and like doing, and what they are told they should do and like.[22]

Yet there are indications that they have been completely won over. A short documentary by a media student which was broadcast on RTE television in 1993 told the story of the initiation of a young woman to prostitution by an older woman. In the end the young initiate left her first client's car and vomited. In Michael Dibdin's novel *Dirty Tricks* which could be taken to reflect some of the more sophisticated 1990s views, oral sex was not expected from 'superior' women only from those regarded as 'inferior'. Yet the mammoth *Sexual Behaviour in Britain* survey found that oral sex was more prevalent among the higher social classes. The researchers found that cunnilingus and fellatio were common experiences for both genders, with 75 per cent of men and 70 per cent of women reporting some experience of one or the other at some time during their lives. More than half of the heterosexual sample reported oral sexual activity, and of these over 80 per cent reported both cunnilingus and fellatio in the previous year, suggesting that it is generally a reciprocal practice.

Eileen McLeod, in her research on prostitution in the early 1980s, found that fellatio was becoming more popular among clients of prostitutes because wives were not prepared to do it. Most prostitutes, at that time, also protested that they were not prepared to do oral sex because they found it intrinsically distasteful; but there was the suggestion that they were, in fact, doing it because they were desperate for money.

Susan Griffin explains the prevalence of fellatio in pornography as another instance of the rage of the male infant against the mother. In the pornographic depiction of fellatio, the 'heroine', under threat of punishment, must always drink the semen of the 'hero'. This evokes, she says, the revenge of the small child who is told to 'eat every bite', who is told if he spits he is 'in trouble', who is forced by his parents to finish his meal.[23]

Most people dislike the terms masturbation, self-abuse and onanism, not just because they are derogatory, but also because the activity has always been condemned as an 'unnatural act' by the Judaeo/Christian culture. (Onanism is usually used as an academic term and is applicable only to men. Onan 'spilled his seed upon the ground' [Genesis 38:9].) The researchers of *Sexual Behaviour in Britain* used the non-judgemental term, non-penetrative sex, meaning genital contact not involving intercourse, or sexual stimulation without intercourse. But non-penetrative sexual activity could also mean non-genital activity such as fondling ('petting', 'necking').

Opprobrium, mainly perpetuated by religions, has surrounded mas-turbation until the present day, without diminishing the practice. Most of the suppression was directed against adolescent boys, and this inquisition of young male sexuality intensified during the eighteenth and nineteenth centuries, and well into this century. The dire results of (male) masturbation which were threatened by 'medicine and pedagogy' in the nineteenth century were listed by Foucault as the gradual exhaustion of the organ, the death of the individual, the destruction of his offspring, and finally, harm to the entire human race. Then he pointed out that onanism was condemned in virtually the same terms by the Greek physician Areteaus in the first century A.D.[24] Yet it was not always condemned in ancient Greece and Rome; in Foucault's perusal of the early literature he found it treated positively as an action of the gods, learned by shepherds from the god Pan.[25]

Male masturbation has always had a much higher profile in society's consciousness than the female activity. Yet, as mentioned above, women were subjected to genital mutilation by their families if they were caught, or suspected of, doing it. I have not come across any reference to men being castrated for the same deed. Among the tribes of Africa where clitor-idectomy is practised, it is said that masturbation is accepted, even encouraged, among *young* girls, so that they can experience the pleasure of sexuality while remaining pure.[26]

It was the feminist movement of this century that gave a measure of acceptability to female masturbation. In the 1930s, Laura Hutton, a physician at the Tavistock Institute in London, treated it in a matter-of-fact way when she wrote about the sexuality of the single woman.[27] Guilt, brought on by cultural attitudes, is the only serious damage to the in-dividual from masturbation. One of Wilhelm Reich's aims in his deification of the orgasm was to remove that guilt; and later came Kinsey and Masters and Johnson who liberated everyone. In the 1977 *Health Education Report* of the British Department of Education and Science, one small, official step was taken to reprieve masturbation - it was harmless if regarded as an adolescent pursuit, but not advisable in adulthood where it might inhibit 'healthy' and 'productive' heterosexual relationships. If slang terms of abuse are an indication of cultural attitudes, then masturbation has not reached the stage of acceptability that is professed by liberals. 'Wanker' still means a 'contemptible person' (*Oxford English Dictionary*).

In the 1970s, masturbation became part of liberated female sexuality, the direct route to orgasm which seemed to elude so many women. In the United States workshops were held to teach women how to do it; 'there is no such thing as a frigid woman', the cry went, 'a frigid woman is one who has not had an orgasm – yet'. By 1988, when the BBC made a series of programmes on sex education, masturbation was treated as a natural phenomenon. It is still, however, forbidden as unnatural and sinful by the Catholic Church and Islam.

Men might have been made to feel guilty by the demonising of masturbation but they always seemed able to innure their consciences. For many women, however, it has denied them a private pleasure, a sexual release and physical relaxant, and, more practically, a method of toning womb and vagina in preparation for childbirth. In Ireland, there has been no public discussion on the subject, while presumably it continues as a private pursuit, but many women would refrain from practising it because of the attitude of the Catholic Church.

As many writers (Segal, Kitzinger, et cetera) have pointed out, masturbation is not the solution to female or male sexuality. It is merely one enjoyable aspect of it, a physical release of sexual tension and has nothing to do with desire, love, or a relationship with another person, except in fantasy. However, denial of the right to it has been another oppression of women through their sexuality.

The practice of casual sexual activity made possible by the pill, is undergoing a retreat due to the danger of HIV, AIDS and sexually transmitted diseases, a reversal which was unthinkable to the warriors of the sexual revolution. Sexual attitudes are beginning to change, and a few are thinking of other expressions of sexuality. Nevertheless, we have what Sally Cline describes as a genitally trapped culture in which celibacy and chastity are almost regarded as deviant. In the popular definition, celibacy and chastity mean refraining from sexual acts; but the *Oxford English Dictionary* defines celibacy as 'not marrying' (from the Latin *caelebs*, a bachelor); and chastity as not engaging in unlawful sexual acts. Therefore, under this definition,

Catholic clergy who have sexual affairs are not breaking their vow of celibacy but offending against chastity.

The denial to women of the right to remain single, without incurring contempt, is widespread. As recent as the 1920s, unmarried females were called 'superfluous women'.[28] A woman who chooses to remain celibate or single is regarded as one who has been unable to attract a mate, a failure, or in more recent times a suspected lesbian, and therefore to be despised. In each case her sexuality is suspect: she is either deficient or 'perverse'.

In *Women, Celibacy and Passion*, Sally Cline wrote a well-reasoned defence of celibacy, an argument against the genital fixation of modern society. On a radio programme where she discussed the book, the male interviewer treated the subject as somewhat offbeat and amusing, but sexy: after all, they were discussing sexuality. The implication was that thirty years after the sexual revolution, this misguided woman was flying in the face of reason. The book, however, was not such an aberration. It was a serious re-assessment of sexual activity, a courageous step in the present climate of genital fixation.

Sally Cline defines celibacy as a form of sexuality, and divides celibate women into two categories: ascetic celibates who reject any form of genital or physical sexuality; and sensual celibates for whom touch is not taboo, and who will indulge in hugging, affectionate intimacy, kissing and masturbation, but will not engage in genital activity with another person. In her research she found many women who had chosen to become celibate, and who saw their celibacy as an expression of their sexuality. She saw their move not as a rejection of sexuality, but as a healthy escape from the genital fixation of society. It is, of course, as valid an option where sexuality is concerned as political lesbianism is in the struggle against sexism. When we proceed to the next phase of feminist consciousness-raising, and re-evaluate the way sexuality has been organised, then analyses like Cline's will be valuable.

In *The Hite Report on Women and Love*, one-third of the 2,300 single women who took part in the survey had chosen celibacy for a period of at least six months after they had been sexually active earlier in their lives; it gave them an emotional break, they said, to focus their energy and attention on other things. None of them felt that it was imposed, or were disturbed by it in any way.

Genital fixation is not as general or cross-cultural as we are led to believe. A glance through the literature of anthropology shows that different cultures have different levels of genital interest and activity. The problem for us is that the cultures we know (and which have colonised a large portion of the planet) have become so genitally fixated, particularly in the second half of this century, that we consider it normal. This fixation has been culturally constructed mainly because of the psychological importance men attach to their genitals, and it is fuelled by a media culture in reporting, advertising and the commercialisation of sexuality and sexual activity. It is the current phase of what Foucault called the deployment of sexuality. In the last century sexuality was deployed in the interests of the conjugal family and reproduction; today reproduction is out and the commercialisation of sexual activity is the fashion.

Female chastity has been regarded as a traditional way of ensuring paternity to one man; a woman's virginity was always tied to family honour. Of course there was always a real and practical need for virginity (and chastity) when a woman could be left with inadequate resources to rear father-deserted offspring. However, recently there emerged another compelling reason for, if not complete chastity, then fastidiousness in sexual relations. While sexually transmitted diseases, including AIDS, have always been associated with promiscuity, gynaecological problems in women including cervical cancer, have not. In what researchers have begun to call 'the male factor' these medical problems have now been associated with the male penis and sperm and refer to hygiene, possible infections carried in the sperm, and frequency of coitus.[29] One wonders why it took so long for that idea to surface.

The gynaecologist Elizabeth Duncan worked with poor women and inadequate facilities in Ethiopia and with wealthy women and superb medical facilities in one of the Gulf States. She found that the women in both places shared the same gynaecological problems – infertility, ectopic pregnancy, puerperal fever, pelvic abscess and cervical cancer; they also shared two causative factors: early sexual experience and 'the male factor'.[30]

In non-Western societies there are additional ways of sexually oppressing women – genital mutilation such as clitoridectomy, infibulation and circumcision;[31] harems; sale of brides and arranged marriage; death for adultery (for which men are not punished).

The official World Health Organisation figure for the genital mutilation of women is more than 75 million, but unofficial figures put it higher. It is widely practised in various forms in Africa and the Middle East (mainly in Muslim populations), and in areas as diverse as Australia, Brazil, El

Salvador, Malaysia, Pakistan, and among the Skoptsi Christian sect in areas of the former Soviet Union.[32]

The 'justification' for clitoridectomy has been that the clitoris has no function in reproduction and, as Mary Daly said, because it does not serve male purposes. Therefore, in some cultures, it is regarded as 'impure' because its only function is female pleasure. Removal of the clitoris is deemed to keep a woman faithful to a husband by removing what is believed to be the seat of her sexual desire. As it happens this may be a mistaken belief; Sheila Kitzinger points out that women mutilated in this way can still experience sexual excitement in the urethra (Ernest Graffenburg's famous G-spot) and perineal spongy areas, and even have an orgasm.[33]

Clitoridectomy is not foreign to Western society; it was practised in Britain and the United States by the medical profession in the nineteenth century as a 'cure' for masturbation, 'nymphomania' and 'hysteria' and was used in both countries as recently as the first quarter of this century.[34] The last reported case took place in the United States in 1948 on a little girl of five to stop her masturbating. Circumcision (removing the hood of the clitoris) became fashionable in the 1970s in the United States as an aid to female orgasm; and episiotomy has been carried out on the grounds that suturing a woman's vagina after delivery makes it tighter and intercourse, therefore, more exciting for her male partner. In the United States it is called 'the husband's stitch'; Sheila Kitzinger calls it genital mutilation.[35]

Meanwhile, clitoridectomy has come to Europe as part of the culture of immigrants from former colonies in Africa and Asia. It has been made illegal in Norway, Denmark and Sweden, but France and Britain have not yet legislated against it, although it is practised in these countries among their immigrant communities and has become a public issue. In Africa infibulation was banned by Sudan in 1946; by Egypt in the 1970s and Kenya in 1982, but it is still practised widely and illegally in these countries, mainly among Muslims. Jomo Kenyatta said that no proper Kikuyu would marry a woman that was not circumcised.

A woman, once she reaches sexual maturity, is constantly concerned about her fertility. If she uses the contraceptive pill, she must remember it daily. She may have to consider abortion, a stressful decision in any circumstances. If she has children, she is at all times solicitous for them and their care. These are constant concerns because men (apart from a considerate few) do not generally concern themselves with such problems.

Women are continually swimming against a tide created by the sexual environment in which the culture imprisons them.

If some would say that a woman is oppressed simply by her reproductive biology, the fact is that her biological condition becomes oppressive only through the agency of men, and the control that men have over her fertility. The laws surrounding women and their reproduction have roots in legal structures set in place thousands of years ago, and invoked in every generation since then, so that men could ensure their paternity and their control of women and children. Male-controlled states often have their own reasons for perpetuating the control of women's fertility. The Catholic Church and Islam are world powers that perpetuate the exploitation of women through their sexuality by legislating to control their fertility, and influencing secular legislatures and populations to follow their dictats, even infiltrating the international assemblies which plan for population control.[36] These controls linger on to a greater or lesser degree all over the world, in marital and family law, in gynaecological practices, and in the everyday abuse of power by men who maintain cultural attitudes against which legislation has been officially enacted.

Women have been slowly getting control of their own fertility. Contraception is now legal in all countries of Europe and North America. Ireland was the last European country to legalise limited contraception in 1978, and that opened the door, in practice, to unlimited use. Although advances have been made in contraceptive methods for women, the condom (used by men) is the most widely used contraceptive device. Vasectomy and coitus interruptus are the other forms of contraception used by men. Devices used by women are barriers like the diaphragm, the cervical cap, spermicides and the spermicidal sponge, and the new female condom. (The female condom has been described as a cross between a [male] condom and a diaphragm, and about as aesthetically pleasing as a vacuum cleaner bag.)[37] The interuterine device (IUD or coil) is not a barrier but works by causing the lining of the womb to reject the fertilised egg. The most popular contraceptive used by women is the contraceptive pill.

With the exception of the condom, all these devices are burdens on women's sexuality; the insertion and removal of material objects into the vagina is at the very least a nuisance, a downright uncomfortable process, and occasionally dangerous. Some of them can be pollutants of her sexual organs (the IUD has a copper coil which deteriorates, slowly, in the uterus) and a high level of hygiene is necessary with all of them. The pill alters a woman's hormonal balance and many women have experienced worrying side effects. 'Health feminists' of the seventies saw the pill as a conspiracy to pollute women's bodies and make them sexually available to men. The sexual benefit to men was incontrovertible, but the paranoid idea of a conspiracy to pollute might be more accurately phrased as a conspiracy to make commercial gain from women's bodies. Promotion of the pill in the United States also represented a separate political agenda: to limit population growth among the black population, and particularly among prospective emigrants from Puerto Rico.[38]

Sterilisation has become a popular method of contraception for both women and men, and a more drastic response to the cultural demands of sexuality can hardly be imagined. It is not without physical and psychological side effects, which may include immediate and subsequent pain and sometimes physiological complications, such as the need for hysterectomy. Like clitoridectomy it is sexual mutilation and similarly an oppression of women, because often it is not freely chosen but undertaken because the women concerned have internalised the wants of a partner for unrestricted coitus. In the case of men, it can sometimes mean painful erection and ejaculation. Defining the effect of sterilisation for men is more problematic as, in their case it is a freely chosen option to sustain a regime of sexual activity that has been constructed by their male culture. That may sound a bit too glib, because men, too, are victims of the sexual culture, but the psychological environment in which they make their decision is different, even when they decide to have a vasectomy for the sake of their partners.

We tend to look at contraception from one point of view only, as a boon to women in their right to control their fertility. And it *is* an advantage; but that ignores other aspects of the situation. Women often feel bound to put up with unpleasant and dangerous side effects of contraception because they see no alternative way to avoid pregnancy. There are alternatives. Male contraceptives could be developed, but there is no great rush in the world of scientific research to do so. A male hormonal contraceptive was developed some time ago but, like the female hormonal pill, it caused headaches and reduced libido; it also reduced the amount of semen and retarded ejaculation (which could be counted as an advantage in a male contraceptive) and therefore was not acceptable to men.[39] In that case, they would certainly not welcome a contraceptive device that was inserted into the urethra.

Prejudice plays a part in attitudes towards different methods of contraception; condoms were despised ('like eating toffee with the paper on') when the pill was introduced. They have now returned to favour, partly due to side effects of the pill which some women found un- acceptable, but mostly due to the need for protection from infection.

Natural birth control (particularly the rhythm method) has had a bad press, for two reasons: it requires of the woman a certain level of com- petence and organisation, and it is considered unreliable. The first should not present problems to the educated women of Western society, but they were the first to criticise the unreliability of these methods. This was due partly to a certain unreliability in some of the methods, but also to a pro- science, pro-technology prejudice, and partly also, I think, because these 'natural' methods were supported by the Catholic Church.

The fallibility of the rhythm method arose because it relied solely on temperature and a calendar calculation of a safe period around the time of ovulation. In most women this calculation was difficult because of the variations in their reproductive cycle. More reliable safe-period calculation became available through the work of various researchers, culminating in the mucothermic method developed by Professor John Marshall, and better known now as the Billings method. It involves monitoring changes in the cervix, in vaginal secretions (mucus), and in temperature. Studies of its reliability 'indicate that motivation and the quality of teaching are crucial factors' and that well-taught users 'have an effectiveness rate comparable to the Pill and IUD'.[40]

Some women who started to question the crude barrier methods of contraception and to worry about the chemical reactions of the pill and the IUD turned again to natural methods. The new revised British edition of the Boston Women's Health Book *Our Bodies, Ourselves*, gave natural birth control (or fertility awareness) equal status with all the other methods. Fiona McClosky of the Bristol Women's Health Group, who contributed the item, argued that natural birth control works with, rather than against, a woman's biology; and that controlling fertility is not a medical problem, but one rooted in the way heterosexuality is organised.[41]

Coitus interruptus is another natural method of birth control that has been widely practised historically, and just as widely disdained in our Western society. Germaine Greer's serious examination of sexuality, *Sex and Destiny*, was scorned and dismissed because she gave 'houseroom' to coitus interruptus. There was a wealth of important information and observations in *Sex and Destiny* that did not get discussed in the media because they seized on coitus interruptus. She was wrongly derided, and her book dismissed, by women who did not stop to examine or think through the point she was making. Men reacted predictably, given the context. However, coitus interruptus is not a satisfactory option for a woman because she is totally dependent on the man involved to withdraw.

Contraception is rarely regarded as a commercialisation of women's sexuality, but, in fact, that is what it is. There are no industrial profits to be made out of *coitus interruptus* or natural birth control, and an insidious campaign of derision has existed against them. And why have safer technological methods not been developed? It is nearly forty years since the pill was launched – a long time in a world of rapidly changing technology!

In many of the poorer East European countries, abortion is the main method of birth control. Abortion is also a significant method in Western countries, arising out of failure to use birth-control measures or failure of the methods used. In Ireland, where contraceptives are readily available (but abortion is illegal), some four thousand women go to Britain each year for abortions. In Britain around two hundred thousand abortions are carried out yearly.

Since the 1960s abortion has been available in most countries in Europe and in the United States and Canada with varying levels of ease or difficulty. It has been available in former Eastern bloc countries even longer. Ireland and Malta are the only European countries where abortion is illegal but the question is being addressed in Ireland in the mid-nineties. Attempts are made periodically in some countries (Britain, the United States, France, Italy, Roumania, Spain) to abolish or limit abortion laws, so far without avail.

Legalised abortion is strongly opposed by the Christian Churches, although it has only been forbidden by them since 1869. Feminists of the current women's movement advocate a woman's right to choose abortion in the case of an unwanted pregnancy. Mary Daly, in her thoughtful and pro-woman analysis of the subject, sums up the attitude of many when she says that the abortion issue represents 'neither the epitome of feminist consciousness nor the peak of religious consciousness'. Abortion, she says, is hardly the 'final triumph' envisaged by the women's revolution; and she asks: Why should women be in situations of unwanted pregnancy? No one, she points out, sees abortion as the fulfilment of her greatest dreams, and many would see it as a humiliating procedure.[42]

Abortion is no picnic for women, and although freely chosen by them, it is another oppression of them through their sexuality, the least onerous of two solutions to the problem of unwanted pregnancy. It is easy for those who are against abortion to talk about it as a slide into immorality, but what woman wants an abortion (with the pain and invasion involved) except for overwhelming or overpowering reasons? Some people are concerned with the moral considerations of destroying life, while others will say that a foetus, particularly an early foetus, only has the *potential* for life, and point to the high incidence of natural abortion that occurs early in pregnancy. Others still, wonder what the fuss is all about when the life is not valued when it is born, and killing people in wars is tolerated with little moral anguish.

Carol Gilligan writes that, in the case of unwanted pregnancy, women's attitude to abortion is mediated by a complex mix of feelings that include relationship, connection and survival. If connection and relationship are not established, and survival is predominant, then a woman will have an abortion; the simplistic view that abortion is the taking of life is not what influences her. Furthermore, Gilligan points out (as does Daly) that the moral codes in society are shaped by the dominant group (men), and not by those to whom they apply (in this case, women). Women usually do not make abortion a moral issue, if they themselves (or a daughter) have an unwanted pregnancy.[43]

As abortions result from unwanted pregnancies, it would seem logical to try to seek a solution to the problem by examining its root causes. How do unwanted pregnancies come about? To a large extent through ignorance, sometimes through carelessness or failure of contraception; also through rape, or through pressures from partners that sometimes are not quite rape but could qualify as coercion.

Absence of thorough sex education is inimical to women, because they, not men, bear the brunt of pregnancy. The deliberate effort to separate sexuality from reproduction, while valid on the level of the right of people to exercise and enjoy their sexuality, becomes irresponsible and dangerous when the thinness of the line between sexual intercourse and conception is ignored or dismissed from consciousness (a line as thin as a condom or as the knowledge of the biology involved). Girls (and boys) are taught the intricacies of mathematics, of physics and chemistry, of language and its uses, of cooking, carpentry and engineering, yet they are not taught about their own sexuality and its workings except in a small number of schools and then generally only in the most rudimentary way. Political campaigns have been carried out by lobby groups in Ireland, Britain and the United States to prevent sex education in schools. Their agenda and purposes are often hard to understand, and are usually centred on preserving the ignorance of adolescents about sexuality, although it is patently obvious that young people have sexuality and that they experiment with it.

Where sex education exists, and the programmes are dominated by medical considerations, success is judged by the level of reduction in unplanned, teenage pregnancies and sexually transmitted diseases. Where moral considerations are important, the programmes are concerned principally with inhibiting adolescent sexuality, and preventing the exploitation of women and children.[44] Both medical and moral approaches are important if the programme for each is well-rounded and comprehensive. For instance, the physiological considerations should also include the diversity of sexual pleasure and not concentrate on genitality.

Social and cultural morals are also important, because they are the cultural rules of right and wrong by which a society regulates itself, for the good of the individual and for the common good. But moral principles (and here I mean social morality not just religious morality) must be informed by knowledge and justice, and accepted by the consent of the society, not imposed by 'moral' juntas. As we have seen, women have always been the victims of hostile 'moral' tyrannies. Sexual morals are only one set of social morals, but they are the source of more repressions than any other. The 'moralists' who narrowly define sexual morality and attempt to deny young people a knowledge of their sexuality are increasing rather than reducing the sexual immorality that they claim to defend.

Another example of the commercialisation of women's sexuality is menopause. Treatment of the symptoms of menopause by hormone replacement therapy (HRT) has spread like wildfire in the United States and at a somewhat slower pace in these islands.

Germaine Greer's *The Change* is a stimulating and well-researched book about menopause, in which she developed one feminist-held approach – that menopause is a natural development of women's biology and should be allowed to take its course. She quotes from the work of Dr Mary Anderson, who says that only one-third of women suffer during menopause from symptoms 'of any degree of importance to them'.[45] Greer argues that the depression which some women suffer at menopause may be a condition from which they are already suffering; and the cultural attitude towards women ageing – the marginalisation of older women, the idea that they have lost their value since they cannot bear children – may exacerbate the condition. This prognosis is also held by sociologist Jane Lewis, who adds that research and surveys on the menopause are usually carried out on women who *report* problems of menopause to their doctors, rather than on the menopausal population in general.[46] The medical profession tended to be dismissive of the problems of the menopause until the advent of HRT. Previously, menopause had been regarded as a 'physiological crisis', a climacteric; but once the possibility of 'treatment' and 'medical management' arose, it became a 'deficiency' or a 'degenerative disease'.[47]

Apart from the psychological problems which afflict them, women who have menopausal problems have distressing physical symptoms, such as headaches, hot flushes, sweats, rheumatic pains, vaginal dryness, and the onset of osteoporosis which is the most serious affliction attributed to menopause. Osteoporosis, a condition of ageing, is the absorbtion of bone into the tissue, leaving the bone porous; and it occurs earlier in small-boned people and those deficient in calcium. It is believed that the reduction of oestrogen which occurs at menopause accelerates this loss of bone, and HRT replaces the oestrogen and slows (or halts) the bone loss.

The administration of hormones is not without side effects, and the worst levelled against regular doses of oestrogen in HRT was that it caused thickening of the lining of the womb and later endometrial cancer. However, this drawback was overcome by administering following doses of progesterone. In effect, the 'normal' menstrual cycle, complete with breakthrough bleeding, was restored. This treatment has other side effects, like those of the contraceptive pill, mainly the increased risk of heart disease and deep-vein thrombosis.

Medical arguments apart, what emerges from assessment of the scientific literature on menopause is that there is little sound research on it and few comprehensive surveys. The research results that exist differ widely from each other, and tend to be based on *medical case histories*, 'so that the menopausal *patient* becomes translated into the menopausal *woman*'. The main cause for complaint seems to be that the process of ageing and the menopause are not sufficiently differentiated, and often the symptoms are treated by doctors as emotional and psychosomatic.[48] Greer and Lewis both recommend that women set out to learn for themselves what is known about HRT and what is involved in its use.

The Boston Women's Health Book *Our Bodies, Ourselves* is no more encouraging than Germaine Greer. HRT, they say, is not *the* answer to menopausal symptoms, nor is it protection against old age; but it does relieve most cases of hot flushes and vaginal dryness. The book lists the side effects and offers alternative self-help approaches to the various symptoms. HRT has not been in operation long enough to discover whether it has any long-term effects.

Nevertheless, many women have found relief through HRT, and many more complain that it is not readily available to them. On balance, I would agree, after reading the literature, that women should be wary. They should acquaint themselves with the category of woman that should not use HRT,[49] then with the possible side effects, and balance them against the symptoms they are trying to alleviate. They should also appreciate that the public relations exercise, the sales pitch for HRT which the pharmaceutical companies have launched, is concerned more with profits than the wellbeing of women. One of the selling points is that it prolongs the active sexual life of women and makes them more attractive to their partner (if they have one). Some HRT preparations even added testosterone to revive the middle-aged woman's flagging libido, as it is assumed (not always correctly) that male libido persists over a longer period of life than that of the female. Germaine Greer takes issue with this assumption, and with the consequent oppression of middle-aged women who are expected to prolong their natural cycle of genital sexual activity. It is an expectation typical of the genitally fixated culture in which we live.

Foucault said that the hysterisation of the female body was achieved by analysing it as 'thoroughly saturated with sexuality', and then integrating it into medical practice because it was intrinsically pathological. It is not difficult to accept that analysis, because women's reproductive organs are the basis for a large area of medical practice – gynaecology.

Our present-day gynaecology grew out of the nineteenth-century discipline, with some of the same attitudes that regarded women's reproductive organs as basically prone to, or the cause of, disease. Removing women's ovaries (castration) for psychological reasons became a fashion a hundred years ago, and today we are outraged by the practice.[50] But ovaries and wombs are still routinely removed, for sound medical reasons, and very little advice is given to women on how to avoid this surgery. One of the causes of diseased wombs and ovaries is 'the male factor'. I have never heard of gynaecologists who take it into account; or if they do, they may have advised the women not to have any more children, or to rest more, especially when they are pregnant, as if women were in total control of both eventualities; or they may have a quiet word with a husband. There is no national campaign for male hygiene or for less frequent coitus to correct 'the male factor'; the removal of womb and ovaries is regarded as a female hazard. Women do not regard the uterus as a sexual organ, or in a woolly way, think of it as part of their sexual organs but not a part of their sexuality. When that organ has always been associated with pain (menstrual, childbirth, things going wrong), and when it has been part of their oppression, then it is likely that women have an ambivalent relationship with it. (I heard a woman remark after she'd had a hysterectomy that she'd got rid of a cradle and replaced it with a playpen. I also heard her daughter twenty years later, when she had a hysterectomy, weep for the loss of part of her womanhood.) I wonder how these operations will be regarded in a hundred years time?

Gynaecology became a male preserve a couple of hundred years ago, and like all branches of medicine it has remained so. Although some women have entered the profession, few of them have questioned the ethos which was established by their male predecessors, and the anti-woman practices remain. Regardless of whether ovaries are being removed unnecessarily or not, some current gynaecological practices, as we have seen in earlier chapters, are oppressions of women through their sexuality.

Then there is the phenomenon of male obscenity. There is very little written in feminist literature about male obscenity as sexual oppression. Mary Daly refers to it in *Gyn/Ecology*; and in *Sexual Politics*, Kate Millett asserts that obscenity is a form of violence, a manner of conveying male hostility, both towards the female (who is sex) and towards sexuality (which is her fault).[51]

The worst insult that can be hurled at man or woman is 'cunt'. It is a very old word, meaning the female external genital organs, and a form of it is found in all the Germanic languages. According to the Oxford English Dictionary it only became 'a term of vulgar abuse' in 1929; perhaps women 'knew their place' in earlier times. The corresponding word for the male external genitalia, 'cock' does not carry any intimation of scorn (that's right, old cock!).

Similarly with the word 'fuck' which means 'to copulate' (with an implication of domination). The *Oxford English Dictionary* says that 'fuck' is 'used profanely as the coarsest equivalent of damn', and the word 'fucking' is used 'as a mere intensive'. Both of these words are sexual, and in a pre-dominantly heterosexual culture refer to the exercise of sexuality by men with women. But while 'fuck' has passed into the vernacular to convey an emphatic previously conveyed by the word 'damn', 'cunt' means what it always meant, but debased into an insult.

There are other sexual slang words used about women, such as 'pussy', 'tail', 'bitch', which constitute obscenity; the legal meaning of obscenity is 'liable to deprave or corrupt' (the British Obscene Publications Acts, 1857, 1959). These sexually disparaging words, which make fetishes of female anatomy, have already corrupted the users who have internalised them as synonymous with 'woman'.

Allied with male obscenity is sexual harassment of women. Now illegal in many Western countries, the extent of it was only realised when courageous women took legal action against the perpetrators. The catcalls and whistles directed towards women in public, bottom-pinching on public transport, sexual personal remarks, remain despite the law.

All of these examples of the oppression of women through their sexuality, which have been absorbed into the culture and survive through centuries of change, are abuses of power by men. Cultural attitudes, many of which have long been legislated against, are used to maintain male power. Sexuality has led to the role that women are allocated in society, and every trick in the book is used to keep women in this 'traditional' role. The current problems of society are blamed on women seeking equality (feminists); women are blamed for violence and crime (bad mothers); for poverty (taking jobs from men and getting paid less for them). The scapegoating of women always avoids pointing the finger at men, at their economic poli-cies, their hierarchal systems, their sexual practices. It is they who exploit and oppress women, who pay them less (or not at all); and it is they who take as little as possible responsibility for the future generation. What role does male sexuality play in these situations, in the exercsie of male power and superiority complex?

15

THE MALE OF THE SPECIES

The dominating sexuality in our society is male, and it is thrusting not only physically but culturally. Female sexuality is defined in relation to male sexuality, as passive, complementary and responsive to it. This chapter discusses male sexuality – *not* men. Manifestations of male sexuality differ from man to man, and all of the elements that go to construct it are not found in every man, but are present in the community of men.

The earliest surviving records of women challenging the double standards of sexuality were the plays of Aphra Behn (*c.* 1640–89). Over the next two centuries other women continued the challenge: Mary Wollstonecraft, in *Vindication of the Rights of Women*;[1] Anna Wheeler (with William Thompson), in *Appeal on Behalf of Women*;[2] Harriet Taylor Mill (with John Stuart Mill) in *The Subjection of Women*;[3] and the nineteenth-century social purity movements on both sides of the Atlantic which sought to curb male sexuality.

What constitutes male sexuality? What is the link between male sexuality and masculinity? What is the relationship between male sexuality and patriarchy, between masculinity and patriarchy?

What is masculinity? According to the men who responded to Shere Hite's report on male sexuality, a man should be self-reliant and self-assured, assertive, dominant and in control of situations especially in relation to wife and children, unemotional, brave, competent at men's work, strong and aggressive, successful, reliable and with moral integrity. He should be 'a man's man' or 'one of the boys'; he should not act like a woman, he should avoid 'woman's' work, and be the provider in the family. He should also be the one to occupy and control positions of influence and power in all spheres of life: family, social, workplace, politics, religion, culture- and opinion-making. But above all he should have sexual intercourse with women; that is what defines him as a man.[4]

(Even if these responses were not the whole truth, this was still the cultural norm which the respondents wished to project.) The list more or less covers the Western cultural definition of masculinity, and in general many women would agree; after all, most of them try to inculcate these characteristics in their sons.

However, there are class differences in the expression of masculinity in our society. Status, power and ambition in their working lives are important to middle-class men; the power often takes the form of arrogance, and knowing better than other men and, of course, all women. Working-class men who are not independent, who are employed and given orders and controlled by other men, need some psychological props to maintain a satisfactory level of domination and therefore self-esteem. Physical strength is important to them, but even more vital is male bonding, which takes place in certain locations and circumstances, such as games, clubs, pubs, building sites and other all-male workplaces. In these situations men ritually and overtly observe a contempt for women in a sublanguage understood by the initiates, or by whistling and cat-calling and all the other well-known examples of sexual harassment addressed to women. Their domination of, and to some extent contempt for, women is carried over into their personal relationships: they must at all times be 'the boss' of the women in their lives, be they lovers, wives or children, and sometimes mothers. In *Goliath: Britain's Dangerous Places*, Beatrix Campbell's alarming, and cautionary book about the alienated males of unemployed Britain, Paul the joyrider declares that his relationship to his woman and his world is about power:

> I've told her that I'm wearing the trousers; I'm the man in this relationship; what I say goes. Everyone wants to be the boss of something, don't they? I want to be the boss of [my local area], only I can't.[5]

In the interviews with working-class women which Fairweather, McDonough and Fadyean carried out for *Only the Rivers Run Free*, it emerged that men objected to contraception because they needed to feel that they had made their women pregnant.[6]

In the small farming communities of these islands there is a variation of this working-class masculine ethos. To the farmer who owns and works the land, physical strength is very important, and self-reliance, assertiveness and all the other masculine characteristics listed above; he must also be boss in his own house, and he will usually avoid a self-assertive wife. But in this society men only come into full estate when they marry, and the unmarried sons who remain on the farm act very much like working-class men in male bonding and overt contempt for women. When they marry, however, while the bonding remains it changes in character, and overt contempt for women is muted.

Male ideology has become the dominant frame of reference, the basic building block of all cultures in the world. (Women live bi-culturally: they live in the world of male supremacy and they live in another world of women where co-operation and caring are important.) Racism, sexism, gender prejudice and class divisions are all different varieties of a basic tenet of male ideology which is essentially one of hierarchy. If men adhere to the rules of male hierarchy, then they believe that they have a natural right to dominate some men, all women, all children and the planet. This is the concept of male pride which makes the struggle of women for equality so intractable. Men find it difficult to conceive of a system other than the hierarchical one, and so if women are challenging their domination, then they believe that women want to *dominate* them. Male sexuality is also shaped by this masculine ideology, and in all cultures and classes, apart from a few tribal societies, male sexuality is related to superiority over women. What role does patriarchy play in the formation of masculinity and male sexuality?

First let's look at patriarchy and power. What is patriarchy and what is its link with male sexuality? The answer depends on whether the context or the theory is psychological, anthropological or sociocultural. Patriarchy is defined as

- the power of the father within the family and, by extension, male domination within society (symbolised in psychoanalytic terms as the phallus by Freud, Lacan, Irigaray, et cetera);
- as the exchange of women to form kinship groups (anthropologists Lévi-Strauss, Rubin);
- as sexual power over women (radical feminists Millett, Firestone, Dworkin, et cetera);
- as a social or cultural system of male domination supported by legal and cultural restraints (cultural feminists Daly, Rich, French, et cetera);
- as a social system organised by men, of which control of women's labour and sexuality is a necessary and important part (socialist feminists Rowbotham, Segal, and others).

In fact, patriarchy is all of these definitions. Socialist feminists say that the social system creates a bond between men which enables them to dominate women. Patriarchy operates, they say, through laws of the male-dominated State and Church, through the culture, the myriad of customs, rules and regulations that govern our lives (also male-dominated), and by male control of women's labour both publicly and privately. Social structures, particularly the dependence of women, and economic systems and practices are all designed and controlled by patriarchy. Women co-operate with this apparatus of male domination because the culture within which they live conditions them to accept it.

Twenty-five years ago, when women examined the laws and culture within which their lives were embedded, they recognised this conditioning, and it became obvious to them who gained from it.[7] The feminist movement has challenged the laws of both State and Church and effected some changes. It has also wrought some changes in social and cultural attitudes and practices, even persuading some men to change the pattern of their lives. But the great majority of men (and women) have not changed and are fighting *against* the liberation of women. Those who claim a post-feminist era are the dupes of the anti-feminist backlash.

Power-seeking is a psychological phenomenon, and we must go to the psychologists (Dinnerstein, Chodorow, et cetera) for a fuller explanation. They have attributed the coerciveness of men's sexual behaviour, their obsession with genital sexuality, and male violence towards women, to fragility of their gender identity – their difficulty in overcoming their attachment to their mothers and, at the same time, their infantile resentment of the mother as the thwarting parent.

These psychologists say that the fragility of masculinity is caused by the way it (or what patriarchal society calls masculinity) is formed, the cultural injunction to be the opposite of feminine. The structure of 'maleness' which is required of the boy conflicts with his original identity which was part of a warm and secure emotional relationship of identification with his mother, an identification which he had to reject in the process of becoming a man. His new masculine identity, therefore, has not got a firm basis, it is in conflict with the roots of his emotional life; it requires constant reassurance that he is conforming to the masculinity which male society expects from him. One way he can affirm his masculinity is through genital sexuality – the use of the organ that makes him male – and that becomes a way of achieving the domination that men feel they should have in society, while at the same time providing the closeness that they need. Violence and rape enter the equation when men feel that they are not being accorded the status and respect which they consider due to their sexuality and masculinity, or when they fall short of this standard themselves.

I have always found small boys delightful little beings. Then in adolescence many of them become louts, and although they generally change in adulthood (on the surface at least), in many of them the seeds of loutishness are transformed into an assumption of superiority over women, and sometimes contempt for them, however well camouflaged. It is intriguing to speculate on the form society might take if fathers were involved in the nurture of children and boys were not required to reject the mother. Would we have an egalitarian society free of conflict? Human beings are complex, and the dynamics are not so simple as that solution might suggest, but it would be an interesting experiment.

Women are not the only theorists who have arrived at the conclusion that obsession with genital sexuality results from weak male gender identity.[8] John Stoltenberg says that for many people the act of fucking makes their sexual identity feel more real than it does at other times; and that this fix lasts for at least a while after the act. Central to the reinforcement of male gender identity, he says, is the sexual objectification of 'people who are born without penises' by 'people who are born with penises'.[9]

And what is sexual objectification? It is, says Stoltenberg, a cultivated habit of regarding a person's body as a thing divorced from the person as a person, and being sexually aroused by that body. He gives a list of examples of objectification leading to sexual arousal:

- scrutinising the body of a known or unknown person with sexual intent;
- studying the body of a film image or photograph of a person's body for the same reason;
- building up certain images in his mind of what shape, colour, age, he finds desirable in a sexual object with no regard to personality;
- recalling these images when engaged in sexual activity with himself or another in order to become aroused.

What does it mean, Stoltenberg asks, when this pattern of behaviour, this objectification, is an important part of a man's life? It means, he says, that the man is 'ordinary' and 'normal'.

He points out that boys are brought up in a society which prizes the penis as the locus of male sexual identity, and essential for the achievement of all sacred and secular power. This culture causes the young boy great gender anxiety in case he does not measure up to the standard of maleness expected of him. The first thing he must do is dissociate from femaleness (this is a layman's version of the Oedipus complex). Then Stoltenberg adds a significant *male* insight. He refers to the involuntary non-sexual erections that young boys have in response to situations of fear, anger, hazard or anxiety (mentioned in Kinsey),[10] what he calls a basic 'fight-or-flight' reflex. These erections, he says, cause the adolescent further anxiety, and as he develops he learns to associate the erections with 'desire'; thus, his gender anxiety and his reflex erections become linked.

When he looks at the sexual parts of other people's bodies as distinct from looking at them as persons (sexual objectification), he has a jolt of anxiety about the authenticity of his own maleness which triggers an automatic erection. That, in turn, says Stoltenberg, confirms his masculinity and is satisfying. So he depends on this gender anxiety, which is generated by sexual objectification and which he knows can be counted on if properly stimulated, to make his penis hard. Violence enters the model when objectification is not enough to arouse the man sexually, and he finds that he can re-create the erection (caused by fear or danger as a child) by becoming threatening and dangerous to his chosen sex object. Because he regards the sex object not as a person but an object, he has no ethical problem about being violent towards 'it'.[11]

This explanation of male sexual violence shows the effect that a male supremacist (patriarchal) society has on the formation of masculinity through sexual identity. It explains how violence helps the man achieve the sexual satisfaction he seeks, and at the same time reinforces his dominance. It also explains why men get violent with women who threaten their sense of masculine or sexual identity and supremacy; and it can explain male violence when a woman annoys a man for other reasons, and his anger triggers a sexual response. In some ways this explanation of male gender anxiety corresponds to the gender fragility of the psychoanalysts, but described in biological terms. It is not clear, however, when or how the young male learns the physical and emotional association between his anxiety and his desire. It may happen through masturbation.

Stoltenberg holds that there is a symbiotic relationship between sexual objectification and male supremacy. Men's habit of sexually objectifying, he says, serves in part to construct a culture of male supremacy; and male supremacy requires men to adapt to that culture by adopting the habit of sexually objectifying. But which comes first: male supremacy or sexual

THE MALE OF THE SPECIES

objectification? A strictly cultural explanation is not satisfactory; it does not explain the widespread male contempt for women that gives rise to the objectification in the first place. That is more adequately explained by the rejection of femaleness, and the deeply unconscious, psychological condition of 'filial spite' against the will of the mother, and hence all women, as described by Dinnerstein. ('Woman is the will's first overwhelming adversary . . . In our first real contest of will we find ourselves, more often than not, defeated. The defeat, is always intimately carnal; the victor is always female.')[12] An explanation must be sought for the significant number of men who do not feel contempt for women and would never consider being violent to them. Have they got a gender identity that is more robust? Men also share in romantic love, they fall just as helplessly in love as women, a state which has an element of lust but also includes a personal love.

The emphasis given to sexuality and society's genital fixation have warped women's (and men's) lives. Men go off and take their pleasures without the same measure of emotional involvement as women; women are tied by the emotional element in their sexuality; but male sexuality is not totally centred on pleasure; they also desire warmth and emotional security, so perhaps there is hope.

The patriarchal nature of society has also caused the alienation of men. They have been denied a role in caring and loving, yet the very structures which their culture led them to erect – authoritarian institutions, multi-national companies, technological advances – these have now rejected large numbers of them, made them redundant without providing any ego-boosting replacement. This, coupled with increased status for women, with women demanding and claiming equality, has left many men angry and alienated; and they blame their loss of status on women as handy scapegoats. Some hold that feminism, not the social and economic structures which they themselves have erected, is to blame for their rejection.

Women are going to need the help of men to solve the problem of male violence against women. Society as a whole deplores male violence against women, yet in recent times it is evident that it is widespread in the community, particularly in marriage. Women have violence in them too. Is their violence the same as men's but kept under control because of their relationship with men, because of their inferior strength or lower status?

The ideology of masculinity not only makes it difficult for many men to love unreservedly but because of its competitive nature it also finds co-operation difficult. Male supremacy is a complex phenomenon; it relies on the old-fashioned mores that have survived from times which are not admired now except in the patriarchal religions. It is also closely related to selfishness and greed, but most of all to power. While women create, through the development of relationships, the social glue that keeps society civilised, men have an almost universal social adhesive of their own: they bond together inside the various strata of their hierarchical structures.

It is also evident that men themselves to a large extent define their identity in terms of their sexuality; even very successful men seem to have a need to demonstrate their sexual prowess. It sometimes seems that the greatest social crime a woman can commit is withdrawal of admiration for men and male sexuality. That is why feminists, lesbians and assertive women are detested; they query male superiority and scorn male sexuality. Germaine Greer had an interesting insight on the sexuality of men in some Muslim societies where women are veiled and kept in harems, and where foreign women who go uncovered risk sexual attack. She suggested that the function of veils and harems is to support the fiction that the men are highly sexed, and women must be hidden so as not to arouse their passions. When foreign women visit their countries, and go about uncovered, they are challenging these cherished notions of male potency.[13]

What, then, is male sexuality? Various definitions are given by different factions of psychology, feminism and sexology. Most sexologists saw male sexuality as compulsive, aggressive, dominant and focused on male orgasm. Freud defined libido as the psychological representation of the sexual instinct, and he saw it as essentially male. Freud's theory of sexuality rested on a build-up of tension, then release and return to equilibrium, the pleasure principle being the release (or in some cases the prolonged deferment of an imminent release), which supports the contention that male sexuality is focused exclusively on male orgasm.

Although feminists generally accept the Freudian analysis that sexuality is psychologically constructed, they reinterpret the evidence and most have decided that the roots of male domination lie in male sexuality. Some of the more forceful among them agree with the sexologists' description, only they use somewhat different terms and a variety of adjectives: they describe male sexuality as compulsive, driven, genitally oriented and potentially lethal, craving power and orgasm, selfish, violent and woman-hating; and they see pornography as its cultural expression.

For Sheila Jeffreys, male sexuality is a ruling-class sexuality that requires a subordinate object on which to act; it is aggressive and separates sex from love. Robin Morgan, speaking for one strand of American cultural feminism, said that male sexuality was compulsive and violent, and placed emphasis on genital sexuality, the objectification of women, promiscuity, emotional non-involvement. Adrienne Rich queried its compulsivity and suggested that this was a myth which gave men a *right* to the sexual use of women: 'In the mystique of the overpowering, all-conquering male sex drive, the penis-with-a-life-of-its-own, is rooted the law of male sex-right to women.' Andrea Dworkin saw male sexuality as sadistic and the stuff of murder not of love.[14]

Susan Griffin described it more elegantly; she said that a male sexuality which was detached from feeling was unnatural and 'the death of the heart': 'It is the nature of sexuality to arouse feeling, and of feeling to arouse sexuality.'[15] Petra Kelly describes the male principle as masculine materialism, waste, alienation, domination, possession; and opposed to a female principle of co-operation and conservation.[16] Simone de Beauvoir took it to a more metaphysical level and claimed that Man was ashamed of the biological aspect of his sexuality – the seemingly involuntary erection – and took pride in it only to appropriate the Other which was Woman; but he gloried in the phallus (meaning the symbolism of having a penis) because it represented transcendence and power.

From a synthesis of replies to *The Hite Report on Male Sexuality*, Shere Hite found confirmation of a cultural situation that is obvious to any social observer: that society's definition of sexuality is culturally created, and masculinity is an ideology that is central to the culture. Therefore to understand male sexuality, she says, it is necessary to understand the culture from which it comes. In a loop like a dog biting his own tail, she declares that

- the culture dictates to men what male sexuality and masculinity are,
- male sexuality is central to the definition of masculinity
- and masculinity as an ideology is central to the culture.

At the same time there are cultural limits placed on the emotions permissible to men and this causes them serious problems in their relationships with women.

Hite says that society tells men to define love as sexual activity, sexual activity as penetration and ejaculation inside a woman, and to do this as often as possible in order to prove themselves men. This ideology is a power structure which looks down on women, and uses sexual activity as a ritual drama re-enacted over and over again. Men are not happy sexually, but that is not the point, she says; they cling to their ideology of masculinity because it gives them power, and therefore they resist change.

'Intercourse is the sublime moment during which the male contribution to reproduction takes place. This is the reason for its glorification.' It is a celebration of 'male' patriarchal culture, Hite continues. In patriarchal society intercourse turns a male into a man before other men, it is symbolic of men's ownership of women, and is a form of male bonding. It has the whole force of society's approval behind it for a man, but not for a woman; a woman is more likely to be blamed than praised for having intercourse, and in that culture there is no role for her orgasm. As Shere Hite said earlier, 'if male orgasm is the sacrament here, the woman functions as the priest ... catering to the series of events which culminates in his orgasm.'[17]

What evidence did Shere Hite obtain to support this analysis? The majority of her respondents believed that to be a proper male a man should be dominant and have a strong sexual drive. They regarded sexual activity ('sex') as foreplay followed by coitus ('intercourse') and ending with male orgasm in the vagina, 'to want sex is by definition to want intercourse'. The surprise of the survey was that, paradoxically, among those same men only a very small number (3 per cent) mentioned orgasm as important in coitus (they could get it more easily and even more intensely with masturbation); most assigned more importance to physical closeness and full-length embracing.[18] However, *machismo* describes the predominant impression which emerges from the report.

There are, however, chinks in this armoured sexuality, as also emerged from the responses, from the horse's mouth, so to speak. It became evident that man's 'sexual drive' is not a biological imperative, and the responses confirmed that 'compulsivity' did not seem to be a problem. Far from being the 'driven' sexual beings they are supposed to be, two-thirds of the respondents said there were times when they were not interested in sex; roughly the same proportion admitted sometimes having difficulty in getting an erection; only one-quarter preferred to lead in love-making. However when it came to other forms of male sexuality (foreplay, masturbation, fellatio, et cetera), it was evident that these, although their approval rating was high, were only adjuncts to 'real' sexual activity, the focus of which was coitus.

Despite the macho image that emerged from this report, it was also evident that male sexual identity is indeed more fragile than men would like to admit. They had feelings of rejection when women did not want sexual activity as frequently as they did; they also felt rejected if women did not initiate it. There were signs of confusion here: while men did not want passive partners because that indicated lack of interest in their performance and affected their potency, the woman should not be too demanding or initiate sex when the man didn't want it; a sexually active woman instead should merely react with enjoyment and excitement to what the man was doing to her. There is also evidence here of the clash between men's needs and what the culture says they should need. More than half didn't get the closeness and warmth in life that they wanted; almost half had resentments against women, and more than half felt guilty about their treatment of women. It would seem that a lot of men (who would rather not) are having to live up to an over-sexualised culture.

One thing that becomes evident from Hite's report is that men's sexual aspirations and feelings are condensed into penis obsession to the detriment of other types of relationship (including sexual relationships) with women. From this it is apparent that male sexuality is in a state of arrested development, arrested at the stage when they discovered as small boys that 'playing with oneself' was pleasurable.

What compulsive elements exist in male sexuality? In a physical or biological sense compulsion in male sexual activity exists only when orgasm has begun. The compulsion of arousal – erection – is dependent on psychological, social and cultural factors, but it is represented as being as powerful, as if it were solely a biological reflex. The biological trigger in men which responds to pheromones released by women during their fertile period has long been overlaid by psychological and cultural prohibitions and inhibitions in the male, the cultural and psychological construction of sexuality, not to mention personal hygiene in the female. A few decades ago 'love-making' generally consisted of 'petting' (kissing, close embrace and some touching), and although men complained in countless cases, they accepted it without progressing to ejaculation and came back for more. In Irish society, and many others, it was only when the sexual revolution arrived in the sixties that sexual relationships began to include coitus as a matter of course.

Ideas of what is 'sexy' in women and a source of arousal in men differ between cultures. Some of the likely causes of breast fetishism in Western society are (1) fashions in women's clothing where breasts are covered or titillatingly, partially exposed, (2) the curtailment, interruption, or absence of breast-feeding in infancy, and (3) cultural ideas of nudity and modesty (tribal African women who normally go barebreasted, do not arouse sexual impulses in the men of their communities); (4) the social re-inforcement of the feteshism, once established. The role of breasts in human sexuality also differs between the sexes; in Western society they titillate men, for psychological reasons; for women, breasts are erogenous zones because of a biological connection between them and the womb, which contributes to its contraction postpartum.

Genitality is now generally expected in sexual encounters, and the difficulties in achieving erection which emerged in the responses to *The Hite Report on Male Sexuality* could arise because sexual activity and coitus is relatively freely available to men in Western society. Foucault's theory that sexuality is manufactured and heightened by controls that bring about selective suppression may apply in these cases. The sexual revolution of the past decades tacitly removed many controls and made genital sexual activity more readily available, indeed, *de rigueur*. This situation may, paradoxically, have removed some of the erotic stimulus. Increasing assertiveness among women may also contribute to male difficulty with erection. The cultural requirement of sexual proclivity and prowess puts further pressure on men to perform. These are all psychological and sociocultural factors, and if they cause men to have difficulty in getting an erection it is obvious that, far from being compulsive and involuntary, male sexual arousal needs certain environmental or psychological conditions.

Still the myth of the compulsive and uncontrollable penis, of erection and ejaculation as automatic motor actions of which man is the passive host, persists; although it is evident that substantial numbers of religious, young and old, choose celibacy (and chastity) and are able to cope. (However, there have always been some who have obviously had difficulties.) Germaine Greer remarks that total celibates are not any more deranged, inefficient, unhappy or unhealthy than any other segment of the population, and that, obviously, the male biological urge is psychologically controllable.[19]

The Hite Report on Male Sexuality indicates that a dominant sexuality is part of what male culture expects of men; this was evident in all the responses despite much confused thinking about their relationships with women. Most men could not visualise a relationship with a woman that did not involve sex. It was also their belief that women were primarily sex objects, and would always remain so. In the context of stable and family relationships, the general attitude was that the man should provide the main economic support in the family even when the woman was also a wage earner; that she should provide 'sex' in exchange for that support; that she should be passive and that he should be dominant and in charge in all phases of life; that they would not like a woman boss; and, one way or another, that women were inferior to men. (True or not, it was the way they believed they should feel.) Only a minority gave answers that conveyed a different message in which equality of status for women had a place.

But when does domination become aggression, and what is the link between male aggression and sexuality? Is male sexuality aggressive and violent, or is it the patriarchal system which makes it so? Listening to harsh, aggressive male pop songs, and observing uncaring, uninvolved, aggressive sex in films and videos, the amount of violent and woman-degrading pornography in circulation, the horrific reports of mass rape of women from war-ravaged areas, the cases of casual rape in the course of other crime or because the women are vulnerable, the amount of violence in families, the women-beating and child abuse that is being uncovered directly and indirectly by the women's movement, from all this evidence it is not difficult to believe that male sexuality is aggressive and violent. But is this contention sustainable?

Freud held that there were two fundamental instincts: sexuality which he called *eros*, and *thanatos*, the death wish. *Thanatos* manifested itself in destructiveness towards oneself or others or the outside world, in sadism, masochism, aggression, violence and destruction. Freud would say that the situation in the world today, war and terror, pollution and destruction, is proof that *thanatos* has superseded *eros*. If so, then, in Freudian terms, something has gone very badly wrong with male sexuality.

Some of the early post-Freudian psychoanalysts believed that aggression was a response learned in childhood: if the child found that docility gained approval he learned to use it; if he got his way by being aggressive then he practised aggression. Dorothy Dinnerstein and Nancy Chodorow said aggression was aroused in the child by the parent who thwarts its desires. This does not explain where the aggression came from, or why some people have a short and others a longer fuse. Wilhelm Reich, said male aggression was the result of sexual repression and urged 'self-regulated genitality' based on 'sexual potency'. By this logic, if genitality could be regulated, so also could aggression.

The sociobiologists call aggression a biological contingency plan, and male aggression as natural and different from female aggression, which should only be defensive. In evolutionary theory aggression becomes a basic survival drive in humans as in many other species: those who did not possess it perished at the hands of those who did. By this process of selection an aggressive drive could become part of the human character. But that theory has within it the seeds of its own destruction, as uncontrolled aggression could also wipe out a species. In fact most mammal species use aggression in a ritualised way, paired with ritualised submission, in the interests of survival. Furthermore many species that are not aggressive to other species, such as rabbits, have survived and thrived.

Susan Griffin regrets the obsession of men of science (from Darwin and Marx to Freud and Lorenz) with the idea that man is competitive and violent. She quotes Erich Fromm as saying that the idea of aggression as an instinct is not tenable.[20] Fromm pointed out that men who defend themselves are found in all cultures; at the same time, destructiveness and cruelty are so minimal in so many people, that these great differences could not be explained if aggression were innate. He has a point.

However, regardless of what causes it, there has to be some root or source for aggression; if there were no mechanism, no hormone, no electrical, chemical or other impulse of the central nervous system from which it arises, then it would not exist. Stress releases adrenaline from the adrenal glands, and this hormone stimulates either fear or aggression (flight or fight) in mammals, including humans. And if we accept that an aggressive drive exists in humans, there is already ample evidence that control or use of it can be learned, or constructed by psychological or sociocultural means.

In *On Aggression* Konrad Lorenz says that humanity defends its own self-esteem with all its might, and the unthinking person does that by being aggressive. Humans, unlike other animals, have the intelligence to regulate and control an aggressive drive which is not always needed in the complex and changing world in which we live. This control, he says, is accomplished by increased self-knowledge and appreciation of the causes of human behaviour, and sublimation of the aggressive drive into some other challenging activity. (But male sexual aggression does not always serve the purpose of defence against some danger; it is mainly used as an instrument of domination.)

On the other hand, Lorenz suggests, suppression of aggression may lead to other psychological problems, but his examples refer only to men. He cites research carried out on the Ute Indians, where a surfeit of aggression was causing psychological problems among the men, the successors of the 'braves'. In the past aggression was necessary for survival. In the present-day world this aggression was unnecessary, so it was dammed up and caused psychological problems.[21] In reply to that thesis, however, all the most aggressive need not necessarily have survived: he who fights and runs away, lives to fight another day. Far from being unnecessary, the reason for the Ute men's aggression could be the conditions imposed on them by the 'white man': the theft of their lands; their lack of status; the racism practised against them for three centuries. Their psychological problems could arise from the frustrations of their situation.

Does Lorenz suggest that men have a greater aggressive drive than women, that women are genetically less aggressive than men, even though they draw on the same gene pool as the male of the species? He charges that if the male of any form of animal life attacks a female of the species, the behaviour of that male is pathological. A lower level of aggression in women could perhaps be explained as hormonal difference, as biologists tend to link testosterone with aggression; but women with a full complement of female hormones can be very aggressive, especially in defence of their young. Women also have severe problems with their self-esteem in a world that constantly denigrates them, and some find a solution not in aggression against others, like the Ute men, but in aggression turned in on themselves which causes them to suffer from depression. So there may not be much difference in the aggressive capacities of women and men, except that women seem to be more in control of theirs.

So is there a difference between *control* and *suppression* of aggression? Perhaps there is. A great number of women, whom one could call well-adjusted, manage to live in a sexist world where they need to suppress aggression, and they do not suffer from depression; and many well-balanced men are not aggressive either in their everyday lives or sexually.

In the traditional culture of male supremacy, freely expressed aggression is an accepted part of masculinity. Society encourages boys to be 'manly', to stand up for themselves, to stand up for their sisters, to fight the bully; to go out into the world and get what they want. It also condemns the boy who is not aggressive, ridicules him, says he lacks courage, calls him a sissy or a wimp. On the other hand, society discourages 'tomboy' activity in girls; it is not acceptable for women to be aggressive. Women are conditioned against violence, against striking or hurting another person. They have been moulded by the culture to suppress their aggression, to believe in the superior strength of men to the extent that they have become inhibited and almost incapable of defending themselves against physical assault. As they are physically weaker than men, they have good reason to fear retaliation, therefore, it makes better survival sense to appease rather than to attack. For women who have not the confidence of self-defence skills, the fear of male strength can be overpowering. Indeed, police advise women not to resist rape in case they are seriously hurt or killed. In the recent decades, however, when women started to attend self-defence classes, not only did they find that they could develop their physical strength but they also gained the self-confidence to defend themselves. What was learned could be unlearned.

If, as Lorenz suggests, the unthinking defend their self-esteem by aggression, then it would seem that there are a lot of unthinking men in the world, and it follows that we must ask ourselves what constitutes their self-esteem? The answer is not a secret; men themselves have given it. It is patriarchy and the expectations which it fosters in men, together with an image of masculinity that is fused with sexuality. These are at the root of male self-esteem; and it is this combination that is destroying society and the planet.

Men themselves link their sexuality with aggression; the imagery of war and colonisation are sexual – virgin soil, the rape of countries – and weaponry is phallic. War is legitimate and institutionalised male aggression (most women see war as a male activity, from which they suffer, and over which they have no control), yet, when men's aggression is examined in the context of war, many incongruities emerge. First, it is not the rank and file of soldiers, those who fight and die, that decide to make wars; it is a patriarchy of military and political strategists, not fighting personnel, who take these decisions. Men obey because of their hierarchical ideology. War is also inimical to the best interests of the majority of men; it is a method used by male power blocs to further their own interests and to persuade or coerce other men to make outrageous sacrifices for those interests. War is a confidence trick played on the great majority of men.

Lynne Segal points out that military aggression is both fostered and protected by military traditions, one of which is insults that impugn the masculinity of the recruit, particularly by the use of the objectified and derogatory word 'cunt'.[22] This might suggest that military aggression has a sexual content but, in fact, in this case it is probably more a question of gender identity and only indirectly sexual.

The development of armies since, and perhaps during, the Second World

War has taken a turn towards dehumanisation. A Canadian television series in the late eighties showed the deliberate, psychological brutalisation of soldiers during their training period. Submissiveness and a willingness to die, as Segal points out, are important requirements on the battlefield. Therefore, it would seem that the objective of military training is not only to *arouse* aggression but also to break the spirit of individuality in order to *harness* aggression. Gender and sexual insults may be the most effective methods of doing so: the recruit would prefer to submit to the will of another male than be called any adjective that means feminine.

How is war associated with male sexuality? Does it enhance it? Do men feel more sexual for having displayed aggressive masculinity? What part does rape play in the sexuality of war? Is male sexuality aggressive, or is male aggression related to sexuality? To examine these questions we must look at men's violence to women. This is a type of violence that is not legitimately triggered by attack or danger – it is generally gratuitous attack for psychological reasons.

There is an epidemic of pathological male sexuality abroad which ranges in virulence through sexual obsession, pornography, violence to sexual partners, to child sexual abuse, rape and sexual murder of women and children. Women, particularly feminists, have undertaken the task of re-educating themselves: of raising their consciousness in regard to their sexuality, their true status, their roles in life; of improving their self-confidence and self-esteem. The project of re-educating men about their own sexuality, about their psychological problems, about male violence and injustice to women, has been attempted by women, yet it is barely considered by men themselves. For them, each man's actions and attitudes are personal to him, and the personal is definitely not political.

There are no absolutely safe places now for women in Western society; the highways and byways, the streets of towns and cities, always contained some danger, but now it seems that the home has been a dangerous place for many. In what has emerged recently to be a significant proportion of family situations, men seem to have no inhibitions about violently abusing partners and children. This violence is almost always sexual, because the men involved generally include forcible sexual activity to reinforce their claim that the woman or child is their property. Until recently, our patriarchal society condoned domestic violence, and had no sanctions against it; indeed, men were urged 'to show her who was boss' or to 'give her a bit of a slapping around to keep her in line'. Through pressure from the women's movement, barring orders were introduced in most Western countries, keeping the violent man out of the home, but not necessarily charging him with any offence. More recently, domestic violence has been made a criminal offence in many countries, even in Ireland. We had to wait until the 1990s to hear a radio campaign which said 'it's a crime to beat a woman'.

Male violence towards women has at all levels an element of coercion and psychological violence. When sexual, it ranges from sexual harassment and the making of pornography, through battering and rape to murder. The enjoyment of pornography is strictly psychological and vicarious violence until it stimulates a man to put the images and fantasies into practice.

Some modern feminists who denounce the nineteenth-century social purity movements also attack those who now campaign against pornography. They oppose limits on personal sexual freedom, even when that freedom encroaches on the freedom of others. Yet they support limits on personal freedom in the areas of economic and property rights, personal safety from violence, or political ideology, and do not find this position incongruous.

Why has Robin Morgan's one-liner 'pornography is the theory and rape is the practice' remained in the literature,[23] in feminist graffiti, in spite of the efforts of many writers and theorists to discount it? It has lived on because women recognise its truth. Adrienne Rich says that pornography depicts women as a sexual commodity to be consumed by men, and its most pernicious message is that a woman is natural sexual prey for men and that she loves it.

Andrea Dworkin, in her blood-curdling polemic *Pornography*, uses stronger terms. First she gives the etymology of the word: it comes from the Greek *porne*, which means 'whore' or the lowest prostitute in the brothel, available to *all* male citizens, and *graphos*, meaning 'writing'. Modern pornography, she says, remains true to its origins; it does not mean writing about sex or the erotic, or depictions of sexual acts, it means 'the graphic depiction of women as vile whores' not just prostitutes. This is an important distinction. She maintains that pornography terrorises women with the threat of rape. Furthermore, pornography reveals that slavery, bondage, murder and maiming have been acts suffused with pleasure for those who committed them, that the history of atrocity is rooted in male sexual obsession. Pornography, she says, reveals that male pleasure is inextricably tied to victimising, hurting, exploiting; that sexual fun and sexual passion in the privacy of the male imagination are inseparable from the brutality of male history.[24]

Strong stuff, and too simplistic, too all-embracing. Yet when one looks around at what is happening in the small wars that plague this planet, or look at the alienated males in city jungles who have nothing to lose but their macho identity, it is easy enough to find truth in Andrea Dworkin's words. Then look at all the decent men we know, who would never rape, strike or demean a woman, those who would not look at pornography, who would find it repulsive, and ask ourselves: are we just lucky enough to know the 10 per cent who do not use it? Who buys all these millions of pornographic journals and videos produced each year, and why do they buy them?[25] (Pornography was estimated as a 10-billion-dollar industry in the United States in 1993.)

Nine out of every ten respondents to *The Hite Report on Male Sexuality* looked at pornography, some regularly, others less frequently, and the majority first saw it when they were very young (eight or nine years old); one-quarter of respondents saw their first pornography in their own homes.[26] Hite's sample relates only to the United States, but if the numbers of pornography users in European countries were only half as large, they would still be alarming. The circulation figures for pornographic material in Great Britain would indicate a large usership. I have no figures for Ireland, where traffic in hard porn is mainly underground, but soft porn is readily available on the newstands and on the video racks.

Most of Hite's respondents, whether regular or infrequent users, preferred what they called 'soft-core', that is, pornography that does not show an erect penis.[27] Pictures that included an erect penis were considered 'hard-core', and most men complained that it was generally of 'poor quality', they resented the way men were depicted as merely 'studs', and they did not want to identify with it.

The most telling revelation that emerged from the survey was that pornography was a 'men together' phenomenon, an aspect of male bonding, even between strangers. It made young men feel that they belonged to the macho club, made them feel good and gave them an ego boost. From this picture, pornography suddenly appears as an important instrument in the reinforcement of male supremacy. There was nothing in any of the responses from most of the men who used pornography to suggest that they saw anything wrong with depicting women as subordinate creatures or objects, nor did they seem to realise in the case of pictorial pornography that what turned them on was an object, a photograph. It was instructive to find that these men took the subordination and objectification of women for granted – that was the way women were – but then they were the same men who in a different questionnaire said that women would always be sexual objects. A small number appreciated that it was demeaning to women, but nonetheless found it exciting. Those that did not use pornography considered that it was unacceptable because it degraded women, and these men showed concern for their relationships with their partners.

Why is pornography wrong? In what way does it degrade women?

First, pornography is the graphic or literary depiction of the domination of women through their sexuality. It describes or shows a woman being dominated sexually by a man, and being fucked in fantasy by the viewer or reader. She is the 'bitch in heat', who exists to be used by any man in any way he wants. If the woman is depicted as dominating a man, as sometimes happens, the message is either the 'bitch' who will dominate a man if she is let, 'but wait until I get to her', or it appeals to an 'errant' masculinity, a damaged, masochistic psyche.

Second, it makes sexual objects of women. A woman depicted in pornography is not an intelligent, thinking, speaking person but an instrument for the satisfaction of a twisted and neurotic sexuality. (Men also make work objects of women when they regard them as instruments of personal service. Women are in a no-win situation, they are either sexual vessels or vacuum cleaners.)

Third, pornography conditions men to women's subordination and it reinforces two cultural messages: that men should dominate women even to the point of violence, and that women are masochistic and enjoy being dominated, being hurt, or being forced into sexual acts. The erotic potential of pornography does not arise from a healthy sexuality (in the way that touches or caresses arouse), but from domination, and it is therefore exploitative, both in relation to its images and in relation to its female participants. It is a social problem with a psychological base.

Why do men use pornography? One answer can be found in object-relations psychoanalysis: the helpless rage of the infant against the all-powerful mother who thwarts him and does not grant his every whim; the reaction of the boy who observes the freedom of his father, his role model, while he suffers the domination of a woman, his mother. These 'wrongs' are not remembered, but are buried deep in the unconscious; they are manifest only as fear, hatred or contempt of women which are also partially suppressed in the adult man (see Dinnerstein and Chodorow in chapter 6).

In her erudite study *Pornography and Silence*, Susan Griffin describes the pornographer as obsessed; chained and enslaved to the past and his image of the past, wanting to exact revenge for all that he has suffered in body and mind. This is why, she says, pornography is so filled with reversal. (The reversal which Griffin refers to here is Melanie Klein's paranoid-schizoid syndrome, discussed in chapter 5, or the projection by the infant of his/her bad feelings on to the mother.) Behind every pornographic fantasy which has reversed reality is the infant's wish to turn the tables on his parents. Here is the child's desire to have the power his parents had, to inflict upon them the longing, rejection, frustration, pain and humiliation that the infant once felt. She says that this is particularly evident in porn-ography that portrays fellatio, where the woman is 'driven to the point of madness out of desire to put a man's penis in her mouth'. The reversal is not hard to spot: the overwhelming need of the child for the mother's breast.[28]

These individual feelings are also fuelled by the similar feelings of other men which they can all release by the sexual subjection of women. In pornography male fantasy can take revenge for these 'wrongs' and share with other men this pretence of controlling women. It also provides a fan-tasy of power for men who are powerless in other spheres of their lives. Pornography is represented as an affair of men and their sexuality, but in fact it is an affair of male domination and women; it is an exercise in power; the sexualising of power; power as an aphrodisiac.

The problem is twofold and an overriding one for women: first, pornography reinforces and reproduces the subordination of women in the minds of men in the real world; it depicts 'the sexiness of inequality', and is an 'unacknowledged motor force of male supremacy'.[29] Second, some men want to re-enact the humiliation of women which they see in pornography in their own real sexual relations. In *The Hite Report on Male Sexuality*, some men regarded pornography as a manual for sexual practice and shared it with their partners before sexual activity. There is something psychopathic about a man using images of dominated or humiliated women to arouse a sexual response in himself, and it is proof, if more were needed, that heterosexual desire, as culturally constructed, is eroticised power for men and eroticised subordination for women.

Passionate arguments are put forward in favour of permitting porn-ography, but they are singularly unconvincing. From the libertarian point of view, these arguments are usually based on the concept of freedom of choice and the sexual 'liberation' that resulted from the sexual revolution. Other feminist arguments against banning pornography centre usually on opposition to censorship and fear of being found on the same platform as the fundamentalist right, although these same women have no objection to occupying the same stance as fundamentalists on murder and rape, robbery and assault. Some, like Lynne Segal, see pornography as a symptom of a situation that exists, and do not see it as an incentive to men to act out with real women the pornography they have enjoyed. Jeffrey Weeks puts forward a male homosexual view: he finds 'very little evidence' that pornography encourages men to act out these fantasies, and comes to the conclusion that the real objection to pornography is moral. He finds the arguments that pornography constitutes a danger for women unconvincing; after all, he says, 'violence against women – economic, social, public and domestic, intellectual and sexual – is endemic in our culture', and too much emphasis is laid on pornography to the neglect of other problems of sexual politics.[30] In a book that otherwise has important insights, his arguments are weak. Pornography is one of the ways that sexual violence is condoned for men, and often how it is introduced to young males.

Most feminists are united against pornography and would like to see it banned in the same way that tracts inciting racial hatred are prohibited. There is a considerable body of closely reasoned, feminist literature advocating the prohibition of pornography, and these arguments carry more weight and conviction than those of people who support it or condone it.

Catharine MacKinnon, the lawyer who took up the case of Linda Marciano, 'star' of the notorious pornographic film *Deep Throat*, calls pornography a breach of women's civil rights. In 1983, with Andrea Dworkin, she formulated a city ordinance for Minneapolis and Indianapolis. This ordinance attempted to halt the production of pornography, by allowing those who felt harmed by it to take legal action against the makers, distributors and sellers once it appeared for sale. The proposed law drew on the Fourteenth Amendment to the United States Constitution which guarantees freedom from discrimination (including sexual discrimination) to all citizens. The categories of people who could take action were those who were coerced, intimidated or fraudulently induced to take part in a pornographic production; anyone on whom pornography was forced in public or private; anyone assaulted or physically attacked as a direct result of pornography; anyone defamed by pornography; similarily any man or child alleging injury by pornography; and, significantly, any woman who wishes to take action against the subordination of women.

In that ordinance pornography was defined as the graphic, sexually explicit subordination of women through pictures or words in which women are presented as one or more of the following: (1) dehumanised as sexual objects, things or commodities; (2) as sexual objects who enjoy pain or humiliation; (3) as sexual objects who experience sexual pleasure in being raped; (4) as sexual objects tied up or cut up or mutilated or bruised or physically hurt; (5) in postures of sexual submission, servility or display; (6) as whores by nature; (7) being penetrated by objects or animals; (8) in scenarios of degradation, injury, torture, shown as filthy or inferior, bleeding, bruised or hurt in a context that makes these conditions sexual; (9) pictures or words in which women's body parts – including but not limited to vaginas, breasts or buttocks – are exhibited such that women are reduced to those parts.

The ordinance declared that pornography was a systematic practice of ex-ploitation and subordination based on sex which harmed women; that the contempt and aggression which it fostered harmed women's opportunities for equality in all areas of civic life (in employment, education, public services, et cetera). MacKinnon and Dworkin claimed that the production and distribution of pornography was sex discrimination and therefore those who took part in that process, or coerced others to take part, at any stage could be prosecuted and were liable to damages.

An amended form of the ordinance was adopted by Indianapolis (not in Minneapolis), but it was challenged in the courts and declared uncon-stitutional because it conflicted with the First Amendment to the Constit-ution which guarantees freedom of speech. The Supreme Court refused to hear an appeal, so MacKinnon and Dworkin failed. If men were depicted in similarly humiliating situations, it would be hard to believe that the courts would have allowed it to continue.

In Ireland although pornography is prohibited by the censorship, it is readily available, despite occasional raids on distribution premises for hard porn; videos which are termed soft porn, are available in most outlets and soft porn magazines are on open sale in most newsagents.

In Britain whatever control of pornography existed came under the Obscene Publications Act of 1959; pornography per se did not exist. In 1979, the Williams *Report of the Committee on Obscenity and Film Censorship* called for restrictions on the sale of pictures of genital and excretory organs, and of violent acts; in 1982 limited legislation was introduced controlling sex shops and cinema clubs. In 1992 Labour MP, Dawn Primarolo introduced a Bill to confine soft porn to sex shops. It failed.

Many British and American feminists (Lynne Segal, Carole Vance, Mary McIntosh, Feminists Against Censorship, et cetera) do not support these anti-pornography moves.[31] Some fear that supporting censorship legislation against pornography would strengthen the powers of the right-wing moralists. Another objection is that anti-pornography has become a single issue, when they believe that it should be only part of an attack on sexism in all its forms. The counter argument to that claim is that feminists have not been physically able to fight on all fronts at once. It became necessary early on in the women's movement for the issues to be shared out – for some women to concentrate on particular issues and others on different ones, such as pornography, battering, rape, equality of work opportunity, equality of pay, et cetera. It seems obvious, however, that those women who have made censorship an issue are reluctant to include pornography in a programme for change.

Some feminists who oppose the banning of pornography are on very shaky ground when they maintain that the research does not show any correlation between its availability and violence against women. In *The Age of Sex Crime*, Jane Caputi shows that the case histories of sex killers almost universally revealed 'not only a regular use of pornography, but also the enactment of a fantasy of making and participating in pornography itself'. She quotes several sociological and psychological reports, and official, judicial and police reports from the United States. In a National Institute of Justice study in which thirty-six serial murderers were interviewed, all of them ranked pornography as their principal sexual interest. I have uncovered no official or scientific studies of the correlation between pornography and rape, but one similarity exists between the relevant statistics: they are both on the increase.[32] The anthropologist Peggy Reeves Sanday linked campus rapes in her own university with pornographic video shows watched every night by male students, and found other anecdotal evidence of a similar nature on other campuses.[33]

Lynne Segal is also concerned for the 'fragility of male sexuality' and sees the current flourishing of pornography not as evidence of men's domination of women but as an expression of men's declining power in Western society. She maintains that in a society where women's power is

increasing because of divorce, single mothers, working wives, women being publicly critical of men, and self-assertiveness in women, pornography
is a compensation, a reassurance, for men's loss of power over women; it is,
she said, the last bark of the stag at bay. Her insight is important but it must
be taken in tandem with the arguments which point out the damage
pornography does; its links with real violence. She does, however, acknowledge 'a dynamic interplay between power and desire ... which
eroticises those seen as inferior'.[34]

The very minor, and localised, changes in the balance of power between
women and men may have contributed in some small part to the increase in
pornography, but its very proliferation militates against better relations
between the sexes. It cancels out the efforts of women to re-educate men,
or the efforts of both women and men to remove the root causes of male
domination, because it infects the minds of boys and young adults at an
impressionable age, and either initiates them into the regime of male
supremacy or causes them great psychological conflict. It is not just a
question of making pornography available for those who wish to enjoy it;
it is a growing industry, constantly seeking new customers and markets.
The pressures on men to avail of it are exploited by the industry in many
ways but particularly in the deification of male supremacy. If sexual
harassment is an area where legal restrictions are considered necessary then
so also is pornography. Legal restrictions would indicate a definite cultural
disapproval or rejection of what it contains and represents.

16

AGAINST OUR WILL

Rape, said Susan Brownmiller in her seminal book *Against Our Will: Men, Women and Rape*, is about power, it is man's basic weapon of force against women, 'it is nothing more or less than a conscious process of intimidation by which all men keep all women in a state of fear'. Brownmiller's book focused attention on rape as an instrument of women's oppression, and repudiated the belief that rape was a matter of compulsive desire. In her 1982 study, *Women Working: Prostitution Now*, Eileen McLeod quotes research which describes rape as an extreme example of man's aggression towards women,[1] and places it on a 'spectrum of sexual insult and assault that women are subjected to throughout their lives', ranging from obscene comments from complete strangers to rape and murder. The Cambridge philosopher Ross Harrison also saw rape as a sort of punishment of women by men, because when applied in a few cases it has the effect of moulding the pattern of all women's social behaviour. Harrison points out that the punishment aspect of rape is reinforced in court proceedings, where the woman victim rather than the man seems to be on trial.[2]

The broad spectrum of feminist and informed analysis agrees with Brownmiller and Harrison, and sees rape as the product of men's power, and most accept that it functions as a sexual control of all women by men. From a woman's point of view, both are correct: all women live in fear of rape, although they may push the concern to the back of their mind. It is also true that all men, whether or not they realise it, benefit from that fear, when women seek their protection against rape, or concede to them for fear of rape.

It would seem at first glance that there are two types of rape – sex-inspired and power-inspired. But on closer examination it is evident that power enters both. The man who believes that a woman has been leading him on and arousing him – 'a cock-teaser' – rapes her partly because he has been aroused, but also to show her 'who's boss', to control her, to take revenge on her. However, it goes further than that in the suppression of women's sexuality; rape is a punishment for women who express their sexuality. It is also a punishment for women who challenge men in what men consider their own areas of superiority; it demonstrates a primitive act of domination, or a simple declaration of man's superiority and power over women, as in the casual rapes of elderly women in the course of burglaries, and of women in other vulnerable situations inside and outside the home.

It has been claimed that women enjoy rape, and it is true that women have rape fantasies which they obviously enjoy. This may seem incongruous when women fear rape. Psychoanalyst Helene Deutsch suggested that there was an innate masochism in women; in her day nobody mentioned the eroticisation of subordination in female and male sexuality. Women's enjoyment of rape fantasies is as pathological as sexual aggression in men, and it is part of the eroticisation of their subordination in the same way that aggression can be erotic to men. The rapist in a woman's rape fantasy is always either a man she finds attractive or the image of one she would find desirable or exciting, the dark handsome one who is going to become her lover. He is forceful, masterful, he may even be a 'bodice-ripper', but not too violent; and, of course, he falls in love with her and desires her as a person. Women's fantasies of rape bear no similarity to real rape.

In some people's minds there is no such thing as rape within marriage, or the rape of a prostitute, or of a woman who dresses in a sexually provocative way. In marriage a woman is considered under an obligation to provide sexual services to her husband. In the case of the prostitute,[3] or the sexy dresser, she has put her wares on display, or is in the business of selling them. The incidence of rape within marriage is not known. Legislation exists which makes it a crime, but few women report marital rape except in cases of violence or where separation or the breakdown of the marriage has occurred. There has been only one court case in Ireland since legislation making it a crime came into force.

Rape is very difficult to prove, because it is rarely performed before hostile witnesses. It is usually the victim's word against the rapist's, unless she has suffered obvious physical injury. Male judges have been notoriously inclined to blame the physically uninjured victim as having led the man on or as having post-coital second thoughts, and have been lenient on men. They are also tougher on rapists who are also guilty of sexual assault or gross indecency, terms which cover buggery, forced fellatio, and the insertion of foreign bodies in vagina or anus of the victim. Their attitude comes from a male view of intercourse that treats rape as an act like a handshake – sometimes welcome, sometimes unwelcome, but not very serious if violence is not involved.

Rape, however, is a very serious act from a woman's point of view. The implantation of sperm is one of the most serious acts in life – the possible creation of a person. In the case of rape it is not just an act of aggression, of invasion, of subjection, it is the colonisation of another person without a shred of responsibility. The satisfaction which this crime brings to the perpetrator is totally incommensurate with the result for the victim. From the man's point of view, a minor victory is won; from the woman's, it is a ravaging of her innermost self, a forced engagement and an unwelcome colonisation that could proceed to the birth of an unwanted child. (This is the philosophy and one of the arguments used by the protagonists of abortion in cases of rape.)

Since the 1970s there has been a dedicated effort by feminists to combat rape, using the media and protest marches to stir the community into action, and setting up of rape crisis centres to help the victims. Newspapers report the court cases, often without naming the accused in order to protect the privacy of the victim. But media reports of rape and violence against women are a double-edged sword; they establish that it takes place and therefore something must be done about it; but they also foster fear among women by amplifying the incidences and convincing women that they are helpless victims.

Most men deplore and condemn rape, and would never perpetrate it, but they do nothing positive to stop it beyond supporting the laws of the state and urging women to be careful and to avoid situations of danger. Yet laws have not reduced the incidence of the crime. Rape within marriage or a relationship and date rape are occasions to boast about in male-bonding groups: 'I showed her who was boss' situations; these men seem not to consider their actions as crimes. In 1975 Susan Brownmiller said that once it is accepted that rape is not a crime of uncontrollable lust, but a deliberate, hostile act of power designed to inspire fear, then something must be done about the attitudes, ideology and psychology that allow it, particularly in the case of 'impressionable, adolescent males, who form the potential raping population'. (As I said in chapter 1, they have the ideas and the vocabulary of rape and sexual oppression, *and a cultural context in which to express them.*) Twenty years later the situation has not changed.

Statistics indeed show that adolescents form the largest age group of rapists. These young men have not yet entered the kingdom of patriarchy, declares Cambridge historian Roy Porter, 'they lack the permanent erections of mature patriarchy – wealth, property, office, "standing"'. Other rapists, he says, come from armies of occupation, and those on the margins of patriarchal society who fail to be 'encultured into normal patriarchal sex'. Rapists, he says, are not the 'shock troops' of patriarchy, as Brownmiller called them, they are 'its wayward sons'.[4] If this sounds like an indulgent male view, it emphasises the lack of urgent concern that men feel about rape. Porter goes on to relate rape to the sexual culture of these times. He insists that society is socially conditioned to this culture, just as many Victorian women were conditioned into an absence of sexuality, and as sexual activity became more 'free and legal', rapes and other sexual offences such as child-molesting, became even more prevalent.

Although Porter says that rape flourishes on the margins and in frontier situations – that is, where there is no rule of law – he does not believe that rape is an instrument of patriarchy to keep women in subjection. (Perhaps it is a question of semantics: while rape may not be a conscious patriarchal instrument of oppression, it certainly acts as such where women are concerned.) He holds that it was not as prevalent in earlier centuries as it is today, that men had such control of women then that they did not need rape as a method of oppression. He bases this thesis on the absence of references to rape in the diaries and writings of women in the sixteenth, seventeenth and eighteenth centuries, and on the small number of prosecutions for rape in those times. He admits, however, that much rape would have gone unreported, but he does not give due weight to the consideration of the shame and ostracisation that women (and their families) suffered as a result of being raped. It became a deep, dark secret in order to preserve reputations, and in many cases vengeance on the rapist was meted out secretly. In regard to its absence in early writings, rape often lurked between the lines in the guise of 'seduction'. Rape was a capital offence in Britain until 1840, and fear of the gibbet could account for its rarity before then.

Although he does not see rape as an instrument of patriarchy, Porter admits that it is about power and domination more than sexuality, and that it arises as much from masculine culture as from the individual rapist. (It could be said that if men regard women as sexual objects, then rape for them is not an abuse of women, it is using them for what they are for.) Porter also admits that in the United States 'with cults of glamourised women and macho men, with the most strident and successful women's movement and the most vicious male backlash ... rape does indeed become male vengeance'.

Lynne Segal agrees and asks: 'Might not rape be the deformed behaviour of men accompanying the destabilisation of gender relations, and the consequent contradictions and insecurities of male gender identity.'[5] There may be an element of truth there, because in stable societies, such as provincial towns and rural areas in Ireland, the incidence of rape is relatively low, no doubt controlled by public opinion and the danger of being found out.

If rape is an element in the male backlash against feminism, we are not without our backlash women. Young, naïve Katie Roiphe in intergenerational reaction against her feminist mother (and looking for attention), questioned the reality of date rape (particularly on campus), suggesting that these episodes may have been only bad sexual experiences.[6] Rape, she says, requires physical force, the strong threat of physical force, or the woman unconscious (passed out drunk). Camille Paglia also says that date rape does not exist, that a woman by consenting to accompany a man is consenting to sexual intercourse. Being iconoclastic about feminism gets both women attention.

Men in general ask what they can do, other than condemn rape, and the answer is, a lot. In the case of ordinary physical attacks in the course of robbery on elderly people living alone, men came together, declared 'Community Alert' and 'Neighbourhood Watch' areas, signposted them and formed community patrols. Such a course may not be feasible in the case of rape, but it was a considered reply. However, there have not been any meetings of men considering how they can combat rape, nor educational courses in schools, like those for drug addiction, teenage pregnancy and AIDS prevention, nor has there been a concerted drive to change cultural attitudes to rape.

In an article examining the steps taken to reform the law in relation to rape in Britain and North America, British Professor of Law Jennifer Temkin remarked on the reluctance of men in all countries, and of traditional women's groups in Britain to campaign for change.[7] Rape has been regarded as a women's issue, and the battle has been left to feminists although the benefits accrue to all women. Male-controlled legislatures everywhere have had to be pushed into making changes in law so that rape victims are not treated like criminals, and sentences for rapists are made more severe. They have sat on their hands in relation to a cultural and social environment which allows rape, and which in the case of pornography promotes it; and they have ignored psychological theories that might help to bring about change. Anthropologist Peggy Reeves Sanday observed during fieldwork in West Sumatra that it was an almost rape-free society. A man who rapes is treated as a pariah, she reports, his masculinity is ridiculed, he is ostracised, exiled or even killed.[8]

Sanday found that there are rape-prone and relatively rape-free societies. In the rape-prone societies personhood for males is expressed in terms of toughness and interpersonal violence, female power and authority is low and men show contempt for women as decision-makers. In rape-free societies women and men are equals, womanly virtues are respected, and the attitude towards nature is one of reverence rather than domination and exploitation.[9]

Lynne Segal says that tackling the problem of rape means tackling the dominant mythology which sees rape as a part of male sexuality or need for dominance. She sees rape as a more complex behaviour, expressing many emotions: anger, inadequacy, guilt and fear of women, all linked with men's attempts to affirm their masculinity. It stems as well, she says, from the economic, political and ideological practices which give men power over women, allow them to abuse women sexually with impunity, and also allow men's violence against women in the home to go unpunished.

In *The Hite Report on Male Sexuality*, a number of rapists replied to the survey; but they were a minority. However most of the respondents had wanted to rape a woman at one time or another. No figure was given for the number of rapist responses, but I counted eighty-two separate replies which comes to something over one per cent of total responses, that is, one man in a hundred is liable to rape. In a town of 30,000 with, say, 10,000 males over sixteen, there could be 100 potential rapists. It is a sobering thought. (Shere Hite applied the designation 'some' to respondents who admitted rape, and in her notes on methodology 'some' lay between 11 per cent and 33 per cent.) The breakdown of those who said that they had at one time or another wanted to rape a woman is interesting:

- In the general sample, of those who had replied anonymously to the survey, only 53 per cent said they wanted to rape, or had fantasies of raping a woman.
- Of those who gave their names 64 per cent entertained the idea of rape.

- The proportion rose to 77 per cent where the respondents thought they were replying to another man.
- It rose further to 81 per cent where they were, or had been, in the military.

Which brings us to the incidence of rape, or mass rape, in war situations.

There has always been rape in war when one army overruns the territory of another; occupying armies have set their seal on the population by raping the women. All armies have raped in all wars; this is a horrific fact that is hidden beneath the victories, rarely reported by war correspondents, and ignored when the history is written. In some wars it has been revealed and in recent times documented by the women involved, but nobody has ever been punished for it. 'Our boys' never rape, only 'the enemy' rapes. But our boys *do* rape; rape took place in the First and Second World Wars by all the armies involved – American, British, German, Russian, et cetera – and in every other local war – Korea, Vietnam, Bangladesh,[10] and so on. There is something about the male ethos of war that allows it, that gives men the wish, the desire or will, the need, to rape; war certainly gives them the opportunity. Is it a celebration of their male dominance in victory? Is it related to a cycle of fear and anger at being put in a situation of fear? Or is it a function of the hierarchal organisation which puts soldiers at the bottom of a chain of command with only 'enemy' women to dominate?

One reason is that it is the culture of war, rape as the spoils of war was endorsed in many Old Testament stories. When Moses, on the 'inst-ructions of God', waged war on the Midianites and captured them and their stock, he instructed his officers to kill all the boys and all the women who were not virgins, 'but the women children that have not known a man by lying with him, keep alive for yourselves'. There are many more biblical accounts, and these are the historical roots, the cultural ratification, for present-day rape and genocide in war.

The latest atrocities in the genocidal war in former Yugoslavia brought home to everyone the reality of rape in war. The Serbian armies were ordered by their superiors to carry out systematic mass rape on Croatian and Muslim women in a declared tactic of 'ethnic cleansing'.[11] This has been acknowledged by Serb spokespersons. Their purpose was threefold: to assert domination over the non-Serb ethnic group, both women and men; to effect 'ethnic cleansing' by 'sowing' Serbian seed, again as a gesture of domination, holding the male contribution to reproduction to be dominant; women were to be kept prisoner until they gave birth to

Chetnik children; as a triumphalist act to strike terror into the population.

The testimony of survivors and refugees was reported in the media worldwide (see Appendix 1). The United Nations Commission on Human Rights declared rape and ethnic cleansing as war crimes. Two New York based international human rights organisations sent a delegation into the war zone to collect evidence. They had little success because it was difficult for the women who had been raped to identify the soldiers who had raped them. Moreover, United Nations peace-keeping soldiers were reported in *Newsday* as patronising the forced-prostitution brothels set up by the Serbian army. The abuse of women in that war makes horrific reading: rape, penetration with truncheons and other objects, mutilation and murder, forced prostitution were commonplace; rapes and tortures were taped for pornographic videos.[12]

Rape is currently being used as a weapon of war and as an unofficial instrument of state power and terror in many countries where dictatorships, oppressive regimes or strongly patriarchal cultures exist. These rapes do not get reported, and are usually kept secret by the victims because of the stigma which attaches to a raped woman. They are only revealed when they make political waves such as this account by the Pakistani journalist, Ahmed Rashid. He reported that 'every year hundreds of women are raped by men connected with the state structure - feudal landlords, politicians and policemen'. Nothing was ever done about this situation until one high-born woman was raped by five armed Criminal Investigative Agency men, who questioned her about her association with Benazir Bhutto and her party. Her family filed a court case against the agency and its director, and brought the scandal out into the open.

Another report by William Dalrymple in the *Observer Magazine* (20 March 1994) told of an Indian woman of the lower (potter) caste, a government-paid health auxiliary, who was raped by the village headman and his two sons as a punishment because she reported the family to the authorities for illegal child marriage. She was obstructed by the police, insulted and ostracised by her village in her attempts to report the rape to the authorities. Social workers took up her cause and created a political lobby, and eventually the rapists were committed to trial, with a strong case brought against them.

There are varying degrees of motivation for rape: power (always), fear, frustration, pride, anger, sexual deprivation (combined with one of the foregoing), but each of these must be backed up by a psychological linkage that stimulates an erection. The activator may be the woman's fear, or the generalised fear that soldiers live with, or sexual need; the erection and the tension caused by one of these triggers demands relief and rape is the solution. Biological determinists would say that aggression is a biological instinct in humans as in other animals, and might see rape as an act of survival, the 'selfish gene' ensuring its reproduction. From the psychological point of view, the idea that man has a rape-prone, animal nature is at variance with the idea of the superior, transcendent creature that male supremacy is supposed to suggest.

In 1975 when Susan Brownmiller wrote *Against Our Will*, the incidence of rape was enough to frighten her. At that stage rape was not reported except in rare cases. Feminism was only beginning to be assertive, so there was no reason for men to feel threatened. There is no way of knowing if rape has increased in the last twenty years, but the number of women who have come forward to the new rape crisis centres and said that they were raped many years ago is very large, and our newspapers report rape cases almost every day. In tackling the prevalence of rape, it is essential that we engage in constructing new definitions and images of women's active sexuality, to which every woman is entitled without courting violence. Similarly we must engage in constructing new images of male sexuality, because, as Lynne Segal says, while it is phallic and assertive, it may also be passive, receptive, diffuse and sensual, expressing all manner of joyful and generous, rather than twisted and vicious, emotions.

To research the subject of the sexual abuse of children throughout the world, in incest, the making of pornography, child marriages, sexual slavery, enforced prostitution, clitoridectomy, infibulation, is to see a pathological male culture.

Incest has always been with us. The Old Testament (Leviticus) forbade it and laid down punishments for certain prescribed forms of incest. It prohibited sexual relations with near kin but in a detailed list of these it does not mention specifically father/daughter incest. The crime seems to lie in a man having sexual relations with his father's wives, daughters and sisters; the crime was against the father, against the patriarchy, not against the woman's person or integrity. All forms of adultery (sexual relations with another man's *wife*) were punishable by death.

The Judaic Ten Commandments only mention adultery (not incest), and the Precepts of the Catholic Church specify only *marrying* within 'the forbidden degrees of kindred'. Even in these commandments and pro-scriptions incest was the hidden sin, and de facto it remained so until the recent efforts of the women's movement to bring it out into the open. But the resistance of society to admitting that it exists still remains. In Britain, when social workers started to uncover sexual abuse of children in the home, they met with great resistance from parents, community and police. In the famous Cleveland case in 1988, social workers were persecuted for their efforts, charged with wrongful accusation, even by the authorities, and legal action was abandoned in nearly all cases.

Freud had problems with incest. In the early 1890s, when he first encountered evidence of child sexual abuse among both male and female patients, he spent several years developing his theory of seduction, which he took into account when seeking the causes of their 'hysteria' or neurosis. The 'seducers' who practised this 'perversion', he wrote, were their fathers when the victims were very young, and older brothers and sisters later on. From 1893 he pursued this seam of research, then in 1897 he declared that he was mistaken and that the 'memories' of his patients were really 'fantasies' arising out of the sexual desire of the child for the father. (How did the child know about the form of such sexual acts if they did not happen?) It was Freud's flight from what he called 'the unthinkable' – and the unthinkable was that the incidence of 'perversion would have to be immeasurably more frequent than the hysteria' because neurosis arises from 'an accumulation of events'.[13]

Florence Rush was one of the first to query Freud's change of mind and to assert that the seduction theory was in reality sexual abuse, not fantasy. She attributed his recantation to his problems with his own father and to his desire to maintain the status of fathers.[14] In *Thou Shalt Not Be Aware*, Alice Miller wrote of her regret that Freud had refused to accept the prevalence of incest.[15] The tendency of parents to use their children to meet their own needs, she says, is so generally accepted that people do not refer to in-cestuous sexual abuse as a perversion, but as one of the many ways adults exercise power over their children.[16] Another critic of Freud's rejection of the idea of incest was Jeffrey Masson, but he accused Freud of intellectual cowardice.[17]

Some of the sexual radicals saw nothing wrong with child incest or sexual activity with children if damage was not done to the child. (Presumably they meant physical damage, because it has been proven that children who have been sexually abused suffer psychological damage.) Reich considered a genital relationship between parent and child as 'normal'. Some libertarians, still maintain that if the child enjoys 'harmless sex' then there is nothing wrong with it. Jeffrey Weeks points out that for moral absolutists such practice is wrong because it breaches the innocence necessary for mature development; but he asks if 'intergenerational' (crossgenerational) sex is a disruption of cultural expectations, or an assault by older people on younger? In answering he remains true to his Reichian leanings.

Weeks shows a tolerance for 'self-declared paedophiles' (and he means pederasts – 'man-boy lovers') who, he maintains, are interested in boys from the age of twelve to nineteen, and provide 'no evidence of either cruelty or violence', and where the boys 'overwhelmingly experienced their sexual experiences as positive'. While he accepts that a sexual relationship between a heterosexual man and a young girl is exploitative, he believes that the power imbalance between a man and a boy is not necessarily so, because 'it does not carry the same sociosexual implications that a heterosexual relationship inevitable does'. He would like to shift the focus of intergenerational sexual activity away from the subject of the sexual activity in itself to the forms of power which are involved and the limits imposed on the free play of consent: 'if the power element were removed from intergenerational sexual activity, then the question of consent could be discussed'.[18]

The use of children in prostitution is one aspect of the Southeast Asian sex industry and moves have been made to curtail it. Following a visit to the Philippines, Australian Senator Margaret Reynolds launched a campaign to stop the sexual exploitation of Asian children by men from her country. After a programme of education and lobbying by her and the Bangkok based group End Child Prostitution in Asian Tourism, legislation was introduced in 1994 prohibiting Australian men from having sex with children (aged sixteen and under) overseas. Some countries have enacted laws which allow them to take legal action against any of their nationals who sexually exploit children in another country. One such case was successfully brought in Sweden, and Irish and British politicians have also raised the question in their respective parliaments.

All women (feminist or not), apart from the rare exception, will condemn adult/child sexual activity

- because of the power difference,
- because children lack maturity,
- and because it is inevitable, in a sexual situation, that young girls and

boys will be exploited by adult men; it is overwhelmingly adult men who sexually abuse children).

There is an inherent and inevitable structural imbalance in the situation because the adult person fully understands the sexual situation, and the child is unaware of it. The revelations of victims of early sexual abuse which have come to light in recent years indicate that the trauma suffered by them lasts well into adulthood. Libertarians might say that the trauma arises because of the cultural climate, because of the attitudes to sexuality, sexual activity and sexual relations which exist. By that logic, then, they should refrain from condoning crossgenerational sexual activity until the culture changes; and their attitude takes no account of the reservoir of anger and hurt that is the legacy of victims who were too young to be aware that incest was condemned by society.

Sheila Jeffreys discusses the 'Lolita' complex, the allegation that the girl child seduces her abuser. Jeffreys points out that child sexuality develops gradually and a child seeking affection from an adult is not 'seeking to service adult male sexuality'; and that as in the case of prostitution, the victim (the woman, the girl child) is cast as the problem, and the male abuser disappears from blame and from the cultural picture. Similarly, she debunks the idea that paedophile groups of the 1970s and 1980s were, as they claimed, interested only in children's liberation, in freeing them from the strictures of parents and allowing their sexuality free rein. They were, she declares, 'demanding sexual access, without legal hassles, to the territory of children's bodies.'[19]

There is another side to the discussion. Incestuous and other sexual abuse of children has been attributed to many causes: sexual inadequacy, cheap sexual relief, the misuse of power, the sexual abuse which the abuser may have experienced in childhood. Incest by fathers has been blamed on mothers who neglect their partners' sexual needs. Psychologists would say that the abuser is also a victim. In her article 'Betrayal' Susie Orbach says that sexual abuse has less to do with sexuality than with complex feelings of powerlessness, vulnerability, anger and longing, which produce a violent reaction and are projected on to the victim. She goes even further, to suggest that sexual aggression is the abuser's call of distress, and an attempt to transfer his pain to the victim as a way to get rid of it, and as revenge for it.[20]

Many male sexual abusers of children, of partners or of women in general, have been abused themselves as children. Some link wife-beating with incest. Women cope with sexual abuse in a different way: some abused girls later become prostitutes and drug addicts. One study quoted in Miller revealed that 70 per cent of all prostitutes and 80 per cent of female drug addicts interviewed were severely sexually abused as children; most suffer from poor self-image and often severe depression, turning their anger in on themselves.[21]

The incest taboo, according to some modern psychoanalysts and anthropologists, is the foundation of civilisation (see Lévi-Strauss in chapter 7), yet incest is a less studied phenomenon than rape. Society is slow to accept that it is widespread (nobody knows how prevalent) because it is a canker in the heart of the family, leaving that institution open to severe criticism. The literary world was shocked to discover that Virginia Woolf was a long-suffering victim of incest;[22] thus the source of her mental illness and the reason for her suicide became evident to researchers – one example of a woman turning her anger in on herself.

When, in the 1970s, women were encouraged to speak out about their experiences, they spoke first of their current experiences, and when the rape crisis centres were established, they catered for current victims. After some time, earlier memories of rape surfaced in the minds of women seeking to explain their psychological problems, and rape crisis centres found increasingly that their clients were women who had been raped in the past. It took longer for incest victims to speak out and not all of them did so. Those who did harboured an anger against the abuser so great that they were ready to hit back, or spoke out to protect siblings.

Social workers became more vigilant in the detection of child sexual abuse in families. Slowly it became evident that incest was widespread in society. According to Segal some social service departments in the United Kingdom suggest that as many as 20 per cent of girls and 10 per cent of boys will have been abused as children, and the vast majority of perpetrators are fathers or (more commonly) stepfathers.[23] Almost one-third of the women who replied to *The Hite Report on the Family* reported having to deal with sexual abuse, either from a father or stepfather, a brother, uncle or grandfather – 'sometimes "just" sexual harassment, sometimes forced coitus'.[24] The Cleveland affair in Britain horrified everyone but it also opened eyes. Even in Ireland, because of some notorious cases, structures are being put in place to uncover and deal with incest and to help the victims, mechanisms designed to encourage children to tell of any abuse, and to help social workers, teachers, mothers and others who come in contact with children regularly to recognise the signs.

Some feminist theorists have asked if male emotional and physical violence against women is a symptom of their general alienation from a loving, caring life, and from an economically and politically insecure society. Others place more emphasis on inequality of power; they say men are violent towards women because they can be, because they have power over them. These theories are part of the answer: inequality of power gives men the opportunity of violence towards women, but it doesn't explain why they should want to be violent. That may result partly because of their alienation from a caring life and an insecure society. But men have brought about this alienating and insecure society themselves, with their multinational industries, their abuse of science, their wars and their weapons of mass destruction – in other words, their power-seeking. Male bonding is a central pillar of patriarchy: men bond together in all the authoritarian institutions – the State, both in politics and civil service, the religions, the various professions, particularly in the upper echelons of the legal profession, the judiciary, medicine and business.

The American sociologist Lionel Tiger said that bonding was a male 'instinct' which made them the natural leaders in society and gave them control over women.[25] All feminist writers point to male bonding as an essential ingredient of male domination, but they see it as a power ploy not as a biological factor. Part of the bonding mechanism is the disparagement of women which is often sexual. Men bond at work and in clubs, through sexual jokes and innuendo, by the denigration of women through their sexuality, by viewing pornography together, in what Dorothy Dinnerstein calls 'a group affirmation of their common maleness' and Segal refers to as sexist sniggering. The disparagement of women is not always overt, it can be merely tacitly assumed, but there is always an assumed superiority to women in these male groups. Ann Ferguson says that men bond together in situations which require the disparagement of women, and not from an initial need to disparage women.[26] Dinnerstein would disagree and point to her 'filial spite' theory, that men need to put down women in order to liberate themselves from their childish antagonism to the mother. This, she says, is the reason they seek refuge from female control in sex-segregated institutions and fight to keep them segregrated.

Some commentators go further and say that male bonding is a substitute or an outlet for homosexuality. Ferguson sees male bonding as part of her system of sex/affective energy, which describes both sexual interest and other affectionate attachments such as friendship, parental and family love, kinship, and all kinds of social bonding with others. Sexual segregation of work, she says, allows for an expression of sex/affective energy between men and between women, a same-sex bonding which is not overtly sexual; and it ensures that male sexual bonding is preserved and hence male power over women.

However, while male bonding is sacrosanct in society, female bonding is discouraged except in tacitly defined situations, particularly in marriage where a woman's prior loyalty is expected to be to her husband and children. This disapproval of female bonding is a divide-and-conquer tactic and is why feminism is criticised by the institutions of the establishment; it is why women will say 'I'm not a feminist but ...' and go on to state a feminist point of view. It is also why men and their institutions always associate feminism with its most extreme manifestations in order to discredit it. If women bonded in the same way as men, they could reduce or remove male domination.

Men bond to maintain male supremacy, and to exercise power over society, but they equate coercion with cohesion. There would be no civilised society without the work of women. Men perpetuate divisiveness, often without realising they are doing so, because they tacitly accept the structures constructed by male supremacy: they may even think that there are no alternatives.

On the other hand, to look on the pessimistic side of this reasoning, universal change may not be possible. If one accepts the theory that pacificism can never win against aggression because the aggressors will wipe out the pacifists, the same argument is applicable to equality. Because if a significant proportion of men seek to perpetuate male supremacy by either coercion or violent means, they will win, unless the men who value equality are prepared to resist.[27] But that is a counsel of despair, and we might do better to take note of the advances that have been made against male supremacy. There will never be grand or sweeping change. It will come about by small increments, legal, social and psychological, through the work of groups and individual women and men who will campaign for it.

A MULTITUDE OF SEXUALITIES?

During the past twenty-five years, an enormous literature has developed on the subject of homosexuality. Much of it has been the work of male homosexuals, but a significant amount has emerged from the women's movement, from both political lesbians and self-identifying or 'sexual' lesbians. The incidence of homosexuality in society is generally accepted as roughly 10 per cent. This was borne out by *The Hite Report on Male Sexuality*, where 9 per cent of the respondents claimed that they were exclusively homosexual and a further 6 per cent claimed bisexuality; and in *The Hite Report on Women and Love*, 11 per cent of women respondents had love relationships only with other women; and an additional 7 per cent sometimes had homosexual relations.

European statistics differ greatly from these American results. In *Sexual Behaviour in Britain*, less than 6 per cent of men claimed some level of attraction to men or had some homosexual experience, but only 0.5 per cent claimed to be exclusively homosexual.[1] Less than 5 per cent of women claimed some attraction to women and only 0.3 per cent claimed homosexual experience. The authors claimed that the British returns were consistent with similar surveys in France and Norway, but they entered a caveat: 'Because of possible reporting and response bias all prevalence figures relating to homosexual activity should be regarded as minimum estimates.' One thing is evident from this survey, that there seems to be a higher level of bisexuality than of homosexuality in the population. A recent American survey found that only 2–3 per cent of the population was exclusively homosexual; and 8.6 per cent reported some homosexual activity, which again shows a higher level of bisexuality than of exclusive homosexuality.[2] I would expect that the same caveat applies to the American survey as to the British one.

In *The History of Sexuality*, Vol. 2 , Michel Foucault points out that the concept of homosexuality as we define it – as a distinct and separate sexual preference – did not exist in the time of the early Greeks. They did not see love of one's own sex and love of the opposite sex as opposed or radically different types of behaviour. The Greeks were, he said, much more interested in the ethical question of the differences between the man of loose morals (one incapable of resisting either women or boys) and the one who practised self-denial, which was held in very high regard. However, he also pointed out that as one man had to be passive in the relationship, homosexuality between two adult men at that time could be the subject of 'irony and criticism'. While passivity was acceptable for women and boys who had not yet finished their education, it was 'disliked' in men.

There are, however, conflicting views on homosexuality in ancient Greece. Some, like Foucault, apply a homosexual frame to close relationships between men. There are also classical scholars who say that pederasty was practised then because the lowly status and uneducated state of women made them poor companions for intellectual men. Others believe that to be 'a gilding of homosexuality' by monastic and effeminate intellectuals, and point to the hetaerae.[3] The hetaerae were educated and independent women who remained unmarried to protect their property rights from the marriage laws, and played a vital part in the intellectual and social life of the time.[4]

In the first and second centuries A.D., the Roman practice of men loving freeborn boys declined but sexual relations with slave boys continued. And while male homosexuality was acceptable, sexual acts (penetration) between women were regarded as 'unnatural', because a woman, as an inferior caste, was usurping the role of a man.[5]

The sexologist Alfred Kinsey also provided a historical vindication of homosexuality by delving into early Jewish history to show that homosexuality and other sexual practices such as fellatio and cunnilingus were included in religious practice. The condemnation of these practices around the seventh century B.C., he said, was a move to establish a Jewish culture different from that of the neighbouring 'heathens'. It was also designed to concentrate sexual activity on reproduction, because the small Jewish nation needed to increase its population in order to survive.[6]

The nineteenth-century psychologist Krafft-Ebing saw homosexuality (which he called 'antipathic sexual instinct') manifest in two forms: congenital and acquired; the latter due to masturbation and occurring in prisons, ships, garrisons and boarding schools because of the absence of females. In the same period Havelock Ellis also saw homosexuality as a congenital inversion, which placed him firmly on the biological side; but like Krafft-Ebing he also recognised it as, in some cases, a temporary condition.

For Kinsey (originally a zoologist) homosexuality was a perfectly normal condition; he said that other mammals have homosexual relations (and masturbate) quite commonly. Kinsey saw sexuality as a continuum on which a person was not necessarily confined to one practice. He devised a scale to measure the degree of homosexuality, bisexuality and hetero-sexuality found in the population, and because of overlapping and varia-tions in tendencies from one person to another, he said that the term 'homosexual' applied to a behaviour pattern rather than to a person. Kinsey's theory refers only to men but is important because it was an attempt at scientific evaluation. Konrad Lorenz (also a zoologist) gave an affecting description of homosexuality among geese, where paired ganders were not just accepted within the flock: they always attained very high, if not the highest, places in the ranking order of the colony.[7]

Foucault dates the birth of the 'homosexual person' (man) from 1870, when homosexuality was designated as a medical or psychological prob-lem; prior to that there were homosexual acts carried out by a male or a female. In the latter half of the nineteenth century, he said, sexology and psychoanalysis dissected the personality of 'afflicted' persons and came up with a sexual type, a category of person (and a stereotype) that was homo-sexual. In fact, said Foucault, homosexuality became a problem of gender as well as of sexuality.[8] Some later writers would say that homosexual prac-titioners colluded with the sexologists and psychoanalysts in order to vindi-cate their activities and preferences.

Is homosexuality psychological, psychocultural, biological, or a perfectly natural condition? Jeffrey Weeks, a homosexual theorist, replies, 'Today it is not clear what homosexuality is: an orientation or a preference, a social role or a way of life, a potentiality in all of us or a minority experience.' His own belief is that there are homosexualities rather than a single homosexuality, and that there are biological sources, psychological disposition and social regulation in the making of sexual identities.[9]

Freud did not regard homosexuality as a 'degeneracy', but as a psycho-logical problem of identification, a faulty transition by the boy when ne-gotiating the Oedipus complex. The adolescent boy with this psychological problem identifies with his mother rather than his father, and then relates to other boys as he would like her to relate to him. He preferred to refer to it as 'inversion', and saw it as one manifestation of the universal bisexuality of humans. His theory wavered between one where the boy identified with his mother and thereafter sought a love object like himself, and another where the boy's revulsion against 'castrated' woman left him seeking a love object with a penis.[10]

This theory of how masculinity is constructed lays all men open to homosexuality, because if woman is inferior then desire and love should be directed towards the superior male. Following that logic, lesbianism should result from an appreciation by women of the superior attributes of women. However, Freud saw female homosexuality as a 'masculinity complex', the girl identifying with her father, but his work on female homosexuality was limited to not much more than two cases. In the 'Dora' case, his most famous, he failed to learn much that he might have, because he insisted in imposing a failed Oedipus transition on Dora (see Appendix 3). With male homosexuality he was on somewhat firmer ground.

Freud also saw a latent or sublimated homosexuality in male bonding in armies, in religion and, by extension we could say, in all-male social groupings such as football teams or male clubs and pubs. This insight into homosexuality, which suggests that homosexuality is not biological, could provide a new and broader insight into sexuality in general, because if sexuality is constructed psychologically and culturally then the original biological function (which remains) can be sidestepped to some extent.

Jung said that male homosexuality was partly 'the consequence of the mother complex, and partly a purposive phenomenon' (which is the prevention of reproduction). Jung defined mother complex as subordination by a strong mother.[11] Zoologist Desmond Morris deserted his own field of study to give a psychosocial explanation for homosexuality. Like Jung he blames 'an unduly masculine and dominant mother, or an unduly weak and effeminate father' for homosexuality in their offspring. But this is a cultural prejudice on his part and has no scientific basis. Another social factor might well be that male homosexuals are questioning the cultural structure of male sexuality, and finding a conflict with their emotions.

Post-Freudians like Dorothy Dinnerstein and Nancy Chodorow see homosexuality as a likely result of a 'father-absence', particularly for girls who can remain in a pre-oedipal state of erotic relationship with the mother. Juliet Mitchell had a humanist view of homosexuality: it was a human condition and therefore acceptable, any other attitude was moralistic and prejudiced.

Ann Oakley cites from two separate studies by sex researchers, endo-crinologists Dr John Money and Drs John and Joan Hampson, who were studying intersexuals (or hermaphrodites) in the 1960s. They found that the sexual orientation of 95 per cent of their study group depended on the sex which was *ascribed* to them, that is the sex in which they were reared, and not on 'their biological sex as determined by chromosomes, hormones, gonads and the formation of the internal and external genitals'. One of the researchers, John Money, decided that 'erotic outlook and orientation is an autonomous psychologic phenomenon, independent of genes and hor-mones, and moreover a permanent and ineradicable one as well'.[12] (The last part of this statement is open to question as feminists who chose political lesbianism, and men in prisons, have shown.)

These researchers have come down in a decided manner on the side of psychosocial influence on sexual orientation. Whatever the 'cause' of sex-ual orientation or preference, stereotypes of both homosexual and hetero-sexual individuals have emerged. Conforming to a stereotype results when persons who find that they differ from the 'norm' consort together and join forces against the rest of society. There is a culture of homosexuality just as there is a culture of heterosexuality, and these cultures lead to stereotyping.

The more likely situation is, as Kinsey suggested and as appears from the surveys quoted above, that a multitude of sexualities lie on a spectrum which runs from undifferentiated heterosexuality at one end and undifferentiated homosexuality at the other. If on the centre of that spectrum there are varying degrees of bisexuality, then it is possible that bisexuality is the norm, and heterosexuality and homosexuality are each extremes at either end. Then sexuality must have a wider definition than reproduction, a subject I will return to later.

Most male theorists who are homosexuals adopt this Kinseyan theory and see a bisexuality of which heterosexuality and homosexuality are con-stituent parts. These positions are not fluid, they say, they are given, but the psychological or biological causes are not yet known. Other researchers are guided by a desire to prove that homosexuality is a natural, biological phenomenon, without producing the convincing proofs, and many male homosexuals prefer this theory.

In recent times medical science has been dissecting the physical body in search of the elusive physiological element that constitutes the homosexual. From this medicalisation has arisen the popular perception of the male homosexual as having an imbalance of some undefined feminine element in his constitution (perhaps hormones), and the female homosexual as having a corresponding masculine imbalance. Sociobiologist Edward D. Wilson flirted with the genetic answer to homosexuality, but he qualified his thesis by saying that if a homosexual gene exists it would need a 'modifier' gene to become active and be dependent on a certain environment.[13]

A report by United States researchers gave the results of a survey carried out in 1993 which suggested that genes played a part in female homosexuality.[14] The scientists studied a group of homosexual women, half of whom had identical twin sisters, and some of the other half had non-identical twin sisters, and others had adopted sisters. They found among the women who had an identical twin that almost half of their twin sisters were also homosexual; among those who had non-identical twin sisters only 16 per cent of the twin sisters were homosexual, and among those who had adopted sisters only 6 per cent of the adopted sisters were homosexual. These findings led the researchers to believe that heredity is an important force in setting sexual orientation, because identical twins share all their genes with one another, while fraternal twins have only half their genes in common, and adopted siblings share no genes. (The same scientists had carried out a previous study in 1992 on men and found also that half of the identical twins of homosexual men turned out to be homosexual.) In explanation the researchers suggested that hormonal fluctuations in the womb affect twins differently in ways that have yet to be gauged.

These results were hardly a resounding endorsement of a genetic theory. First of all, the women were not randomly selected but canvassed through lesbian periodicals, and it is not indicated whether any or many of them were political lesbians. Then presumably the various pairs of sisters were reared together and so experienced a similar social and psychological environment which could have affected their sexual preference. Moreover, intimacy between twins is observably greater than between other siblings, and there is a greater intimacy between identical twins than between non-identical twins. That intimacy could lead to a breaking down of the cultural barriers against homosexual intimacy.

There have been reports that neuro-biologists have recently identified discrepancies between homosexual and heterosexual men in the hypothalamus and other brain structures that could help determine sexual behaviour. In 1990 Dick Swaab, director of the Netherlands Institute for Brain Research in Amsterdam, and his colleagues found that the volume of the suprachiasmatic nucleus of the brain (the part that regulates the 'biological clock' – the mechanism that controls daily cycles of sleep, and may have a role in sexual activity) was almost twice as large in homosexual men as in heterosexual men, and had double the number of cells. This research has been strongly challenged by other scientists.

In 1991, Simon LeVay, a researcher at the Salk Institute for Biological studies in San Diego, found that an area of the brain called INAH-3 was more than twice as large in heterosexual men as in homosexual men. INAH-3 is part of the anterior hypothalamus, a region known to regulate sexual behaviour in male monkeys. Two other anatomical researchers, Laura Allen and Roger Gorski, at the University of California at Los Angeles, reported that a structure in the brain called the anterior commissure, which contains nerve fibres connecting the halves of the brain, was larger in homosexual men than in heterosexual men. This area of the brain has no role in sexual behaviour. All of the men in this last study had died of AIDS, and the abnormalities could have resulted from AIDS, but the researchers did not believe that AIDS was responsible, they thought it more likely that the differences in size result from the way the brain responds to sex hormones in its development very early on in life.

This looks like a tendency to fit results to a preconceived theory, one that links male homosexuality to femininity. In that case how do they explain macho male homosexuals whose sexuality is obviously male? Similarly it was found that in tests on spatial and verbal ability homosexual men scored closer to women than to men, suggesting some biological difference related to hormones. This is far from being in any way conclusive. Significance can be found in that result only if the researcher is prejudiced to believe that women generally lack spatial ability and men lack verbal ability. I know many heterosexual women who are as good as men in spatial ability, and many heterosexual men who have verbal ability as good as women's. I also know women who have poor verbal ability, and men who have poor spatial ability. Until recent years women have been generally segregated from mathematics, science and engineering skills; moreover, as a subordinate group, they have needed to develop their verbal ability. Jeffrey Weeks writes that the disturbing thing about the revived search for biological explanations of social behaviour is 'that the urge to fill a conceptual gap is stronger than an adherence to theoretical consistency and political judgement'.

The idea that homosexuality results from a hormonal imbalance with a surfeit of oestrogens in the man and a surfeit of testosterones in the woman has long been conventional wisdom: the female imprisoned in a male body or vice versa. But the development of homosexuality in recent times would dispute that contention.

In *Slow Motion: Changing Masculinities, Changing Men*, Lynne Segal refers to the changes that occurred in attitudes to homosexuality in the nineteenth century and the emergence of a gay rights movement in this century, what she calls the progress from 'camp' to 'gay' to 'super-macho'. (Camp was a pose of pseudo-femininity which was an exaggeration of what society deemed homosexuality to be; it was a fashion comparable to male macho posturing which is also an exaggeration.) Segal says that some radical homosexual men saw 'camp' as a way men could become more woman-identified and thus declare the conventions of masculinity oppressive. She sees the transition from 'camp' to 'gay' as political, and part of the sexual and women's liberation revolution. The Gay Liberation Front of the early seventies included both men and women. Gay men, she says, identified with the oppression of women and allied themselves with the emerging women's movement. This alliance did not last long, as the men, despite their early idealism, were unable (or unwilling) to shed their sexism. Lesbians left the Gay Liberation Front to concentrate on work within the women's movement, and homosexual men moved on to the leather-and-denim phase of super-machismo. Again this phase has been defined by some gay theorists as cocking a snoot at heterosexual males, an irony. Others suggest a more credible theory, that super-machismo is the introduction of eroticised difference within the homosexual community, and a challenge to the assumption that homosexuality means effeminacy.

Like their female counterparts, male homosexual theorists have provided important insights into sexuality. Jeffrey Weeks says that male homosexuals abandoned their identification with effeminacy in order to define themselves not as sexual deviants but in terms of 'object choice'; and adds that there is some evidence that the macho style arouses more hostility in heterosexual men than effeminacy in men because it 'gnaws at the roots of a male heterosexual identity'. Weeks discusses how homosexuality as practised today evolved from, first of all, study and discussion of its basic origins to the later establishment of its own culture and identity, and its different roles and categories. Historically, there arrived a time and a climate in which homosexuality could be discussed, then came discussion, and liberalisation followed.

Weeks does not believe that homosexuality is biological or that there is a biological explanation in the 'essential, internal characteristics' of homosexuality. He is more inclined to think that it has a cultural cause, that homosexuality results from 'complex socio-historical transformations'. He also says that male and female homosexual identity are political as well as sexual – 'identity is not a destination but a choice'; and, he says, the new gay consciousness challenges the traditional, oppressive view of homosexuality and makes it possible for everyone to enjoy different types of sexuality. But he has reservations about the tactics of modern political homosexuals. Having challenged the sexual status quo and the idea that sexual identity is fated and fixed, he says, they 'have become key definers of a homosexual role and its minority status, thus leaving heterosexuality as a "norm" '.

Segal also welcomes this political dimension. She extols the 'affirmation of sexuality', of pleasure in bodies, that is evident in the lifestyles of male homosexuals and says that it is likely to have a profound effect on masculinity in general. In her analysis of the effect of AIDS on the male homosexual community she points to the rapid adjustments in their sexual behaviour in order to avoid infection, and to their new attitudes to nursing and caring. Here, of course, is another proof of the cultural construction of sexuality. If homosexual men could adjust so quickly to the threatening situation of AIDS, then it is evident that sexuality is to a large extent culturally defined.

Until recent times most of the scientific research has been directed towards male homosexuality, much of it guided by a desire to prove homosexuality a natural phenomenon. In general, female homosexuality has been ignored or considered of little cultural or social importance.

In Greece of the seventh century B.C., Sappho wrote her poetry, and conducted a school on the island of Lesbos, acclaimed and unmolested. The specific, derogatory terms of 'sapphist' or 'lesbian' did not appear until relatively modern times: sapphist in 1890 and lesbian in 1908 (*Oxford English Dictionary*) – no doubt under the influence of the male classical scholars. In Roman times homosexual relations between women were regarded as unnatural; in medieval times lesbians and male homosexuals were, like witches, burned at the stake; and in the seventeenth-century New World the death penalty was decreed in New Haven for lesbians. More recently, in the eighteenth and nineteenth centuries, close friendships between women (often called 'passionate' without any suggestion that they were sexual) were widely accepted. In *Surpassing the Love of Men* Lilian Faderman records many of these relationships.[15] In modern times it was not until after the First World War that homosexuality or bisexuality among women became a factor and was stigmatised. This happened, feminist writers believe, because they constituted a threat to male power by symbolising women's ability to function happily independent of men.[16]

The founding fathers of sexology, Havelock Ellis, Edward Carpenter, *et al.*, regarded lesbians as pseudo-men, women who adopted the manner and attitudes of men. Freud had trouble with lesbianism, but then he had trouble with female sexuality; it did not fit in with his theory of male homosexuality. He saw lesbianism as a masculinity complex. In his Dora case he decided that his patient identified with her father and therefore adopted a masculine identity. (With hindsight, Dora showed more signs of the sexually abused child than of any other syndrome.)

Broadly speaking, female homosexuals divide into two main strands: 'sexual' lesbians, whose sexual orientation and identity correspond in female terms to the male homosexuality described above; and 'political' lesbians, who are feminists and choose their sexual identity primarily for political reasons. Bisexuality, as seen above, is also evident among women as well as men.

Sexual lesbians hold that their sexual identity or orientation is intrinsic. Some are feminists, but for sexual lesbians their sexuality supersedes their politics. Among them are found butch-femme relationships, and the more radical of them are the libertarians who put no limits on preference.

Political lesbians are separatists who believe that the feminist agenda cannot be achieved if women continue to have sexual relations with the 'enemy': their politics influence their choice of sexual partner rather than their original sexuality. Most of them are, in fact, bisexual. Some political lesbians hold that women are essentially different to men in their innate characteristics: that they are more caring, less aggressive, creative in a more integrated and less destructive way, and that women gain from separation from men. Other political lesbians dismiss that philosophy; they hold that women are more caring because they have been subordinated. Similarly, they believe that the libertarians enjoy sado-masochism because their subordination has been eroticised.

The first political lesbian manifesto, 'Woman-identified Woman', was launched in 1970 by the New York Radicalesbians. In it they gave many quotable quotes to future writers, such as 'A lesbian is the rage of all women condensed to the point of explosion.' Feminists, they said, should not consort with the enemy. In Britain, in the late seventies, The Leeds Revolutionary Feminist Group broke away from the socialist feminists in the Women's Liberation Movement and in 1979 issued their own manifesto which accused heterosexual women as 'collaborators with the enemy', and did not mince words: 'Our definition of a political lesbian,' they wrote, 'is a woman-identified woman who does not fuck men. It does not mean compulsory sexual activity with women.' But, in fact, most of them have emotional or sexual relations with women.

Political lesbians are an important part of the women's movement, particularly on the question of the definition of sexuality. Their sexual identity, because it is deliberately chosen and because sexually it works, supports a more flexible theory of a general human bisexuality in which positions on the spectrum can be chosen. They show that sexuality is not fixed, that it can be fluid and malleable. (On the other hand, some might say that those who become political lesbians may have always been disposed to be lesbian, but that does not rule out a theory of bisexuality.) They have critics in the women's movement and in the gay liberation movements who accuse political lesbians of seeing men, rather than male-dominated institutions, as the enemy. That attitude indicates a certain amount of hairsplitting; after all, the male-dominated institutions are constructed and controlled by men, and men in general do little to change them. Sexual lesbians say that political lesbians deny them their identity, but their attitude is also illogical, and perhaps resentment that some heterosexual women can decide to assume a lesbian identity.

Political lesbians, in turn, are highly critical of the libertarians among the sexual lesbians. They say that the libertarians have adopted a male power model of sexuality; and that they are preoccupied with genital sexual activity rather than the politics of female/male relations. Janice Raymond writes: 'For all its perpetual talk about sex, libertarian lesbian discourse is silent about the connection of sex to the rest of a woman's life and therefore silent about sex itself.'[17]

Libertarian lesbians are following in the footsteps of the sexologists who tried to impose a male-type practice of sexuality on women, until the women's movement recognised it for what it was. For them the inclusion of pornography and sado-masochism in the blueprint for lesbian sexuality has become part of 'the politics of desire'.[18] Their argument is, that denying women sado-masochism is controlling women's sexuality. By the same token it could be said that stopping a man from raping a woman could also be described as controlling a man's sexuality. They fail to take into consideration that sado-masochism or even lesser forms of 'submission' are likely to be desires into which they were conditioned by patriarchy and male domination. These desires may not be easy to expel because they have been sown deeply in the unconscious and reinforced by the culture; some really serious consciousness-raising or psychotherapy may be necessary to expunge them.

In *Sexuality and Its Discontents*, when writing about what he calls 'the sexually oppressed' and the libertarian agenda, Weeks asks – is sado-masochism just a theatrical ritual of power relations or an acceptance of socially constructed fantasies? Are butch-femme relations freely chosen erotic roles or the continuation of domination and subordination? In discussing the emergence of an acknowledged subculture of sado-masochism among both male and female homosexual groups, he is ambivalent. He examines the arguments which lesbian sado-masochists put forward to justify their practices: they say that these practices provide unique insights into the nature of sexual power; that they are therapeutic and cathartic and release people from their violent and potentially anti-social fantasies; and that they show the nature of sex as ritual and play. But libertarian writer Pat Califia claims that lesbian sado-masochism is consensual, that it is power without privilege, and that it reveals the repressed sexuality behind power.[19] Weeks questions the role of power in sado-masochistic encounters and sees it as part of the old repressive culture of eroticised power. He also queries whether people need to live out each fantasy in order to be free of it. While he finds the arguments for sado-masochism not entirely convincing and consistent, he nevertheless finds it a challenge to a repressive culture and a standard-bearer for a culture of sexual activity as pleasure. In fact, he sees it as a retreat from genitality in favour of a sexuality that is not confined to any part of the body; and, following in the footsteps of Reich, he sees the sexual minorities as forces for liberation in society.

Political lesbianism is not a new phenomenon. In *Compulsory Heterosexuality and Lesbian Existence* Adrienne Rich lists the women's groups that historically resisted patriarchy or marriage: the Sapphic school of women in the seventh century B.C., the Chinese marriage-resisting sister-hoods, African sororities, and the Beguine of twelfth-century Holland (a community of women who were not religious), and of course nuns and communities of religious women that have existed for the past fifteen hundred years. These women led lives relatively free from the daily control of men. Nuns were, of course, under the rule of the local bishop or abbot.

Rich's definition of lesbianism is obviously much broader than the limited, clinically sexual meaning (a genital experience with another woman) which is usually applied to it; it falls somewhere in the space between the political and sexual lesbians. She expands the term beyond sexuality to include what she calls 'woman-identified experience': forms of primary intensity between and among women, such as sharing a rich inner life, bonding against male tyranny, the giving and receiving of practical political support. She postulates a female sexuality (or 'the erotic in female terms') that is 'unconfined to any single part of the body or solely to the body itself', that is, a diffuse energy and a joyous sharing between women. She would say that female sexual liberation is the freedom to bond together.

Rich sees no similarity between lesbianism and male homosexuality (nor indeed do male homosexual writers such as Weeks). It is, she says, 'like motherhood, a profoundly female experience with particular oppressions, meanings and potentialities we cannot comprehend as long as we bracket it with other sexually stigmatised existences'. She bases this definition of lesbianism on Nancy Chodorow's analysis of the psychosexual development of the small girl, her first close and emotional relationship with her mother, the most important person in her early life.[20] She sees lesbianism as a natural condition for women and more than a political situation, and holds that heterosexuality is the sexuality that is learned.

In presenting her alternative and thoughtful view of sexuality Adrienne Rich puts a persuasive case for the thesis that our male-dominated culture has made heterosexuality compulsory, and outlawed or marginalised homosexuality. Moreover, while the motivation of political lesbians is tactical, she provides them with a philosophical basis. Her definition suggests a continuum of sexuality stretching from friendship and pleasure in the company of another, to cuddling, petting and genital activity. But there is no reason why the same continuum should not apply to male sexuality, and no reason why eroticism should be strictly heterosexual.

Ann Ferguson disagrees with Rich that compulsory heterosexuality is the central mechanism of male domination, or that women are 'naturally' lesbian because of their original love-preference for the mother. This is due, she says, to the fact that women, not men, mother; therefore lesbianism is no more 'natural' than heterosexuality. If humans are bisexual or pansexual at birth, she says, it will not do to suggest that lesbianism is the more authentic sexual preference for feminists. Ferguson believes that compulsory heterosexuality (which she does not deny) is central to women's oppression only where women are dependent on men (an immensely widespread condition of women worldwide). 'From the fact that compulsory heterosexuality is oppressive, it does not therefore follow,' she says, 'that all heterosexuality is oppressive, nor that heterosexuals cannot be true feminists!' She describes a lesbian as 'a woman who has sexual and erotic-emotional ties primarily with women or who sees herself centrally involved with a community of self-identified lesbians whose sexual and erotic-emotional ties are primarily with women; and who is herself a self-identified lesbian'.[21]

In *Beyond God the Father* Mary Daly, the American Catholic theologian and feminist, saw the terms 'heterosexuality' and 'homosexuality' as patriarchal classifications, designed to maintain male supremacy by regulation of emotions and attachments. She saw men's fear of homosexuality, and hostility to it, as evidence of their anxiety over losing the power and social control which was based on the stereotyping of sex roles. These attitudes could be changed, she says, simply by allowing the word to mean 'a deep and intimate relationship with a person of the same sex, with or without genital activity'. Lilian Faderman said that women who identify themselves as lesbians see the term as a synonym for sisterhood, solidarity, affection and, as such, a basic aspect of feminism.

It is possible to think of a world in which women consort together and with their children, and consort with men at intervals; there are primitive societies in which that happens. But is it much different from the formalised, cultural sex segregation of the decades before feminism, with women in the home and men in the world of enterprise? And would men still rule?

There is one strong argument against political lesbianism: the opposite of compulsory heterosexuality is compulsory homosexuality. The alienation by political lesbians of women who regarded themselves as heterosexual has retarded the women's movement. The vast majority of women, who see themselves as heterosexual and attached to a man, will not change or adapt, whether that attachment has a psychological, social or biological base. If you tamper with structures, you have to be very careful with their replacements. Laying down rules about tactics will never recruit more than a tiny minority of women. Moreover, the biological content of sexuality, the desire to have children, however repressed, oppressed or occluded by social and psychological accretions, lies buried, ready to betray or subvert any constructed edifice.

Whatever original reasons existed for forbidding homosexual relations, they should now have vanished. In a world increasingly mechanised, large populations are not necessary; in fact they are a burden and a strain on resources. It could be argued that homosexuality has a political role in this much-abused planet. But whereas many homosexual women (of whatever motivation or inclination) wish to have children, there is not much evidence of such desire among male homosexuals. In fact, as Weeks said, they are absorbed in constructing a minority society; and it is obvious from their writings that this society is outside the main pulsating drive of the mass of human society which is to reproduce.

Reproduction is sexual and biological, and requires heterosexual coitus, but this does not rule out other other forms of sexuality. If sexuality as we experience it is psychologically and socially constructed, then different forms are bound to exist and are equally valid. If we look at sexuality as a set of bodily feelings and pleasures, biological and undirected until they are developed psychologically and culturally, then it has many possibilities. In that case there are millennia of conditioning to be undone if we are to arrive at a sexuality of the same integrity as that of the other mammals. It is as difficult as that, and as simple as the rearing of a new generation. Of course, if that situation is ever achieved, we may need to institute a new regulatory framework, necessary to preserve the civil and human rights of others and in the interests of the greater good of society, but it could be more firmly rooted and a more authentic sexuality than we enjoy now.

BISEXUALITY

When bisexuality is discussed it is almost always in the context of Freud's 'polymorphous perversity' – unfocused, undifferentiated, infant sexuality – or as one of the 'deviant' sexualities. But in early Greek and Roman cultures male bisexuality was considered normal. In our culture bisexuality is practised among men to a greater extent than is generally known. Many men can switch between homosexuality and heterosexuality depending on the opportunities available to them; yet they can call themselves heterosexual and believe that they have a heterosexual identity. The army, prisons, and other places of male concentration provide opportunities for homosexual activities that break down the cultural barriers. Increasingly, in court cases, we hear of homosexual and heterosexual rape perpetrated by the same man. In such cases, it is not a question of sexual choice but of power, the imposition of the rapist's will on the victim.

The practice of bisexuality, the apparent ease with which some men can slip from one 'identity' to another, is another indication that sexual identities are constructed psychosocially. Is there a hidden stream of bisexuality in society that surfaces only occasionally? The self-conscious practice of bi-sexuality by men has become established in pornographic films and videos during the last decade. (Images of female homosexuality have long been a part of mainstream heterosexual pornography.) Its success is evidence that bisexual fantasies already existed, and the commercialisation of sexual act-ivity ensured that it was only a matter of becoming accustomed to the idea. Whether one opposes or supports pornography it must be admitted that it has helped to throw light on the complexity of sexuality, and in this case it provides another indication of the existence of a bisexual nature in humans.

There is a strong case to be made that bisexuality is the human norm as writer and feminist Sue George does in *Women and Bisexuality*.[22] This is a view of sexuality as a human characteristic which is non-directed; one which, like affectionate love, is not confined to the opposite sex but is also involved in reproduction, although not exclusively confined to that end. There are two historical situations which suggest that sexuality can be non-directed: the bisexuality of men in ancient Greece, and in prisons; and the modern situation of political lesbianism where women who previously had been heterosexual, turned from men to women in the exercise of their sexuality for political reasons.

THE PASSION OF LOVE

There are three main sexual relations between people: lust (also known as sexual love or desire); romantic love or sexual passion; and gender relations within which platonic friendship and conjugal love would be included. Sometimes the word 'desire' (*Oxford English Dictionary*: a physical appetite; lust) is confused with romantic love; but while desire is generally associated with romantic love, romantic love is not always associated with desire. In many of the texts on the subject the word 'desire' is used in a somewhat confused manner to mean lust on its own *or* lust and romantic love.

First of all what is love? The *Oxford English Dictionary* defines it as 'that state or feeling with regard to a person which arises from recognition of attractive qualities, from sympathy, or from natural ties, and manifests itself in warm affection and attachment'. It also defines it as 'that feeling of attachment which is based upon difference of sex', and 'the sexual instinct and its gratification'. A versatile word – like 'sex', much used and abused – it is often confusing in its usage.

These definitions give no indication of the genesis of love. Is it of biological origin like, say, hunger, or of psychological origin like envy, or of social or cultural origin, a feeling learned from cultural norms, like say, dislike? Freud and psychoanalysts like Melanie Klein regarded love as an instinctual endowment already implanted in the infant at birth. They also say that the quite discrete 'sexual love' (desire, lust) is also a drive or instinct of paramount importance to psychological development. The problem is that the word 'lust' comes loaded with a baggage of psychological, social and moralistic attitudes as one of the seven deadly sins, which obscure its biological genesis, its biological role in all mammals to respond to the pheromones that stimulate the urge to procreate. In humans this basic instinct is mediated and controlled by psychological factors, by intelligence and its creation, culture, and it ebbs as the years advance and the sexual hormones decrease. Freud saw 'the compulsive character of the process of falling in love' as a development of the child's fixation on the parents and the problems of her/his relationship with them.

Love has a history as old as human time and a literature to match. The Song of Solomon, a collection of erotic love poems in the Old Testament, is variously dated from the eleventh century B.C. to the third century B.C. Love has engaged the professional interest of writers of all kinds: novelists, philosophers, social theorists, psychologists, psychoanalysts and historians. Aristotle called 'the passion of love' a longing for delight working upon the emotions (he looked on sexual love as a biological phenomenon and not a subject for analysis). Plato held that there could not be desire without the want of the thing desired, without privation and a certain amount of suffering. For the Greek philosophers 'the passion of love' was often an intense friendship between men; where men and women were concerned, in their estimation, perfect love was not possible because they were not equals. Sappho, however, wrote of romantic love for both sexes, but is best remembered for her love of women and, of course, for her eloquence: 'Love has obtained for me the brightness and beauty of the sun', and 'Love shook my heart like a wind falling on oaks on a mountain.'

Romantic love in medieval sociological history, referred to as courtly or chivalrous love, is attributed exclusively to the nobility. Undoubtedly this was because only the upper classes were literate and in a position to leave an account of their passions; it would be hard to believe that passionate attraction did not exist between the sexes at all levels of society. Courtly love was almost always unrequited, a 'knightly' game rather than a serious emotion, highly ritualised and usually involving an unmarried knight and a married woman or betrothed damsel.

Mary Wollstonecraft, one of the illustrious foremothers of feminism, was more realistic; in the late eighteenth century she described romantic love as a 'common passion in which chance and sensation take the place of choice and reason'. It 'draws the mind out of its accustomed state and exalts the affections,' she wrote, but the security of marriage allows the fever to subside, 'the calm tenderness of friendship, the confidence of respect' replaces 'blind admiration and the sensual emotions of fondness'.

Friedrich Engels maintained that true romantic love existed only among the proletariat, where women as well as men were in the labour market and therefore on terms of equality. For Alexandra Kollontai, in the early days of post-revolutionary Russia, romantic love was ' "winged Eros" whose love

is woven of delicate strands of every kind of emotion', but which makes one
suffer from sleepless nights, saps one's will and entangles the rational workings of the mind. Her 'wingless Eros' was where men and women of the
revolution came together without great commitment and parted without
tears or regret, in a period when there was no time or energy for love's
'joys and pains'. If there was no room in the early days of the revolution
for romantic love, by 1923 she was urging Russian youth to 'make way
for winged Eros and more commitment'.

History has been unkind to Kollontai, as it always has been to outspoken
feminists, and has branded her as the apostle of 'free love'; however her
'wingless Eros' was an expedient in times of stress and privation. She
herself knew both kinds; and love, she said, is not just a biological factor, it
is a profoundly social and psychological phenomenon.[1]

The French have always had the reputation of holding *l'amour* in special
regard; but Charles Fourier, early-nineteenth-century social theorist and co-
operativist, was practical: he held that love was both spiritual and physical.
The twentieth-century French novelist Paul Bourget also took a sober view
of love as 'a mental and physical state during which everything is annulled
in us, in our thoughts, in our hearts and in our senses'. Philosopher Denis de
Rougement argues that romantic love is not about sexuality but about a
mystical longing for an ideal that sounds sexual to our oversexualised ears.
For Sartre, love was an attempt to overcome separation and therefore self-
defeating; it sought the appropriation of the loved one's freedom and
therefore the end of her/his individuality, which, presumably, made them
attractive in the first place.

The eighteenth-century German philosopher Immanuel Kant also
admitted a tension between respect and love: 'The principle of *mutual* love
admonishes men constantly to *come nearer* to each other; that of the *respect*
they owe each other, to keep themselves at a *distance* from each other.'[2] In
The Mermaid and the Minator, Dorothy Dinnerstein agrees with Sartre and
Kant when she says: 'It is impossible wholly to monopolize the erotic
interest of another person without crushing the untameable part of that
person which makes her/him erotically interesting.'

Lawrence Stone, social historian and expert on marriage and the family,
says that the key elements of romantic love are the following:

- the notion that there is only one person in the world with whom one
  can unite at all levels;
- the personality of that person is so idealised that the normal faults and

follies of human nature disappear from view;
- love is often like a thunderbolt and strikes at first sight;
- love is the most important thing in the world, to which all other considerations, particularly material ones, should be sacrificed;
- and lastly, the giving of full rein to personal emotions is admirable, no matter how exaggerated or absurd the resulting conduct may appear to others.[3]

These perceptions are generally held in Western society.

The psychoanalyst Eric Fromm wrote a book on the subject, *The Art of Loving*, and said that there is no such thing as love, that it is an abstraction. To him, there is only the act of loving, which is a productive activity and an art which requires effort and knowledge.[4] And one can see that in Fromm's terms love needs to be learned, since it includes caring for, knowing, responding, affirming, enjoying the loved one. He paints a dismal picture of the demise of romantic love, when a couple ceases to make the same effort to be attractive that they did in the initial flush of courtship. Since he is concerned with a continuing act of loving, and considers the extraordinary emotion of falling in love as a temporary phenomenon which is aided by sexual attraction and consummation, his contribution to a discussion on romantic love is only marginal. Other writers, who do not include the satisfaction of desire in their definition, believe, like Plato and Sartre, that unavailability is necessary for romantic love, and that intimacy destroys it.

Desmond Morris, suggests that a capacity for falling in love was part of the evolution of the human species. This capacity, which he called 'sexual imprinting', was necessary, he said, for the evolution of a pair bond, a man and a woman forming a family unit to rear children. The pair bond in turn was necessary, he maintained, in order to avoid sexual rivalries between males. Pair bonding serves the family unit now, and falling in love serves pair bonding, but his thesis ignores the fact that for millennia, falling in love was not a prelude to marriage or family.

In *Romantic Love and Society*, anthropologist Jacqueline Sarsby quotes sociologist William J. Goode who sees romantic love as potentially common to all societies, but suggests that societies can be placed along a continuum of attitudes to love. At one end are those in which a strong love attraction is viewed as laughable or tragic; at the other end are societies such as ours where it is considered mildly shameful to marry without being in love. Sarsby points out that love has to be controlled or obstructed in some societies because sexuality and procreation have to be regulated for various social reasons such as power, property or alliance. This occurs especially where young people are controlled by their elders. She asks a very pertinent question: should we regard the existence of romantic love in Western culture as a liberating influence on feelings which have been dammed up in other societies because they would endanger the social structure? Or should we see it 'as a phenomenon thrown up by the tensions and inadequacies of our social system, [which is] lacking in stable communities and kin?' Will it wither away, she asks, when women are no longer economically dependent, when childcare is properly socialised and people are not divided into economically competitive family units; or will it, alternatively, come into its own in such circumstances?[5]

Feminist writers who were influenced by the sexual revolution saw romantic love as a blend of some of these hypotheses, as a liberating but purely sexual emotion which is intensified and warped by the subordination of women, particularly those who are alienated from the extended family. ·A liberated sexuality, many of them say, would enjoy sexual activity without the shackles of idealising the partner.

Shulamith Firestone believed that falling in love was not possible for women because of the inequality between men and women. She described romantic love as an 'alteration of male vision', through an idealisation of the woman involved, which temporarily cancelled her 'class inferiority'. Men have difficulty loving, she said, because of the Oedipus complex, their first rejection by a mother, but they need love, so they obtain it through the process of romantic love. She considered romantic love in men to be a combination of repressed eroticism, the identification of a woman's sexuality with her individuality, and a current ideal of beauty; a tool of male supremacy for keeping women from knowing their true condition.[6] While there are elements of truth in Firestone's theories (romantic love *is* used to keep women in subjection), these statements only define aspects of it, and they don't explain the autonomous, obsessive and overwhelming emotion that strikes both women and men.

Germaine Greer agreed with Plato (and Shulamith Firestone) that love is only possible between equals; but she described romantic love as an aberration, an obsession, a mania, a disease, which was the result of repressed sexuality, and used to make sexuality transcendent. Such obsession, she says, is a perversion of real love and, what's more, it is the 'opiate of the supermenial' used to enslave women.[7]

Mary Daly describes the fulfilled woman (meaning fulfilled by marriage) as the perfect tool of patriarchy:

> Because of her frustration and low self-image she craves romantic love and marriage, religion, alcohol and pills, professional help, and all kinds of man-made things. She lacks energy to fight back or to move ahead, and has an insatiable desire for male approval. She is psychically impotent.[8]

There is a certain Grundyism in all these definitions of romantic love, a jaded attitude that does not correspond with the fresh, new, exhilarating, exciting feeling that is romantic love in the falling in love stage, when being in love is like a long orgasm of emotion. I can't help feeling for instance, that under the influence of the sexual revolution Germaine Greer had a rather skewed view of romantic love, of falling in love; she has mellowed since then. The liberated or overemphasised genital sexuality, with which she then equated romantic love, masks another aspect of it that is evident in cultures where genital sexuality is controlled, socially or voluntarily (repressed, she would say); the repression allows this other aspect to surface. Later on in the 1980s feminist writers took a more realistic line. Sheila Rowbotham (who equates desire with romantic love) had a more rhapsodic view:

> Desire has the capacity to shift us beyond commonsense. It is our peep at the extraordinary. It is the chink beyond the material world . . . True it can land us down with a bump. Folly, fear, embarrassment, humiliation, violence, tumble about with ecstasy and bliss. Desire is a risk, but so is freedom.[9]

For the post-Freudian psychoanalysts romantic love is psychological. Juliet Mitchell said that being in love is about the Great Unknown; 'to be in love is not to understand it; if you understood it you would not be in it'. Drawing on 'all the greatest portrayals of romantic love', she decided that it seeks an ideal; if it attains its idealised object, then it ceases to be romantic love and may turn into affectionate love. She has, however, a very interesting insight into its nature when she says that romantic love relates to the pre-oedipal stage of narcissism, bisexuality and a sexuality that is non-genital – the polymorphous infant sexuality that Freud referred to, which finds pleasure dispersed over the whole body.

But Mitchell goes further and relates it also to Freud's 'death drive', or *thanatos*, the destruction of the species, because, she explains, romantic love is not concerned with procreation and the future of the species but only with the satisfaction of the individual:

> One might almost say that where interpersonal, procreative love ... is the
> triumph of sexuality over death, the species over the individual, romantic
> love, being only about the individual, is the triumph of death over life.[10]

This seems to me a rather specious argument, casting about to justify Freud's
'death drive'. The modern requirement in our society that romantic love
precedes marriage and procreation would negate the idea that it is
connected with a death drive even in the most tenuous, semantic way. At
the same time Mitchell's oedipal explanation of romantic love has several
points in its favour: it does relate to a sexuality that is not necessarily
genital, a polymorphous sexuality; it may indeed hark back to infantile
sexuality and have narcissistic elements.

Most of these writers, both male and female, have a transcendent view of
humans. In the eagerness of the feminists among them to shed the old
dichotomous earthy/transcendent view of femaleness/maleness, they have
abandoned the earthiness of femaleness to embrace a totally transcendent
view of the female, when they should hold on to both (and, indeed, add
the earthy dimension to maleness). Perhaps a biological element in
romantic love is the missing link. Sociologist Bob Mullan quotes from an
article in the *New York Times* which uses many sources to claim that
romantic love is a chemical reaction, like an amphetamine high. When a
person is in love, the article suggests, the brain produces phenylethylamine,
its own intoxicating substance, and conversely when a person is spurned it
ceases this production and the body has withdrawal symptoms.[11]

In *The Chemistry of Love*, Dr Michael Liebowitz attributes the excitement
of romantic love to three other chemical substances, dopamine, neoepine-
phrine (noradrenaline), and in cases of very intense attraction, serotonin.
These are neuro-transmitters which carry messages between the brain and
the nervous system; serotonin is involved in moods and dispositions.
When activated by the sight or memory of someone attractive (the psychological connection), the pleasure centres of the brain become awash with
these chemicals, causing the well-known symptoms of falling in love.
Liebowitz also cites the causes of the depression which follows the end of a
love affair as the withdrawal of these chemicals. He associates endorphins
(neuro-transmitters which have a mildly narcotic effect on the system)
with companionate love, and the same withdrawal symptoms when separation occurs.[12] It is as likely a theory as any other, combining psychology, culture and biology. If stress can cause adrenaline to be produced in
the human system in order to induce a fight or flight reaction, and pain

induces the brain to secrete endorphins for pain relief, then sexual attraction might also generate a helpful chemical.

People talk about a love which they refer to as 'the real thing', an emotion which seems to be a blend of all types of love – romantic, sexual and affectionate – but mainly the 'madly-in-love romantic' type. It is important to examine it because it is so closely identified with sexuality; and in Western culture so many women (and men) attempt to build their lives on what has been described as an erratic, uncontrolled emotion. Sex and love seem to be inextricably entwined for women; Byron said: 'Man's love is of man's life a thing apart, 'Tis woman's whole existence.'

Simone de Beauvoir agrees with Lord Byron that the word 'love' has by no means the same sense for both sexes, and she quotes Nietzsche expressing the same idea. I will give the Nietschean extract here, if only to remind women of how bad things were:

> The single word love, in fact, signifies two different things for man and woman. What woman understands by love is clear enough: it is not only devotion, it is total gift of body and soul, without reservation, without regard for anything whatever. This unconditional nature of her love is what makes it a *faith*, the only one she has. As for man, what he wants is that love from her; he is in consequence far from postulating the same sentiment for himself as for the woman; if there should be men who also felt that desire for complete abandonment, upon my word, they would not be men.[13]

Of course Simone de Beauvoir rejects the idea that romantic love is a law of nature. 'It is the difference in their situations,' she says, 'that is reflected in the difference that men and women show in their conceptions of love.' According to her, it is women eroticising their subordination. Her explanation is that romantic love is narcissistic, and she explains the narcissism as the reinforcement of a self-image – the woman who is loved considers herself a person of worth; then women eroticise their subordination.

In one way it would be comforting if romantic love and the desire for it could be explained away as a conditioning of women in their subordination. In the preface to *The Hite Report on Women and Love*, where professor of psychology Naomi Weisstein writes of her lifelong resistance to 'the oppression and dehumanisation of women that went along with our pursuit and achievement of love', she reminded me of what had been the Irish social convention of the dancehall, where young women waited patiently for a man to notice them and ask them out to dance.

Still, de Beauvoir's definition of love (with psychoanalytic overtones) may fit the generality of the lives of many women, but it does not explain the unbidden emotion of falling madly in love with one man or woman while passing over dozens who are equally qualified and personable. Nor does it explain the lasting nature of some of those passions when unrequited, especially in cases where the woman or man knows rationally that the loved individual is, in fact, totally unsuitable socially, and perhaps, psychologically. Moreover, a passion for someone may be one-sided, but nonetheless real for all that.

'Is being passionately in love a neurosis?' asks Shere Hite in her report, *Women and Love*. 'And are physical and spiritual passion as easily separable as our culture tries to make them?' Echoing Sartre and others, she says that sometimes a desire for romantic love, for more spiritual closeness, a lack of aloneness, is in part a longing for the impossible, a longing to end the solitariness of the soul, a longing for the completing of the soul. Then she asks the loaded question: is the desire to have children with someone when in love a feeling of the soul's desire for unity, or a biological trick on women triggered by the mechanics of sexual arousal?

Shere Hite found that most women who were in love when they married say that the in-love feeling subsides into a loving or caring feeling after a year or two, as part of a natural development. This seems to vindicate some of the theories given above; yet women look back with great nostalgia on the period of their lives when they were in love and mourn its passing. Hite asks if this is an inevitable progression. Does passion die automatically, or is it killed because of lack of support, respect or communication? Is it the result of a culture that puts men and women in unnecessarily adversarial situations destroying the intensity of romantic love? And, on the results of her survey, she decides that the dynamics that kill romantic love basically involve inequalities in the emotional contract; that the emotional contract itself must be changed before relationships can be stable *and* happy – whether based on 'loving' or 'being in love'.

I found the responses in Shere Hite's survey very sad – not because the women were missing something in their lives, but because they were conditioned to expect something in their lives that wasn't there and that could not be there. They were conditioned by a cultural attitude to a sexuality that is distorted. Their main complaints were the lack of emotional support from men, and that they suffered a loss of identity because of their subordination.

What about jealousy: is sexual jealousy the obverse of romantic love? Is it a resentment for losing control of the loved one; would equality in a sexual relationship eradicate jealousy? We are told that it is an ugly emotion, not worthy of 'good' and 'proper' people. For such a powerful emotion, there is very little scientific writing about it. According to Freud, it is born during the oedipal stage of the child's sexual development and he regarded female jealousy as one of the character weaknesses that resulted from 'penis envy' and woman's physical, sexual 'deformity'; but with his usual sexism he also saw male jealousy as the natural care and consideration which a man should provide as owner of his womenfolk.

The psychotherapist Susie Orbach described jealousy as one of the most unpleasant feelings in the world:

> One feels suspicious, distrustful and mean. One feels threatened. Desperately insecure. Guilty at one's possessiveness. Alternately angry and clingy. We feel so powerless, so overcome that the only soothing that seems possible is to want the person who has provoked the feeling to renounce all interest in the outside world and to focus on us.[14]

Jealousy is, indeed, a most powerful emotion: sexual jealousy is the most frequent cause in the battering and murder of women. It has also driven women to murder lovers or rivals, though less frequently than men. Orbach agrees that the roots of jealousy start in childhood when feelings of insecurity and loss occur for a variety of reasons, usually in relations with parents, sometimes the birth of a new baby. If these feelings are not handled as a part of the child's development, helping her/him with re-assurance to realise that loss is a part of life, then they will return, she says, to plague the person in later life. If the child learns to adjust to loss and is reassured of his/her worth, although jealousy will occur again in times of insecurity and loss, she/he will be able to adjust and cope. This is a more generalised Freudian explanation of jealousy; another is given by Janet Sayers when she says that a woman's sexual jealousy is often a projection of her own desire to be unfaithful. This theory is based on Freud's analysis of delusions of jealousy in the Schreber case and relates to transference and paranoia where homosexuality is concerned.[15] This complex manifestation of jealousy may also occur, but it is more likely that unresolved insecurity is the more frequent cause. Most commentators link jealousy with self-esteem and self-worth.

Feminist writer Sally Cline links jealousy more directly to genital sexuality, and she approaches the question from the point of view of celibacy. In *Women, Celibacy and Passion*, she quotes examples of jealousy disappearing when celibacy entered the frame and genitality departed.

If there is an unconscious link between sexual jealousy and infant–parent attachment, then the strength of sexual jealousy, the fact that it can lead to horrific violence, certainly helps to strengthen the importance of infant sexuality. It provides one more indication that the subordination of women through their sexuality is deep-seated and will be difficult to change.

Sexuality is not meant to be ardent all through one's life. It has different cycles and a variety of manifestations: romantic love, desire, childbirth and child-rearing, loving relations between individuals. If women's or men's identity does not depend on a narrow definition of sexuality, why worry if genital desire wanes? Our tastes and desires in other aspects of life wax and wane as we grow older, why should genital sexuality continue to be the overwhelming, all-pervading, central point of life? There are other delights, such as intelligence which is our special human characteristic. Still nobody who has experienced romantic love would banish it; it cannot be rationalised or legislated out of our lives.

If romantic love is just sexual, part of the mechanics of arousal, then it is biological. When we examine the physiology of romantic love, it definitely shows some of the symptoms of sexual arousal; racing pulse, constricting heart, blushing; but one of the interesting things about romantic love in women is that these symptoms can occur without genital excitement. Hite's respondents describe it as pleasure and pain, terrifying, risky, exhilarating, magic excitement, a heart-racing, breathtaking, body-melting, intense feeling.

If we are aware of this state of ecstasy and of its implications then psychology also plays a part. The fact, too, that some women choose sexual partners who resemble their fathers in character, and some men pick partners that resemble their mothers, happens far too often in life to be ignored; psychology is undoubtedly at work there. There are social factors also involved in romantic love, although they are not quite as simple as Eric Fromm believed. He maintained that what makes a person attractive depends on the fashion of the time, and that two people fall in love when they have got the best bargain available to them. To Fromm's 'fashion of the time' can be added other social or sociopsychological factors such as ideas of physical or psychological attractiveness, or the attraction of wealth or power. But romantic love can be more spontaneous than that, and more overwhelmingly consuming; there is no doubt that many people experience it like a tornado.

It is accepted almost universally that women have a greater desire for romantic love in their sexual relations than men. In common parlance men have sex lives and women have love-lives. Dorothy Dinnerstein finds the reason for this phenomenon in 'the muting of women's erotic impulsivity' and in 'female dominated childhood'. Dinnerstein's theory of men's problems with love are discussed in chapter 6: how women refrain from being sexually demanding so as not to recall to men their old love–hate relationship with their mothers; how men keep love superficial, et cetera. On first reading, Dinnerstein's theory sounds far-fetched, but on deeper consideration it could explain why the culture teaches and expects women to restrain or repress their sexuality while men are allowed more rein. In *The Hite Report on Male Sexuality* most men said that they did not trust passionate love, and that they did not marry the women that they had most deeply and passionately loved.

Dinnerstein also says that because women remain 'attached' to the mother (or feel that they should), when they become detached from her, they spend a lifetime trying to regain a similar attachment with a man, because that is what the culture deems correct. They rarely succeed; women, as a rule, do not get from their partners the same caring attention that they received from their mothers.

Luise Eichenbaum and Susie Orbach, the psychotherapists who follow Nancy Chodorow's objects-relation theory, are concerned with the great deficiency of love and caring in women's lives. In childhood and young girlhood, they say, they are encouraged, consciously or unconsciously, to put others, mainly men – fathers and brothers – before themselves, to be 'unselfish' both materially and emotionally, and they grow up emotionally needy. Boys are brought up to expect care and attention from women; only 'warped' or 'man-hating' women will deny them this nurture. Women, on the other hand, they point out, are often disappointed at the lack of nurturing attitudes in the men with whom they have relations.[16]

Women only admitted to this lack of reciprocity when in the consciousness-raising sessions of the women's movement they found that they were not alone in their predicament; that many other women felt neglected because the men in their lives showed little concern for their emotional and/or physical needs. Susan Brownmiller said that women read romantic fiction as a way of compensating for this neglect and as a means of diffusing their anger against men. More than three-quarters of the women who responded to Hite's survey on women and love said that their 'husband or lover rarely tried to draw them out or get them to speak about their thoughts or feelings the way women do (or try to do) for men'. Women, she says, find this maddeningly unfair, because they provide these services so congenially and unobtrusively. However, men seem to have the impression that this is natural behaviour for women, and they often don't realise how much they depend on and use women's emotional support.

A more serious threat to romantic love emerged as feminists began to examine relations between men and women, and particularly when they came to analyse pornography. It soon became evident to them that 'desire' (meaning, lust with some elements of romantic love or sexual passion) depended to a significant degree on a power difference between those in- volved: men's power and women's powerlessness or subordination. Sex- ologists had already recognised this phenomenon when they emphasised that male sexuality was dominant and women's passive or submissive, and that equality in the relationship between women and men would dampen male ardour. Running through a majority of the responses to *The Hite Report on Male Sexuality* was a tacit acceptance that they were in control, in charge, that sexual activity was a validation of their masculinity and membership of a man's world. Few of the respondents acknowledged explicitly that power difference was a factor in their desire, but they assumed the power difference of the 'man's world' as the air they breathe. And in *The Hite Report on Women and Love*, 95 per cent of respondents said that men assume they will take first place psychologically in a relationship.

This power difference is deeply embedded in the culture: men are expected to fall in love with women who are younger and smaller than them, women who earn less than they do and have less responsible jobs. Men who contravene these unwritten codes are diminished in the eyes of their fellow men. Women are also conditioned to these cultural expec- tations. They find power erotic because, as Sheila Jeffreys says, they have never had the opportunity to eroticise equality; their only experience of the erotic has been as subordinates.[17] Indeed some feminists of the 1970s found it difficult to sustain desire in the presence of their antagonism to the overt sexism of men. Others found it difficult to 'democratise' their hidden yearnings; they found that equality in sexual relations was not 'sexy'.[18] These observations would tend to support the idea that romantic love is connected in some way with the oppression or subordination of women. Lynne Segal called this a blow to the heart indeed!

But what of the 'hidden yearnings'? Where do they come from, before culture and the psyche take control of them? Romantic love, like sexuality of which it is a part, has a biological basis which has been mediated and moulded by culture and the psyche. It is likely that it is not a direct cause of women's subordination, but that it is used as an element in the edifice of male supremacy. Like the sexuality of which it is a part, the ecstasy which is romantic love can survive equality, when its psychological trappings have changed, when we cleanse the pathology of eroticised power from the unconscious. Feminists like Sheila Rowbotham, who had difficulty with the idea of eroticised subordination, were merely discovering that not all aspects of feminist reform were easy, that undoing the conditioning of their previous life was not as simple as discovering it.

19

CONCLUSION

So where does all that leave human sexuality? If we return again to the meaning of the word 'sex' as the physiological difference between women and men, we find that the difference results from the *balance* of sexual hormones; both sexes have the same type of sexual hormones but in different proportions. Therefore there is a masculine element in women, and a feminine one in men, which the culture requires them to suppress. Starting with these biological differences, sexuality is constructed psychologically and culturally.

A rational study of the material available cannot but accept that the polymorphous sexuality (or bisexuality) of the child has been moulded psychologically, socially and culturally into the diverse 'sexualities' and into the various oppressions and perversions which we see around us. What has been regarded in female sexuality as passiveness is, in fact, a sexuality that is autonomous in a bodily way, that is diffuse, and includes childbirth and nurturing as sexual bodily functions. Women are more adjusted to their sexuality than men; but it can also be said that part of female sexuality is a hunger for contact that would be active and demanding if the conventions allowed this freedom. On the other hand, male sexuality need not always be aggressive but could enjoy a similar type of diffuse sensuality, again if the conventions allowed.

Radical feminists (and sexologists) want to increase the value of, and the freedom of, sexuality in our lives, but they continue to narrow it down to the male, genital interpretation. When feminists (especially the radical feminists) set out to redefine female sexuality, they went only part of the way. They proclaimed the clitoral orgasm, celebrated masturbation and adopted lesbian practice. But they stopped there because they had retained the prevailing male idea of sexuality.

Lesbianism, especially political lesbianism, was important in giving significant impetus to the task of discovering female sexuality. By detaching from men, even temporarily, women could evaluate the sexual and political relationship that existed between women and men; freedom from male power and influence allowed them to discover certain aspects of their own sexuality that were masked in heterosexual relationships, and some made their own arrangements to enjoy motherhood, if not the Great O of birthing. If it denied them the complementarity of female/male sexuality, they would say that male sexuality needed reform before it could be complementary.

No proper theory of sexuality can be independent of feminism – no more than it can be independent of male scrutiny and theory. There are two distinct strands to the enquiry into sexuality, one carried out by men, the other by women. The members within each strand often hold varying and even conflicting theories, and the strands have their own distinguishing marks. The male approach to the definition of sexuality is almost exclusively male-centred and based on a male sexuality that has been warped by cultural and psychological influences. On the other hand, women are breaking new ground, getting away from the almost universal male-centred definition of sexuality and focusing on a broader definition.

The psychoanalysts in the women's movement who reinterpreted Freud, and deconstructed his theories, declared that sexuality was psychologically formed, that it determined personality development which in turn influenced the way society was formed and designed; but they dismissed any biological dimension. Those who followed the social and cultural road held that sexuality was determined by the prevailing culture. And while some of these feminists acknowledged the biological roots of sexuality, they then went on to ignore them in the prodigious job of analysing the cultural reality that caused the subordination of women.

I believe that we cannot lose sight of any of these dimensions of sexuality: the biological, the psychological and the cultural are all important in the construction of our human sexuality. Feminists have been fighting the battle against sexual subordination on two fronts: first, on 'the right to choose', which is linked principally to reproduction rights such as contraception and abortion; and second, on the right to sexual autonomy, integrity and pleasure. However, these two aims have been virtually divorced from each other. While contraception and abortion help to solve the problem of 'the right to choose', it is a campaign which marginalises or excludes reproduction from sexuality in the interests of sexual autonomy.

On the other hand, by focusing on genital intercourse, the battle for sexual equality is being fought on territory defined by male perceptions of sexuality. These are narrow and restrictive; narrow in terms of male sexuality, and ignoring a large area of female sexuality.

Most feminists have allowed sexuality to be divorced from its biological roots, as if humans, because of their intelligence, should forget their mammalian genesis. They partitioned reproduction, treating conception as sexual and separate from the rest of the reproductive cycle, which they regarded as non-sexual and consigned to a biological purgatory.

Others refused to engage in battle on male terms, and turned to lesbianism; they, too, are trying to distance themselves from, or are attempting to deny, the biological aspects of their sexuality. Yet the desire of women for children survived even the righteous anger of heterosexual feminists against the oppression of mothers;[1] and lesbian feminists, like their heterosexual sisters, are increasingly including reproduction in their life plan.

Both male and female sexuality are complex with an instinctive unconscious/conscious drive to reproduce embedded in a desire for emotional intimacy and various physical pleasures. Women also have the great orgasm of birth, and a sensual/emotional bond with the child which they can share with men. It is true that the values women attach at present to sexuality differ from those men attach to it. Women connect sex with warmth, affection, loving, caring, as well as with arousal and orgasm; men connect it principally with male orgasm, but underneath the machismo they too are looking for affection and emotional security. If female sexuality has been repressed by patriarchy, then so has male sexuality.

An overview of human sexuality finds it, if not in a pathological state, then severely warped by various psychological and cultural influences and manipulations. Often these sexuality or 'gender' constructions are postures and people go around presenting a false persona, like a Noh mask, to the world. The task of discovering and defining female sexuality still goes on, but where previously getting rid of the double standard meant that women could act in the same way as men, it now means that a new standard of sexual equality, a new definition of sexuality for both sexes, could and should be found. It means that men must rediscover, and not reject, the loving intimacy of childhood. It also means that they must learn to take women's sexual needs into account; 'wham, bang and thank you ma'am' or the perfunctory tweaking of nipple and clitoris before penetration is not enough.

What are the cultural myths that surround sexuality? The main notions are that sexual desire is purely genital; that women's sexuality is passive, and not autonomous but a response to male sexuality (women know that their sexuality is autonomous but they are conditioned to believe that a positive sexuality for them is sluttish, so they hide the fact or suppress it); that birthing is *necessarily* painful and is divorced from sexuality; that male arousal is uncontrollable and therefore women must respond to it or suffer the consequences.

THE FAMILY

These are cultural myths which (apart from the question of painful birthing) feminism is striving to eliminate, but with them they have also mounted a strong assault on the family. The current attack on the family did not start with this latest wave of feminism, but with the ideas of Reich and Marcuse who saw the family as the instrument of a repressive state in forming submissive people. Mid-to-late-twentieth-century feminism borrowed anti-family theory from the sexual revolution and fuelled it from the well of its own experience and consciousness-raising on the plight of women in the family. Their opposition to the family has been often misinterpreted; it was not the family per se that feminism opposed, although the popular media, male theorists (Jeffrey Weeks) and anti-feminists maintained that it was. It was the traditional, patriarchal family that feminists had in their sights. Their constant assaults were on the family in which the man considered that he held a superior and dominant position, in which he had privileges not accorded to his partner, and in which he sometimes used the fist to enforce his domination.

Foucault maintained that the deployment of sexuality was exercised in the family in two ways: through the relationship between husband and wife, and between parents and children. Parents and relatives, he said, became the chief agents of a deployment of sexuality with the outside support of doctors, teachers and later psychiatrists. He said that the frankness about sexuality which existed at the beginning of the seventeenth century gradually disappeared. By the nineteenth century sexuality was confined to the home, located in the parent's bedroom, and limited to the conjugal couple in the interests of reproduction. As we have seen, women as wives, partners and mothers are prisoners in that bedroom and slaves in that home. They may be willing prisoners and slaves, but the family, as presently constituted in most societies is not a liberating or fulfilling place for a woman.

The fact that women leave sexist and oppressive partners in droves (taking their children with them) and set up single-woman families is due, in large part, to the raised consciousness which feminism brought to *all* women; they realised that they did not have to put up with such unjust treatment. (Roughly three-quarters of divorce petitions in Britain and the United States are initiated by women.) Most women suffer economically by their exodus from oppressive relationships; Western capitalist economies are not organised to accommodate women rearing children. But when these women walked away from oppressive men, they were not abandoning the idea of family, but eliminating men from it: the family unit of mother and children remained. Feminist criticism of the family refers to one form of family, a unit of organisation where injustice prevails. The family, where the rights and welfare of all members are served on equal terms, where partners share equally the rearing of children and both are accorded the same opportunities to self-development and self-esteem, is a civilised institution, but all too rare in practice. An important stage in the development of civilisation was the domestication of the human animal. Females were domesticated early on because of the rearing of children, but the domestication of the male is not yet completely realised.

Although men dominate in most societies and absent themselves from housework and the nurturing of children (and one must admit that they do it because they can), there are some isolated, primitive groups where this does not apply. Margaret Mead found among the Arapesh men *and* women 'a personality that we would call maternal in its parental aspects, and feminine in its sexual aspects'. She found no evidence that sex was a powerful driving force for men or for women. But among the Mundugumor she found that 'both men and women developed as ruthless, aggressive, positively sexed individuals', with little maternal characteristics. In the third tribe, the Tchambuli, she found a reversal of the sex roles, where women were 'the dominant, impersonal, managing partner, the man the less responsible and emotionally dependent person'.[2] These variations in behaviour patterns demonstrate what is possible in our societies if we were prepared to change or modify our culture.

Men, too, are in bondage in the family, but they can usually dictate some of their terms. Their lives in the world outside the home, where they spend most of their waking hours, are the best that society will permit them, given their ability to earn a living. And when life gets unbearable they seem to be able to leave the family, leave their children, much more easily than women can. The number of family desertions by men is vastly greater than desertions by women; a woman can leave a sexual relationship with a man, but she finds it very difficult to leave children. The mother/child bond is a stronger part of a woman's sexuality.

Worldwide, the basic family unit is a woman and her children; but family or household structure can vary from one culture to another. In some cultures there are extended families of three generations in one household (a type that existed in Ireland until comparatively recently), in another, women living in community with their children and men living apart. The extended family living in one household is found mainly in sub-sistence or low income societies, and is prevalent in Asia, Africa, Eastern Europe and in some pockets of traditional communities in the developed world. Communities of women with men living apart (the Long House of some African villages where men live apart from women) are disappearing and remain only in the reports of anthropologists on isolated tribes, or in the tiny number of new communes set up by feminist separatists. The breaking away of the nuclear family of Western society from the extended family was a product of the Industrial Revolution and the need for mobility of labour. In it women have had gains and losses: the young wife has more autonomy than in the household of her mother-in-law, but she is also isolated from female solidarity and from sharing of housework and child-rearing.

Single mothers, who chose to be such, are a new trend in family structure, and they divide into several categories:

- young women who, whether they become pregnant through accident or design, retain their independence by not marrying or living with the father of their child;
- young women who deliberately become pregnant to gain independence from parents in the knowledge that the social services will provide them with housing and support;[3]
- women who decide to have a child, but have not met a man with whom they want to live (these women are usually financially secure);
- women with children who seek divorce from their partners and become single parents.

Nancy Chodorow quotes a theory which holds that young women who choose to be single mothers come from families where children are an exclusively mother/daughter affair, and fathers are irrelevant in the home. These young women identify too closely with their mothers and have problems of detachment from them.[4] This theory could explain the actions of some young women, but not those who are anxious to leave home and become independent, when independence also means *not* having a male partner, and can mean poverty. Other theorists maintain that the satisfactions and gratifications of motherhood, the intense relationship with the child, even in difficult circumstances, replace the need for heterosexual relationships, especially when men tend not to provide a loving intimacy.

Ann Ferguson says that rational self-interest does not explain why women predominate in single-parent families; but agrees that there is a genuine interest in motherhood because of the sensual and social union it promises between mother and child, which is particularly exemplified by breast-feeding. However, she sees mother love as a form of sex/affective energy that is neither a substitute for heterosexual intercourse nor a mere acting out of a desire for male power (Freud's mistaken idea of the child as a 'penis substitute').[5]

These ideas reinforce the theory that birthing and nurturing are a part of women's sexuality when sexuality is understood in a broader context than genitality. It also points to the great social and cultural misunderstanding of sexuality by both sexes, which causes mental suffering to both women and men. Dorothy Dinnerstein points out that it is not a physical tie with the new baby that makes fatherhood, but an intellectual one, and one that is of great importance to the father. Otherwise, she says, why would men go to such lengths in the control of women's sexuality in order to ensure that the children they rear really are theirs; 'the tenuousness of their physical tie to the young clearly pains men,' she states. Their need to identify with their children is another reason why men's involvement in the rearing and nurture of their children is important. She also quotes from a research experiment[6] which found that male rats, given a sufficiently intense exposure to rat pups, show the same nurturing behaviour as the mothers. This observation would indicate some other (biological?) stimulus (perhaps the baby's dependence or its unformed appearance) to 'maternal' behaviour for which no label exists. I have found no research into the generation of fatherhood, but men who have minimal contact with children live in an artificial world which lacks an essential part of human experience.

In this proposed new world of female freedom and equality what will substitute for the present family in the rearing of the next generation? At present the cultural justification for the family is

- that it enables a woman to remain with the child in its formative early years, in order to ensure her/his physical and cultural development;
- that it provides better economic security for the child, even when only one parent is earning, and more so when the two parents are earning;
- that the family is consolidated by the sexual relationship between the parents, and monogamy provides the stability which, psychologists say, is important to the psychological health of the future adult;
- that this stability is undermined by divorce and serial monogamy and by single-parent rearing;
- that children of single mothers are likely to be economically deprived (the economic situation of single-mother families could be improved if the legal requirement that fathers support their children were enforced everywhere);
- and because of the absence of a father, children will have a skewed knowledge of society which is both male and female.

No research exists which indicates how the children of single-mother families develop, but the situation begs the question: would a woman-reared child, when she/he became an adult, bring about the changes necessary to liberate women? Dinnerstein and Chodorow and other psychologists say no, and maintain that the monopoly of mothers in the rearing of children is the reason that misogyny persists in society.[7]

Does a child need to know her/his father, or is it instead a want which arises because society is structured into nuclear families and other children have one? Was it an advance psychologically and culturally to know one's parents? What kind of society would we have if men reared the boys and women reared the girls? Human young, because of their extended dependency, have always known their mother; and in previous, less economically developed centuries, fathers took over the rearing of boys and their integration into the economy, after a certain age. However, that division of labour helped to strengthen and perpetuate patriarchy.

Human history has shown that civilisation, progress and development took place when people co-operated. But in the process of civilisation women and some groups of men were enslaved, and men gave up a 'domestic' dimension to their lives, they also gave up fatherhood except in a symbolic way, for the power of material success.

Women have not consented to leave the running of the world to men as compensation for their peripheral role in the continuity of the species, as Margaret Mead claimed. If she were alive today she might revise that opinion, because it was a superficial observation made about an enslaved or subordinated section of the population who had internalised their enslavement. The desire of women to take part in the public face of history-making during the last quarter of the twentieth century and at several other periods through history, their manifest pleasure in challenging the status quo, contradicts Mead's statement. Her own life also contradicts it; she ensured herself a part in public history-making. That claim was made in the context of a defence of, or plea for, the family, which, she said, was 'a patterned arrangement of the two sexes in which men play a role in the nurturing of women and children'.

Far from being an agency for subordination, the family has within it the necessary ingredients for the liberation of women. Sharing the rearing of children is the only way that women can participate on equal terms with men in the public history-making. The other methods of family organisation – the present situation of absent fathers, single-mother families, the kibbutz-style communal rearing of children, extended families where the unliberated older women bear some domestic burden to free the younger women for involvement outside the home – do not take into account the strength of mother love; the existence of a suppressed or stultified father love; the psychological need of men to know their children; or the psychological development of the child. The British experience in the upper/ruling classes, where children were reared by nannies and the boys were sent to boarding school at an early age, often led to psychologically damaged males, sometimes with sexual problems. What must be guarded against is too large a psychological, emotional or physical investment on the part of the parents in the child, and the consequent expectation of a dividend. Overinvestment restricts the child's and the parents' own development, particularly that of the mother.

We have constructed our culture piece by piece, layer by layer, much of it in order to regulate our actions for very good reasons. Because we have intellect and memory of things past, we try to control our aggressions against others, we instil a sense of personal justice, a social conscience, into the culture, particularly in the prohibition on stealing and damage to person or property. Sexual regulation has also been part of the culture for reasons of hygiene and, in some cases, population control. Unfortunately these prohibitions were also used to control people in other aspects of their lives, particularly women, and so they were rebelled against. In that rebellion good ideas were thrown out with the bad. In a new construction of rules for sexual behaviour for the good of everyone, factors like hygiene, population control,[8] and, most importantly, the abuse of power must be considered.

In *Beyond Power: Women, Men and Morals,* Marilyn French discusses how power became a value that replaced Nature. As we now see in a world suffering from overexploitation and pollution, Nature was unforgiving. While we have exercised our minds on great technological developments, we have sacrificed Nature to the achievement of power. Within that scenario are the seeds of our own unhappiness and even destruction.

APPENDICES

APPENDIX 1

Summary of Mothers' Manifesto demands:

- Remuneration, insurance, pensions for mothers at home.
- Neighbourhood infrastructure of crèches, mothers' centres, communal dining/living rooms, et cetera.
- Flexible access to work: shorter hours, part-time work, lifting age barriers to training and education, recognition of social experience of mothering.
- 50–70 per cent of women's quota positions for mothers, in politics and employment.
- Timetabling of political life to suit mothers, with paid child care.
- The right to fulfil the desire for children without constraints, to allow spontaneous life rhythms.
- Male participation to be encouraged, under direction of mothers; involvement of childless women. 'The couple' cannot cope alone.
- Better provisions for disabled and for carers of the elderly; for example, pay, suitable housing, insurance, right to return to work. (Chamberlayne, 1990).

APPENDIX 2

Catharine MacKinnon's article in *Ms* magazine (vol. 4, no. 1, July/August 1993) gives a representative account of such reports collected with detailed references by members of a Croatian women's group. (More testimonies of Bosnian refugees were reported in *Ms*, vol. 3, no. 4, January/February 1993 and in *Ms*, vol. 3, no. 5, March/April 1993.) MacKinnon records the inaction of the United Nations on the question: an all-male commission set up to investigate the first reports was given funds for administration but none for the collection of testimonies; and the commission described the testimonies which were volunteered as lacking in the necessary details (dates, locations, names of victims and perpetrators) to sustain criminal charges. Like the political intervention to stop the genocide, the effort was half-hearted and a blot on the record of the United Nations.

A United Nations *ad hoc* group sent to investigate a well-documented and testified report (Roy Gutman, *Newsday*, November 1993) that UN soldiers were patronising a Serb brothel where Muslim and Croatian women were sexually enslaved, returned to say that they could find no evidence to support the report. The International Women's Human Rights Clinic, the Centre for Constitutional Rights, and the International League for Human Rights (all New York based) filed a multimillion dollar civil suit against the Bosnian Serb leader, Radovan Karadzic, charging him with legal responsibility for the human rights violations committed by his soldiers. Catharine MacKinnon and the United States National Organisation of Women took the legal action one step further, filing a civil suit in a New York federal court on behalf of a Croatian Muslim woman and two Bosnian women's groups (*Ms*, vol. 3, no. 6, May/June 1993).

APPENDIX 3

Dora's name was Ida Bauer. She was the daughter of Philip and Käthe Bauer and she had a brother who was more than a year older than her. Her father had been ill with tuberculosis at various times during his life and also suffered from conditions related to advanced syphilis and other venereal diseases. He had attended Freud as a patient and had been impressed by him. From the account given by Philip Bauer Käthe, the mother, was described by Freud as having a 'housewife psychosis' by which he meant that her preoccupation with her household chores made her frigid and took precedence over her relationship with her family. She also suffered from venereal disease and bouts of depression. From the age of eight Ida showed various 'hysterical' symptoms – nervous asthma, migraine, depression, coughs, breathing difficulties and loss of speech and suicidal tendencies. Freud found that she also suffered from a vaginal discharge. During analysis, Ida told Freud of the involvement of their neighbours the K family; of her own close friendship with Frau K; how her father had embarked on an affair with Frau K, which Freud interpreted as compensation for his wife's frigidity; and how Herr K made sexual advances to Ida when she was fourteen, when he forced a kiss on her, which disgusted her, and at sixteen, when he proposed that she have intercourse with him. Ida was upset that her father did not believe her and assumed that her father had made her available to Herr K in exchange for tolerating his relationship with Frau K. Freud agreed with her perception but he thought that her reaction to Herr K's advances was neurotic, that if she was normal she would have experienced sexual excitement, and that her 'hysteria' was due to her repression of that feeling. He also maintained that she was really in love with Herr K. Later, with a foot in two camps, he changed his diagnosis to declare that it was possible that the root of Ida's problem was a 'deep-rooted homosexual love of Frau K', and that her attachment to Frau K resulted from her identification with her father.

Some feminist commentators see Ida's position as a rejection of heterosexuality in spite of a culture that was forcing her into a 'feminine' (as defined at the time) mode. This is the political lesbian argument; Ida was rejecting, heterosexuality because of the infection that it caused in her mother. There is another way to look at the 'Dora' story. It is possible that Ida's father was sexually abusing her. But Freud had already rejected the idea that this ever occurred when in 1897 he decided to discount as fantasy the accounts of sexual abuse which his female patients were telling him. It was no wonder that she should become revolted by the sexuality of men because of venereal disease. She also had a discharge which was never fully explored in the case. Where did she get infection from? Ida terminated her analysis with Freud after three months, probably because he refused to accept her refusal to accept his diagnosis. She did not believe that she was in love with Herr K. But, perhaps, she had not yet reached the stage of uncovering her own suppressed knowledge of sexual abuse, or because she was approaching the stage of uncovering it and balked. We will never know.

NOTES

CHAPTER 1

1 The term 'patriarchy' has become
   unfashionable in a 'post-feminist' era;
   but I will use it throughout this book
   because whether or not the word is in
   vogue, we live in a patriarchal world.
2 *See* Kaplan (1984), pp. 321-36
3 Lévi-Strauss (1949, 1969)
4 Caroline Humphrey review of *Blood
   Relations: Menstruation and the Origins of
   Culture*, Chris Knight, *London Review
   of Books*, 27 February 1992
5 Stoller (1968)
6 MacKinnon (1989)
7 Oakley (1985), pp. 158-71
8 *Oxford English Dictionary*
9 Greer (1984), p. 199
10 The scientific revolution developed
   along mechanistic lines, ignoring the
   gestalt ('the ways in which each part at
   any given instant take their meaning
   from the whole'), which is difficult to
   measure. Because of this development,
   modern science is still at an elementary
   level of knowledge, in the
   kindergarten, so to speak. It will not
   advance until it takes a more holistic
   approach to scientific study, looking at
   the interaction of the parts rather than
   studying the parts in isolation from the
   whole.
11 Walker, Alice (1993), p. 24

CHAPTER 2

1 Millett (1970), p. 45n.
2 Rich (1977)

3 Smith (1989), p. xvi
4 Daly (1973), p. 45
5 Spender (1983), p. 59
6 Faludi (1992)
7 Segal (1990), p. 103
8 de Beauvoir (1953); Millett (1970);
   Faludi (1992); French (1992), et cetera
9 Dinnerstein (1987), p. 125
10 In *A History of Their Own: Women in
   Europe from Prehistory to the Present*,
   Bonnie Anderson and Judith Zinsser
   (1988) give a well-documented
   account of misogyny through the
   ages.
11 Rowbotham (1973); Spender (1982);
   and many, many more
12 Walker, Barbara G. (1983), pp. 767-8
13 Quoted in de Beauvoir (1972), p. 112;
   and in Rose and Rose (1976b)
14 Sherfey (1970) in Humm ed. (1992), p.
   265
15 Ranke-Heinemann (1991)
16 *Epistle to Timothy*, 2:11–12. Paul was
   not the out-and-out misogynist that
   he has been made to appear by the
   selective interpretation of his writings
   by the Church Fathers. For every text
   condemning women there are others
   (rarely quoted) that support them. Ute
   Ranke-Heinemann (1991) shows how
   in many instances Paul had been
   deliberately mistranslated,
   misrepresented and taken out of
   context by translators, transcribers and
   preachers, in order to further their
   own ideas of behaviour and the role of

women. However, Paul was infected by the Gnosticism of the time with an antagonism to the physical world.

17　St Augustine, *De Civitate Dei*, A.D. 426

18　Russell, Letty M., ed. (1985); Anderson and Zinsser (1988); Ranke-Heinemann (1991)

19　Ehrenreich and English (1973), p. 28

20　MacCurtain and O'Corrain (1978), p. 9. These designations stand at odds with the apparent liberal Brehon Laws on marriage and property until one realises that the liberality was framed to preserve and guard the clan's property. A woman retained ownership of her marriage dowry and divorce was allowed, but if she divorced she could return with all or part of her dowry of land and cattle to her father's house.

21　Ehrenreich and English (1973) p. 33

22　Christine de Pizan (1365–1430) is credited with being the inspiration behind the feminist movement which began in the fifteenth century and has continued sporadically ever since. In her *Book of the City of Women* (1405), she told how she became aware of the injustices of men to women and decided to oppose them (Anderson & Zinsser, 1988, pp. 341–3).

23　Hufton (1995), p. 27

CHAPTER 3

1　For much of the material in this chapter I am indebted to the many feminist researchers and historians of the past twenty-five years who have retrieved this history.

2　Both women have lost favour with some modern feminists because of what is termed their exhibitionism and egocentricity, their cavalier attitude towards the standards of devices, their lack of scientific reporting on the results of their work, and their assent to eugenics (Greer, 1984, p. 135; Forster, 1984, p. 271). This is less than fair to both of them and smacks of

anachronistic nit-picking. A new biography of Marie Stopes has helped to restore her reputation (Rose, June, 1993).

3　Epstein in Snitow, Stansell and Thompson, eds (1984), p. 161; Jeffreys (1985), pp. 134–5

4　Spender (1982), pp. 340–1; Forster (1984), p. 170

5　Trimberger in Snitow, Stansell and Thompson, eds (1984), pp. 174–8

6　Kollontai (1923a) in Holt (1977), pp. 276–93

7　Holt (1977), pp. 116, 118, 212; Porter, Cathy (1980), p. 347. Lenin called it, in the circumstances, 'an inevitable evil' (Porter, Cathy, 1980, p. 348). Kollontai (1923b), in Holt, pp. 148–9, also considered abortion a necessary evil. It derived, she said, from the insecure position of women, and would disappear when Russia had a broad and developed network of institutions protecting motherhood.

8　Russell, Dora (1977), pp. 162–96

9　Rowbotham (1973), p. 142

10　Malthus argued that population had a natural tendency to increase faster than the means of subsistence and efforts should be made to cut the birth rate by self-restraint, or nature would keep the population in balance with the means of subsistence by poverty, war and pestilence.

11　'Branks': a scold's bridle, having a hinged iron framework to enclose the head and a bit or gag to fit into the mouth and compress the tongue (*Chambers Twentieth Century Dictionary*, 1936).

CHAPTER 4

1　Researchers and psychoanalysts differ on whether Freud meant a biological instinct or a psychological drive. The confusion arose when the two German words *Trieb* (drive) and *Instinkt* (instinct) were both translated as 'instinct' by Freud's English translator.

2   Freud (1905)
3   Freud (1923)
4   Freud (1939)
5   Freud (*Three Essays on Sexuality*, 1916)
6   Freud (*Three Essays on Sexuality*, 1917)
7   Freud (*A General Introduction to Psychoanalysis*, 1916–17)
8   Freud (1939)
9   Freud (*Three Essays on Sexuality*, 1905–20)
10 Freud (1961)
11 The idea of a racial unconscious was carried further by Jung. Freud arrived at it through the influence of Lamarck, whose ideas of inherited characteristics were discredited (perhaps too precipitately) by Darwinians. Until we know more about genes, we cannot reject (or accept) the thesis. Weeks (1985), pp. 159–60, challenges the racial memory theory for two reasons: because it presupposes already fixed sexualities when Freud had earlier posed a theory of bisexuality; and because Freud does not say how the sons-versus-the-father-in-control-of-many-women situation came about.
12 Freud (1931)
13 Jung (1961), p. 147
14 Fromm (1959)
15 Freud (1905, 1926, 1932)
16 Freud (1931)
17 Freud (1923)
18 Freud (1925)
19 Freud (1932)
20 Irigaray (1985); Rich (1977); Ferguson (1989); et cetera
21 Freud (*Three Essays on Sexuality*, 1917)
22 Mitchell (1984), p. 250
23 Freud (1939)
24 Freud (1935)
25 Freud (1939)

CHAPTER 5
1   Jung (1927)
2   Erikson (1968), quoted in Millett (1977), pp. 210–20
3   Reich (1983), pp. 169 ff., 180

4   Reports from the UK Family Policy Centre (1992–3)
5   Reich (1983), pp. 368–86
6   These ideas are to be found in Reich's *The Sexual Struggle of Youth* (1931), *The Discovery of the Orgone: The Function of the Orgasm* (1942), and *The Sexual Revolution* (1945), all of which have been republished in recent times.
7   Marcuse (1955), pp. 190–214
8   Deutsch (1944)
9   *Ibid.*
10 Bonaparte (1953)
11 *Ibid.*
12 Horney (1932)
13 Horney (1931). Kate Millett (1969), p. 258, thought that womb envy was Karen Horney's malicious response to Freud's penis envy until she read D.H. Lawrence's *The Rainbow*.
14 Horney (1935)
15 Klein (1945)
16 Miller (1990); Rush (1980); Masson (1984)
17 Klein (1952)
18 Klein (1957)
19 'We have never prided ourselves on the completeness and finality of our knowledge and capacity. We are just as ready now as we were earlier to admit to imperfections of our understanding, to learn new things and to alter our methods in any way that can improve them'. Sigmund Freud 1919; quoted in Grosskurth, 1986, p. 320.

CHAPTER 6
1   Later published in the UK under the title *The Rocking of the Cradle and the Ruling of the World*.
2   Dinnerstein (1987), pp. 111–12
3   Chodorow (1978)
4   Sayers (1986), p. 70
5   Eichenbaum and Orbach (1982)
6   Sayers (1986), pp. 71–2
7   On politics and war; on the organisation of work; on attitudes to scientific research where men tend to

concentrate on constituent parts rather than the whole. The physicist Evelyn Fox Keller uses Chodorow's work to explain men's tendency in science to focus on the independent operation of the constituent parts of the phenomena they investigate, whereas women (like the biochemist Barbara McClintock), she says, seem to be more open to recognising the dynamic interplay of the constituent parts of their objects of investigation. Sayers (1986), pp. 72–3.

8 Sherfey (1970, 1973); in Humm, ed. (1992), p. 265

9 Humm, ed. (1992), p. 266

10 *The Drama of Being a Child* (1979); *For Your Own Good: The Roots of Violence in Child-rearing*, (1980); *Thou Shalt Not Be Aware: Society's Betrayal of the Child*, (1981)

11 Miller (1990), p. 122

CHAPTER 7

1 Structuralism tries to identify and define the rules and constraints within which meaning is generated and communicated. But it goes further in that it elevates structure above function, which means, in this context, that the way culture is organised is more significant for understanding it than its purpose.

2 Some saw Lacan's use of the word 'language' as meaning speech, others saw it as meaning all forms of communication, and that is the sense in which I interpret it here.

3 Lévi-Strauss (1969)

4 The anthropologist Nancy Tanner (1981) argues that male tenderness and female bonding led to the evolution of Homo sapiens; that it was not hunting that led to the development of early society but the gathering of plant food. Mothers who gathered plant food in groups with other women, and who learned to walk upright and carry implements, were most likely to have children who survived to contribute to the gene pool. Natural selection would have favoured those with the intelligence to gather and the sociability to share with others. Quoted in Sanday (1986), pp. 100–101. The wars and break-up of society in former Yugoslavia and other places demonstrate the stability of women as the core of family first, and society second. Men make periodic attempts to destroy both.

Adrienne Rich (1984) quotes Susan Cavin on an alternative definition of patriarchy in which the band of women and children eject the adolescent males; the males return and overpower the women, so rape of the mother by the son is the start of patriarchy [or just rape of the women by the men].

Chris Knight (1991) puts forward a counter theory that it was females, not males, who invented culture and socialisation. Evolving females banded together to control their own fertility by synchronising their menstruation, and allowed sexual access only to males who supplied them with food for themselves and their offspring. This social unit and common objective changed females into women. There is evidence that when women live together their menstrual periods tend to coincide, which would clear the first obvious question. All other questions are unanswerable, but it is as valid a theory as that of Lévi-Strauss.

5 Lacan is the most unintelligible of theorists. A surrealist, he allowed the surrealism of dreams to invade his language. In keeping with his view of himself as the new messiah of Freudian psychoanalysis, he developed a new and matching language (or jargon). Those who study his writings, however, seem to achieve a plane of comprehension; they elide the details and extract the theory with a certain

measure of intelligibility. Lacan's most respectful reviewer (Bär, 1974; quoted in Oliner, 1988, p. 118) admits that he is confusing and his terminology ambiguous. According to another critic, Lacan's complexity 'hides confused thinking and fundamental errors' (Oliner, 1988). Perhaps an example of the emperor's new clothes.

6   Lacan (1975), quoted in Irigaray (1985), p. 87

7   Mitchell (1974)

8   Mitchell (1984), p. 251

9   Freud (1933)

10 Irigaray (1985), p. 28

11 *Ibid*, p. 33

12 Grosz, Elizabeth, 'Julia Kristeva', in Elizabeth Wright, (ed.), *Feminism and Psychoanalysis*, Blackwell, 1992

13 Foucault.(1976, 1984a, 1984b)

14 Foucault (1976), p. 103

15 It is difficult to decide what meaning Foucault gives to the word 'sex', whether he means 'biological difference' or 'sexual activity'. From the context it could be either, but I assume he means sexual activity, (Foucault, 1976, p. 152).

16 Jeffreys (1990), p. 167

17 Freud (1930)

18 Freud (1935)

19 Mitchell (1984), p. 250

20 It is the *existence* of intelligence, not its level, that matters in this case.

CHAPTER 8

1   Jeffreys (1990), pp. 5–6, 11–12

2   Friedan (1963), p 181

3   History repeated itself in the 1980s in a backlash against the progress of career women. The media launched a campaign, based on, in many cases, distorted information, warning women about the 'biological clock' and the dangers of leaving childbearing too late, and also about the burnout of women trying to hold down positions previously held by men (Faludi, 1992, pp. 125–8).

4   David Mace, *Marriage Crisis*, Delisle 1948; Eustace Chesser, *Love and Marriage*, Pan, 1946, (reprinted 1957) and *Sexual Behaviour: Normal and Abnormal*, Key Publishers, 1949; Frank Caprio, *The Sexually Adequate Female*, Citadel, 1953 (reprinted 1963); Maxine Davis, *The Sexual Responsibility of Woman*, Fontana, 1957 (reprinted 1965); Sybil Neville-Rolfe, ed., *Sex in Social Life*, Geare Allen & Unwin, 1949; et cetera

5   *See* the biography of Kinsey written by his colleague, W.B. Pomeroy (1972)

6   Kinsey (1948; 1953)

7   Dworkin (1981), p. 180

8   Reich (1983), pp. 368–93

9   Masters and Johnson (1966)

10 The vaginal wall is a non-sensitive area.

11 Stoltenberg in Itzin, ed. (1992), p. 148

12 This situation, which is more evident in the UK than in Ireland, continues to the present day, and blame for it is laid not on men or on the sexual revolution, but on the independence of women which resulted from feminism. This attitude totally ignores the fact that women live in a political and economic system which keeps them and their children disadvantaged, and forces the majority of women to require the help of a man in order to rear their children in a financially secure situation.

13 Spender (1982; 1983), and others

14 Coote and Campbell (1982), p. 18

15 Rubin (1974); after promulgating this important (but partial) insight, Rubin came under the influence of Michel Foucault, and of homosexual male philosophy, and rejected her earlier interpretation of the relationship between sexuality and gender (in Vance, ed., 1989). By that time she had also become involved with a strand of libertarian lesbianism which defended sado-masochism and pornography.

16   Millett (1970); Greer (1970)
17   Dworkin (1981); Griffin (1981)

CHAPTER 9
1   Segal (1987, 1990, 1994)
2   Ferguson (1989)
3   Coote and Campbell (1982), pp. 31–3
4   MacKinnon (1982), quoted in Segal, 1987, p. 70. Catharine MacKinnon (1987) continued to hold that view: 'Feminism is a theory of how the erotization of dominance and submission creates gender, creates woman and man in the social form in which we know them'; and Segal (1992) continued to criticise it.
5   Firestone (1979), pp. 183–224
6   Bernard (1982), p. 140; Rowbotham (1984)
7   Griffin (1978); Morgan (1982)
8   Segal (1987), p. 68; Echols in Snitow, Stansell and Thompson, eds (1984), pp. 63–9
9   Coote and Campbell (1982), p. 29
10   Raymond in Itzin, ed. (1992), pp. 166–7
11   Andea Dworkin (1981; 1987) held the same view, if more trenchantly, as did Catharine MacKinnon (1982; 1987) and John Stoltenberg (1990).
12   Hite was criticised by other researchers for her methodology and feminist bias, ignoring the fact that all the other surveys had a male bias; and by feminists for a behaviouristic and mechanistic approach to sexuality. It could be said in her defence that she was then working within the confines of a sexology already defined by her predecessors. She responded to the criticism and in subsequent reports she explored love, affection and relationships.

CHAPTER 10
1   Merchant (1980), pp. 164–90
2   Mittwoch (1988). The knowledge that all mammalian embryos were anatomically female in the early stages of foetal life was known in the early 1970s. In 1970 Dr Mary Jane Sherfey quoted the embryological research that establishes it in 'A theory on female sexuality' (Morgan, ed., 1970, and Humm, ed., 1992).
3   Morris (1967), pp. 56–7
4   Wilson blamed 'the evil influence of Marxism' for all radical criticism of sociobiology. In his review of *Promethean Fire*, Stephen Jay Gould mischieviously quotes Engels who speculated on the influence of labour on the development of speech and intelligence, and the influence of intelligence on labour.
5   Wilson (1975), pp. 547–75. Edward O. Wilson's most recent book, *The Diversity of Life*, Harvard University Press, 1992, has restored his reputation.
6   Gould (1987), p. 119
7   *Behind the Mirror* (1973) and *The Waning of Humaneness*, (1983)
8   Myrdal quoted in Gould (1987), p. 216
9   Rose and Rose (1976b), p. xx
10   Gould (1987)
11   Gould (1987), p. 113
12   Dr Barbara McClintock discovered that some genes control other genes, and that they are not static as was thought by the discoverers of DNA and RNA, but that they can move about to achieve their purpose.
13   *Signs* vol. 7 (1982), quoted in Sayers (1986), p. 73
14   Weeks (1985), pp. 96–123

CHAPTER 11
1   Asexual reproduction involves the splitting of the organism by fission, budding, spore formation or vegetative propagation (such as plant cuttings) and therefore less variation. New research has shown that sexual reproduction for the species, such as humans, that practice it is an important factor in combating disease by increasing the variation of the

genetic pool and therefore resistance to parasites such as viruses, bacteria, et cetera (Ridley, 1993).

2   A degree of sexism has lingered on in the language of reproduction. I have not used the words 'fertilise' or 'fertilisation' in relation to the sexual fusion of genetic material. The process is usually described by saying that a male spermatozoon 'fertilises' an 'unfertilised' female ovum or egg. This gives the impression that the female egg is inert until the benefit of life is conferred on it by the male sperm; the implication is that the male sperm has 'life' and is not inert. It is a belief that has lingered on from ancient times when men sought superiority over women, convincing themselves that they were the authors of life, and women were mere vessels of reproduction. The truth is that both spermatozoa and ova are 'live' but unfertilised until they fuse.

3   Morris (1967)

4   Havelock Ellis in 1929, and Niles Newton in 1955, made similar reports.

5   Masters and Johnson (1966)

6   Quoted in de Beauvoir (1972), p. 522. Helene Deutsch maintained in *The Psychology of Women* (1944) that maternal love is a sentiment, a conscious attitude, not an instinct. This belief follows from her attachment to her theory of female masochism.

7   Male religion has always regarded sexuality as dirty, therefore it cannot be associated with motherhood. Paradoxically, religion has also considered giving birth as 'unclean'; women had to be purified afterwards before they could resume religious practice. This practice continued until very recently in the Catholic Church.

8   High levels of endorphins have been found in the placentas of animals and humans after birth (Kimball *et al*, 1981; Odent, 1981, quoted in *Our Bodies,*

Ourselves 1989, p. 379).The production of endorphins is linked with strenuous effort; they have been found also in the blood of joggers.

9   Dr Wagner was speaking at a seminar organised by the Association for the Improvement of Maternity Services (AIMS) in Cork on 7 October 1995; report in *Irish Times*, 9 October 1995.

10 Rich (1977), p. 176

11 Article by Dr Patricia McNair in *Guardian*, 4 February 1992

12 Adrienne Rich identifies the monopoly of the forceps by male doctors as decisive in the takeover of childbirth by the male medical establishment. The forceps appeared in surgery in the seventeenth century, when women were barred from the practice of medicine or surgery. The takeover of healing by men started much sooner; the fourteenth–seventeenth-century persecution of witches was an organised attack on women in medicine; (Rich, 1977, pp. 142–50).

13 Foucault had no sympathy with feminism. He rarely mentioned women (his interests were homosexual) and his knowledge of female sexuality sparse. In his *History of Sexuality* (as referred to earlier), he was concerned mainly with power, and the deployment of sexuality.

14 Oakley (1972), p. 197

15 Kitzinger (1983), p. 210

16 *Ibid.*, pp. 211–18

17 Quoted in *Our Bodies, Ourselves*, p. 393

18 *British Journal of Obstetrics and Gynaecology* (April 1981)

19 Rich (1977); Daly (1978); Ehrenreich and English (1973); Boston Women (1971, 1989); Anderson and Zinsser, (1988)

20 Morgan (1982), p. 53

21 In Ireland in 1961 there were 450 maternal deaths, and 2,100 deaths of infants under 4 weeks old, per 100,000 births; in 1987 there were 2 maternal

296 NOTES TO PAGES 152-173

deaths, and 400 neo-natal deaths, per 100,000 live births. These figures compare favourably with those for European Union countries and were among the best in Europe.

22 Rich (1977), p. 183

23 Rossi (1976), quoted in Rich (1984), p. 212

24 Rossi (1973), quoted in Rich (1977), p. 183

25 Saunders (1983), p. 91

26 Spender (1982)

27 Greer (1984), p. 198

CHAPTER 12

1 Simone de Beauvoir was an existentialist, and in existential terms transcendence means a rising above the human condition, a seeking after knowledge and understanding, or in de Beauvoir's own words, an achieving of liberty through 'a continual reaching for other liberties'. There is no justification for present existence, she said, other than its expansion into an indefinitely open future. Every individual who is concerned to justify his existence feels that his existence involves an undefined need to transcend himself, to engage in freely chosen projects. Immanence is the opposite of transcendence. It is stagnation, 'the brutish life of subjection to given conditions', a giving in to oppression. *The Second Sex*, 1972, pp. 28–9.

2 Gordon (1990), p. 127

3 Mitchell (1984), pp. 30–1

4 Myers (1977), quoted in Rowbotham (1989), p. 85

5 *Feminist Review*, no. 40 (Spring 1992)

6 Dinnerstein (1987), p. 77

7 Segal (1987), p. 215

8 Quoted in Chodorow (1978), p. 203

9 Transition to Parenthood Project, Thomas Coram Research Unit, 1982. Channi Kamur, Prospective Study of Sexual Activity during Pregnancy and After Childbirth, University College

Hospital, reported in AIMS paper on Pregnancy, Parenthood and Sexuality Conference, London, January 1982; quoted in Saunders in Cartledge and Ryan, eds (1983), p. 96.

10 Quoted in Deborah Holder, 'No Sex Please, I'm a New Mother', *Independent on Sunday* 5 September 1993

11 Gordon (1990), pp. 121–2

12 McLaren (1984), p. 67

13 Faludi (1992), pp. 101–39

CHAPTER 13

1 In Britain the Married Women's Property Acts, 1881, 1964; the Marriage and Divorce Act, 1857; the Matrimonial Causes Act, 1884; Married Women's (Maintenance in Case of Desertion) Act, 1886; the Divorce Act, 1923; the Custody of Infants Acts, 1839, 1873; Guardianship of Infants Act, 1973. In Ireland the Married Women's Status Act, 1957, and the Divorce Act, 1996.

2 From the German newspaper, *Bild*, 9 January 1991, quoted in *Feminist Review*, no. 39. (1991)

3 Quoted in Daly (1973), p. 61

4 Daly (1973), p. 61

5 McLeod (1982)

6 Spender (1982); Foster (1984); Rowbotham (1973); Anderson and Zinsser (1988), et cetera

7 Spender (1982), p. 342; Forster (1984), pp. 169–202. Told by one woman to Josephine Butler who published the story in *The Shield*, the newspaper of the Ladies' Association against the Contagious Diseases Acts. Under these acts a woman or girl suspected of being a prostitute was taken to the police station and medically examined. She was put on a surgical couch and her legs parted by clamps, her ankles tied in leather stirrups, and held down while a speculum or other medical instruments dipped in boiling water were used to inspect her vagina.

8   Spender (1982), p. 342; Forster (1984), p. 170
9   Kollontai (1921) in Holt (1977), p. 265
10 Leghorn and Parker (1981), p. 129
11 *Ms*, vol. 2, no. 6 (1992), p. 11
12 Gayle Kirshenbaum and Marina Gilbert in *Ms*, vol. 4, no. 6 (1994), p. 13
13 The members of the delegation were Robin Morgan (US), Mahnaz Afkhami (Iran), Keiko Higuchi (Japan), Madhu Kishwar (India) and Marilyn Waring (New Zealand).
14 Morgan (1993), pp. 260–2
15 Personal communication
16 The Collective of Prostitutes (COP) and the Programme for the Reform of Soliciting Laws (PROS) in Britain; Red Thread in the Netherlands; Hydra in Berlin; the Prostitutes' Collective and the International Committee on Prostitutes' Rights in Australia, et cetera.
17 Anthony (1992), pp. 86–7
18 Women Hurt in Systems of Prostitution Engaged in Revolt, an anti-prostitution organisation of ex-prostitutes which campaigns for abolition.
19 Anthony (1992), p. 87
20 Bono and Kemp (1991), pp. 65–8
21 Overs (1994), pp. 114–15
22 In Australia, New Zealand, Germany, the Netherlands, the United States of America, and Canada.

CHAPTER 14
1   Faludi (1992), pp. 140–70
2   *Ibid.*, pp. 184–87
3   *Ibid*, pp. 181–2
4   Kaplan (1984), pp. 321–2
5   Malcolm Gluck, *Cosmopolitan*, July 1992. The author worked for thirty years in advertising agencies.
6   *See* Faludi (1992), pp. 203–36 for women's backlash against the fashion industry in the late eighties, when fashion houses lost billions trying to 'feminise' women's clothes.

7   Foucault (1984b), p. 23
8   Hite (1981), p. 703
9   Interview *Irish Times* 13 January 1994
10 Greer (1984), p. 127
11 Reinisch, *et al.*, in Voeller, Reinisch and Gottlieb, eds (1990)
12 Anal penetration is a neutral term; buggery and sodomy carry a social and cultural baggage of depravity and sinfulness.
13 George (1993), p. 17
14 *Sexual Behaviour in Britain: The National Survey of Sexual Attitudes and Lifestyles*, Wellings, Field, Johnson and Wadsworth (1994), pp. 156–60
15 Kitzinger (1983), p. 142
16 Foucault (1984b), pp. 23–4
17 Jeffreys (1990), pp. 109–10
18 *Ibid.*, pp. 113–15
19 *Ibid.*, p. 255
20 Hite (1976), pp. 371–9
21 Newton and Walton (1989), pp. 242–50
22 Cline (1993), p. 25
23 Griffin (1981), pp. 60–1
24 Foucault (1984a), p. 16
25 Foucault (1984b), p. 140
26 From Jacques Lantier's *La Cité magique*, quoted in Daly (1978), p. 168
27 Jeffreys (1990), p. 43
28 Jeffreys (1985), p. 146
29 D.C.G. Skegg, P.A. Corwin, C. Paul. 'The importance of the male factor in cancer of the cervix', *Lancet ii*, 1982. And research continues on the effects of 'the male factor'.
30 Duncan (1988)
31 Genital mutilation includes circumcision, which is the removal of the prepuce or hood and sometimes the tip of the clitoris; clitoridectomy, which is the removal of the clitoris and all or part of the labia minora, and sometimes part of the labia majora; infibulation, also called pharaonic, which is the removal of the clitoris, the labia minora and much of the labia majora. The remaining sides of the vulva are pulled together and secured

with thorns or sewn, leaving a small opening for urine and menstrual flow. The mutilated woman must be cut open for intercourse and childbirth and sewn up again afterwards.

32 Morgan (1993), pp. 93–4
33 Kitzinger (1983), p. 57
34 Barker-Benfield (1976); quoted in Daly (1978), p. 451, n30
35 Kitzinger (1983), p. 25
36 In 1984 at the World Conference on Population in Mexico City, the Vatican influenced the US government to withdraw support from the United Nations Fund for Population Activities and the International Planned Parenthood Federation. In 1992 at the United Nations Conference on Environment and Development (UNCED – Earth Summit) the Vatican lobbied successfully to have population control dropped from the agenda. In 1994 at the next UNCED conference in Cairo, the Vatican persisted with the same line. At the UN Women's Conference in Beijing in 1995, Vatican delegates abstained from proposals concerning the use of condoms as protection against AIDS.
37 O'Hanlon, *Irish Times* 25 January 1993
38 Greer (1984), pp. 130–58. *See also* Grant (1993)
39 Kitzinger (1983), p. 195
40 Boston Women, *Our Bodies, Ourselves* (1989), p. 279
41 *Ibid*.
42 Daly (1973), pp. 106–14
43 Gilligan (1982), pp. 71–4
44 Thomson (1994), p. 41
45 Greer (1991), p. 80
46 Lewis (1993), p. 45
47 'Climacteric': a critical period in human life; an unexplained disease of advanced life, characterised by loss of strength and sleeplessness (*Oxford English Dictionary*); Greer (1991), pp. 14–20
48 Greer (1991) and Lewis (1993).

Germaine Greer accuses the (male) medical professional of anophobia (an irrational fear of old women), which, she says, has more to do with a male doctor's relations with his mother and wife than with the demeanour of his patient.
49 Those who have had breast, ovarian or vaginal cancer, breast cysts, heart disease, stroke, thrombo-embolism, high blood pressure, diabetes, fibroids, migraine, endometriosis, or gall-bladder disease; those who are overweight or smoke heavily. This list narrows down the number of middle-aged women who would qualify.
50 Barker-Benfield (1976), quoted in Daly (1978), p. 228
51 Daly (1978), pp. 323–4; Millett (1970), p. 307

CHAPTER 15
1   Wollstonecraft (1792, 1982)
2   Thompson and Wheeler (1825, 1983)
3   Mill and Mill (1851, 1983)
4   Hite (1981), pp. 60–83
5   Campbell (1993), p. 265
6   Fairweather, McDonough, McFadyean (1984), p. 121
7   Friedan (1963); Millett (1970); Greer (1970); Rowbotham (1973); Mitchell (1966); French (1985); Faludi (1991); et cetera
8   Andy Metcalf and Martin Humphries (1985) come to the same conclusion.
9   Stoltenberg (1990), pp. 55–6
10 Kinsey (1948)
11 Stoltenberg (1990), pp. 56–61
12 Dinnerstein (1987), p. 166
13 Greer (1984), p. 205
14 Morgan (1993); Rich (1977); Dworkin (1980)
15 Griffin (1981), p. 87
16 Kelly, Petra (1984)
17 Hite (1981), pp. 478–80
18 *Ibid*, pp. 322–472
19 Greer (1984), p. 204
20 Griffin (1981), pp. 95–6
21 Lorenz (1966), pp. 210–11

22 Segal (1987), p. 187
23 Morgan (1993), p. 88
24 Dworkin (1981)
25 2.5 million pornographic magazines are produced each month in the UK in 1990 (Itzin, ed (1993), p. 39).
26 Critics have questioned Shere Hite's method of collecting data, saying that she used the male sexual magazines, *Playboy* and *Hustler*, to distribute her questionnaires. In *The Hite Report on Male Sexuality*, only 11 per cent of the respondents came from readers of these magazines, and their circulation would indicate that much more than 11 per cent of the male population read them.
27 There are different definitions of 'soft-core porn'. Some hold that it is pornography without violence, but which would include 'bondage', but most pundits define hard-core porn as that in which the male penis (erect, of course) is visible.
28 Griffin (1981), p. 60
29 Jeffreys (1990), pp. 251–2
30 Weeks (1985), p. 233
31 Segal and McIntosh, eds (1992)
32 Caputi (1987), pp. 164–6
33 Sanday in Tomaselli and Porter, eds (1986), p. 99
34 Segal and McIntosh, eds (1992), pp. 107–8

CHAPTER 16
1 Collins, *et al* (1978), quoted in McLeod (1982)
2 Harrison in Tomaselli and Porter, eds (1986), p. 45
3 In fairness I must say that changes have occurred where the rape of a prostitute is concerned. In recent cases in Dublin, men were convicted of such a rape, but in each case considerable violence was used and injury was sustained by the woman.
4 Porter, Roy, in Tomaselli and Porter, eds (1986), p. 235
5 Segal (1990)
6 Roiphe (1993)
7 Tomaselli and Porter, eds (1986), pp. 37–8
8 *Ibid.*, pp. 85, 93–8
9 *Ibid.*, p. 85
10 From a report in *Ms* magazine, August 1972, entitled 'The women of Bangladesh' by Joyce Goldman, which documents the rape of 200,000 Bengali women during that war by West Pakistan soldiers. When the author investigated the reports of the unremitting rape and murder of those women, she was told by Pakistani officers that they raped them until they died, or raped them and then killed them. Any survivors were better off dead because they were regarded as 'unclean' and ostracised in their own societies.
11 The Serbs at that time were the occupying armies; even the Serbian anti-war group Women in Black admitted that Serbian fighters had been the initiators and primary perpetrators of systematic rape as part of their 'ethnic cleansing' campaign (Isadora Sekulic, *Ms*, vol. 4, no. 5, 1994) We do not know if Croat and Muslim armies also raped. There were reports (unsubstantiated) from Serbian sources that they did, but they did not have the same opportunities then as the Serbs.
12 It was reported by eyewitnesses that some of the videos were used on Serbian news broadcasts and termed rapes of Serbian women by Muslim or Croatian men. While they were being filmed the women were made to sing Serbian songs or wear the Serbian cross. Did Serbian audiences not ask how it had been possible to video these supposed rapes of Serbian women?
13 Freud's letter to Wilhelm Fleiss, 21 September 1897. An underlying reason for this change of mind, he said, was that he found what turned out to be a better explanation in the theory of

child sexuality which was important and otherwise might not have been developed. Reproduced in Masson (1984), pp. 108–10.

14 Rush (1974)

15 Miller (1990), pp. 309–16

16 Alice Miller, a German psychoanalyst who came to the attention of English-speaking countries in the 1980s, has discarded Freud's idea of an infant sexuality. A defender of the child, she has written intensively and with great integrity on all forms of child abuse, and 'poisonous pedagogy', which is the term she applies to 'good upbringing' or power of parents over children which benefits the parents not the children (1987a, 1987b, 1990). She wrote *Thou Shalt Not Be Aware* in 1981, (published in English in the US in 1984 and in Britain in 1985). She was ten years ahead of these islands in recognising the prevalence of the sexual abuse of children.

17 Masson (1984)

18 Weeks (1985), p. 231

19 Jeffreys (1990), p. 189

20 Orbach (1994), pp. 99–102

21 Miller (1990), p. 326

22 In his biography of Virginia Woolf, Quentin Bell revealed for the first time her sexual abuse by her step-brother. Louise DeSalvo's (1989) examination of the evidence in greater depth revealed the Stephen family as grossly dysfunctional, where all the older men sexually abused all the women. DeSalvo took a less relaxed view of the situation than did Bell, and drew conclusions that Bell had not drawn. She blamed the brutal physical and sexual treatment the men of the family had received as boys in the public schools to which they were sent, treatment which is well documented elsewhere and drew the conclusion that Virginia carried the effects of her trauma literally to the grave.

23 Segal (1990), p. 258

24 Hite (1994), p. 215. The large number concerned may have arisen because the survey took the form of an essay questionnaire and women who had bad experiences would have been more inclined to reply to a survey in that particular form.

25 Tiger (1968)

26 Ferguson (1989), pp. 42–3

27 The ferment of research into sexuality in the seventies, which was mainly carried out by women, challenged a response from men in the eighties which was more rational and reasoned than many of the replies received by Shere Hite. The work of these men to a large extent echoed and confirmed that of feminists. Lynne Segal provides a useful synthesis of their work in *Slow Motion: Changing Masculinities; Changing Men*, Virago Press, 1990.

CHAPTER 17

1 Wellings, *et al.* (1994)

2 *Sex in America: A Definitive Survey*, Robert Michael, John Gagnon, Edward Laumann and Gina Kolata, Little Brown, 1994

3 Brain (1976), p. 67

4 Walker, Barbara (1983), p. 400

5 Foucault (1984b), pp. 190, and pp. 24–5

6 'The men of Sodom were wicked and sinners before the Lord' (Genesis 13:13, *c.* 19 B.C.); they wanted to 'know' the two men who were given lodgings by Lot. Similarly the old man of Gibeah protected the Levite from the wickedness of the sons of Belial who wanted to 'know' him (Judges 19: 20, *c.* 13 B.C.). In each case neither of these saviours saw any wickedness in sacrificing the women of their households to the appetites of the attackers. In Lot's case, he offered to the importunate mob of Sodomites his 'two daughters who have not known man ... and abuse you them as

it shall please you, so that you do no evil to these men' (Genesis 19: 8). In the case of the old man of Gibeah, he offered the sons of Belial his maiden daughter and the Levite's concubine 'to humble them and satisfy their lust, only I beseech you commit not this crime of nature on the man' (Judges 19: 24). Then the sons of Belial took the concubine and abused her until she died.

7   Lorenz (1963), p. 168
8   Foucault (1976), p. 43
9   Weeks (1985), pp. 195–7
10 Freud (1905, 1909, 1910, 1918)
11 Jung (1963), p. 247
12 Oakley (1985), pp. 164–6
13 Wilson (1975), p. 555
14 J.M. Bailey and R.C. Pillard in *Archives of General Psychiatry*, March 1993
15 Faderman (1980)
16 Leghorn and Parker (1981), p. 131
17 Raymond in Itzin, ed. (1992), pp. 176–7
18 Snitow, Stansell and Thompson, eds (1984); Vance, ed (1984)
19 Califia (1979), quoted in Weeks (1985), p. 238
20 Rich, in Snitow, Stansell and Thompson, eds. (1984). Adrienne Rich, while accepting that particular section of Chodorow's thesis, does not agree with much of the rest of it.
21 Ferguson (1989), pp. 189–95
22 George (1993)

CHAPTER 18

1   Holt (1977), pp. 276–92
2   Quoted in O'Neill (1989), p. 115
3   Stone (1977), p. 282
4   Fromm (1975)
5   Sarsby (1983), p. 9
6   Firestone (1970), pp. 121–38
7   Greer (1970), pp. 139–70
8   Daly (1984), p. 204
9   Rowbotham (1984), p. 21

10 Mitchell (1984), p. 111
11 Mullan (1984), p. 226; de Courcy Hinds in the *New York Times*, 14 February 1981, p. 15
12 Quoted in Masters, Johnson and Kolodny (1992)
13 Quoted in de Beauvoir (1972), p. 652
14 Orbach (1994), p. 75
15 Freud's *Psycho-Analytic Notes Upon Autobiographical Account of a Case of Paranoia (Dementia Paranoides)*, 1911
16 Eichenbaum and Orbach (1982; 1984)
17 Jeffreys (1990), pp. 299–312
18 Rowbotham (1984), p. 21

CHAPTER 19

1   Rowbotham (1984)
2   Mead (1935)
3   The social and political practice of supporting single mothers is not necessarily the reprehensible or corrupting practice alleged by some social critics. It is, in fact, a move towards a system of paying women for maintaining a home and rearing children; children's allowances are a similar kind of payment. The fairness or otherwise of the system relates to the fairness or otherwise of the taxation system. It might seem unfair that all taxpayers pay for the rearing of some families; and it might be fairer if all home-makers and child-rearers, like teachers, were paid a state wage which was collected from all taxpayers, and if child-minding facilities were as institutionally established as schools.
4   Chodorow (1978), pp. 202–3
5   Ferguson (1989), pp. 170–87
6   Rosenblatt (1967)
7   Dinnerstein (1987); Chodorow (1978)
8   Control of populations is necessary if the species is to advance, to develop their intelligence and live the fulfilling lives that their intelligence demands.

SELECT BIBLIOGRAPHY

Anderson, B.S., and J. Zinsser. *A History of Their Own: Women in Europe from Prehistory to the Present*, vols 1 and 2, Harper & Row, 1988

Anderson, Mary. *The Menopause*, Faber & Faber, 1983; quoted in Greer, 1991

Anthony, Jane. 'Prostitution as "choice"', *Ms*, vol. 2, no 4 (January/February 1992)

Bär, E.S. 'Understanding Lacan', *Psychoanalysis and Contemporary Science*, vol. 3 (1974)

Barker–Benfield, G.J. *The Horrors of the Half-Known Life: Male Attitudes Towards Women and Sexuality in Nineteenth-Century America*, Harper & Row, 1976; quoted in Daly, 1979

Beauvoir, Simone de. *The Second Sex*, Penguin, 1972 (first published in French in 1949; English edition, Jonathan Cape, 1953)

Bernard, Jessie. *The Future of Marriage*, Yale University Press, 1982

Bonaparte, M. *Female Sexuality*, International Universities Press, 1953

Bono, Paola and Sandra Kemp. *Italian Feminist Thought*, Basil Blackwell, 1991

Boston Women's Health Book Collective, *Our Bodies, Ourselves*, British edition, (eds) Angela Phillips and Jill Rakusen, Penguin, 1989

Bourget, P. *Physiologie de l'amour*, Modern, 1890

Brain, Robert. *Friends and Lovers*, Paladin, 1976

Brownmiller, Susan, *Against Our Will: Men, Women and Rape*, Secker & Warburg, 1975

Califia, Pat. 'Unraveling the sexual fringe. A secret side of lesbian sexuality', *The Advocate* (December 1979); quoted in Weeks, 1985

Campbell, Beatrix in *Feminist Review*, vol. 5 (1980)
  Goliath: Britain's Dangerous Places, Methuen, 1993

Caputi, Jane. *The Age of Sex Crime*, The Women's Press, 1987

Cartledge, Sue and Joanna Ryan. (eds). *Sex and Love*, The Women's Press, 1983

Chamberlayne, Prue. 'The Mothers' Manifesto and disputes over Mütterlichkeit', *Feminist Review*, no. 35 (1990)

Chodorow, Nancy. *The Reproduction of Mothering*, University of California Press, 1978

Cline, Sally. *Women, Celibacy and Passion*, André Deutsch, 1993

Cohen, David. *Being a Man*, Routledge, 1990

Collins, W., E. Friedman, and A. Pivot. *The Directory of Social Change*, Wildwood House, 1978; quoted in McLeod, 1982

Connell, Robert, *Gender and Power*, Polity Press, 1987; quoted in Segal, 1990

Coote, Anna and Beatrix Campbell. *Sweet Freedom*, Picador, 1982

Coward, Rosalind. 'Sexual politics and psychoanalysis', in Rosalind Brunt and Caroline Rowan (eds), *Feminism, Culture and Politics*, Lawrence & Wishart, 1982

Our Treacherous Hearts, Faber & Faber, 1992

Daly, Mary. *Gyn/Ecology*, The Woman's Press, 1979 (first published 1978)

Pure Lust, The Women's Press, 1984

Beyond God the Father, The Women's Press, 1986 (first published 1973)

Dawkins, Richard. *The Selfish Gene*, Oxford University Press, 1976

de Courcy Hinds, M. 'They fell in love at first sight', *New York Times*, 14 February 1981; quoted in Mullan, 1984

de Rougement, Denis. *Love in the Western World*, 1940 and 1956, cited in Juliet Mitchell, *Women: The Longest Revolution*, Virago, 1984

DeSalvo, Louise. *Virginia Woolf: The Impact of Childhood Sexual Abuse on Her Life and Work*, The Women's Press, 1989

Deutsch, Helene. *The Psychology of Women*, Grune & Stratton, 1944

Dinnerstein, Dorothy. *The Mermaid and the Minator*, Harper & Row, 1976; also published as *The Rocking of the Cradle and the Ruling of the World*, The Women's Press, 1987

Duncan, M. Elizabeth. 'An alternative to Condomania' (1988)

Dworkin, Andrea. *Take Back the Night*, (ed.), Laura Lederer, Morrow, 1980

Pornography, The Women's Press, 1981

Intercourse, Secker & Warburg, 1987

Echols, Alice. 'The new feminism of Yin and Yang', in Snitow, Stansell and Thompson (eds), 1984

Ehrenreich, Barbara. *For Her Own Good: One Hundred and Fifty Years of Experts' Advice to Women*, Doubleday, 1979

Ehrenreich, Barbara and Deirdre English. *Witches, Midwives and Nurses*, Writers' and Readers' Publishing Cooperative, 1976 (first published 1973)

Eichenbaum, Luise and Susie Orbach. *Outside In, Inside Out*, Penguin, 1982

What Do Women Want?, Fontana, 1984

Ellis, Havelock. *Man and Woman*, Houghton Miflin, 1929

Engels, Friedrich. *The Origin of Private Property and the State*, in *Karl Marx and Friedrich Engels*, Foreign Languages Publishing House, Moscow, 1962 (first published in Zurich, 1884)

Epstein, Barbara. 'Family, sexual morality, and popular movements in turn-of-the-century America', in Snitow, Stansell and Thompson (eds), 1984

Erikson, Erik. 'Womanhood and the inner space', in Erik Erikson, *Identity, Youth and Crisis*, Faber & Faber, 1968

Evans, Mary. *The Woman Question*, Fontana, 1982

Eyles, Leonora. *The Woman in the Little House*, 1922; quoted in Rowbotham, 1973

Faderman, Lilian. *Surpassing the Love of Men: Romantic Friendship and Love between Women from the Renaissance to the Present*, Junction Books, 1980

Fairweather, Eileen, Roisín McDonough and Melanie McFadyean. *Only the Rivers Run Free, Northern Ireland: The Women's War*, Pluto, 1984

Faludi, Susan. *Backlash*, Chatto & Windus, 1992 (first published 1991)

Ferguson, Ann. *Signs*, vol. 7, no. 1 (1981)
  Blood at the Root, Pandora, 1989

Firestone, Shulamith. *The Dialetic of Sex*, The Women's Press, 1979 (first published 1970)

Flax, J. 'Theorizing motherhood', *Women's Review of Books*, vol. 1, no. 9 (1984)

Forster, Margaret. *Significant Sisters*, Secker & Warburg, 1984

Foucault, Michel. *The History of Sexuality*, vol. 1, Penguin, 1990 (first published 1976)
  The Uses of Pleasure: The History of Sexuality, vol. 2, Penguin, 1990 (first published 1984a)
  The Care of Self: The History of Sexuality, vol. 3, Penguin, 1990 (first published 1984b)

French, M. *Beyond Power, Women, Men and Morals*, Jonathan Cape, 1985
  The War Against Women, Hamish Hamilton, 1992

Freud, Sigmund. *The Complete Works of Sigmund Freud*, standard edition, (trans.) James Strachey, Hogarth Press and the Institute of Psychoanalysis, 1955
  Letter to Wilhelm Fliess, 1897, in *The Complete Works*, 1955
  Three Essays on Sexuality, 1905 and footnotes on later dates; revised 1916, 1917, 1920, in *The Complete Works*, 1955
  'Analysis of a phobia of a five-year-old boy (Little Hans)', 1909, in *The Complete Works*, 1955
  Leonardo da Vinci and a Memory of His Childhood, 1910, in *The Complete Works*, 1955
  'From the theory of an infantile neurosis (The Wolf Man)', 1918, in *The Complete Works*, 1955
  A General Introduction to Psychoanalysis, 1916–17, in *The Complete Works*, 1955
  Lines of Advance in Psychoanalytic Therapy, 1919, in *The Complete Works*, 1955
  The Ego and the Id, 1923, in *The Complete Works*, 1955
  Some Psychical Consequences of the Anatomical Distinction Between the Sexes, 1925, in *The Complete Works*, 1955
  The Question of Lay Analysis, 1926, in *The Complete Works*, 1955
  Female Sexuality, 1931, in *The Complete Works*, 1955
  Letter to Carl Muller Braunscheig, 1935, published in 'Freud and female sexuality: an unpublished letter', *Psychiatry*, (1971); quoted in Mitchell, 1984
  New Introductory Lectures, 1933, in *The Complete Works*, 1955
  'Femininity', *New Introductory Lectures*, 1932–36, in *The Complete Works*, 1955

An Outline of Psychoanalysis, in *The Complete Works*, 1955

The Interpretation of Dreams, 1930, (trans.) James Strachey, George Allen & Unwin, 1961

The Complete Introductory Lectures on Psychoanalysis, (trans. and ed.) James Strachey, George Allen & Unwin, 1971

Freud, Sigmund and Josef Breuer. *Studies on Hysteria*, 1895, in *The Complete Works*, 1955

Friedan, Betty. *The Feminine Mystique*, Penguin, 1965 (first published 1963)

Fromm, Eric. *Sigmund Freud's Mission*, Harper, 1959

The Art of Loving, George Allen & Unwin, 1975

George, Sue. *Women and Bisexuality*, Scarlet Press, 1993

Gilligan, Carol. *In a Different Voice*, Harvard University Press, 1982

Gilman, Charlotte Perkins. *Women and Economics*, Harper & Row, 1966 (first published 1898)

Goode, W.J. 'The theoretical importance of love', *American Sociological Review*, vol. 24 (1959); cited in Sarsby, 1983

Gordon, Tuula. *Feminist Mothers*, Macmillan, 1990

Gould, Stephen. J. *An Urchin in the Storm*, Norton, 1987

Grant, Linda. *Sexing the Millennium*, Harper Collins, 1993

Greer, Germaine. *The Female Eunuch*, Paladin, 1971 (first published 1970)

Sex and Destiny, Secker & Warburg, 1984

The Change, Hamish Hamilton, 1991

Griffin, Susan. *Pornography and Silence*, The Women's Press, 1981

Woman and Nature, The Women's Press, 1984 (first published 1978)

Grosskurth, Phyllis. *Melanie Klein, Her World and Her Work*, Hodder & Stoughton, 1986.

Harrison, Ross. 'Rape – a case study in political philosophy', in Tomaselli and Porter (eds), 1986

Hays, H.R. *The Dangerous Sex*, Pocket Books, 1972

Hite, Shere. *The Hite Report on Female Sexuality*, Pandora, 1989 (first published 1976)

The Hite Report on Male Sexuality, MacDonald Optima, 1981

The Hite Report on Women and Love, Viking, 1988

The Hite Report on the Family, Bloomsbury, 1994

Holt, Alix. *Alexandra Kollontai: Selected Writings*, Alison & Busby, 1977

Horney, K. *The Flight from Womanhood*, Norton, 1926

The Distrust Between the Sexes, Norton, 1931

The Dread of Woman, Norton, 1932

The Problem of Feminine Masochism, Norton, 1935

New Ways in Psychoanalysis, Norton, 1939

Hufton, Olwen. *The Prospect Before Her: A History of Women in Western Europe, Vol. 1, 1500–1800*, Harper Collins, 1995

Humm, Maggie (ed.). *Feminisms, A Reader*, Harvester/Wheatsheaf, 1992

Humphrey, Caroline. Review of *Blood Relations: Menstruation and the Origins of Culture* by Chris Knight in *London Review of Books*, 27 February 1992

Hunt, Margaret. 'The de-eroticization of women's liberation: social purity movements and the revolutionary feminism of Sheila Jeffreys', *Feminist Review*, no. 34 (1990)

Irigaray, Luce. *The Sex Which is Not One*, (trans.) Catherine Porter, Cornell University Press, 1985 (first published in French, 1977)

Itzin, Catherine (ed.). *Pornography: Women, Violence and Civil Liberties, A Radical View*, Oxford University Press, 1993 (first published 1992)

Jack, Dana. *Silencing the Self: Women and Depression*, Harvard University Press, 1991

Jeffreys, S. *The Spinster and Her Enemies: Feminism and Sexuality, 1880–1930*, Pandora, 1985
Anticlimax: A Feminist Perspective on the Sexual Revolution, The Women's Press, 1990

Jung, C.J. 'Woman in Europe', in *Collected Works*, Routledge & Kegan Paul, 1927
Memories, Dreams, Reflections, recorded and edited by Aniela Jaffé. 1961, Collins and Routledge & Kegan Paul, 1963

Kamur, Channi. 'Prospective study of sexual activity during pregnancy and after childbirth', University College Hospital, reported in AIMS paper on Pregnancy, Parenthood and Sexuality Conference, London, January 1982; quoted in Gordon, 1990

Kanter, Hannah, Sarah Lefanu, Saila Shah and Carole Spedding (eds). *Sweeping Statements*, The Women's Press, 1984

Kaplan, E. Ann. 'Is the gaze male?', in Snitow, Stansell and Thompson (eds), 1984

Kelly, Joan. 'The doubled vision of feminist theory', in *Sex and Class in History*, Judith L. Newton, Mary P. Ryan and Judith R. Walkowitz (eds) Routledge, 1983

Kelly, Petra. 'Women and the future', in Cambridge Women's Peace Collective edited by Petra Kelly, *My Country is the Whole World*, Pandora, 1984

Kimball, C.D., C.M. Chang, S.M. Huang and J.C. Houck, 'Immunoreactive endorphin peptides & prolactin in umbilical vein & maternal blood', *American Journal of Obstetrics and Gynaecology*, vol. 140, no. 2 (May 1981)

Kinsey, Alfred C. *Sexual Behavior in the Human Male*, Saunders, 1948
Sexual Behavior in the Human Female, Saunders, 1953

Kitzinger, Sheila. *The Experience of Childbirth*, Penguin, 1984 (first published 1962)
Woman's Experience of Sex, Penguin, 1985 (first published 1983)

Klein, Melanie. 'The Oedipus complex in the light of earlier anxieties, in *The Writings of Melanie Klein*, Hogarth Press, 1975 (first published 1945)
'Some theoretical conclusions regarding the emotional life of the infant', in *The Writings of Melanie Klein*, Hogarth Press, 1952
'On observing the behaviour of young infants', in *The Writings of Melanie Klein*, Hogarth Press, 1952
Envy and Gratitude, Tavistock, 1957

Knight, Chris. *Blood Relations: Menstruation and the Origins of Culture*, Yale University Press, 1991

Koedt, Ann. 'The myth of the vaginal orgasm', 1970, reprinted in *Radical Feminism*, New York Times Books, 1973

Kollantai, Alexandra. 'The fight against prostitution', 1921, in Holt, 1977
'Make way for the winged Eros', 1923a, in Holt, 1977
'The labour of women in the evolution of the economy', 1923b, in Holt, 1977

Krafft-Ebing, Richard von. *Psychopathia Sexualis*, 12th edition, (trans.) F.S. Klaf, Staples Press, 1965 (first published, 1886)

Lacan, Jacques. 'Encore, Le Séminaire XX', 1975, quoted in Irigaray 1985

Lederer, Wolfgang. *The Fear of Women*, Grune & Stratton, 1968

Leghorn, Lisa and Katherine Parker. *Woman's Worth: Sexual Economics and the World of Men*, Routledge & Kegan Paul, 1981

Lévi-Strauss, Claude. *The Elementary Structure of Kinship*, 1969 (first published 1949)

Lewis, Jane. 'Feminism, the menopause and hormone replacement therapy', *Feminist Review*, no. 43, (1993)

Lorenz, K. *On Aggression*, Methuen, 1966 (first published 1963)
Behind the Mirror, Methuen, 1977 (first published 1973)
The Waning of Humaneness, Unwin Hyman, 1988 (first published 1983)

Lumsden, Charles L. and Edward O. Wilson. *Promethean Fire: Reflections on the Origin of the Mind*, Harvard University Press, 1984

Maccoby, Eleanor E. and Carol N. Jacklin. *The Psychology of Sex Difference*, Stanford University Press, 1974

MacCurtain, Margaret and Donncha O'Corrain. *Women in Irish Society: The Historical Dimension*, Arlen House, 1978

MacKinnon, Catharine. 'Feminism, Marxism, method and the State', *Signs*, vol. 7 no. 3 (1982)
Feminism Unmodified: Discourses on Life and Law, Harvard, 1987
Towards a Feminist Theory of State, Harvard, 1989

McLaren, Angus. *Reproductive Rituals*, Methuen, 1984

McLeod, Eileen. *Women Working: Prostitution Now*, Croom Helm, 1982

Marcuse, H. *Eros and Civilisation*, Beacon Press, 1955

Masson, Jeffrey. *Freud: The Assault on Truth: Freud's suppression of the Seduction Theory*, Faber & Faber, 1984

Masters, William H. and Virginia E. Johnson, *Human Sexual Response*, Little Brown, 1966
Human Sexual Inadequacy, Little Brown, 1970

Masters, William H., Virginia E. Johnson and R.C. Kolodny. *Human Sexuality*, HarperCollins, 1992

Mead, Margaret. *Male and Female*, Gollancz, 1949
Sex and Temperament in Three Primitive Societies, Routledge & Kegan Paul, 1948 (first published 1935)

Merchant, Carolyn. *The Death Of Nature*, Wildwood House, 1980

Metcalf, Andy and Martin Humphries. *The Sexuality of Men*, Pluto Press, 1985

Mill, John Stuart (with Harriet Taylor Mill). *The Subjection of Women*, Virago Press, 1983 (first published 1851)

Miller, Alice. *The Drama of Being a Child*, Virago Press, 1987a (first published in German in 1979)

    For Your Own Good: The Roots of Violence in Child-rearing, Virago Press, 1987b (first published in German in 1980)

    Thou Shalt Not Be Aware: Society's Betrayal of the Child, Pluto Press, 1990 (first published in German in 1981)

Millett, Kate. *Sexual Politics*, Virago Press, 1977 (first published 1969)

Mitchell, Juliet. 'Women: the longest revolution', in *New Left Review* (1966)

    Psychoanalysis and Feminism, Penguin, 1974

    Women: The Longest Revolution, Virago Press, 1984

Mitchell, Juliet and Jacqueline Rose. *Feminine Sexuality: Jacques Lacan and the Ecole Freudienne*, Macmillan, 1982

Mittwoch, Ursula. Department of genetics and biometry, University College London, in *New Scientist*, vol. 120, no. 1, 635 (22 October 1988)

Morgan, Robin. 'Theory and practice: pornography and rape', in *The Word of a Woman: Selected Prose 1968–1992*, Virago Press, 1993 (first published 1975)

    The Anatomy of Freedom, Martin Robinson, 1983 (first published 1982)

Morris, Desmond. *The Naked Ape*, Jonathan Cape, 1967

    The Human Zoo, Jonathan Cape, 1969

Mullan, Bob. *The Mating Game*, Routledge & Kegan Paul, 1984

Myers, Nell. 'Sometimes a sad adventure', *Morning Star*, 28 June 1977; quoted in Rowbotham, 1989

Neville-Rolfe, Sybil (ed.). *Sex in Social Life*, George Allen & Unwin, 1949

Newton, Esther and Shirley Walton. 'The misunderstanding: towards a more precise sexual vocabulary', in Vance (ed.), 1989

Newton, Niles. *Maternal Emotions*, Hoeber, 1955; quoted in Rich, 1977

Newton, Judith L., Mary P. Ryan and Judith R. Walkowitz. *Sex and Class in Women's History*, Routledge & Kegan Paul, 1983

Oakley, Ann. *Sex, Gender and Society*, revised edition, Gower, 1985 (first published 1972)

Odent, Michel. 'The evolution of obstetrics at Pithiviers', *Birth and Family*, vol. 8, no. 1 (Spring 1981)

Oliner, Marion M. *Cultivating Freud's Garden in France*, Jason Aronson, 1988

O'Neill, Onora. *Constructions of Reason*, Cambridge University Press, 1989

Orbach, Susie. *What's Really Going On Here?*, Virago Press, 1994

Overs, Cheryl. 'Sex work, HIV and the state', *Feminist Review*, no. 48 (1994)

Owens, Rosemary Cullen. *Smashing Times*, Attic Press, 1984

Pomeroy, W.B. *Dr Kinsey and the Institute for Sex Research*, Harper & Row, 1972

Porter, Cathy. *Alexandra Kollontai: A Biography*, Virago Press, 1980

Porter, Roy. 'Does rape have a historical meaning?', in Tomaselli and Porter (eds), 1986

Radicalesbians. 'Woman-identified woman', 1970; quoted in Jeffreys, 1990

Ranke-Heinemann, Ute. *Eunuchs for the Kingdom of Heaven*, Penguin, 1991 (first published in German in 1988, (trans.) Peter Heinegg for Doubleday, 1990)

Raymond, Janice. 'Pornography and the politics of lesbianism', in Catherine Itzin, (ed.), *Pornography: Women, Violence and Civil Liberties, A Radical View*, Oxford University Press, 1993 (first published 1992)

Reich, Wilhelm. *The Function of the Orgasm*, (trans.) Vincent R. Carfagno, Souvenir Press, 1983 (first published 1942)

Reinisch, J.M., M. Ziemba-Davis and S.A. Sanders. 'Sexual behaviour and AIDS: lessons from art and sex research', in B. Voeller, J.M. Reinisch and M. Gottlieb (eds), *AIDS and Sex: An Integrated Biomedical and Bio-behavioural Approach*, Oxford University Press, 1990

Rich, Adrienne. *Of Woman Born*, Virago Press, 1977 (first published 1976)
    'On compulsory heterosexuality and lesbian existence', in Snitow, Stansell and Thompson (eds), 1984 (first published in *Signs*, vol. 5, no. 4, 1980)

Richards, Janet Radcliffe. *The Sceptical Feminist*, Routledge & Kegan Paul, 1980

Ridley, Mark. *Explanation of Organic Diversity*, Oxford University Press, 1993

Roiphe, Katie. *The Morning after: Sex, Fear and Feminism on Campus*, Hamish Hamilton, 1994 (first published 1993)

Rose, Hilary and Stephen Rose. *The Political Economy of Science*, Macmillan, 1976a
    The Radicalisation of Science, Macmillan, 1976b

Rose, June. *Marie Stopes and the Sexual Revolution*, Penguin, 1993 (first published 1992)

Rosenblatt, Jay. 'Nonhormonal basis of maternal behavior in the rat', *Science* (June 1967); quoted in Dinnerstein, 1987

Rossi, Alice. 'Maternalism, sexuality and the new feminism', in *Contemporary Sexual Behaviour*, J. Zubin and J. Money (eds), John Hopkins University Press, 1973
    'Children and work in the lives of women', paper delivered at the University of Arizona, Tucson, 1976

Rothman, Barbara Katz. *Women, A Feminist Perspective*, Mayfield, 1979

Rowbotham, Sheila. *Hidden from History*, Pluto Press, 1973
    'Passion off the pedestal', *City Limits*, no. 26 (1984)
    'Dilemmas of mothering', *Feminist Review*, no. 31 (Spring 1989)

Rubin, Gayle. 'The traffic in women: notes on the political economy of sex', in R. Reiter (ed.), *Towards an Anthropology for Women*, Monthly Review Press, 1974
    'Thinking sex: notes for a radical theory of the politics of sexuality', in Vance (ed.), 1989

Rush, Florence. 'The sexual abuse of children: A feminist view', in The Radical Therapist Collective, *The Radical Therapist*, Penguin, 1974

'Freud and the sexual abuse of children', *Chrysalis*, no. 1 (1977); quoted in Tomaselli and Porter (ed.), 1986

The Best-Kept Secret: Sexual Abuse of Children, Engelwood Cliffs, 1980; quoted in Tomaselli and Porter (eds.), 1986

Russell, Dora. *The Tamarisk Tree*, vol. 1, Virago Press, 1977

Russell, Letty M. (ed.). *Feminist Interpretation of the Bible*, Basil Blackwell, 1985

Sanday, Peggy Reeves. 'Rape and the silencing of the feminine', in Tomaselli and Porter (eds.), 1986

Sarsby, Jacqueline. *Romantic Love and Society*, Penguin, 1983

Saunders, Lesley. 'Sex and childbirth', in Sue Cartledge and Joanna Ryan (eds), *Sex and Love*, The Women's Press, 1983

Sayers, Janet. *Sexual Contradictions*, Tavistock, 1986

Scott, Hilda. *Working Your Way to the Bottom: The Feminization of Poverty*, Pandora, 1984

Segal, Lynne. *Is the Future Female?*, Virago Press, 1987

Slow Motion: Changing Masculinities; Changing Men, Virago Press, 1990

'Introduction', in Lynne Segal and Mary McIntosh (eds), *Sex Exposed: Sexuality and the Pornography Debate*, Virago Press, 1992

Straight Sex, Virago Press, 1994

Sherfey, Mary Jane. 'A theory on female sexuality', in Robin Morgan (ed.), *Sisterhood is Powerful*, Vintage Books, 1970; and in Humm (ed.), 1992

The Nature and Evolution of Female Sexuality, Vintage Books, 1973

Smith, J. *Misogynies*, Faber & Faber, 1989

Snitow, Ann, Christine Stansell and Sharon Thompson (eds). *Desire: The Politics of Sexuality*, Virago Press, 1984

Spender, Dale. *Women of Ideas and What Men Have Done to Them*, Routledge & Kegan Paul, 1982

There's Always Been a Women's Movement this Century, Routledge & Kegan Paul, 1983

Stanton, Elizabeth Cady. *The Woman's Bible*, Polygon Books, 1985 (first published 1895)

Stoller, Robert J. *Sex and Gender*, Science House, 1968

Stoltenberg, John. *Refusing to Be a Man*, Fontana, 1990 (first published 1989)

'Pornography, homophobia and male supremacy', in Catherine Itzin, (ed.), *Pornography: Women, Violence and Civil Liberties, A Radical View*, Oxford University Press, 1993 (first published 1992)

Stone, Lawrence. *The Family, Sex and Marriage in England 1500–1800*, Weidenfeld & Nicolson, 1977

Strachey, Ray. *The Cause: A Short History of the Women's Movement in Great Britain*, Virago Press, 1978 (first published 1928)

Tanner, Nancy. *On Becoming Human*, Cambridge University Press, 1981

Temkin, Jennifer. 'Women, rape and law reform', in Tomaselli and Porter (eds), 1986

Thompson, William (with Anna Wheeler). *Appeal on Behalf of Women*, Virago Press, 1983 (first published 1825)

Thomson, Rachel. 'Moral rhetoric and public health pragmatism: the recent politics of sex education', in *Feminist Review*, no. 48 (1994)

Tiger, Lionel. *Men in Groups*, Random House, 1968

Tolson, Andrew. *The Limits of Masculinity*, Tavistock, 1977; quoted in Segal, 1990

Tomaselli, Sylvana and Roy Porter (eds). *Rape: An Historical and Social Enquiry*, Basil Blackwell, 1986

Trimberger, Ellen Kay. 'Feminism, men, and modern love: Greenwich Village 1900–1925', in Snitow, Stansell and Thompson (eds), 1984

Vance, Carole (ed.). *Pleasure and Danger: Exploring Female Sexuality*, Pandora, 1989 (first published 1984)

Viney, Ethna. *Ancient Wars: Sex and Sexuality*, Attic Press, 1989; also in *A Dozen Lips*, Attic Preiss, 1994

Walker, Alice. *Warrior Marks*, Jonathan Cape, 1993

Walker, Barbara G. *The Woman's Encyclopedia of Myths and Secrets*, HarperCollins, 1983

Weeks, Jeffrey. *Sexuality and Its Discontents*, Routledge & Kegan Paul, 1985

Weiner, G. and M. Arnot. *Gender Under Scrutiny*, Unwin Myman, 1987

Wellings, K., J. Field, A.M. Johnson, and J. Wadsworth. *Sexual Behaviour in Britain: A National Survey of Sexual Attitudes and Lifestyles*, Penguin, 1994

Williamson, Judith. 'Seeing spots', *City Limits* (February/March 1983); quoted in *Sweeping Statements*, Kanter et al., (eds), 1984

Wilson, Edward O. *Sociobiology*, Harvard, 1975

Woodworth, Robert S. and Mary R. Sheehan. *Contemporary Schools of Psychology*, Methuen, 1965

Wollstonecraft, Mary. *A Vindication of the Rights of Women*, Penguin 1982 (first published 1792)

INDEX